Lecture Notes of the Institute for Computer Sciences, Social Informatics and Telecommunications Engineering 120

Kan Zheng   Mo Li   Hongbo Jiang (Eds.)

Mobile and Ubiquitous Systems: Computing, Networking, and Services

9th International Conference, MobiQuitous 2012
Beijing, China, December 12-14, 2012
Revised Selected Papers

 Springer

Volume Editors

Kan Zheng
Beijing University of Posts and Telecommunications
Beijing 100088, China
E-mail: zkan@bupt.edu.cn

Mo Li
Nanyang Technological University
Singapore, 637698
E-mail: limo@ntu.edu.sg

Hongbo Jiang
Huazhong University of Science and Technology
Wuhan 430074, China
E-mail: hongbojiang2004@gmail.com

ISSN 1867-8211　　　　　　　　　　e-ISSN 1867-822X
ISBN 978-3-642-40237-1　　　　　　 e-ISBN 978-3-642-40238-8
DOI 10.1007/978-3-642-40238-8
Springer Heidelberg New York Dordrecht London

Library of Congress Control Number: 2013946650

CR Subject Classification (1998): C.5.3, H.3, C.2, C.3, K.4, H.5, H.4, I.2, D.2, H.2.8

Typesetting: Camera-ready by author, data conversion by Scientific Publishing Services, Chennai, India

Printed on acid-free paper

Springer is part of Springer Science+Business Media (www.springer.com)

Preface

The 9th International Conference on Mobile and Ubiquitous Systems: Computing, Networking and Services (Mobiquitous 2012) was successfully held in Beijing, during December 12–14, 2012. It brought together the world's leading researchers from academia and industry working in areas of systems, applications, social networks, middleware, networking, data management and service. The keynote speeches presented new ideas to the attendees. Researchers, developers, practitioners, and business executives from all over the world had intensive discussions on the new topics during the conference, generating fruitful results.

Kan Zheng

Organization

General Co-chairs

Haila Wang Orange R&D center, Beijing, China
Wenbo Wang Beijing University of Posts
and Telecommunications, China

General Vice-Chair

Kan Zheng Beijing University of Posts
and Telecommunications, China

Publicity Chairs

Min Chen Seoul National University, Korea
Jaime Lloret Polytechnic University of Valencia, Spain

Technical Program Committee Chairs

Francesco De Pellegrini Create-Net, Trento , Italy
Hongbo Jiang Huazhong University of Science and Technology
China
Mo Li Nanyang Technological University, Singapore
Xing Zhang Beijing University of Posts
and Telecommunications, China

Web Chair

Hang Long Beijing University of Posts
and Telecommunications, China

Program Committee

Aaron Quigley University College Dublin, Ireland
Alois Ferscha University of Linz, Austria
Andrea Tomatis Hitachi Europe - ERD
Andrzej Duda Grenoble INP, France
Branislav Kusy CSIRO, Australia
Chris Gniady University of Arizona, USA
Christian Becker University of Mannheim, Germany
Danny Soroker IBM T.J. Watson Research Center, USA
Erik Wilde EMC, USA

Table of Contents

Traffic Density Estimation Protocol Using Vehicular Networks

Adnan Noor Mian[1], Ishrat Fatima[1], and Roberto Beraldi[2]

[1] National University of Computer and Emerging Sciences,
Block-B, Faisal Town, Lahore, Pakistan
{adnan.noor,ishrat.fatima}@nu.edu.pk
[2] DIS, Università di Roma *"La Sapienza"*
via Ariosto, 25, Roma, 00185, Italy
beraldi@dis.uniroma1.it

Abstract. Traffic density estimates on maps not only assist drivers to decide routes that are time and fuel economical due to less congestions and but also help in preventing accidents that may occur due to the lack of not being able to see far ahead. In this paper, we propose a protocol that exploit vehicle-to-vehicle ad hoc communication for the estimation of vehicular density and the amount of congestion on roads. The protocol forms cluster heads by a voting algorithm. These cluster heads aggregate density information and spread it to the network via few selected forwarding vehicles. The protocol does not assume all vehicles to be equipped with Global Positioning System. We analytically study the cluster head formation part of the protocol and then simulate the proposed protocol using network simulator NS2 to understand different characteristics of the protocol.

Keywords: Vehicular networks, traffic congestion, wireless ad hoc networks.

1 Introduction

Congestion estimation can be used in providing the efficient route information to the drivers. Generally two approaches can be employed for getting traffic congestion information using vehicular network. The first approach uses road side infrastructure in addition to the vehicles and the second only exploit the vehicles on the road and uses only vehicle-to-Vehicle (V2V) communication for estimating traffic congestion. In this paper we focus on the second approach.

There are many protocols available for collecting road traffic information using V2V communication, however, most of them work by generating large amount of network traffic [6][12][9]. Huge network traffic adversely effects the performance of the protocol in many ways. Firstly, large network traffic results in collisions of packets which may eventually lead to loss of information[17], [5], such as dropping of critical messages generated by emergency and safety services [2]. Secondly, security is another reason to avoid higher network traffic generation

K. Zheng, M. Li, and H. Jiang (Eds.): MOBIQUITOUS 2012, LNICST 120, pp. 1–12, 2013.
© Institute for Computer Sciences, Social Informatics and Telecommunications Engineering 2013

in case of vehicular networks. Each packet in the network is digitally signed and checked using its digital signature to ensure that it was received from legitimate sender. This security clearance takes some milliseconds for each packet thus introducing large delays in the processing which in turn affects processing real time capabilities of vehicular networks [7]. Lastly, due to large network traffic the CSMA/CA mechanism of IEEE 802.11p, which is now a widely adapted standard for vehicular communication, a node has to wait before being able to send its information. This becomes a serious issue when vehicular density is high, resulting in large latencies in broadcasts.

Moreover the existing road traffic estimation protocols depend on the GPS readings and assume that all the vehicles have GPS installed. Their performance will be drastically affected in scenarios where the number of GPS equipped vehicles are less. For example, mostly in the developing countries small number of vehicles may have GPS installed. Even if the GPS is installed, the GPS outages can occur in different areas like tunnels and hilly areas[4]. There are techniques like dead reckoning [13] and infrastructure assisted localization [10] that aim to find the position during GPS outages but these solutions are computationally intensive. Such reasons motivates for a protocol that can work fairly even when the GPS availability is not 100% in the vehicular network.

In this paper, we present a Traffic Density Estimation Protocol (TDEP) which utilizes minimum bandwidth by generating minimum network traffic. The protocol works by electing cluster heads. These cluster heads gather the road traffic information for a certain period of time and then broadcast this information. Only the vehicles decided by the cluster heads rebroadcast this information. The protocol does not require every vehicle to have GPS. The vehicles that do not have GPS can only transmit their ids to cluster heads to inform about their presence. We show by our simulations that the proposed protocol works well even if there are only 50% of the vehicles have GPS. We not only do simulations to analyze the behavior of the protocol under different traffic scenarios but also provide a mathematical analysis of the cluster head formation part of the protocol, which forms the core of the protocol.

2   Related Work

Our approach is based on cluster head formation but is different from the Connected Dominating Set (CDS) approach[3]. In this approach the vehicles in the virtual backbone of CDS may become congested with network traffic and may drop packets whereas in the proposed protocol each cluster head will select few vehicles for forwarding packets thus distributing the load. Also it incurs no cost for maintaining the virtual backbone, which is otherwise expensive in such scenarios [15].

Porikli and Li [14] propose an algorithm that exploit traffic videos for the estimation of congestion. In [16], Singh and Gupta assume that the vehicles in proximity contribute more for congestion. Pattara et. al. [18] exploit the cellular technology and use Cell Dwell Time (CDT) to determine the congestion. If a mobile cell has larger CDT the longer the vehicle remains in contact with one base station and the higher is the probability of congestion. Hang et. al. [8] use shockwaves to identify congestion on a road. Shockwave is produced when an unusual event e.g., an accident occurs at the road. In Padron [12] approach when a vehicle considers its speed to be smaller than a threshold, it votes for their own speed to be lower. If a certain number of vehicles around this vehicle also vote for the same, the congestion is supposed to occur and the information is then flooded to the network. The CASCADE protocol [9] aggregate data and rebroadcast the aggregated data for the purpose of developing a position map of vehicles. It divides the area in front of a vehicle into 12 clusters and aim to display the exact position of vehicle on the map. TrafficView [11] protocol display the traffic scenario to the driver by aggregating a vehicle's neighborhood information and flooding it to other vehicles. Chang et. al. [6] Trafficgather protocol forms cluster of vehicles and finds cluster heads but there is no criteria for becoming a cluster head. A node that wishes to collect information declares itself as cluster head. Furthermore Trafficgather use TDMA to avoid collision whereas TDEP use widely proposed IEEE 802.11p CSMA protocol.

The research works presented so far is different in many ways from the work proposed in this paper. We assume that each vehicle has only IEEE 802.11p protocol wireless support and do not use any other devices like directional antenna, camera or support from cellular network. The proposed protocol does not explicitly declare the presence of congestion, instead it displays approximate vehicle density road ahead to the drivers from which they can judge the amount of congestion at different places. Besides, we have done a mathematical analysis on the expected number of cluster heads, which lacks in the previously proposed protocols.

3   Proposed Protocol

The proposed protocol is given by algorithm 1. The protocol runs on each vehicle i in the network. Its different phases run asynchronously and concurrently as described below.

Cluster Head Selection. Cluster head is selected on the basis of the number of neighbors d, i.e., the number of vehicles in the transmission range. The vehicle which has more d has more chance of being selected as a cluster head. The cluster head aggregate information about its neighbor vehicles and then forward this information to other vehicles and cluster heads. The timer vehInfoTimer on each vehicle expires periodically after a specified time interval (line 1-3) to broadcasts VehInfoPkt packet. This packet contains the id of the vehicle, its GPS position if available and its no. of neighbors d. Each vehicle receiving VehInfoPkt stores the packet to its VehInfo cache (line 34-35).

The election of cluster head is done periodically, triggered by timer voteCast-Timer. In this phase, each vehicle determines its d and adds this information to the VehInfo cache. The VehInfo cache is periodically searched to find the id

---

Algorithm 1. Protocol running on a vehicle i

 1: **ScheduleEvent(vehInfoTimer)**
 2: $d \leftarrow$ number of vehicles in Location cache
 3: bcast VehInfoPkt.i.d
 4:
 5: **ScheduleEvent(voteCastTimer)**
 6: $elected\_vehicle \leftarrow$ vehicles with max d in VehInfo Cache
 7: **if** $elected\_vehicle > 1$ **then**
 8:     $elected\_vehicle \leftarrow$ random selection from $elected\_vehicle$
 9:     bcast VotePkt.$elected\_vehicle$
10: **end if**
11:
12: **ScheduleEvent(locationUpdateTimer)**
13: $location \leftarrow \emptyset$
14: **if** GPS is avaliable **then**
15:     $location \leftarrow$ coordinates of vehicle i from GPS
16:     bcast LocationPkt.i.$location$
17: **end if**
18:
19: **ScheduleEvent(clusterHeadInfoTimer)**
20: **if** $clusterhead = 1$ **then**
21:     $d \leftarrow$ number of vehicles in Location cache
22:     $Fnodes \leftarrow$ forwardingNodes()
23:     $location \leftarrow$ coordinates of vehicle i from GPS
24:     bcast ClusterHeadInfoPkt.i.d.$Fnodes$.$location$
25: **end if**
26:
27: **ScheduleEvent(mapDisplayUpdateTimer)**
28: **for all** records in ClusterHeadInfo cache **do**
29:     display point at record.$location$
30:     compute rectangular area $A = \frac{2rb}{mapScale}$ with its center positioned at $location$
31:     display record.d uniformly distributed points in A
32: **end for**
33:
34: **OnReceive(VehInfoPkt)**
35: save VehInfoPkt in VehInfo cache
36:
37: **OnReceive(LocationPkt)**
38: save LocationPkt in Location cache
39:
40: **OnReceive(VotePkt)**
41: **if** VotePkt.$elected\_vehicle = i$ **then**
42:     $vote \leftarrow vote + 1$
43: **end if**
44: **if** $vote \geq t_f \times d$ **then**
45:     $clusterhead \leftarrow 1$
46: **else**
47:     $clusterhead \leftarrow 0$
48: **end if**
49:
50: **onReceive(ClusterHeadInfoPkt)**
51: save ClusterHeadInfoPkt in ClusterHeadInfo cache
52: **if** ClusterHeadInfoPkt.$Fnodes = i$ **then**
53:     **if** ClusterHeadInfoPkt.$ttl > 0$ **then**
54:         ClusterHeadInfoPkt.$ttl \leftarrow$ ClusterHeadInfoPkt.ttl - 1
55:         $Fnodes \leftarrow$ forwardingNodes()
56:         bcast ClusterHeadInfoPkt.$Fnodes$
57:     **else**
58:         drop ClusterHeadInfoPkt
59:     **end if**
60: **end if**

---

of the vehicle which has a maximum value of d. If the found id is not the id of vehicle itself, then a VotePkt packet is formed which has the id having maximum d in the vote field. The packet is then broadcasted (line 5-10). When a vehicle receives a VotePkt packet, it checks if the packet has its id in the vote field. If this is the case, then the number of vote of the vehicle is incremented by one. A vehicle is decided to be the cluster head when $vote \geq t_f \times d$ where $0 \leq t_f \leq 1$ is the threshold fraction (line 40-48). This is further explained in section 4.

Density Calculation around Cluster Heads. Each vehicle periodically broadcasts a Location packet after a time interval Lt given by locationUpdateTimer. This Location Packet contains id of the vehicle and its location taken from the GPS (lines 12-17). When a vehicle receives a Location Packet, it saves this information in its Location Cache (lines 37-38). This Location Cache is maintained till the timer clusterHeadInfoTimer expires after interval Ct on the cluster head. The expiry intervals of locationUpdateTimer and clusterHeadInfoTimer follows the following condition $Ct \geq 2 \times Lt$ to refrain from redundant traffic. On expiry of clusterHeadInfoTimer timer, Location cache is traversed to calculate the number of vehicles within the range (we assume 250m) of cluster heads. The cluster head also calculates the forwarding vehicles which will be responsible for rebroadcasting the ClusterInfo packets. Cluster head broadcasts a ClusterInfo packet and initializes it with its current GPS coordinates, number of vehicles around and list of ids of forwarding vehicles (lines 19-25).

Density Estimation Propagation. When a vehicle receives a ClusterHeadInfoPkt packet, it saves the location of the cluster head and its neighbor ids into its ClusterHeadInfo Cache. It then checks the list of forwarding vehicles inside ClusterHeadInfoPkt to find out if this vehicle is the forwarding vehicle and if this is so then the packet is accepted otherwise discarded. After accepting the ClusterHeadInfoPkt, the vehicle calculates its own forwarding vehicles and replaces the list of ids of these forwarding nodes with the previous one in the ClusterHeadInfoPkt packet. The packet is then broadcasted (lines 50-60).

Map Display. The map display on each vehicle is refreshed after a certain time period. The protocol (line 27-32) identifies a rectangular area $A = r \times b$ on the map where r is the length of transmission range r and b is the breadth of road and the center of the rectangle being positioned at the cluster head. The number of neighbors of each cluster head is read from the ClusterHeadInfo cache and corresponding to each cluster head, location points are uniformly distributes points in A. We take 250m as the range for both calculating the information about cluster and then distributing its information on the map. If we increase this range then it would mean that we are aggregating information from a larger area at just one cluster head resulting in more error between the actual road scenario and the estimated map. If we decrease this range, the error again increases as we will be aggregating information of very small area at one cluster head resulting in large number of cluster heads. This will again lead to the flooding scenario, requiring too many vehicles to generate information packets and broadcast them.

Forwarding Vehicles Selection. Cluster heads and forwarding vehicles compute their forwarding vehicles for forwarding information packets to the network. The basic idea is to divide the communication range of 250m around the cluster head into equal sectors and then choose one farthest vehicle from each sector. We choose one vehicle from each sector so that we can cover most of the area around the cluster head and information can propagate in all the directions with minimum redundant packets. The number of sectors can vary. Here we have set the number of sectors equal to 4.

4   Analysis of Expected Number of Cluster Heads

We know that the number of cluster heads effect the performance of the protocol. The expected number of cluster heads, in turn depends on the value of the threshold in the protocol. In this section we shall derive an analytical expression for the expected number of cluster heads when the threshold is varied. Let us take a snap short of an urban congested scenario. In such a case vehicles are positioned such that we can assume each vehicle to have approximately the same number of neighbor vehicle d. For such a case we present the result as follows.

  Result: Let the protocol given by algorithm 1 be running on N vehicles forming a connected network such that each vehicle has the same number of neighbor vehicles d with which it can communicate. The expected number of cluster heads H_{t_f} formed by the protocol at a threshold t_f where $0 \leq t_f \leq 1$, is given by

$$H_{t_f} = N \left[1 - \sum_{v=0}^{\lceil t \rceil - 1} \binom{d+1}{v} p^v (1-p)^{d+1-v} \right] \tag{1}$$

where $p = 1/(d+1)$ and $t = t_f \times (d+1)$

Proof. The protocol in the algorithm 1 makes a vehicle cluster head when the vehicle gets votes from its neighbor greater than or equal to a threshold t. A vehicle **B** votes for a vehicle **A** if vehicle **A** has the maximum contacts (neighbors) in **B**. If there are two or more vehicles in **B** neighbor list with the same number of maximum contacts then a vehicle is chosen randomly for casting the vote. A vehicle can also vote for itself. If d is the number of neighbor vehicles of a vehicle then a vehicle can get maximum of $(d+1)$ votes. The total possibilities of votes are thus $(d+2)$ i.e., 0 vote, 1 vote, ..., d votes, $(d+1)$ votes.

  Let p be the probability that a specific vehicle **A** is voted by one of it neighbor vehicle **B**. Since **B** has $d+1$ options to cast its vote out of which voting to **A** is one of them, we thus have $p = 1/(d+1)$. As we have assumed that all vehicles have the same number of neighbor vehicles d, p is same for all vehicles. It is thus easy to see that the probability that a vehicle i is voted exactly v times by any one of its d neighbors and also by itself, is given by

$$P[\text{vote}_i = v] = \binom{d+1}{v} p^v (1-p)^{d+1-v} \tag{2}$$

The probability that the vehicle i becomes a cluster head i_H is the probability that the vehicle is voted at least t times i.e.,

$$P[i = i_H] = P[\text{vote}_i \geq t]$$
$$= 1 - P[\text{vote}_i \leq (t - 1)]$$

The second term on the right hand side is cumulative probability of $P[\text{vote}_i = v]$. We can thus write

$$P[i = i_H] = 1 - \sum_{v=0}^{t-1} P[\text{vote}_i = v] \tag{3}$$

Let the threshold t be written in terms of threshold fraction t_f given by $t = t_f \times (d+1)$ where $0 \leq t_f \leq 1$, as in the line 44 of algorithm. In such a case t will be a real number. The probability $P[i = i_H] = 1$ for $t_f = 0$ since due to 0 threshold t each vehicle i will be a cluster head. The $P[i = i_H]$ for $t_f > 0$ remains same for t intervals $]0,1],]1,2], ...$ which is same as taking ceiling of t i.e., $\lceil t \rceil$.

From above and equations 2 and 3 the probability that any vehicle i is a cluster head can thus be written as

$$P[i = i_H] = 1 - \sum_{v=0}^{\lceil t \rceil - 1} \binom{d+1}{v} p^v (1-p)^{d+1-v} \tag{4}$$

Since the probability of being a cluster head H is same for all vehicles since we have assumed that d is same for vehicles, the expected number of cluster heads H_{t_f} at a threshold t_f is given by

$$H_{t_f} = N \times P[i = i_H]$$

From equation 4, the above equation leads to equation 1.

To validate the analytical result we developed a simulator for the cluster head formation part of the protocol. To have a topology in which all vehicles have the same number of neighbors, we placed the vehicle in a grid in such way that edge vehicles are neighbors of opposite edge vehicles thus forming a closed grid. Such a topology is far from real but nevertheless, since all vehicles have the same numbers of neighbors, it helped to do the analysis. Moreover generalization of the analysis to a case where d is variable can be done following the same approach. Each value of H_{t_f} is calculated by taking an average of 1000 iterations. Fig. 1(a) shows six plots, analytical and simulation for $d = 4$, $d = 8$ and $d = 12$ for 100 vehicles. We see that the analytical and simulated plots completely overlap, thus validating the analysis. We note that the plots are step function. This is because the probability given by equation 2 is a step function depending on d.

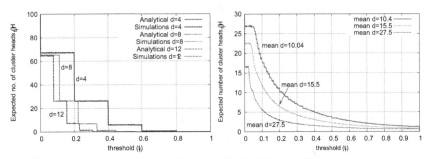

(a) Vehicles with constant no. of neigh-(b) Vehicle at uniform random locations
bors validating analysis

Fig. 1. Expected number of cluster heads as a function of threshold for 100 vehicles

The number of steps in the plots are $(d+2)$, as discussed in the proof. These steps are quite notable from the data but not much visible from the plots since the steps are very close to each near higher values of t_f. We also note that for higher d the plot is shifted left. This can be understood from equation $t = t_f \times (d+1)$. As d increases, t_f should decrease to have same t and H_{t_f}.

The importance of the analysis is that it gives us an insight about the cluster head selection algorithm and how the number of cluster heads vary with the threshold. This understanding can help us to understand the protocol behavior in more realistic topologies, which are otherwise difficult to model. Fig 1(b) shows simulation plots of the expected number of cluster heads formed in a real scenario by randomly placing 100 vehicles on a 1000x1000 area. Each point was plotted after 1000 iterations. We had 3 plots for $0 < t_f \le 1$, with a mean d by changing the transmission radius. Note that for $t_f = 0$ the number of cluster heads will be N. For threshold $t_f > 0$ the step size in the plots is very small. This can be explained by considering the analysis done before. As we know that the number of steps and hence step size in the plots depend on d, in randomly placed vehicles the neighbor distribution d has a wide range of values thus increasing wider range of possibilities of H_{t_f}. Similarly the shifting of plots to left for higher values of mean d can be explained due to the reason described earlier for the plots in Figure 1(a). The result obtained for the random placement of vehicles can be used to tune the protocol in a real scenario to get the best compromise between number of cluster heads and accuracy of display of traffic congestion by setting the parameter t_f.

5 Simulation Setup

We have simulated the proposed protocol using network simulator NS2 version 2.35 [1]. We have used IEEE 802.11p protocol for V2V communication. The transmission range of each vehicle is 250m. For each packet, we set $ttl = 30$ hops. We have done simulations for a straight road of 5 km and with different

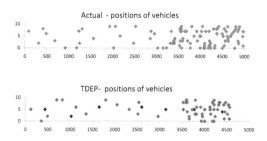

Fig. 2. Display of actual 100 vehicle positions and positions computed from TDEP as seen by a vehicle at $x = 0$

traffic densities scenarios. The vehicles have different velocities ranging from 15 km/hr to 60 km/hr and can overtake each other, thus may form clusters. We allow simulations to take place for 2 minutes and then measure the actual positions of the vehicles in the network. To analyze the accuracy of the protocols we divide the road into segments and measure the root mean square error of all segments. Formally if dA_j is density of jth slot in the actual network and dE_j is the estimated density of jth slot, we define mean square error e_{rms} of difference of densities of all the slots as follows

$$e_{rms} = \sqrt{\sum_{\forall j}(dA_j - dE_j)^2} \tag{5}$$

6   TDEP Characteristics

In the following we describes some of the important characteristics of the protocol obtained from the simulations.

Visualization of the Vehicle Density. The proposed protocol aims to display a map of traffic density to the driver. The purpose is to give driver a close approximation of the actual situation and not to display the exact position of vehicles since the drivers are not interested in the actual position of the vehicles. They are only interested in knowing where there is likely to be more traffic in real time. Each vehicle is shown by a point. More traffic is represented by more points per unit area on the map. When drawing map, the protocol takes the accurate positions of the cluster heads. The position of all other vehicles is approximated with respect to their nearest cluster heads. Figure 2 shows the positions of vehicles as calculated by TDEP. These positions are seen from a vehicle at zero x-axis. We see that the results produced by TDEP are good enough to give a good estimate of the traffic density. The actual error in the representation is calculated by equation 5. This error in display under different conditions is discussed as follows.

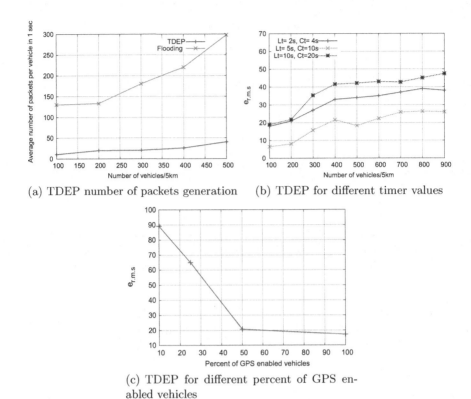

(a) TDEP number of packets generation   (b) TDEP for different timer values

(c) TDEP for different percent of GPS enabled vehicles

Fig. 3. TDEP performance characteristics

Number of Packets Generated. Figure 3(a) shows the number of packet generated per second per vehicle for different vehicular densities. The plots show a comparison between a flood based protocol, in which each node forwards packets and TDEP. We see that TDEP generates far less number of packets. This is clearly due to the aggregation property of the cluster based protocol. The interesting fact is that the number of packets generated by TDEP are not much effected by higher vehicular densities. This can be explained with the help of the analysis done in section 4. In the plots of Figure 1(b) we see that for $t_f = 0.5$, when $d = 10.4$, $H_{t_f} = 3.4$, when $d = 15.5$, $H_{t_f} = 2.2$, and when $d = 27.5$, $H_{t_f} = 1.2$ that is, the increase in the vehicular density d is compensated by a decrease in the expected number of cluster heads consequently resulting a less increase in the rate at which packets are generated.

Effect of the Varying Protocol Timers. Figure 3(b) shows the error for TDEP protocol for different values of the timer and densities. We note that the error is higher in case of high or low values of the timers. This is due to the fact that for small time intervals the information is updated more frequently thus generating large number of packets which result in collisions and drop of packets and thus loss of information. On the other hand, when timer values are large the current positions of the vehicles are not updated timely thus introducing error and displaying a density map to the user which is far from real. We see that the best is obtained when $Lt = 5$ and $Ct = 10$.

Effect of Decrease in GPS Information. Figure 3(c) shows the plot when GPS information decreases from 100% to 10%. For the simulations we selected the timer values that gave comparatively better results as discussed previously, that is, $Lt = 5s$ and $Ct = 10s$. The plots of Figure 3(c) shows that the accuracy of the protocol is reduced when the GPS information becomes less available. The interesting point is that the accuracy is not much effected until the GPS enabled vehicles reduce to 50%. This can be explained by considering the fact that cluster head not only aggregate number of neighbor vehicles but also their GPS information. When cluster head or any one its neighbors have GPS information, then during aggregation this can compensate for all those neighbors who do not have GPS. Thus even if 50% of vehicles do not have GPS, their positions can still be approximated with the help of neighboring vehicles and error in displaying the position of cluster head is not much effected.

7   Conclusion and Future Work

In this paper, we have proposed a Traffic Density Estimation Protocol using Vehicular Networks which first selects some vehicles as the cluster heads by a voting mechanism. These cluster heads aggregate the information about the vehicles in their transmission range and then select few vehicles for forwarding this information to the rest of the network. We have simulated our proposed protocol using NS2 network simulator. Simulations shown that the proposed protocol give fairly accurate results under different road traffic scenarios. The proposed protocol is better able to take advantage of GPS enable vehicles. As the number of GPS enabled vehicles increases, the accuracy of the the proposed protocol is also increased. We have also done mathematical analysis of the cluster head selection part of the protocol and have analytically determined the estimated number of cluster head formed.

In future we plan to simulate the protocol on curved roads also having multiple road crossings and in real map scenarios. We also plan to see the effect of changing the transmission range on the accuracy of the protocol.

Acknowledgements. This work was partially funded by grant 'Progetti di Ricerca, La Sapienza', prot. C26A129S3Y, 2012.

References

1. Network simulator ns-2, `http://www.isi.edu/nsnam/ns/`
2. Ababneh, N., Labiod, H.: Safety message dissemination in vanets: Flooding or trajectory-based? In: Med-Hoc-Net, pp. 1–8. IEEE (2010)

3. Almahorg, K., Basir, O.: Simulation-based performance comparison of vanets backbone formation algorithms. In: 12th IEEE/ACM International Symposium on Distributed Simulation and Real-Time Applications, DS-RT 2008, pp. 236–242 (October 2008)
4. Hofmann-Wellenho, H.L.B., Collins, J.: Global positioning system: Theory and practice, vol. 4. Springer (1997)
5. Bilstrup, K., Uhlemann, E., Ström, E.G., Bilstrup, U.: On the ability of the 802.11p mac method and stdma to support real-time vehicle-to-vehicle communication. EURASIP J. Wirel. Commun. Netw., 5:1–5:13 (January 2009)
6. Chang, W.-R., Lin, H.-T., Chen, B.-X.: Trafficgather: An efficient and scalable data collection protocol for vehicular ad hoc networks. In: 5th IEEE Consumer Communications and Networking Conference, CCNC 2008., pp. 365–369 (January 2008)
7. Hsiao, H.-C., Studer, A., Chen, C., Perrig, A., Bai, F., Bellur, B., Iyer, A.: Flooding-resilient broadcast authentication for vanets. In: Proceedings of the 17th Annual International Conference on Mobile Computing and Networking, MobiCom 2011, pp. 193–204. ACM (2011)
8. Huang, D., Shere, S., Ahn, S.: Dynamic highway congestion detection and prediction based on shock waves. In: Proceedings of the Seventh ACM International Workshop on VehiculAr Inter-NETworking, Systems, and Applications, VANET 2010, pp. 11–20. ACM (2010)
9. Ibrahim, K., Weigle, M.: Cascade: Cluster-based accurate syntactic compression of aggregated data in vanets. In: 2008 IEEE GLOBECOM Workshops, November 30–December 4, vol. 30, pp. 1–10 (2008)
10. Lee, E.-K., Yang, S., Oh, S., Gerla, M.: Rf-gps: Rfid assisted localization in vanets. In: IEEE 6th International Conference on Mobile Adhoc and Sensor Systems, MASS 2009, Macau, pp. 621–626 (2009)
11. Nadeem, T., Dashtinezhad, S., Liao, C., Iftode, L.: Trafficview: traffic data dissemination using car-to-car communication. SIGMOBILE Mob. Comput. Commun. Rev. 8(3), 6–19 (2004)
12. Padron, F.M.: Traffic congestion detection using vanet. Master thesis, Florida Atlantic University, USA (2009)
13. Parker, R., Valaee, S.: Vehicle localization in vehicular networks. In: 2006 IEEE 64th Vehicular Technology Conference, VTC-2006 Fall, pp. 1–5 (September 2006)
14. Porikli, F.: Traffic congestion estimation using hmm model without vehicle tracking. In: IEEE Intelligent Vehicles Symposium, pp. 188–193 (2004)
15. Ros, F., Ruiz, P., Stojmenovic, I.: Acknowledgment-based broadcast protocol for reliable and efficient data dissemination in vehicular ad hoc networks. IEEE Transactions on Mobile Computing 11(1), 33–46 (2012)
16. Singh, R.P., Gupta, A.: Traffic congestion estimation in vanets and its application to information dissemination. In: Aguilera, M.K., Yu, H., Vaidya, N.H., Srinivasan, V., Choudhury, R.R. (eds.) ICDCN 2011. LNCS, vol. 6522, pp. 376–381. Springer, Heidelberg (2011)
17. Tonguz, O.K., Wisitpongphan, N., Parikh, J.S., Bai, F., Mudalige, P., Sadekar, V.K.: On the Broadcast Storm Problem in Ad hoc Wireless Networks. In: 3rd International Conference on Broadband Communications, Networks and Systems, BROADNETS 2006, pp. 1–11 (2006)
18. Pattara-atikom, R.P.W., Luckana, R.: Estimating road traffic congestion using cell dwell time with simple threshold and fuzzy logic techniques. In: IEEE Intelligent Transportation Systems Conference, pp. 956–961 (2007)

Mobile-to-Mobile Video Recommendation

Padmanabha Venkatagiri Seshadri, Mun Choon Chan, and Wei Tsang Ooi

National University of Singapore, Computing 1, 13 Computing Drive 117417, Singapore
{padmanab,chanmc,ooiwt}@comp.nus.edu.sg

Abstract. Mobile device users can now easily capture and socially share video clips in a timely manner by uploading them wirelessly to a server. When attending crowded events, however, timely sharing of videos becomes difficult due to choking bandwidth in the network infrastructure, preventing like-minded attendees from easily sharing videos with each other through a server. One solution to alleviate this problem is to use direct device-to-device communication to share videos among nearby attendees. Contact capacity between two devices, however, is limited, and thus a recommendation algorithm is needed to select and transmit only videos of potential interest to an attendee. In this paper, we address the question: which video clip should be transmitted to which user. We proposed an video transmission scheduling algorithm, called *CoFiGel*, that runs in a distributed manner and aims to improve both the prediction coverage and precision of the recommendation algorithm. At each device, CoFiGel transmits the video that would increase the estimated number of positive user-video ratings the most if this video is transferred to the destination device. We evaluated *CoFiGel* using real-world traces and show that substantial improvement can be achieved compared to baseline schemes that do not consider rating or contact history.

Keywords: mobile-to-mobile communication, memory based collaborative filtering, coverage.

1 Introduction

Mobile devices are increasingly capable in their abilities to sense, capture, and store rich multimedia data. Multiple wireless interfaces facilitate users to upload and share their experience with friends and public. In this work, we are interested in mobile video sharing among attendees of an event. As an example, consider product exhibitions, malls, museums, game events such as the Olympics, where people have to move around in a large area and could benefit from receiving video clips of a small portion of the event so that they can decide whether to attend it.

This information sharing paradigm emphasizes both spatial locality and timeliness and is different from archived video sharing services such as those provided by YouTube. A straight forward approach to enable such video sharing is to have users upload the videos captured to a central server through 3G/HSPA networks. Users can then search for or browse through the uploaded videos through the server. While this approach can provide good performance in terms of delivering the right videos to the right users, it has obvious drawbacks. First, when user density is high, there is likely to be insufficient aggregate upload bandwidth for the combination of large amount of data

K. Zheng, M. Li, and H. Jiang (Eds.): MOBIQUITOUS 2012, LNICST 120, pp. 13–24, 2013.

and large number of users. Next, the use of 3G/HSPA network for upload is relatively inefficient, since the network is optimized for download. Finally, videos stored in the central server have to be downloaded to individual mobile phone for viewing and rating, further straining the 3G/HSPA network.

The approach adopted in this work is to circumvent the cellular network infrastructure and transfer videos directly, from one mobile device to another mobile device, via short range connection such as WiFi or Bluetooth. A user captures a video and indicates the mobile application to share it. The video is pushed to nearby devices when connections to these devices becomes available. A user can choose to watch and rate videos accumulated in the video inbox of the device. The device can also forward the videos through a mobile-to-mobile network.

Besides alleviating the network infrastructure bottleneck, direct mobile-to-mobile communication may also reduce power consumption [9]. In addition, the much shorter RTT for direct mobile-to-mobile transfer allows significantly higher throughput compared to transferring large amount of data over the Internet through the 3G/HSPA network, where the median ping latency has been observed to be almost 200ms [2].

The use of short range communication among mobile devices results in intermittent connectivity. These devices, in essence, form a delay-tolerant network (DTN). As mobile devices have limited contact time, pushing the right video to a neighboring device is especially important. Ideally, we want videos that a user is interested in to end up in its inbox within a given time period. As such, our system uses a collaborative filtering (CF) based recommender system to predict the user preference. The use of this algorithm, however, requires collection of sufficient number of user-item ratings to work. In other words, pushing a video to a user now has two purposes: for the user to watch and for the user to rate. The decision to select which video to transfer should thus consider the needs of the CF algorithm as well.

To address this challenge, we propose *CoFiGel*, a video transfer scheduler in the DTN context that integrates CF-based recommender system. CoFiGel effectively utilizes the limited contact capacity among mobile devices to filter and disseminate user-generated videos published by mobile users to other mobile users. CoFiGel is designed to (i) increase the prediction coverage, which is the ability of the algorithm to predict ratings for items, and (ii) route videos in such a way that increases the item precision, i.e., the percentage of items recommended to users that are rated positively.

We evaluate CoFiGel through trace-based simulation using RollerNet human mobility trace [6] and an user rating data set from MovieLens[1]. Our evaluation shows that CoFiGel can provide 80% more prediction coverage in comparison to the baseline algorithms, detecting at least 74% of positive ratings in the process, and delivers at least 59% more positive (liked by user) items in comparison to the baseline algorithms that do not take into account either ratings or contact history.

The rest of the paper is organized as follow. Section 2 discusses related work. Section 3 describes our mobile-to-mobile video transfer application and motivates the need for CoFiGel. CoFiGel is presented in Section 4 and is evaluated in Section 5. Finally, Section 6 concludes.

---

[1] MovieLens Dataset, http://www.grouplens.org/node/73

2   Related Work

Collaborative Filtering (CF). The most prominent and popular recommendation technique that has seen extensive research and wide deployment is collaborative filtering (CF) [3]. CF techniques can be broadly categorized into memory-based or model-based. Memory-based CF (MCF) utilizes rating history of users to identify neighbourhood patterns among users or items. This pattern facilitates the prediction of ratings for hitherto unrated user-item pairs. Model-based CF uses the user ratings in conjunction with standard statistical models such as Bayesian belief nets and latent semantic model to identify patterns in the ratings of user-item pairs. The resultant model is then used to make predictions for future ratings. There exists much research on using CF on peer-to-peer (P2P) systems. PocketLens [14] is a recommender system for portable devices that uses item-item collaborative filtering for making recommendations. It proposes a rating exchange protocol for both distributed P2P architecture and centralized server architecture, where nodes rely on a central server for storing rating information. A probabilistic model-based CF is proposed by Wang et al. [8] for a P2P network. Other related work focuses on the security and privacy aspect, including providing user incentive [5], trust of rating protocol and privacy [7].

DTN Content Dissemination. There are many unicast DTN routing schemes designed to improve point-to-point delivery probability and/or minimize delay [15]. These protocols, however, do not address the issue of information dissemination. A common problem studied in DTN content dissemination is how to maximize the freshness of dynamic content [10]. A subset of mobile devices download internet content and exchange among themselves so as to maximize freshness. Caching schemes where nodes refresh/reshuffle their cached content based on a voting process can also be exploited, as done by Ioannidis et al. [10]. In [11], predefined preferences are used to route items to users. However, preferences are static and not predicted. Another approach for content discovery and dissemination in DTN uses tags [12]. Tag metadata is propagated in the network and user interest is determined by matching tags.

Unlike previous work, *CoFiGel* provides a framework to integrate MCF and DTN routing, focusing on utilizing limited contact capacities in DTN to improve rating coverage and item recall. *CoFiGel* does not assume any specific MCF algorithm. Instead, it defines an abstract model of how MCF works and how the MCF should interact with the DTN routing protocol. We are not aware of any MCF that specifically takes into account the intermittent contact capacities of mobile nodes, nor any DTN mechanism that takes into account usefulness of item transferred to improve coverage and item recall of the MCF algorithm.

3   Mobile-to-Mobile Video Sharing

Motivation. We now motivate our work by demonstrating the efficacy and advantages of mobile-to-mobile video transfer.

Mobile data usage has outgrown available bandwidth in 3G/HSPA network, resulting in severe congestion in the cellular network in some cases[2]. A popular approach to reduce such congestion is to offload data traffic to the WiFi network whenever possible[3]. Communication over WiFi also consumes less power than 3G/HSPA network (four to six times less power for file transfer [9]). We further measure the performance of file transfer between a mobile device and a central server using 3G/HSPA network and between two mobile devices directly using WiFi.

To quantify the performance of mobile-to-server transfer, we upload and then download a 14.3 MB video clip to YouTube using a HSPA network, which provides a maximum download and upload rate of 7.2 Mbps and 1.9 Mbps respectively. The average download and upload throughputs measured (average of 5 trials) are 1125.2 kbps and 57 kbps respectively. To quantify the performance of mobile-to-mobile transfer, we use two Samsung Nexus S phones that support IEEE 802.11n (link rate is 72.2 Mbps) to exchange the same video file directly over a TCP connection. The measured throughput is 22.6Mbps (average of 5 trials). The 20-fold difference in measured throughput can be attributed to the differences in link rate and RTT observed (70ms for mobile-to-server and 5.5ms for mobile-to-mobile). This superior throughput motivates our study on mobile-to-mobile video sharing.

Mobile-to-Mobile Video Sharing. A user of mobile-to-mobile video sharing can share video content either generated or already available on the mobile device through a *video outbox* and watch and/or rate video available in a *video inbox*. When a device is within communication range through WiFi or Bluetooth, the scheduler uses the MCF to choose the subset of videos (interesting to the user) in the inbox to transfer within the limited contact time. The scheduler also manages the limited inbox space. Each device maintains a user-video rating matrix, which is updated either when a video is rated on the device, or when the device receives a rating matrix from another device. The rating matrix is one of the two meta-data (the other is contact history among devices) being exchanged between two devices when devices make contact with each other. Upon update of the matrix, predictions of interest-level of videos are recomputed and video transfers are rescheduled accordingly.

Memory-Based Collaborative Filtering. We now detail how MCF works. MCF is a class of recommender algorithms that is model independent and is able to capture the abstract user preference on a set of items. Typical MCF techniques have the following structure. A training data set is used to build a rating matrix consisting of ratings given for items by users. The rating matrix is used to identify the similarities between users-items and to predict the ratings of hitherto unrated items by a given user. Items that are predicted to have high ratings are shown to the user; Feedback from the user on these items is then used to update the rating matrix. The assumption is that *users tend to behave in the same way as they behaved in the past.*

---

[2] http://www.fiercewireless.com/europe/story/o2-germany-admits-network-meltdown-smartphones-blamed/2011-11-23
[3] http://www.telecomasia.net/content/3g-wifi-offload-pipes-singapore

Table 1. Rating matrix for Cosine-based similarity metric, ◇ denotes ratings that could be predicted and ★ denotes unknown ratings

Users	i_1	i_2	i_3	i_4	i_5	i_6
u_1	1	◇	★	★	◇	◇
u_2	1	◇	★	★	◇	◇
u_3	1	1	★	◇	◇	1
u_4	◇	1	◇	1	1	1
u_5	★	◇	1	1	◇	◇
u_6	1	◇	★	◇	1	1
u_7	1	0	★	◇	0	1

For concreteness, we will use the Cosine-based similarity metric ([13]) in the rest of this paper to illustrate how CoFiGel works. Cosine-based similarity is a popular item-based MCF and has been used in large scale real-world applications such as the recommendation system used by *Amazon.com*. Note that CoFiGel can also work with other MCF algorithms, such as Slope One [3]. Since MCF works for recommendation of any kind of items, we will use the term *items* in the rest of the discussions to refer to videos in our application.

In general, ratings can be represented as integer values. For simplicity, we assume that ratings are binary and are expressed as either 1 (positive/like) or 0 (negative/dislike). In computing Cosine-based similarity, unrated items are assigned ratings of 0. After a user has rated an item, the item will not be recommended to the user again.

Let U and I be the set of all users and items respectively and I_u^+ and $I_u^?$ be the set of items that are rated positive and unrated by a user $u \in U$ respectively. Let the actual rating of an item $i \in I$ for user u be $r_{u,i}$. Cosine-based similarity metric computes $R_{u,i}$, the *rank* of an unrated user-item pair (u,i), in the following way. First, the similarity between two items i and j is computed using $Sim(i,j) = \left(\frac{\sum_{u \in U} r_{u,i} \cdot r_{u,j}}{\sqrt{\sum_{u \in U} r_{u,i}^2} \cdot \sqrt{\sum_{u \in U} r_{u,j}^2}} \right)$ and $R_{u,i} = \sum_{j \in I_u^+} Sim(i,j)$ Obviously, the rank of item i for user u can be computed only if there is at least one user who has rated both i and another item that user u has rated positively. If the rank cannot be computed, then we say that the particular user-item pair is *unpredictable*.

Table 1 shows a rating matrix with items that are rated (positively and negatively), predicted and unpredictable. Typically, the top-k items $i \in I_u^?$ with highest rank are recommended to user u. We say that the prediction of i is *positive* for u if i is among the top-k items in $I_u^?$, and *negative* otherwise. A prediction of i is said to be *correct*, if the predicted rating is consistent with the user rating eventually. Note that the notion of whether a prediction is positive or not changes over time (and thus whether it is correct or not changes over time as well).

The performance of MCF algorithm is measured by several standard metrics [3]. For instance, *precision* and *recall* are used to measure the classification performance of a MCF algorithm. Precision is a measure of recommended items that are relevant to the users, and recall is a measure of the number of relevant items that are recommended to the users. Another common performance measure used is *prediction coverage*, (or coverage for short), defined as the percentage of *the number of predictable user-item pair*.

MCF for Mobile-to-Mobile Recommendation. When two mobile devices meet, they need to select which items to be transmitted over the intermittent contacts based on the meta-data information available. As mentioned, since contact capacity is precious, items that are likely to be liked by other users should be transfer and propagated with higher priorities. Running MCF in the context of mobile-to-mobile video sharing, however, leads to another issue: since each user is likely get a chance to rate only a small subset of all videos available, selecting which items for users to rate is also important, to increase the coverage.

For the rating matrix shown in Table 1, item i_1 has three common user ratings with items i_2, i_5 and i_6. i_3 has only one common user rating with i_4. Using Equations for $Sim(i, j)$ and $R_{u,i}$, we can compute R_{u_4,i_1} and R_{u_4,i_3} as follows: $R_{u_4,i_1} = Sim(1, 2) + Sim(1, 4) + Sim(1, 5) + Sim(1, 6) = \frac{1}{\sqrt{5}\sqrt{2}} + 0 + \frac{1}{\sqrt{5}\sqrt{2}} + \frac{3}{\sqrt{5}\sqrt{4}} \approx 1.30$ and $R_{u_4,i_3} = Sim(3, 2) + Sim(3, 4) + Sim(3, 5) + Sim(3, 6) = 0 + \frac{1}{\sqrt{1}\sqrt{2}} + 0 + 0 \approx 0.71$. i_1 has a higher rating than i_3 with respect to u_4.

The coverage consideration, however, is different. It can be observed from Table 1 that all users except u_4 and u_5 have already rated i_1. Knowing the value of r_{u4,i_1}, allows only at most one more rating, R_{u_5,i_1}, to be computed. The gain in rated and predictable items is 2. On the other hand, i_3 has been rated only by u_5. Knowing the value of r_{u_4,i_3}, allows the rating of 3 users (u_3, u_6 and u_7) for item i_3 to be computed. The gain in rated and predictable items is 4. Therefore, the rating of i_3 by u_4 has a higher gain in rated and predictable items than rating i_1.

This example illustrates the trade-off between improving user satisfaction and improving coverage when not all data transfer can be completed within a contact. If user satisfaction is more important, then i_1 will be chosen for transfer. If coverage has higher priority, then i_3 should be chosen. Note that when there is a centralized server with continuous connectivity to users and has access to all rating information and data items, the impact of this trade-off is not significant. Such a trade-off, however, plays an important role in a resource constraint environment where the contacts between mobile devices are intermittent, contact capacities are limited and only subsets of data items can be stored in the local buffers. *The execution of MCF on mobile devices with intermittent contacts presents a new challenge that is not present in traditional application of MCF in a centralized or peer-to-peer environment where connectivities are not intermittent.*

4   CoFiGel

The MCF algorithm runs locally on each mobile device based on available meta-data information, which consists of the user-item rating matrix and contact history. We denote the element $m_{u,i}$ as the rating of item i by user u at any given time. The status of $m_{u,i}$ can be either **rated**, **predicted** or **unpredictable**. A rating $m_{u,i}$ is rated if i has be transferred to and rated by u, and the rating can be either 1 or 0. A rating $m_{u,i}$ is predicted if it has not been rated yet, but the rank $R_{u,i}$ (see section 3) can be computed. The predicted rating is 1 if i is among the top-k item according to $R_{u,i}$ for user u, and 0 otherwise. A rating $m_{u,i}$ is said to be *correct* if the predicted rating matches the user rating eventually.

Recall that there are two naive methods to pick an item to transfer to another device. The first method, considering only item recall, picks a predicted item that gives the highest rank $R_{u,i}$ to maximize the probability that the rating $m_{u,i}$ is correct and positive. The second method considers only the prediction coverage, and picks a predicted item such that *if* the item is rated, then the number of unpredictable items becoming predictable is maximal. To consider both recall and coverage, we consider the following metric: for an item i, we are interested in the number of correct positive prediction for i eventually, i.e., when i has been rated by all users. Before i is rated by all users, this quantity is considered as a random variable, denoted as Ω_i. At any round t, we know the current number of correct positive rating for i, denoted r_i^+. We also know is the number of positive predictions for item i, g_i^+. Ideally, we would like the following inequality to be true: $\Omega_i > r_i^+ + g_i^+$, i.e., all the positive predictions for i are correct, and there are additional new positive ratings for i. The key question is thus to estimate the probability that the above condition is true if i is transferred.

In the following, we present approximations on the potential positive ratings for an item and the probability of delivery of items with positive ratings to the users. The goal is to derive approximations that can be used as input to guide and motivate the design of *CoFiGel*.

Let, n be number of users, g_i^+ number of positive prediction for item i currently, r_i^+ number of correctly predicted positive ratings for item i currently, Ω_i random variable for number of correct positive ratings for item i when all users have rated i, $\sigma_q(i)$ the queue position of item i at node q, B average device contact capacity, λ average device contact rate, H_i set of devices with item i.

First, we present an equation to bound $P\{\Omega_i > g_i^+ + r_i^+\}$, the probability that the number of correct positive predictions for item i would increase if i is transferred, is given as follows:

$$Pr\{\Omega_i > r_i^+ + g_i^+\} \leq \min\left\{1, e^{\frac{r_i^+ E[\Omega_i]}{n-r_i^+}}\left(1 - \frac{r_i^+}{n}\right)^{r_i^+ + g_i^+}\right\} \tag{1}$$

For the ratings and items to be useful, the item should reach a user before some time deadline. Estimated probability of delivery an item i late after the time deadline t is:

$$Pr\{Y_i \geq t\} > 1 - \min\{1, \frac{|N_i|}{B\lambda t|H_i|} \sum_{v \in H_i} \sigma_{i,v}\} \tag{2}$$

The proofs and discussions of Equations 1 and 2 are available in [1].

We now present the workings of CoFiGel based on Equation 1 and 2. At each device, CoFiGel decides which item to transmit by computing a utility U_i, which incorporates the number of positive ratings (rated or predicted) for i, the probability of gain in ratings, and the probability of delivery within the deadline: $U_i = (g_i^+ + r_i^+) \cdot G_i \cdot D_i$, where G_i is the right-hand-side of Equation 1, and D_i is the right-hand-side of Equation 2. The utility increases if either (i) the total number of correctly predicted positive ratings we get eventually $(g_i^+ + r_i^+)$, increases (ii) the likelihood of the number of correct predictions increases (G_i), or (iii) the likelihood of delivering an item within the deadline t increases. Note that since the bounds provided are very loose, we do not expect these computed utilities to reflect the true value of the rating gain. For scheduling, only relative ordering is important and we transfer items in decreasing order of utility.

Table 2. Simulation Parameters

Parameter	RollerNet
Number of Publisher and Subscriber Nodes	10 and 30
(Item publisher rate)/publisher and item lifetime	40 items/Hr and 1 hour 15 min
Simulation duration, warmup and cool down time	Approx.3 Hrs, 1 Hr and 0.5 Hr
Item size and Buffer size	15MB and 1GB
Default contact bandwidth	3Mbps

5   Simulation Evaluation

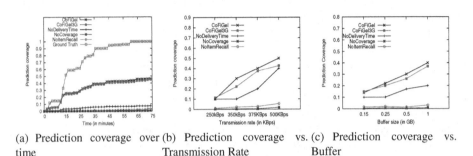

(a) Prediction coverage over time

(b) Prediction coverage vs. Transmission Rate

(c) Prediction coverage vs. Buffer

Fig. 1. RollerNet trace (total ratings = 11536)

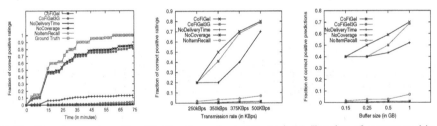

(a) Fraction of correct positive predictions over time

(b) Fraction of correct positive predictions vs. Transmission Rate

(c) Fraction of correct positive predictions vs. Buffer

Fig. 2. RollerNet trace (total positive ratings = 6400)

5.1   Simulation Setting

To evaluate *CoFiGel*, we use the MovieLens data set[4] as the underlying user ratings. The data set chosen has 100,000 ratings, 943 users and 1,682 items. We use the RollerNet trace ([6]) as the human mobility traces. It consists of about 60 Bluetooth devices carried

---

[4] http://movielens.umn.edu

by groups of roller bladers in a roller tour over three hours. The average contact duration is 22 seconds, with an average of 501 contacts made per node over 3 hours.

Video size of user generated content such as those found in popular sites like YouTube is 25MB or less (98% of videos are 25MB or less [4]). We choose data size of 15MB. The buffer size and item generation rate are similarly adjusted to ensure sufficient loading in the system. As some nodes in the trace have very limited contacts with the rest of the trace, we avoid selecting these nodes as the publisher or subscriber nodes (though they can still act as relay nodes). These nodes are identified as nodes which do not have sufficient number of node contacts and contact bandwidth to support meaningful data exchange. After removing these nodes, 10 publishers and 30 subscribers were chosen. In order to reduce simulation time, we reduce the MovieLens data set selected by randomly choosing 900 items (movies) and 500 users from the original data set. All user-item ratings associated with these chosen user-item pairs from the original dataset are also included. Finally, as the rating data set and the mobility trace are generated independently, we map the rating data to the mobility trace in the following way: Every item in the reduced data set is randomly assigned to a publisher node in the mobility trace. This node will act as the publisher for the item. Every user in the reduced data set is randomly mapped onto a mobile subscriber node. The actual user-item rating is known only when the item reaches the given mobile node where the user is located.

Table 2 are used as default unless otherwise specified. Each simulation point is run at least 3 times with different random seeds. The performance objectives used are prediction coverage, precision, recall and number of satisfied users and latency, as described in Section 3.

We compare the performance of *CoFiGel* with four other algorithms, namely: **(1)** A scheme that knows the ground-truth of data available. The ground-truth is available from the MovieLens data set. This scheme provides the actual rating coverage and gives an upper bound on the system performance. This scheme is used only in the coverage comparison since ground-truth is not applicable in the user satisfaction evaluation. **(2)** An epidemic-based algorithm that is similar to *CoFiGel* except that it does not take into account contact history and time constraints. We called this algorithm **NoDelivery-Time**. The performance difference between **NoDeliveryTime** and *CoFiGel* indicates the improvement provided by exploiting contact history. **(3)** An algorithm that uses only the rating information available. This is referred to as **NoCoverage**. The ratings of the items are predicted using the MCF, but the rating update and the potential coverage increase is not considered. By using only limited rating information, **NoCoverage** is expected to perform the worst. **(4)** An algorithm which tries to schedule an item so as to acquire prediction coverage of hitherto unrated users and to satisfy as many more users as possible. This is called the **NoItemRecall**. While this approach also uses contact history, it does not perform multi-round predictions as in the case of *CoFiGel*. It only acts using the current rating information. **(5)** **CoFiGel3G** is a modification of *CoFiGel* such that it uses the cellular network to upload/download ratings and a central server to run the MCF. However, the data are still sent over the DTN. By exploiting the cellular network as control channel, ratings information propagate quickly among the nodes and

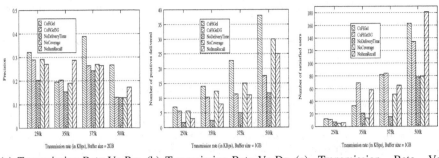

(a) Transmission Rate Vs Pre- (b) Transmission Rate Vs De- (c) Transmission Rate Vs
cision   livered positive items   Users

Fig. 3. RollerNet trace

is always up-to-date. However, it is important to note that faster rating propagation does not always translate to higher rating coverage. This is because an actual rating can only be discovered after an user has access to the actual video and provides the rating.

5.2 Coverage

We now evaluate the performance of *CoFiGel* and the other algorithms in terms of prediction coverage, a commonly used metric for MCF. In addition, we also measured the fraction of correctly predicted positive (or FCPP) items, which measure the ratio of correctly predicted positive item to the total of number of positive ratings rather over all ratings. Given that we are simulating a DTN environment, FCPP provides a better gauge for what is achievable by good algorithms in more challenging environments.

Figures 1(a) and 2(a) show how positive ratings increase over time. The actual number of ratings for the items published so far (*Ground-Truth*) are shown to illustrate the best possible outcomes. In terms of overall ratings, CoFiGel discovers 45% of the ratings. In terms of FCPP, *CoFiGel* discovers 84% of the positive ratings. In fact, the performance of *CoFiGel* measured using FCPP closely matches the actual ratings in the first 15 minutes and the gap remains small throughout the simulation. The results shows that *CoFiGel* has the best performance, followed by *CoFiGel3G*.

This result can be somewhat surprising since *CoFiGel3G* uses the same algorithm as *CoFiGel* but uses the control (3G) channel for centralized rating computation and sharing. We explain the result as follows. Since *CoFiGel3G* performs centralized rating, the rating matrix gets updated much faster. This fast rating update has the (unintended) consequence that the variable G_i in utility function approaches the value of 1.0 much faster than the case for *CoFiGel*. As the value of G_i gets close to 1 and saturates around this value, this variable becomes useless in term of providing information for relative ranking to decide which video data item is more important. However, since propagation of video data item lags behind rating data, the loss of this rating information results in *CoFiGel3G* performing worse than *CoFiGel*.

The higher contact rate and capacity turn out to have adverse effect on **NoDeliveryTime**, **NoCoverage** and **NoItemRecall**, since each algorithm only looks at one aspect of the problem. In terms of FCPP, **NoDeliveryTime** discovers 13% of the positive ratings, while **NoCoverage** discovers 0.6% or less of the positive ratings and **NoItemRecall** discovers around 1%.

The coverage for the **NoCoverage** is very low, showing that it is important to take into account additional information beyond ratings. Figures 1(b) and 2(b) show how coverage varies with transmission rate. While increase in contact capacity results in increased coverage because more items get rated, *CoFiGel* is able to exploit the increase in transmission rate much better than **NoDeliveryTime**, **NoCoverage** and **NoItemRecall**. In the results shown, *CoFiGel* performs better than **NoDeliveryTime** by up to 105% and discovers at least 50 times more ratings than **NoCoverage** and **NoItemRecall** consistently. In general, more improvement comes from taking into account rating coverage gain (from **NoCoverage** to **NoDeliveryTime**) than taking into account contact history. The effort by **NoItemRecall** to increase the number of user ratings is also ineffective due to the absence of rating gain which is capitalized by *CoFiGel*. Nevertheless, substantial improvement is still observed between **NoDeliveryTime** and *CoFiGel*. The performance with respect to different buffer sizes is shown in Figures 1(c), 2(c). There are two observations. First, for very small buffer size of less than 150MB, very few items make it to the next hop and hence, the FCPP remains same for *CoFiGel* and **NoDeliveryTime**. For larger buffer sizes, FCPP of *CoFiGel* is higher than **NoDeliveryTime** by up to 36% and for **NoCoverage** by 50 to 60 times.

5.3   User Satisfaction

While coverage indicates the predictive power of the system, the actual user satisfaction has to be measured by looking at how many items reach users that like them. In order to ensure that the nodes have accumulated enough training data before making the measurement, we consider items generated after first 1.5 hours and before the last half hour. The first 1.5 hours serve as the training phase, while the last half hour is ignored to make sure that items generated later in the trace do not bias the measurement.

Figure 3(a) shows the results for precision of items reaching the users. It is clear that *CoFiGel* performs very well, except for one case (350K), it has the highest precision. In addition, note that even though **NoItemRecall** has a higher precision, from the results in the previous section, it has very low coverage. Due to the disconnected nature of DTN and the large number of data items and users available, it is also useful to look user utility in two other ways. First, we look at the average number of positively rated items that reach any user. The result is shown in figure 3(b). *CoFiGel* clearly outperforms the other two algorithms by a very large margin once the bandwidth exceeds some threshold required for data dissemination. At the highest transmission rate experimented, improvements are 117% compared to **NoDeliveryTime** and 225% more useful items than **NoCoverage**. Another way we measure recall is to look at the number of users who have received at least one useful item. The result is shown in figure 3(c). Again, *CoFiGel* performs well, in particular, at higher bandwidth. At 4Mbps, *CoFiGel* delivers twice as many useful items to users than **NoCoverage** and **NoDeliveryTime**.

6   Conclusion

We have presented *CoFiGel*, a novel approach that combines collaborative filtering and DTN routing in a distributed environment with intermittent connectivity. It is designed for sharing of locally stored contents that have *spatial and temporal relationships*. Results show *CoFiGel* ensures timely deliver of items with higher prediction coverage gain, discovers more ratings and delivers more items that are rated positively by users, than baseline strategies.

References

1. Seshadri, P.V., Chan, M.C., Ooi, W.T.: Mobile-to-Mobile Video Recommendation, (November 12, 2012), http://arxiv.org/abs/1211.2063
2. Huang, J., Xu, Q., Tiwana, B., Mao, Z.M., Zhang, M., Bahl, P.: Anatomizing Application Performance Differences on Smartphones. In: MobiSys, pp. 165–178 (2010)
3. Su, X., Khoshgoftaar, T.M.: A survey of collaborative filtering techniques. In: Advances in Artificial Intelligence, vol. 2009. Hindawi Publishing Corp. (2009)
4. Xu, C., Cameron, D., Jiangchuan, L.: Statistics and Social Network of YouTube Videos. In: IWQoS, pp. 229–238 (2008)
5. Vidal, J.M.: A Protocol for a Distributed Recommender System. In: Falcone, R., Barber, S.K., Sabater-Mir, J., Singh, M.P. (eds.) Trusting Agents. LNCS (LNAI), vol. 3577, pp. 200–217. Springer, Heidelberg (2005)
6. Tournoux, P.U., Leguay, J., Benbadis, F., Conan, V., Dias de Amorim, M., Whitbeck, J.: The Accordion Phenomenon: Analysis, Characterization, and Impact on DTN Routing. In: INFOCOM, pp. 1116–1124 (2009)
7. Shlomo, B., Tsvi, K., Francesco, R.: Distributed collaborative filtering with domain specialization. In: RecSys, pp. 33–40 (2007)
8. Wang, J., Pouwelse, J., Lagendijk, R.L., Reinders, M.J.T.: Distributed collaborative filtering for peer-to-peer file sharing systems. In: SAC, pp. 1026–1030 (2006)
9. Balasubramanian, N., Balasubramanian, A., Venkataramani, A.: Energy Consumption in Mobile Phones: A Measurement Study and Implications for Network Applications. In: IMC, pp. 280–293 (2009)
10. Ioannidis, S., Chaintreau, A., Massoulie, L.: Optimal and Scalable Distribution of Content Updates over a Mobile Social Network. In: INFOCOM, pp. 1422–1430 (2009)
11. Lin, K.C.-J., Chen, C.-W., Chou, C.-F.: Preference-Aware Content Dissemination in Opportunistic Mobile Social Networks. In: INFOCOM, pp. 1960–1968 (2012)
12. Lo Giusto, G., Mashhadi, A.J., Capra, L.: Folksonomy-based reasoning for content dissemination in mobile settings. In: CHANTS, pp. 39–46 (2010)
13. Linden, G., Smith, B., York, J.: Amazon.com recommendations: item-to-item collaborative filtering. In: Internet Computing, vol. 7, pp. 76–80. IEEE (2003)
14. Miller, B.N., Konstan, J.A., Riedl, J.: PocketLens: Toward a Personal Recommender System. In: Transactions on Information Systems, vol. 22, pp. 437–476. ACM (2004)
15. Lee, K., Yi, Y., Jeong, J., Won, H., Rhee, I., Chong, S.: Max-Contribution: On Optimal Resource Allocation in Delay Tolerant Networks. In: INFOCOM, pp. 1136–1144 (2010)

DualCodes: Backward Compatible Multi-layer 2D-Barcodes

Martin Werner and Mirco Schönfeld

Mobile and Distributed Systems Group
Ludwig-Maximilians-University Munich, Germany
{martin.werner,mirco.schoenfeld}@ifi.lmu.de
http://www.mobile.ifi.lmu.de/

Abstract. Matrix codes enable a coupling between virtual and physical worlds for ubiquitous computing applications. With this paper, we propose a technique, which can be used to increase the amount of information contained in a matrix barcode in a backward compatible way. This enables applications to fully utilize the wide spread of QR Codes or Data Matrix Codes for service discovery or basic service, while being able to transmit much more information during one scan for advanced applications. We present the approach, explain difficulties in decoding typical camera images, a simulatory evaluation of decoding performance, and application examples.

Keywords: Matrix code, Two-Dimensional barcode, Pervasive systems, Ubiquitous computing.

1 Introduction

Matrix barcodes play an important role in ubiquitous computing applications due to various reasons: Matrix codes enable a deep integration of physical and virtual worlds without advanced infrastructure components for localization. Matrix codes can be printed, can be shown on displays, can be read from larger distances as compared to RFID or NFC, and are well-known. For all major smartphone platforms, there are free high-quality barcode reading applications available. One of the most widely known matrix barcodes is the Quick Response Code (QR Code).

In 2000, the International Organization for Standardization (ISO) published a specification of the QR Code, which has been initially developed by Denso Wave in 1994 [1]. The most important invention are the finder patterns, which allow for a simple, fast, and rotation-invariant registration of QR Codes inside camera images. Meanwhile, the QR Code was widely adopted. In June 2011, for example, 14 Million American users of mobile camera phones scanned QR Codes. These are 6.2% of the mobile audience [2]. A Japanese survey conducted in 2005 revealed that nearly 90% of the mobile users younger than 20 years have had experience with QR Codes [3].

K. Zheng, M. Li, and H. Jiang (Eds.): MOBIQUITOUS 2012, LNICST 120, pp. 25–36, 2013.

However, QR Code readability with camera phones is limited by the effective resolution of the camera, such that decoding becomes more difficult with increasing information content. For simple Internet applications, there are URL shortening services, which can be used to increase readability of QR Codes. But for pervasive computing applications, it is important to include the complete service information inside QR Codes, because Internet access is often limited inside buildings and privacy concerns restrict a central communication given by an Internet link.

Consequently, there are many approaches, which try to increase the information capacity of a matrix code while keeping a comparable scanning performance in terms of scanning speed and robustness. One common idea is to use multiple different colors [4–8]. While this clearly increases information density as compared to black-and-white codes, it is not clear, whether common smartphone cameras have sufficient color reproduction capabilities. Another drawback of using colors is an increased complexity in normalization and the need for color printing.

Unfortunately, these approaches did not yet converge to standards nor found wide adoption. One exception might be Microsoft Tag, a limited, cloud-based color tagging system using HCCB [5, 9]. However, Microsoft Tag does not allow the dissemination of information without interacting with a cloud service. Therefore, it is not well-suited for pervasive computing applications.

With this paper, we want to bring together the wide-spread QR Code as a publicly standardized basis with an extending technique increasing information density. Therefore, we introduce the so called dual coding technique, which provides two main advantages over using classical matrix codes: First of all, a higher spatial information density can be achieved using modified scanning software without locking out classical barcode scanners from basic functionality. Second of all, hybrid applications are possible, where the service for classical scanning software is different from the service for informed readers and special applications, which make use of the second layer of information.

The next Section 2 introduces the dual coding scheme in general and defines requirements for the underlying matrix code encoding functions. Section 3 describes an enhanced decoding algorithm for dual matrix codes, which explains upcoming challenges in real world scanning situations and gives solutions to them. This Section is followed by an evaluation of the dual QR Code decoding performance with respect to perspective correction, image noise, and blur. Section 5 explains applications, which show the strengths of using a dual encoding scheme. Section 6 concludes this paper.

2   The Dual Coding Scheme

Let $\mathcal{E}_m(s)$ denote the encoding function of some matrix barcode m, which takes a string s as an argument and generates a complete matrix barcode including finder patterns. Let $\mathcal{D}_m(I)$ denote the corresponding decoding function, which takes an image I given as an intensity distribution and returns the content of the

(a) QR Code Layer 1: $\mathcal{E}_m(s)$ (b) QR Code Layer 2: $\mathcal{E}_m(t)$ (c) Dual QR Code $E_d(s,t)$ with $\alpha = 0.7$

Fig. 1. Example of the dual QR Code for $s = $ NTKDLTMMBYAXOGSZEMIHKHTUM and $t = $ DHEVRZOTMRLNXIELEBJUSNDYM

matrix barcode, which is allowed to be contained somewhere inside the possibly noisy image. There is no assumption made about possible perspective distortion, noise, and blur. Consequently, the decoding might fail returning an empty string.

A matrix encoding function $\mathcal{E}_m$ is called *DC-compatible*, if it has the following properties:

– It is *left-unique*: For two equal strings $s = t$, the encoding is also equal: $\mathcal{E}(s) = \mathcal{E}(t)$. Note, that typically left-uniquess is part of the mathematical definition of a function. But there are code systems where the encoding is not left-unique such that two different codewords have the same preimage under the encoding relation.
– The functional properties (i.e., finder patterns for registration, version codes) are kept intact under addition and scalar multiplication of images.

An example for a DC-compatible encoding function is given by the widely adopted QR Code [1, 10], when the version, redundancy level, encoding and block size are chosen the same and the string argument is limited to strings of a fixed length.

The encoding function $\mathcal{E}_d(s,t)$ of dual codes is given as a linear interpolation of two DC-compatible encoding functions applied to the arguments s and t.

$$\mathcal{E}_d(s,t) = \alpha\mathcal{E}_m(s) + (1-\alpha)\mathcal{E}_m(t) \qquad (1)$$

When choosing α significantly larger than 0.5, such that the first code is sufficiently stronger than the second code, compatibility implies, that the result can be decoded by the matrix code decoder:

$$\mathcal{D}_m(\mathcal{E}_d(s,t)) = s, \text{ if } \alpha \text{ large enough.}$$

This fact can be used in two ways: First of all, the dual code can be decoded by any decoder software, which can handle noise. In this way, the first information layer s in the dual code $\mathcal{E}_d(s,t)$ can be used compatibly with the basic versions

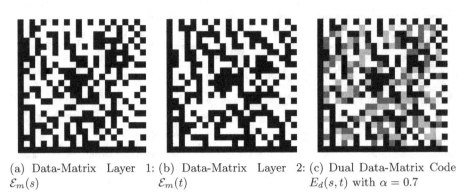

(a) Data-Matrix Layer 1: (b) Data-Matrix Layer 2: (c) Dual Data-Matrix Code $\mathcal{E}_m(s)$ $\mathcal{E}_m(t)$ $E_d(s,t)$ with $\alpha = 0.7$

Fig. 2. Example of the dual Data-Matrix Code for $s =$ NTKDLTMMBYAXOGSZEMIHKHTUM and $t =$ DHEVRZOTMRLNXIELEBJUSNDYM

of the matrix code. The second use enables decoding of the second layer of information. This can be achieved by encoding the decoded result again leading to a noiseless coding of the first information layer and removing this layer. Let I be the intensity distribution of a dual code. Then the following three-step algorithm decodes both information layers:

$$s = \mathcal{D}_m(I)$$
$$I_2 = \frac{1}{1-\alpha}\left(I - \alpha\mathcal{E}_m(s)\right)$$
$$t = \mathcal{D}_m(I_2)$$

This coding scheme has been implemented in a simulation environment for the case of QR Codes generated by the open source software qrencode [11] and decoding provided by ZXing barcode scanning software [12]. Without any image noise and disturbances, the ZXing QR code scanning software was able to decode the stronger part s for $0.67 \leq \alpha$ and the weaker part t for $0.67 \leq \alpha \leq 1 - \epsilon$, where ϵ is a small positive value large enough, such that $I - \alpha E_m(s)$ is non-zero for non-zero pixels in $E_m(t)$. It might seem a bit odd, that there is a lower bound on α, but no (real) upper bound. But as we are working in a perfect environment without noise or amplitude degradation, a successful decoding of the stronger code leads to a 100% correct reconstruction of the weaker code, i.e. I_2 is actually identical to $\mathcal{E}_m(t)$, as long as *alpha* is strictly smaller than 1. An example with two random strings of length 25 is given in Figure 1.

Basically, this coding scheme allows for embedding a second layer of information keeping the first layer of information intact and decodable by software, which is not informed about the existence of the second layer. Furthermore, a given amount of information (s concatenated with t) can be transmitted with less spatial resolution. On the other hand, the image intensity has to be measured in more detail. While the basic QR Code is a binary code, the DQR Code contains four levels of intensity, namely $0, \alpha, 1 - \alpha$, and 1 which have to be

(a) Layer 1: $\mathcal{E}_m(s_1, s_2, s_3)$ (b) Layer 2: $\mathcal{E}_m(t_1, t_2, t_3)$ (c) Dual Code $E_d(s_i, t_i)$ with $\alpha = 0.7$

Fig. 3. Example of the dual Color Superposition Code for six random strings of length 25 assigned to the six color components of two independet RGB images

distinguishable. In summary, the dual coding scheme allows for a flexible payoff between spatial resolution and color space resolution.

The same coding scheme is also applicable to the well-known Data-Matrix Code [13]. Figure 2(c) depicts an example. The stronger symbol also decoded correctly for $\alpha \geq 0.67$. The reason for this equal value is the binary nature of the code and the fact, that the threshold settings in the local histogram binarizer giving the first common stage of decoding are the same. The weaker code could then again be reconstructed for $0.67 \leq \alpha \leq 1 - \epsilon$. Even a superposition code in the color domain (compare [7, 14, 15]) is suitable for this framework.

For a very simple color coding scheme, where three independent QR Codes are put into the three color components of an RGB image, the framework works well. See Figure 3 for an example of such a code. However, for real world applications one should keep in mind, that the detecting camera has to be able to correctly distinguish all three color channels in high quality making decoding under changing light conditions much harder.

In the following section, we explain in more detail, how this theoretical framework was applied for the case of the Quick Response matrix code. The dual version of this code, encoded as above, is called DQR Code.

3   DQR Codes in Real-World Scanning Situations

Figure 4(a) shows a typical smartphone camera image containing a DQR Code. The first step in decoding is the localization of the three position patterns inside the picture. This is classically done using a scanline algorithm searching for the characteristic 1-1-3-1-1 pattern in a binarized version of the camera image. Afterwards, the smaller alignment patterns are localized at the expected positions. This results in at least four locations inside the image.

These define the perspective transformation of the code in the camera image, which is used to reproject the code to known dimension and orientation. Now, this code I can be decoded as usual, as we have taken care that the combined

(a) Camera image   (b) Reprojected and combined image Norm$(I - \alpha J)$ (c) Binarized second layer

Fig. 4. Real-world scanning situation and artefacts

code decodes to layer 1. The result of this decoding step $s = \mathcal{D}_m(I)$ is then re-encoded to $J = \mathcal{E}_m(\mathcal{D}_m(I))$, hence correcting possible bit errors. After normalizing both codes, the reprojected code portion of the camera image and the freshly generated code for layer 1, we can substract and decode layer 2:

$$t = \mathcal{D}_m(\text{Norm}(I - \alpha J))$$

In these equations Norm denotes a normalization of the resulting image with respect to intensity. This step is needed, because the second step of the algorithm, $I - \alpha \mathcal{E}_m(s)$, results in $(1 - \alpha)\mathcal{E}_m(t)$ under ideal conditions and normalization is given by multiplication with $1/(1 - \alpha)$ in this case. But in reality, the image I consists of the encoded data and a noise term as in

$$I = \mathcal{E}_d(s, t) + V$$

such that the normalization factor is unknown.

Due to the high noise level after substracting the re-encoded QR Code J and due to inaccuracies in the locations of the finder patterns, the image Norm$(I - \alpha J)$ suffers from the following problems prohibiting a naive decoding. Figure 4(b) shows an example.

- Finder patterns can be corrupted by addition of neighbouring pixels due to numerical problems with perspective correction.
- Small high intensity edges appear between the matrix blocks, again due to inaccuracies of perspective correction, which heavily influence binarization.
- A higher bit error rate while binarizing is to be expected, as the signal energy of the second code is significantly lower as compared to the signal energy of the first code.

As a countermeasure for the first problem, one can simply correct the corrupted structural elements of the code. For the second problem, one can use a Gaussian filter centered at the known locations of the matrix blocks emphasizing their

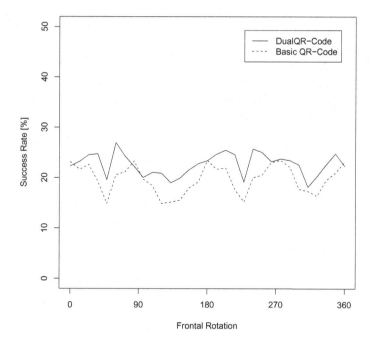

Fig. 5. Decoding performance of DQR Codes compared to classical QR Codes with respect to perspective distortion

center intensity and weakening the effects between adjacent blocks. To deal with the higher bit error rate, the redundancy level of the barcode should be chosen high enough. To further enhance the decoding performance for the second layer, it is advisable to try different binarization methods and thresholds in a loop, Figure 4(c) shows the resulting binary code for the second layer of the example image.

4   Evaluation

A first consideration with respect to evaluation of the dual coding system is the robustness concerning perspective distortion. For pervasive computing applications, it is to be expected that the barcode is scanned from different viewing angles and distances. For comparison of classical QR Codes with dual codes, we conducted a complex evaluation experiment, where the matrix code is rendered rotating around its three axis using the technique described in [16]. Figure 6(a) shows an example of a QR Code rotated around its three axis. Figure 5 depicts the results of this experiment, where the y-axis shows the decoding success rate for images rotated around the pitch axis and the yaw axis from $[\frac{-\pi}{2}, \frac{\pi}{2}]$. The decoding sucess rate is defined to be the fraction of the sucessfully decoded

(a) Three degrees of freedom rotation of a QR Code

(b) A white image containing 10% of random image noise

(c) A DQR Code containing blur with $\sigma = 0.3$ matrix blocks

Fig. 6. The effects of perspective distortion, Gaussian noise, and blur

images out of all rotated images. The x-axis gives the rotation around the rotational axis, which does not affect the spatial extensions of each matrix block. For comparision, the basic QR Code contains a string, which is twice as long as each individual string of the DQR Code, such that it contains the same amount of information. One can clearly see, that the DQR Code performs better with respect to perspective distortion as compared to the basic QR Code. This is due to the fact, that the blocks inside the basic QR Code are smaller due to the longer content.

With smartphone cameras, another source of problems is image noise. To evaluate the effect of image noise, a random image (White Gaussian Noise) was generated and used to create sequences of blendings with clean QR and DQR codes for varying noise amounts. The basic QR Code is able to deal with a noise amount of less than 48%. The dual code, of course, is more sensitive with respect to image noise, as it has to distinguish between more intensities. The message in layer 1 decodes for a noise amount of less than 33% and both layers decode successfully for a noise amount of less than 10%. This is slightly below the theoretically achievable value of 14.4% (i.e., 48% of 30%, for $\alpha = 0.7$), which is due to the fact, that image binarization is more difficult due to the artefacts coming from inaccurate projection. Nevertheless, 10% of image noise is quite a high amount of noise, as one can see in picture 6(b).

Another important effect affecting image quality is blur. For evaluation purposes, we apply a Gaussian blur filter to the matrix code image with varying standard deviation σ and radius 3σ. The block size of the source image is ten pixels and the standard deviations in the following are relative to the pixel domain and not relative to the matrix code blocks. For the DQR Code, a Gaussian blur with σ up to 2.4 pixel (i.e., 0.24 blocks) did not affect the decoding. For $\sigma \in [2.4 \ldots 4.2]$, only the stronger layer 1 was decoded sucessfully. For $\sigma > 4.2$ pixel, the system is unable to decode any of the two layers. The classic QR Code, containing the same amount of information, is decoded for $\sigma < 1.7$ pixel. The big difference is partly induced by a reduced block size of 8 pixel, which is needed, as the QR Code contains the concatenation of the strings of both layers of the dual code. Figure 6(c) shows the effect of blur applied to a DQR Code.

Furthermore, the system has been implemented for Android smartphones and been thoroughly tested in two use-cases: Scanning dual codes from paper and from screens. Both cases worked well, however accuracy problems with perspective correction before substracting a freshly generated code and a scanned code led to some interesting artefacts, which needed a Gaussian filtering step as already described in Section 3.

5   Applications

Dual matrix codes can be used to increase information density in matrix codes. But they also allow for advanced applications, where the individual layers of the dual matrix code have different functionality. In the following, we explain one application, which increases privacy for matrix code based positioning in a location based service scenario. The second application below explains, how DQR codes can be used to provide a higher security level for the adoption of matrix code technology in business environments, where some functions (e.g., adding a contact) can be limited to properly signed barcodes on informed devices, while a non-informed device can still be used with the same matrix code without this security enhancement.

5.1   Privacy-Enabled Location Based Services Using Matrix Codes for Positioning

Due to the tremendous growth of location based services, as for example forecast to grow to US10.4 billions in 2015 [17], the interest in reducing the barriers for large-scale, local provisioning of location based services is growing. However, location based services are nowaday typically provided outdoors, where GPS positioning is available. Inside buildings, however, there is no cheap positioning technology available. To solve this problem, there have been proposals to use barcode technology for location tagging. That is, to bring out different barcodes in the surroundings and to infer the position of a mobile device by scanning a barcode [18]. Unfortunately, Internet access is not available in many buildings and, from a privacy perspective, it is not a good idea to let barcodes point to Internet addresses providing location information. Because then, the time and position of each user can be independently tracked by the location based service platform. Furthermore, the presentation quality is limited by current web technology and a deep integration with smartphone content, such as contacts and calendar, is impossible.

Therefore, future location based services for navigation inside buildings should rely on mobile applications, which hold maps and navigation information on the smartphone. But then, the provisioning of location based services becomes a problem: On the one hand, the barcode could contain an Internet address, which could give hints on how to get the application. But then, location information has to be encoded into this Internet address with one severe implication: The location information is sent over the Internet and the location based service platform could collect this information. On the other hand, the distributed tags could contain only location information. But then, a user, which does not yet have the application, will have difficulties to locate and install the needed software.

With the framework of dual codes, however, one can integrate both approaches and let the stronger barcode point to an Internet address, where the user can download the application and let the weak barcode provide location information. In this way, a user, which does not yet have the application, can use any barcode reading software to locate and install the location based service application, while a user, which already has got the software, will directly get the location based service as provided by the mobile application.

For buildings, where mobile Internet access via a cellular network is problematic, the stronger code could also contain information for authenticating with a wireless local area network, which could provide information and Internet access to the user, while the second layer again contains location information which is not automatically transmitted, as common barcode readers only read the stronger part.

To summarize, with dual matrix codes it is possible to decouple location information from service and application discovery information and hence to realize privacy-friendly location based services with matrix codes.

As a side effect, depending on the information encoded in each barcode, the size of the the matrix code will be smaller than if both types of informations would have to be encoded in one layer.

5.2   Digitally Signed Matrix Codes

Scanning matrix codes, in general, raises some security risks. The reader software could be vulnerable to various attacks, which could lead to system intrusion. Furthermore, the content of the Internet address specified inside the matrix code could exploit flaws in the mobile device browser or simply trick the user to download malware [19–21]. Another risk is that users could be provided with wrong contact information inside modified barcodes enabling man-in-the-middle attacks.

For a company, the dual coding technique allows for a transparent, flexible matrix barcode authentication scheme, where smartphones are equipped with a special matrix code reader, which only allows the user to follow a QR Code, if the second layer in the dual coding scheme is a qualified digital signature over the first layer using a predefined certificate chain. These restrictions can flexibly depend on the actual content of the matrix code, such that risky operations like modifying contact information or adding WiFi credentials are impossible without a correctly signed dual matrix code, while the display of the content of the matrix code might always be allowed.

In this way, smartphones and paper documents can be easily integrated in a working environment without the risk of drive-by infection by unauthorized matrix codes.

6   Conclusion

In this paper, we have proposed a general technique, which enables the encoding of multiple information layers for most matrix codes. With this general approach, backward compatibility is combined with advanced service capabilities, such as a higher spatial information density and advanced applications using for example optional signatures. The dual encoding scheme was evaluated against the most important image distortions for smartphone cameras and a prototypical smartphone implementation based on ZXing barcode scanning library [12] was implemented. The presented dual encoding technique showed good results in simulation and practical experiments.

References

1. Automatic identification and data capture techniques – Bar code symbology – QR Code, ISO/IEC 18004:2000 (2000)
2. 14 Million Americans Scanned QR Codes on their Mobile Phones (June 2011), http://www.comscore.com/Press_Events/Press_Releases/2011/8/14_Million_ Americans_Scanned_QR_or_Bar_Codes_on_their_Mobile_Phones_in_June_2011
3. Kato, H., Tan, K.T.: Pervasive 2D barcodes for camera phone applications. IEEE Pervasive Computing 6(4), 76–85 (2007)
4. Sali, E., Lax, D.M., et al.: Color bar code system. US Patent 7210631 (2006)
5. Parikh, D., Jancke, G.: Localization and segmentation of a 2D high capacity color barcode. In: IEEE Workshop on Applications of Computer Vision, WACV 2008 (2008)
6. Grillo, A., Lentini, A., Querini, M., Italiano, G.F.: High capacity colored two dimensional codes. In: Proceedings of the 2010 International Multiconference on Computer Science and Information Technology (IMCSIT 2010), pp. 709–716 (2010)
7. Dean, T., Dunn, C.: Quick layered response (qlr) codes (2012)
8. Hao, T., Zhou, R., Xing, G.: COBRA: color barcode streaming for smartphone systems. In: Proceedings of the 10th International Conference on Mobile Systems, Applications, and Services, pp. 85–98. ACM (2012)
9. Microsoft Tag (2012), http://tag.microsoft.com/
10. Automatic identification and data capture techniques – QR-Code 2005 bar code symbology specification, ISO/IEC 18004:2006 (2006)
11. qrencode - QR Code encoder (2012), http://fukuchi.org/works/qrencode/manual/index.html
12. ZXing - Multi-format 1D/2D barcode image processing library with clients for Android and iPhone (2012), http://code.google.com/p/zxing/
13. Automatic identification and data capture techniques – data matrix bar code symbology specification, ISO/IEC 16022 (2006)
14. Tan, K.T., Chai, D., Wu, K., Kato, H., Ong, S.K.: Data storage device and encoding/decoding methods. WO Patent WO/2010/031,110 (2010)

15. Kato, H., Tan, K.T., Chai, D.: Novel colour selection scheme for 2D barcode. In: International Symposium on Intelligent Signal Processing and Communication Systems, pp. 529–532 (2009)
16. Scheuermann, C., Werner, M., Kessel, M., Linnhoff-Popien, C., Verclas, S.: Evaluation of barcode decoding performance using ZXing library. In: Proceedings of the Second Workshop on Smart Mobile Applications, SmartApps 2012 (2012)
17. Pyramid Research. Market Forecast: Location-Based Services (Preview) (2011), http://www.pyramidresearch.com/store/Report-Location-Based-Services.htm
18. Mulloni, A., Wagner, D., Barakonyi, I., Schmalstieg, D.: Indoor positioning and navigation with camera phones. IEEE Pervasive Computing 8(2), 22–31 (2009)
19. AVG Community Powered Threat Report (2011), http://aa-download.avg.com/filedir/press/AVG_Community_Powered_Threat_Report_Q4_2011.pdf
20. Zhou, Y., Jiang, X.: Dissecting android malware: Characterization and evolution. In: Proceedings of the 33rd IEEE Symposium on Security and Privacy (2012)
21. Maslennikov, D.: Malicious QR Codes Pushing Android Malware (2011), https://www.securelist.com/en/blog/208193145/Malicious_QR_Codes_Pushing_Android_Malware

A Collaborative Framework of Enabling Device Participation in Mobile Cloud Computing

Woonghee Lee, Suk Kyu Lee, Seungho Yoo, and Hwangnam Kim[*]

School of Electrical Engineering, Korea University
Seoul, Korea
{tgorevenge,sklee25,pen0423,hnkim}@korea.ac.kr

Abstract. Cloud Computing attracts much attention in the community of computer science and information technology because of resource efficiency and cost-effectiveness. It is also evolved to Mobile Cloud Computing to serve nomadic people. However, any service in Cloud Computing System inevitably experiences a network delay to access the computing resource or the data from the system, and entrusting the Cloud server with the entire task makes mobile devices idle. In order to mitigate the deterioration of network performance and improve the overall system performance, we propose a collaborative framework that lets the mobile device participate in the computation of Cloud Computing system by dynamically partitioning the workload across the device and the system. The proposed framework is based on it that the computing capability of the current mobile device is significantly enhanced in recent years and its multi-core CPU can employ threads to process the data in parallel. The empirical experimentation presents that it can be a promising approach to use the computing resource of the mobile device for executing computation-intensive tasks in Cloud Computing system.

Keywords: Mobile Cloud Computing, Multi-Thread, Parallel Computing.

1 Introduction

Cloud Computing is the technology, the service or the system for serving computing and storage capacity to the end-recipient [1]. One of important usage scenarios for Cloud Computing system is that the system executes computation-intensive tasks instead of the mobile device with the data which a user provides. This scenario assumes that the Cloud server has very high computational power and it produces the required results in a shorter time[1]. Mobile Cloud Computing (MCC) is the system concept added the mobility feature to Cloud Computing, where the transmission involves to wireless connectivity [2]. Therefore, the transmission delay becomes an additional important factor determining the overall system performance.

On the other hand, the hardware and the software of mobile devices have been developed significantly in recent years. For example, the smart-phone equipped with

---

[*] Corresponding author.

[1] Note that we focus on this scenario in this paper.

K. Zheng, M. Li, and H. Jiang (Eds.): MOBIQUITOUS 2012, LNICST 120, pp. 37–49, 2013.

quard-core-CPU and 2GB RAM has been released recently. The enhanced mobile device can do multitasking -- it can run several programs at the same time such as surfing the Internet with listening to music -- and it can process the data in parallel with the multi-thread. Users can thus exert high performance and the latest mobile device can handle much higher computation than those of the past. Therefore, the MCC system should pay attention to this development at the mobile device side in order to overcome the current limitations that (*i*) the network delay may negatively affect the overall performance when the entire user data is transferred back and forth between the Cloud server and the mobile device and (*ii*) the mobile device wastes its computing cycles till it receives any response from the server.

These observations motivate us to devise a collaborative framework on computation for MCC, which exploits the mobile device as an additional computing element of MCC. Thus, we propose in this paper a collaboration framework of using the computational power of the mobile device as an additional resource of MCC in order to improve the system performance by using the mobile device's resource to the fullest. We constructed an empirical test-bed to present that the proposed framework can outperform the traditional computing framework for Cloud Computing. The experimentation results indicate that the proposed framework can enhance the performance of most Cloud Computing system. Note that the proposed framework can be applied to computation-intensive services, not simple browsing or accessing data services.

The remaining part of this paper is organized as follows. We briefly explain the MCC system and the related works in Section 2. We then present the proposed framework and detail the process of framework in Section 3. We evaluate the proposed framework and also state a brief scheduling scheme in Section 4. We conclude the paper with Section 5.

2   Preliminary

In this section we describe some features of Mobile Cloud Computing system, remind that the fundamental strength of parallel computing for computation-intensive tasks, even in the mobile device, and summarize the relevant work that are used in subsequent sections.

2.1   Computation-Intensive Service at Mobile Cloud Computing

The MCC is the newest mobile computing technology for overcoming the limitation of resource shortcomings at the mobile device [3]. As for the computation intensive services at MCC, the entire data is transferred to the Cloud server from the mobile device, the server then processes it with its own resources, and finally the device receives the processed data. In this procedure, MCC has the following features:

1. Network environment dependency: MCC is a concept that the wireless feature is added to Cloud Computing, so that the data transmission involves to the wireless medium. Therefore, the transmission delay dependent on underlying network conditions becomes a more important element of MCC. Note that the wireless network condition is time-varying and hard to estimate [4].
2. Cloud server dependency: To overcome the limitation of the mobile device such as processing and memory capabilities, almost the whole data processing is

performed on the Cloud server, so that the entire processing performance relies on Cloud server's capability. However, the capability may dynamically change with several reasons such as the difference in number of users, which also cannot be controlled and managed by the end mobile device.

3. Service availability: The Cloud server is responsible for responding to millions of user's requests with processing the massive data simultaneously. It is an essential prerequisite to continuously support the MCC services even when the number of users exceeds the maximum allowable limit, which should be possible with acceptable performance degradation [5].

We can discover additional features derived from the above main features. (*i*) We cannot expect the constant service turn-around time because the number of service users and the amount of resources for each user request are dynamically changing. (*ii*) Computing resources of the mobile device may be wasted till any response from the Cloud server arrives even though it can be used and more productive in the service provisioning. (*iii*) The communication procedure between the MCC system and the user is fixed, regardless of the device capability, the service type, the network condition, and the current usage of the Cloud server.

2.2   Parallel Processing Schemes for Mobile Device

We briefly explain the current state of the art of parallel processing that we would like to apply to the proposed framework.

Threads. Due to the development of software and hardware, the average size of data is bigger than before and a number of computation-intensive processes appear. Especially, any work that deals with images or videos such as the digital image processing needs many arithmetic operations in handling big data and furthermore requires real-time processing. Therefore, it is possible to process the data using multi-core or multi-thread owing to improvement in hardware like CPU and memory. Parallel computing using multi-thread to process the work divided up into small segments is suitable for computation-intensive processes and it has become the essential method for improving the computing performance [6].

Simultaneous Processing and Transmission. We conducted a simple experiment for processing and transmission using multi-thread simultaneously before we propose a collaborative framework. There are the sender and the receiver in the experiment. The sender starts the process with setting to work. The sender does processing and sends some parts of the processed data at the same time, and then the receiver receives them from the sender and simultaneously does other processing with the received data. All processes are performed by using multi-thread.

2.3   Edge Detection and Discrete Cosine Transform

We used two tasks in our empirical studies in order to demonstrate the benefit of the proposed collaborative framework. One is Edge Detection and the other is Discrete Cosine Transform (DCT). Edge Detection is a fundamental tool in the computer vision and image processing and it is a process for extracting the significant properties of objects in the image. It can be used to do feature detection, feature extraction and identification of the physical phenomena, and therefore it can be employed by any application in 3D reconstruction, motion recognition, image enhancement, image restoration, image compression and so on [7]. DCT is a mathematical tool to express a sequence of finite data using the combination of cosine functions. It is very important in science and engineering such as image processing and compression of audio/image data [8].

Both tasks are widely used for image processing and image compression. Image processing on mobile devices is a new field because the latest phones are equipped with camera, and high performance CPU [9]. Additionally, in terms of the wireless network, image compression is an essential process. Therefore, we choose them as feasible tasks in mobile devices. However, the proposed framework can be applied to any other task in mobile computing environment in order to achieve performance improvement.

2.4   Advantages of Parallel Processing

In order to present the advantages of the proposed framework of letting the mobile device participate in computation in Mobile Cloud Computing environment, we conducted an empirical test with two scenarios. In case A, Sending/receiving are performed after processing is complete, and in case B, they are performed simultaneously. Each of the sender and the receiver has the 4 threads for processing and 1 thread for sending/receiving in case B. As for the task, we use the Discrete Cosine Transform. The DCT for image is generally performed for the block resulted from splitting the image. The block is a square 8 pixels on a side. The sender performed 2D-DCT using 4 threads in parallel and sent the processed blocks, and then the receiver received the processed blocks and performed 2D inverse DCT using 4 threads in parallel. This experimentation was performed in a single PC using two terminals for the sender and the receiver.

We present the empirical result in Table 1. The total processing time of Case B is much shorter than that of Case A. These results show that it is very efficient to do processing image blocks and sending/receiving them simultaneously.

Table 1. The result for processing and sending/receiving simultaneously

	A		B	
	Sender	Receiver	Sender	Receiver
1	240	253	42	69
2	237	257	42	59
3	240	253	52	75
4	239	257	54	61
5	237	253	53	77
6	238	257	56	56
7	241	248	46	61
8	242	260	46	70
9	246	263	54	73
10	238	254	49	67
mean	239.8 ms	255.5 ms	49.4 ms	66.8 ms

Since the latest mobile devices are able to deliver high performance and to use multi-thread like PCs, we were motivated to use the computation capability of the mobile device to improve the overall performance of MCC.

3   Collaborative Framework

As shown in Section 2.4, we have got a hint that we could improve the service performance by letting the mobile device take some parts of the high computational processes.

3.1   Assumed Configuration

It is fundamental to employ threads for all processing in the proposed framework. There are two thread types. One is the task thread for processing the data and the other is the transmission thread for sending/receiving the data. We just use one thread for transmission thread, but one or more number of task threads for processing the data. Even though the processing performance is generally increased with the number of threads, the improvement becomes stalled and then degraded after reaching a threshold. The main reasons of such the degradation are stretching the CPU to handle too many threads and managing the memory access [6]. We found through much experimentation that the optimum number of threads is in the range between 3 and 5 in our experiments. Naturally, the tasks (edge detection and DCT) that we have chosen for the experimentation are processed in parallel.

There is a pair of the server and the client, the server takes the role of MCC and the client takes the role of user's mobile device. *The server is a virtual server whose capability represents the overall capability of the Mobile Cloud Computing infra.* The total processing starts if the client initiates the processing and it ends when the client has total processed data. The overall performance means the turn-around time, meaning the time required for finishing all processes. The overall performance is influenced by network conditions because MCC is running in wireless network environment in which there are many unpredictable variables. Note that the underlying network is assumed to have a wireless connectivity.

The client can choose the amount of data to process at the client and the rest of data is processed at the server. Therefore, the amount of data to be processed at the client varies depending on the situation: network conditions, the mobile device's performance, and the server's state.

3.2   Operational Procedure

The procedure of the proposed framework is described in what follows. (*i*) First of all, the client partitions the task into two parts (where the one is to be processed in the server and the other is to be done at the mobile device). The ratio varies depending on factors influencing the performance of the system such as the capability of the client and the server, and network situations. It is the most important stage for improving the efficiency for the client to decide the optimal ratio. (*ii*) After the ratio has been chosen, the client transfers the server part of data to the server via the transmission thread and starts processing the rest of data with the task threads simultaneously.

Client   Server

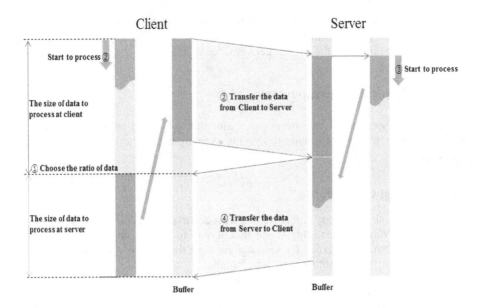

Fig. 1. An execution flow of the proposed framework

(*iii*) The server starts the work with received data. Once all the data is processed, the transmission thread sends the data back to the client. (*iv*) The client receives the server data from the server. When all processes of both sides are finished, the client converges the two parts from different locations into the final data. After that, all of the processes are done. Figure 1 shows the procedure briefly.

The pseudo code of the proposed framework is presented in the Algorithm 1.

4   Performance Evaluation

We employed two evaluation scenarios according to the amount of data processing in order to evaluate the proposed framework. One is the low computational task (Task A) and the other is the high computational task (Task B). Edge detection is used for the low computational task, and DCT is added to the low computational task for the high computational task. Edge Detection mainly consists of integer computations and has few processes, whereas DCT is composed mainly of real number computations and has a large amount of processes. The PC is equipped with 'Intel core i5-2410M', DDR3 4GB RAM, and the mobile device runs Google Android OS version 4.03 in the platform of 'Qualcomm 1.5GHz dual-core MSM8660 Snapdragon', 1GB DDR2 SDRAM. Table 2 shows the approximate average run-time difference between the PC and the mobile device used in the experiment.

Table 2. The average run-time in diverse cases

	Task A	Task B
Mobile device	1000 *ms*	12600 *ms*
PC	80 *ms* (x 12.5)	280 *ms* (x 45)

Algorithm 1. *Pseudo code of the framework*

Server	Client

```
   A = The data assigned to the server;
   B = The data assigned to the client;
   byte buf[]; // buffer array for receiving the data
   byte Dprocess[]; //array for the processed data
1  class ProcessThread{              class ProcessThread{
2     P = first position;              do processing B;
3     while (true){                    P = first position;
4       if(P >= size of A)then         while(true){
5       break;                           if(P >= size of A)then
6       if(buf[P] != null)then           break;
7       do processing buf[P];            if(buf[P] != null)then
8       save the processed               move the data in
9        data to Dprocess[P];             place;
10      P += next position;              P += next position;
11    }                                }
12 }                               }
13 class TransThread{             class TransThread{
14    connect to client;             connect to server
15    receive the A;                 send the A;
16    while(true){                   T = 0;
17      if(Dprocess != null)then     while(true){
18      send Dprocess to Client;       if(T >= size of A)then
19      break;                         break;
20    }                                receive the data;
21 }                                   T += received data;
22 class Mainclass{                 }
23    void main(){               }
24      ProcessThread Pthread;    class Mainclass{
25      TransThread Tthread;         void main(){
26      Pthread.start();               ProcessThread Pthread;
27      Tthread.start();               TransThread Tthread;
28      Pthread.join();                Pthread.start();
29      Tthread.join();                Tthread.start();
30    }                                Pthread.join();
31 }                                   Tthread.join();
32                                   }
33                               }
```

PC's performance is much better than that of the mobile device. In comparison with the run-time, the PC shows better computation capability in Task B (45 times) than in Task A (12.5 times). It means high computational processes such as real number computations overhead much upon the mobile device and processing the high computational operations at the server is more desirable. As mentioned in Section 3, there are the server and the client in our experiments. The PC takes the role of the server and the mobile device takes the other.

Performance Evaluation w.r.t. Low Computational Task. First experiment is performed with 7 configurations in each of which the ratio of data partitioning is changed by 1/6. Both the server and the client have 3 threads for processing. We conducted 5 experimentation runs for each configuration, and so the experimentation results in subsequent explanation are average values. Connectivity between the server and the mobile device is established through Wi-Fi.

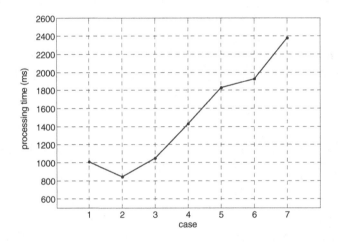

Fig. 2. Turn-around time for each configuration of task partition for Task A

Figure 2 presents the turn-around time of the whole task for each configuration. As shown in the figure, the case 1 (where the entire data is processed at the mobile device) took shorter time than case 7 (where the server is entitled to process the total data). This is because the transmission part took more time than the processing part due to wireless environment; in other words, the delay in the transmission part became the dominating value because of the short processing time.

Additionally, we observed that the time required for sending/receiving total data is over 1 second and the time required for processing total data at mobile device took 1 second approximately, and so it looks inefficient using Mobile Cloud Computing.

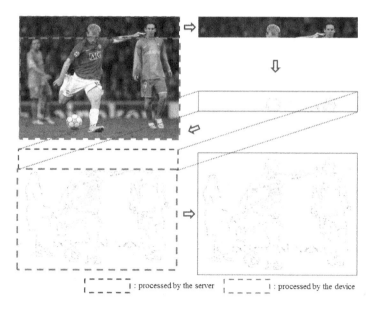

: processed by the server   : processed by the device

Fig. 3. An execution procedure at case 2 for Task A

However, the computational power of the PC (Server) is much better than mobile devices as shown Table 2, so that it could improve the overall efficiency of processing if the proper allocation of data processing is made for the server. It is shown in the case 2 where one sixth of the data is processed at the server and results in the shortest total processing time. The turn-around time of case 2 is shorter than that of the case 1 by about 150*ms*. It means one sixth of the data is the best allocation between processing and sending/receiving in this experiment. Figure 3 shows the execution procedure for the case 2 of task A.

Performance Evaluation w.r.t. High Computational Task. The next experimentation is done with the high computational Task. Figure 4 shows the result of the experiment in this case. The experiment was conducted in the similar way to the previous one. As shown in the figure, the case 7 where the entire data is processed at the server took shorter time than the case 1 where the data is processed only at the mobile device. This comparison shows that mobile device's computational capability could be overwhelmed by the plenty of computation such as DCT. It is more efficient to exploit server computation facility to the fullest. It looks like the advantage assumed in general Cloud Computing system. However, it is not quite the same with that. Even though the case 7 has to show the most efficient result (according to the intention of the current Cloud Computing system), the case 6 (where the mobile device took part in the required computation) shows the shortest time in this experiment. Thus, the ratio of data in case 6 is most pertinent.

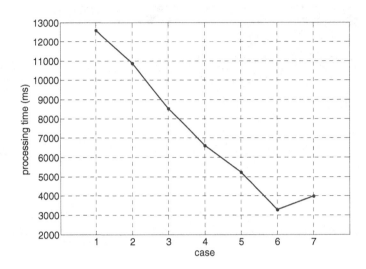

Fig. 4. Turn-around time for each configuration of task partition for Task B

Remarks on Advantages. Recall the issues of existing Mobile Cloud Computing presented in Section 2. The proposed framework can alleviate those issues as follows.

- Low network dependency: The mobile network environment is relatively unstable so its quality cannot be guaranteed. As the occasion, transmission time can be a more dominant factor deciding the overall performance than processing time as shown above. When the network state is stable, sending more data to the server is reasonable. If not, processing more data at the mobile device improves the overall system performance. Also, it can be entirely processed by the mobile device in the extreme case that any connection is not feasible.
- Low Cloud server dependency: Cloud Computing aims at improving the overall performance of processing using the server's computation capability and resources but it is useless if the server could not provide those sufficiently. In this case, it is better to use more resources of the mobile device. Mobile device's resource can be controlled by users and its state is easily ascertainable than that of the server. Processing the data at the mobile device reduces the Cloud server dependency.
- Maximization of mobile device's resources: Entrusting the server with the entire task causes mobile devices idle. Processing some parts of data at the mobile device is one of the ways that optimize the resource usage at the device.
- High flexibility: Factors influencing the performance of Cloud Computing are various. The fixed way for providing services to users is one of causes degrading the overall stability of the service. Users can choose the degree of participation of the user's device in computation in the light of the mobile network condition, device's and server's performance, characteristics of processing. Therefore, these make system flexible and stable, which allows the Cloud server to provide more guaranteed services for users.
- Optimization of Efficiency: It is most important to determine the optimal workload partitioning as shown above, and the efficiency can be achieved by changing the

ratio. The empirical results show that the optimal ratio can be determined and to what extent the optimization is possible.

- Reducing the burden of the server: Distributing the workload across the server and the mobile device can save the server capacity, so that the server is able to serve other users' requests and thus it achieves higher service availability.

A Sketch on Scheduling Algorithm. There are several factors that influence on the proposed framework: the processing capability of the mobile device and the server, network conditions, and characteristics of processing. By considering those factors, we can present a sketch on how to partition workload across the device and the Cloud server based upon the premise that the server maintains steady-state.

Firstly, we determine scheduling parameters as specified in Table 3, which can be estimated by the current network conditions and the computational capability of the server and the device, and then we decide the optimal ratio with those parameters as follows.

Table 3. Scheduling parameters

Notation	Description
T_d	The time required for processing the entire data at the device
T_s	The time required for processing the entire data at the server
T_t	The time required for sending the entire data between the server and the device
T_c	The time required for converging the two parts from different locations.
X	The ratio of work for processing at the server ($0 \leq X \leq 1$)

The total time required at the server is shown in equation (1), whereas the total time required at the device is shown in (2).

$$2XT_t + XT_s . \tag{1}$$

$$(1-X)T_d + XT_c . \tag{2}$$

If the work of the server is finished earlier than that of the device, it means that we do not utilize the server's resource efficiently. On the other hand, if the work of the device is finished earlier than that of the server, it means that the more work can be processed at the device. Therefore, the work can be done most efficiently when either the server or the device is not idle. The optimal ratio X is obtained by using (4).

$$2XT_t + XT_s = (1-X)T_d + XT_c . \tag{3}$$

$$X = T_d / (2T_t + T_s + T_d - T_c) . \tag{4}$$

In Eq. (4), $2T_t + T_s$ means that the time required in case 7, and T_d stands for the time required in case 1. T_c can be negligible for obtaining the X approximately in (4) because T_c is much smaller compared to T_d, T_s, T_t. Therefore, we disregarded T_c to obtain the X more easily. The ratio X is roughly 0.29 in the experimentation for low computational Task and it is between 1/6 and 2/6. Additionally, The X is roughly 0.75 in the experimentation for high computational Task and it is between 4/6 and 5/6. Therefore, the optimal ratio obtained by using (4) accords closely with results of our experiment.

Figure 5 shows the change of X depending on the alteration of T_t, T_s, and T_d. The bigger T_d/T_s means that the Cloud server has more computational power than the device and the smaller T_t/T_s means that the network condition is better. Therefore, the bigger T_d/T_s or the smaller T_t/T_s is, the more data can be processed at the Cloud server more efficiently.

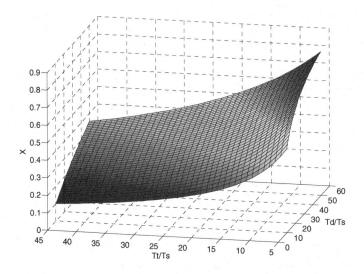

Fig. 5. The change of X depending on the alteration of factors

5   Conclusion

Based on the observation that there are several disadvantages of existing Cloud Computing such as high network environment dependency, high Cloud server dependency, idle mobile devices, low flexibility, and large burden of the server, we proposed a new collaborative framework of letting the mobile device participate in computation-intensive tasks in Mobile Cloud Computing environment. The participation ratio is determined depending on the factors of the system capability, the mobile device's performance, the network state, and characteristics of processing. We ascertained with empirical studies that the proposed framework makes the system achieve better performance and more flexible. It can also alleviate the server workload by using the device capability.

We have several directions as future work. We will elaborate the scheduling algorithm for the proposed framework. We plan to implement the proposed framework in the specific Mobile Cloud Computing infra such as Hadoop-based Cloud Computing system. We also would like to implement the proposed framework in various mobile device platforms such as iPhone and Windows phone.

Acknowledgement. This research was supported in part by the National Research Foundation of Korea (NRF) Grant funded by the Korea government (MEST) (No. 2010-0014060), and in part by the KCC (Korea Communications Commission) Korea under the R&D program supervised by the KCA (Korea Communications Agency) (KCA-2012-08-911-05-001).

References

1. Buyya, R., Yeo, C.S., Venugopal, S.: Market-Oriented Cloud Computing: Vision, Hype, and Reality for Delivering IT Services as Computing Utilities. In: 10th IEEE International Conference on High Performance Computing and Communications, HPCC 2008 (2008)
2. Sanaei, Z., Abolfazli, S., Gani, A., Khokhar, R.H.: Tripod of requirements in horizontal heterogeneous Mobile Cloud Computing. In: Proc.1st Int'l Conf. Computing, Information Systems, and Communications (2012)
3. Sanaei, Z., Abolfazli, S., Gani, A., Shiraz, M.: SAMI: Service-Based Arbitrated Multi-Tier Infrastructure for Mobile Cloud Computing. In: Mobicc. IEEE Workshop on Mobile Cloud Computing, Beijing, China (2012)
4. Woo, S., Kim, H.: Estimating Link Reliability in Wireless Networks: An Empirical Study and Interference Modeling. In: 2010 Proceedings IEEE INFOCOM (2010)
5. Zhu, J., Jiang, Z., Xiao, Z.: Twinkle: A fast resource provisioning mechanism for internet services. In: Proceedings of IEEE INFOCOM (2011)
6. Tullsen, D.M., Eggers, S.J., Levy, H.M.: Simultaneous multithreading: maximizing on-chip parallelism. In: Proceedings of the 25th Annual International Symposium on Computer Architecture, ISCA 1998, pp. 533–544 (1998)
7. Vincent, T.: On Edge Detection. IEEE Transactions on Pattern Analysis and Machine Intelligence (1986)
8. Ahmed, N.: Discrete Cosine Transform. IEEE Transactions on Computers (1974)
9. Wells, M.T.: Mobile Image Processing on the Google Phone with the Android Operating System, http://www.3programmers.com/mwells/main_frame.html

Design and Evaluation of a Publish/Subscribe Framework for Ubiquitous Systems

Zigor Salvador, Alberto Lafuente, and Mikel Larrea

University of the Basque Country UPV/EHU
Donostia-San Sebastián, Spain
{zigor.salvador,alberto.lafuente,mikel.larrea}@ehu.es

Abstract. This paper describes the design and evaluation of a novel publish/subscribe communication framework for ubiquitous systems and applications. The motivation of this work is the realization of the fact that the publish/subscribe communication model has several features that make it suitable to serve as a communication substrate for ubiquitous systems. In particular, we argue that a publish/subscribe framework that is scalable and supports client mobility is a valuable asset for the development of ubiquitous applications. We present a reference implementation, Phoenix, that supports the deployment of publish/subscribe components in mobile devices such as smartphones. In addition, we evaluate the functionality of Phoenix and its performance, in order to determine its operational constraints for server and mobile platforms.

Keywords: publish/subscribe, client mobility, ubiquitous environments, software implementation, empirical validation, performance evaluation.

1 Introduction

The client/server model has played a foundational role in the ongoing success of distributed systems and the Internet. However, distributed systems that are based on the traditional client/server model exhibit a tight coupling of components. Consequently, the deployment and maintenance of large-scale distributed systems based on the client/server model is a complex task. This becomes even more evident when the distributed systems are composed of heterogeneous services, devices and flows of information, as is the case with ubiquitous systems.

The publish/subscribe *communication model* or *interaction paradigm* overcomes this limitation by introducing an indirection layer that decouples components, i.e., producers and consumers of information [21]. This enables the creation of flexible and robust distributed systems that exploit the benefits of space, time and synchronization decoupling of components. The decoupling of components increases scalability by removing all explicit dependencies between the interacting participants [7]. Removing these dependencies reduces coordination and synchronization requirements and makes the publish/subscribe communication model suitable for distributed environments that are asynchronous by nature, such as ubiquitous systems that seek to integrate mobile devices [10].

K. Zheng, M. Li, and H. Jiang (Eds.): MOBIQUITOUS 2012, LNICST 120, pp. 50–63, 2013.

In publish/subscribe *systems*, information producers are known as *publishers* and information consumers are referred to as *subscribers*. Publishers generate information in the form of *events* while an independent Event Notification Service handles the task of delivering those events to a subset of the subscribers. The use of an explicit layer of indirection provides an overall separation of concerns and is what makes publish/subscribe systems inherently flexible and scalable.

Publish/subscribe *applications* are the result of using a publish/subscribe communication model to orchestrate distributed application components. In essence, publish/subscribe applications employ publishers and subscribers to implement a series of information flows or *content streams* [30]. Content streams are continuous flows of information that are transported from a publisher component to subscriber components by the publish/subscribe infrastructure. In order to shape the content streams of a publish/subscribe system, the use of content-based filtering mechanisms can be requested by subscriber components.

Publish/subscribe applications are characterized by the number of client components they employ and the content streams or events they exchange. Assuming the availability of a broker infrastructure, a minimal application can be created with a publisher, a subscriber and a single content stream. However, real applications exhibit a higher cardinality with regards to both the number of client components and the volume of content streams they employ. Depending on the application domain, the amount of publish/subscribe components can range from a handful to tens of thousands. This is often the case with ubiquitous systems and their applications, where having a large number of components is expected.

In general, the decoupled and data-centric nature of the publish/subscribe interaction paradigm makes it a suitable foundation for a wide variety of applications. In particular, the most suitable applications for this communication model are the ones that require the timely, efficient and scalable dissemination of information between large numbers of components [16]. Note that large-scale systems can result either from the geographic distribution of nodes or from the concentration of nodes on a relatively small area [23]. Examples of publish/subscribe application domains include network monitoring, financial services, mobile computing, industrial automation, social networks, smart environments, scientific computation, content distribution and sensor networks [13] [23] [29].

Taking into account that the software architecture of a ubiquitous system has to overcome a series of specific issues and challenges [6], we argue that the underlying communication infrastructure of a ubiquitous system should provide:

- Heterogeneity: allowing a variety of devices and services to operate.
- Dependability: avoiding severe failures that happen frequently.
- Scalability: enabling the deployment of large-scale systems.
- Mobility: enabling the users to roam the environment.

The publish/subscribe communication model not only provides these features but also supports relevant concepts such as *localised scalability* [27] and *content-centric networking* [11]. As a consequence, we conclude that ubiquitous systems and applications can benefit from the use of *content-based* publish/subscribe [7].

The present work documents a foray into this idea, with the objective of validating the applications of our previous work in the field [25]. To that end, we introduce *Phoenix*, a novel publish/subscribe communication framework for ubiquitous systems, and illustrate the empirical evaluation process and first-hand experimentation that has been carried out in order to validate our approach.

The remainder of this paper is structured as follows: in Section 2 we describe the context and features of our publish/subscribe implementation. In Section 3 we present the process that has been carried out to validate the implementation with a ubiquitous application that includes mobile clients. In Section 4 we introduce a timeliness model for our framework and measure the performance of the system. Finally, Section 5 outlines our findings and concludes the paper.

2   The Phoenix Publish/Subscribe Framework

In this section we describe our approach to publish/subscribe and client mobility. We also cover the reference implementation, Phoenix, and key related work.

2.1   Service Interface

Publish/subscribe is a communication model where information producers (publishers) and information consumers (subscribers) exchange information (events) by means of an Event Notification Service that is composed of a set of *brokers*. Publishers publish events and subscribers make use of predicate-based filters to subscribe to specific kinds of events. The distributed network of brokers *matches* published events and subscriptions, routing them as required. Figure 1 shows the interface provided to the clients of a content-based publish/subscribe system.

```
public void publish(Event notification);
public void subscribe(Filter subscription);
public void unsubscribe(Filter subscription);
```

Fig. 1. Interface for publish/subscribe applications

2.2   Client Mobility

Publish/subscribe clients have a *reference broker* that mediates between them and the rest of the system. When a client is hosted in a mobile device, sudden disconnections can take place as a result of limited wireless coverage. As a result, the link between a client and its reference broker will break and publish/subscribe service will be disrupted. Upon the recovery of wireless connectivity, clients may connect to the same reference broker and resume their operation. However, the physical mobility of a device may prevent this and a client could be required to migrate to a new reference broker. In order to cope with these situations, the Event Notification Service needs to handle client mobility and disconnections.

To that end, we propose the use of a publish/subscribe routing algorithm that warrants the transparent reconnection of clients [25]. Based on a Simple Routing strategy [1] our custom routing algorithm ensures that the routing tables of brokers are updated to reflect the mobility of their clients. In addition, our routing algorithm can optionally replay published events that may be pending delivery as a result of a disconnection. A detailed description of the contributed routing algorithm and its correctness proof can be found in [26]. Figure 2 shows the mobility related interface provided to subscribers. Note that publisher mobility is transparent to the system as a result of extending a Simple Routing strategy.

```
public void migrate(boolean replay);
public void resume(boolean replay);
```

Fig. 2. Interface for migration and resumption operations

2.3 Design and Implementation

In order to evaluate our approach, we have implemented a reference content-based publish/subscribe framework known as Phoenix [24]. The main objective of Phoenix is to provide a robust and scalable communication infrastructure for ubiquitous systems where mobility plays a key role. Therefore, it takes into account the requirements that have already been outlined and implements a custom routing algorithm that supports communication efficient client mobility.

Phoenix has been implemented in Java in order to enable the use of publish/ subscribe application components in a wide variety of devices and platforms. In particular, Phoenix supports the deployment of publishers and subscribers in Android devices. Phoenix makes use of the Apache MINA network application framework to provide asynchronous communication capabilities to both the publish/subscribe components and, by extension, the high-level services and applications that are built on top of them. Internally, the publish/subscribe components of the framework communicate by means of JSON formatted message passing over TCP/IP streams. Other noteworthy features of Phoenix include:

- Optimal routing of events and communication efficient client hand-offs.
- Automatic discovery of brokers by means of multicast and unicast.
- Interoperable message serialization/deserialization mechanism.
- Graphical user interface for the management of brokers.

The middleware layer of the Phoenix framework incorporates over 7,000 lines of code and provides developers with simple interfaces such as the ones depicted in Figures 1 and 2. Note that Phoenix has been released[1] under the MIT license.

---

[1] The Phoenix source code repository is https://github.com/zigorsalvador/phoenix

Indeed, a key motivation behind the development of Phoenix stems from the fact that although several academic contributions have been published in the field, few open source implementations are available and none of them provides key features such as client mobility support and/or full integration with Android.

2.4   Related Work

JEDI was the first publish/subscribe system to support client mobility [5]. In particular, JEDI implements a client hand-off or migration protocol that requires clients to proactively inform the middleware before moving away from a broker. This initial *move out* operation must then be followed by a *move in* operation that triggers the reconfiguration of the system. As a consequence, the client mobility protocol of JEDI is not suitable for situations where clients suffer sudden disconnections from the infrastructure [29]. Additionally, it must be noted that in order to support migrations, JEDI requires the reissuing of subscriptions and the availability of out-of-band communication between the pair of brokers involved in the migration. Furthermore, migrations in JEDI often result in the delivery of *duplicate events* due to the coexistence of old and new delivery routes.

The Siena publish/subscribe system was also among the first to support client mobility [3]. In particular, a generic Mobility Service was implemented in order to validate a client hand-off protocol that could be used with any publish/subscribe system or implementation. The Mobility Service relies in client proxies and explicit *move in* and *move out* operations and due to its generic nature requires no changes to the application programming interface of the system. On the other hand, the use of the Mobility Service results in a high messaging overhead, due to the fact that it has to rely on message flooding to locate *source* and *destination* brokers. Indeed, the high signalling cost of this approach was modelled and found to be excessive [29], which severely limits its value for ubiquitous systems.

The REBECA publish/subscribe system was eventually extended to cope with client mobility [8] [9] [17] [32]. In particular, an algorithm for Roaming Clients was proposed in the context of a publish/subscribe system based on an acyclic graph topology with advertisement semantics. Note that REBECA does not support publisher mobility, due to the choice of advertisement semantics and the lack of a specific publisher mobility protocol. Moreover, the REBECA algorithm relies in the reissue of subscriptions upon migration, which is inefficient.

Client mobility support has also been an active research topic in the context of the PADRES publish/subscribe system. In particular, several contributions were targeted at publisher mobility and represent the first foray into this relevant aspect of client mobility support [18] [19] [20] [22]. Additionally, several performance evaluations were carried out regarding publish/subscribe scenarios where client mobility is generalized. One of the most interesting findings is that in most mobile scenarios the replay of buffered events dominates the signalling cost of subscriber hand-off protocols in real-world deployments of client mobility [2].

All in all, Phoenix builds upon previous contributions introduced by the aforementioned systems. However, the custom routing algorithm [25] employed by Phoenix has some advantages with respect to the preceding systems. For one,

Phoenix supports both publisher and subscriber mobility. For another, Phoenix implements a client hand-off protocol that is communication efficient, i.e., minimizes the amount of traffic generated as a result of client mobility. Furthermore, the formal correctness of our custom routing algorithm has been established and therefore Phoenix provides a solid foundation for incremental work in the field.

3   Validation

In this section we describe the empirical validation of the new communication framework with a combination of synthetic tests and application prototypes.

3.1   Synthetic Tests

Resumption and migration mechanisms have been validated using mobile devices. Figure 3 illustrates the Android application that has been developed to conduct the validation. The Mobility application is composed of a subscriber component and a user interface that enables researchers to request subscriptions, resumptions and migrations. Normally, the user launches the application and enables the wireless communication interface of the mobile device. Once the network interface is up, the user triggers the discovery of a broker in the local area network. If a broker has been found, the user can request the submission of a subscription to that broker, initiating the delivery of events. After an arbitrary amount of time, the user will disable the network interface, disrupting the communication channel between the subscriber and the broker. Then, the user will have to re-enable the network interface, and repeat the discovery procedure. When the identity of the broker that is discovered matches that of the broker that was available before the disconnection, the application will request a resumption. If, on the other hand, a new broker is discovered after the disconnection period, the application will issue a migration request. In either case, the broker will resume the delivery of new events and will replay any events that were not delivered during the disconnection. The Mobility application will check that all expected messages were successfully delivered. Figure 4 illustrates the traffic profiles of *source* and *destination* brokers during an example migration.

3.2   Functional Prototypes

The overall functionality and performance of the framework have been validated using realistic publish/subscribe application prototypes. Figure 5 shows a screenshot of a prototype developed for that purpose: the Tracker application. The idea behind the Tracker application is to implement a real-time visitor tracking system using the Phoenix communication framework. The web application is composed of a single subscriber component and a user interface that enables researchers to visually manage subscriptions and track the location of visitors on a map. In the figure, the red circles represent location-based subscriptions,

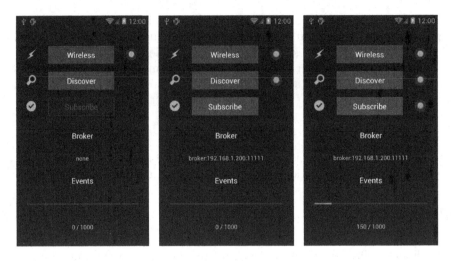

Fig. 3. Screenshot sequence of the Mobility application during a migration test

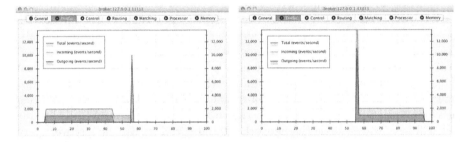

Fig. 4. Traffic profiles of source and destination brokers during a migration test

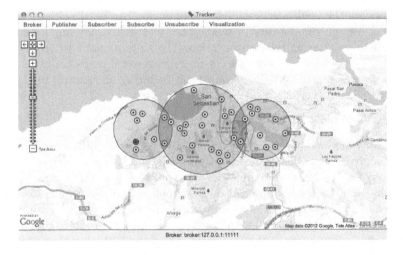

Fig. 5. Screenshot of a web browser rendering the Tracker application

while the small dots represent the real-time location of visitors. In order to generate location data, the mobile devices of visitors are equipped with publisher components that periodically publish the GPS location of these mobile devices and their owners. Using the web application, users can generate fine-grained location-based subscriptions which enable the system to filter incoming events and only deliver those that match a given subscription. The Tracker application has been tested with real subjects using Android devices. However, in order to validate the scalability of the application, virtual visitors can be created by the system and instructed to update their location with an arbitrary periodicity.

4   Performance

In this section we analyse the performance of Phoenix from three perspectives. First, we adopt a theoretical approach and perform an analysis of content-based publish/subscribe performance. Then, we present the results obtained in a series of experimental tests. Finally, we evaluate performance using Android devices.

4.1   Timeliness Model

We assume that the number of brokers is finite and their connection graph G is acyclic and static. Therefore, we can define the diameter of the broker graph as:

$$d = diameter(G)$$

We assume that the communication links in the system are timely, i.e., message transmission delays are bounded. As a result, we can model the communication times involved in the operation of the system and combine them with several assumptions regarding the processing times for different messages in order to model the performance or *average message dispatching times* of a our system. Let δ_c be the average time required for a message to traverse a link that connects a broker and one of its local clients and let δ_b be the average time required for a message to traverse a link that connects a broker and one of its neighbour brokers. If we assume that brokers will benefit from high capacity network links:

$$\delta_c \gg \delta_b$$

Once a given message reaches a process, the message has to be processed, involving changes to data structures and/or event matching calculations. Consequently, we can define the average processing time for each publish/subscribe primitive:

- σ_{SUB}: average time required for a broker to process a subscription message
- σ_{UNS}: average time required for a broker to process a unsubscription message
- σ_{PUB}: average time required for a broker to process a publication message

Based on the fact that the event matching problem is regarded as the main potential bottleneck of a publish/subscribe system [12] [13] [15], we assume that:

$$\sigma_{PUB} \gg \sigma_{SUB} \simeq \sigma_{UNS}$$

And based on the previous, we can model *average message dispatching times* for subscription, unsubscription and publication messages, respectively, as follows:

$$\Delta_{SUB} \simeq \delta_c + \sigma_{SUB} + d(\delta_b + \sigma_{SUB})$$

$$\Delta_{UNS} \simeq \delta_c + \sigma_{UNS} + d(\delta_b + \sigma_{UNS})$$

$$\Delta_{PUB} \leq \delta_c + \sigma_{PUB} + d(\delta_b + \sigma_{PUB}) + \delta_c$$

Finally, based on the assumptions that have been noted, we can now assert that:

$$\Delta_{PUB} \gg \Delta_{SUB} \simeq \Delta_{UNS}$$

This realization underlines the importance of the matching process in publish/subscribe systems. Furthermore, it motivates us to conduct a performance analysis that is focused in Δ_{PUB} scalability and the impact of different optimizations.

4.2   Empirical Evaluation

In order to measure the performance of Phoenix, we have deployed our publish/subscribe system in a dedicated cluster composed of eight server nodes running Ubuntu 11.10 with dual 2.4 GHz Xeon CPUs and 24 GBytes of RAM. Six of the nodes are exclusively dedicated to the execution of a broker overlay with a star topology. The two remaining nodes are dedicated to the execution of a *benchmarking application* and a *workload generator*. The benchmarking application is composed of a publisher and a subscriber component that exchange *probe messages* which traverse the broker overlay. Probe messages are time-stamped and enable the benchmarking application to measure two performance metrics: *probe latency* and *probe throughput*. The *workload generator* orchestrates the execution of synthetic clients and generates arbitrary amounts of background traffic. Probe messages and workload messages are, respectively, 286 and 886 bytes long.

In its basic, non-optimized form, the algorithm in [25] makes heavy use of event matching, which limits the scalability of the system. As a result, two optimizations have been implemented in Phoenix and considered in the experiments. The first optimization, *Filter Poset*, aims at reducing the *number of filters* that are involved in the matching operation of a given event. To do so, it exploits the relationship among the filters stored in the routing tables by maintaining a partially ordered set of filters [4] [31]. The second optimization, *Single Matching*, aims at reducing the *number of matching operations* that are involved in the delivery of a given event. To do so, it exploits global knowledge by having the front-end broker of each publisher compute the set of matching subscriptions on behalf of the rest of the brokers. This optimization is similar to the approach followed in [13] [14] [28]. The combination of the two optimizations results in four benchmarking configurations: $C1$ (no optimization), $C2$ (Single Matching), $C3$ (Filter Poset) and $C4$ (both optimizations). The workload consists of a set of publish/subscribe clients that generate various degrees of synthetic background traffic, in the form of spurious events that need to be dispatched. The performance factors that dimension workloads are: R_p: the rate of background publications in the

Table 1. Average probe throughput (events/second)

Workload	(R_p, N_s)	C1	C2	C3	C4
$W1$	$(0,0)$	24,687	20,626	23,955	21,421
$W2$	$(0,250)$	10,089	11,639	17,522	20,557
$W3$	$(0,500)$	6,843	8,631	18,158	17,050
$W4$	$(5,000,0)$	25,198	22,506	22,197	21,806
$W5$	$(5,000,250)$	7,324	11,305	15,942	18,394
$W6$	$(5,000,500)$	3,905	8,365	14,327	15,996
$W7$	$(10,000,0)$	22,848	21,843	21,693	21,788
$W8$	$(10,000,250)$	5,448	11,474	15,031	16,597
$W9$	$(10,000,500)$	2,746	8,071	11,956	15,221

Table 2. Average probe latency (milliseconds)

Workload	(R_p, N_s)	C1	C2	C3	C4
$W1$	$(0,0)$	1.002	1.118	1.079	1.137
$W2$	$(0,250)$	1.247	1.109	1.060	1.175
$W3$	$(0,500)$	1.451	1.168	1.030	1.144
$W4$	$(5,000,0)$	1.063	1.079	1.022	1.229
$W5$	$(5,000,250)$	1.827	1.462	1.583	1.634
$W6$	$(5,000,500)$	2.873	1.630	1.764	1.573
$W7$	$(10,000,0)$	1.048	1.092	1.063	1.047
$W8$	$(10,000,250)$	3.121	1.749	1.926	1.556
$W9$	$(10,000,500)$	38.891	1.740	2.108	1.649

Table 3. Average smartphone throughput (events/second) and latency (miliseconds)

Interface	Throughput	Latency
WIFI	148	11
UMTS	185	151

Table 4. Average smartphone battery life (minutes)

Scenario	Duration	Percentage
Baseline	582	100%
Publisher	252	43%
Subscriber	267	46%
Combination	215	37%

system and, N_s: the amount of global subscriptions in the system. Note that three discrete levels have been considered for each of the two cited performance factors. In particular, R_p can be one of 0, 1,000 or 2,000 events/second and N_s can be one of 0, 50 or 100 subscribers for each of the five border brokers. This translates into a global publication rate of 0, 5,000 or 10,000 events/second and a total of 0, 250 or 500 concurrent subscribers in the system. Note that two metrics, four configurations and nine workloads require 72 unique experiments.

Tables 1 and 2 show average probe throughputs and average probe latencies, respectively. Throughput measurements involve the publication of 50,000 events and were repeated 10 times. Latency measurements require a single event and were repeated 10,000 times. Based on these results, we can highlight that the performance of the non-optimized configuration ($C1$) stalls under load ($W9$). However, in the highly-optimized configuration ($C4$), Phoenix manages to dispatch over 15,000 messages per second with an average latency of under 2 milliseconds, which represents a significant improvement and a good degree of scalability.

4.3 Android Performance

In order to complete the performance analysis of the Phoenix communication framework, we have conducted additional experiments using Android mobile devices. In particular, we have used a Google Nexus S smartphone as a reference, running Android 4.1.1 with a 1 GHz ARM CPU and 512 MBytes of RAM.

The first set of experiments was aimed at measuring the performance of the Phoenix communication framework when using wireless communication interfaces. Table 3 illustrates the average probe throughput and average probe latency that were measured using both WIFI and UMTS hardware interfaces. Note that probe messages were 280 bytes in size, throughput tests were repeated 25 times and the latency values represent the averages out of 100 measurements. Based on the results, we can assert that our Phoenix cluster is well capable of serving hundreds, if not thousands, of mobile devices running Phoenix clients.

The second set of experiments analysed the energy consumption derived from the use of the Phoenix in a mobile device. In particular, we conducted several experiments where the battery level of the smartphone was monitored during the execution of different communication routines. Table 4 shows the average duration of the battery under four different scenarios. In the first scenario, the device is in standby mode with the screen set to 5% brightness. In the second scenario, a publisher component generates 100 events/second while in the third scenario a subscriber receives 100 events/second. Finally, the fourth scenario combines the publication and the reception of 100 events/second. Based on the results, the impact of using Phoenix is moderate and its energy efficiency is fair.

5 Conclusion

In this paper, we have described the overall design and evaluation of a novel communication framework for ubiquitous systems. The framework is based on the publish/subscribe communication model and has taken into account the requirements of ubiquitous systems. In particular, we have tried to design a communication framework that supports client mobility and provides a good degree of scalability. To that end, we have leveraged a routing algorithm [25] that provides optimal event routing and communication efficient client mobility.

The implementation of the Phoenix publish/subscribe framework has been motivated by the lack of suitable open source implementations that provide what we believe are key features of a communication infrastructure for ubiquitous systems, namely client mobility support and full integration with mobile devices. The reference implementation of Phoenix enables researchers and application developers to create ubiquitous systems and applications using wireless communication interfaces and nowadays common devices such as Android smartphones.

In addition, we have conducted both an empirical validation process and a thorough performance analysis and, based on the results, can assert that Phoenix is a valid and fairly scalable communication framework for ubiquitous systems.

Acknowledgements. The authors wish to note that this research has partially been supported by the Spanish Research Council, under grant TIN2010-17170, the Basque Government, under grants IT395-10 and S-PE11UN099, the Provincial Government of Gipuzkoa, under grant 2012-DTIC-000101-01, and the University of the Basque Country UPV/EHU, under grant UFI11/45.

References

1. Banavar, G., Chandra, T., Mukherjee, B., Nagarajarao, J., Strom, R.E., Sturman, D.C.: An Efficient Multicast Protocol for Content-Based Publish-Subscribe Systems. In: ICDCS, pp. 262–272 (1999)
2. Burcea, I., Jacobsen, H.-A., de Lara, E., Muthusamy, V., Petrovic, M.: Disconnected Operation in Publish/Subscribe Middleware. In: Mobile Data Management, pp. 39–50. IEEE Computer Society (2004)
3. Caporuscio, M., Carzaniga, A., Wolf, A.L.: Design and Evaluation of a Support Service for Mobile, Wireless Publish/Subscribe Applications. IEEE Transactions on Software Engineering 29(12), 1059–1071 (2003)
4. Carzaniga, A.: Architectures for an Event Notification Service Scalable to Wide-Area Networks. PhD thesis, Politecnico di Milano, Italy (1998)
5. Cugola, G., Jacobsen, H.-A.: Using Publish/Subscribe Middleware for Mobile Systems. Mobile Computing and Communications Review 6(4), 25–33 (2002)
6. da Costa, C.A., Yamin, A.C., Geyer, C.F.R.: Toward a General Software Infrastructure for Ubiquitous Computing. IEEE Pervasive Computing 7(1), 64–73 (2008)
7. Eugster, P.T., Felber, P.A., Guerraoui, R., Kermarrec, A.-M.: The Many Faces of Publish/Subscribe. ACM Computing Surveys 35(2), 114–131 (2003)
8. Fiege, L., Gärtner, F.C., Kasten, O., Zeidler, A.: Supporting Mobility in Content-Based Publish/Subscribe Middleware. In: Endler, M., Schmidt, D.C. (eds.) Middleware 2003. LNCS, vol. 2672, pp. 103–122. Springer, Heidelberg (2003)

9. Fiege, L., Zeidler, A., Gärtner, F.C., Handurukande, S.B.: Dealing with Uncertainty in Mobile Publish/Subscribe Middleware. In: Middleware Workshops, pp. 60–67. PUC-Rio (2003)

10. Huang, Y., Garcia-Molina, H.: Publish/Subscribe in a Mobile Enviroment. In: MobiDE, pp. 27–34. ACM (2001)

11. Jacobson, V., Smetters, D.K., Thornton, J.D., Plass, M., Briggs, N., Braynard, R.: Networking Named Content. Communications of the ACM 55(1), 117–124 (2012)

12. Jayram, T.S., Khot, S., Kumar, R., Rabani, Y.: Cell-Probe Lower Bounds for the Partial Match Problem. Journal of Computer and System Sciences 69(3), 435–447 (2004)

13. Jerzak, Z.: XSiena: The Content-Based Publish/Subscribe System. PhD thesis, Technische Universität Dresden, Germany (2009)

14. Jerzak, Z., Fetzer, C.: Prefix Forwarding for Publish/Subscribe. In: Jacobsen, H.-A., Mühl, G., Jaeger, M.A. (eds.) DEBS. ACM International Conference Proceeding Series, vol. 233, pp. 238–249. ACM (2007)

15. Kale, S., Hazan, E., Cao, F., Singh, J.P.: Analysis and Algorithms for Content-Based Event Matching. In: ICDCS Workshops, pp. 363–369. IEEE Computer Society (2005)

16. Mühl, G., Fiege, L., Pietzuch, P.R.: Distributed Event-Based Systems. Springer (2006)

17. Mühl, G., Ulbrich, A., Herrmann, K., Weis, T.: Disseminating Information to Mobile Clients Using Publish-Subscribe. IEEE Internet Computing 8(3), 46–53 (2004)

18. Muthusamy, V., Jacobsen, H.-A.: Small Scale Peer-to-Peer Publish/Subscribe. In: Horrocks, I., Sattler, U., Wolter, F. (eds.) P2PKM. CEUR Workshop Proceedings, vol. 147. CEUR-WS.org (2005)

19. Muthusamy, V., Petrovic, M., Gao, D., Jacobsen, H.-A.: Publisher Mobility in Distributed Publish/Subscribe Systems. In: ICDCS Workshops, pp. 421–427. IEEE Computer Society (2005)

20. Muthusamy, V., Petrovic, M., Jacobsen, H.-A.: Effects of Routing Computations in Content-Based Routing Networks with Mobile Data Sources. In: Porta, T.F.L., Lindemann, C., Belding-Royer, E.M., Lu, S. (eds.) MOBICOM, pp. 103–116. ACM (2005)

21. Oki, B., Pflügl, M., Siegel, A., Skeen, D.: The Information Bus - An Architecture for Extensible Distributed Systems. In: SOSP, pp. 58–68 (1993)

22. Petrovic, M., Muthusamy, V., Jacobsen, H.-A.: Content-Based Routing in Mobile Ad Hoc Networks. In: MobiQuitous, pp. 45–55. IEEE Computer Society (2005)

23. Pietzuch, P.: Hermes: A Scalable Event-Based Middleware. PhD thesis, University of Cambridge, United Kingdom (2004)

24. Salvador, Z.: Client Mobility Support and Communication Efficiency in Distributed Publish/Subscribe. PhD thesis, University of the Basque Country, Spain (2012)

25. Salvador, Z., Larrea, M., Phoenix, A.L.: Phoenix: A Protocol for Seamless Client Mobility in Publish/Subscribe. In: NCA, pp. 111–120. IEEE Computer Society (2012)

26. Salvador, Z., Larrea, M., Phoenix, A.L.: Phoenix: A Protocol for Seamless Client Mobility in Publish/Subscribe. Technical Report EHU-KAT-IK-02-12, University of the Basque Country UPV/EHU (April 2012), http://www.sc.ehu.es/acwlaalm/

27. Satyanarayanan, M.: Pervasive Computing: Vision and Challenges. IEEE Personal Communications 8(4), 10–17 (2001)
28. Shen, Z., Tirthapura, S.: Faster Event Forwarding in a Content-Based Publish-Subscribe System through Lookup Reuse. In: NCA, pp. 77–84. IEEE Computer Society (2006)
29. Tarkoma, S.: Efficient Content-Based Routing, Mobility-Aware Topologies, and Temporal Subspace Matching. PhD thesis, University of Helsinki, Finland (2006)
30. Tarkoma, S., Kangasharju, J.: Handover Cost and Mobility-Safety of Content Streams. In: Boukerche, A., Leung, V.C.M., Chiasserini, C.-F., Srinivasan, V. (eds.) MSWiM, pp. 354–358. ACM (2005)
31. Tarkoma, S., Kangasharju, J.: Optimizing Content-Based Routers: Posets and Forests. Distributed Computing 19(1), 62–77 (2006)
32. Zeidler, A., Fiege, L.: Mobility Support with Rebeca. In: ICDCS Workshops, pp. 354–360. IEEE Computer Society (2003)

Where am I? Using Mobile Sensor Data to Predict a User's Semantic Place with a Random Forest Algorithm

Elisabeth Lex, Oliver Pimas, Jörg Simon, and Viktoria Pammer-Schindler

Know-Center, Graz, Austria

Abstract. We use mobile sensor data to predict a mobile phone user's semantic place, e.g. at home, at work, in a restaurant etc. Such information can be used to feed context-aware systems, that adapt for instance mobile phone settings like energy saving, connection to Internet, volume of ringtones etc. We consider the task of semantic place prediction as classification problem. In this paper we exploit five feature groups: (i) daily patterns, (ii) weekly patterns, (iii) WLAN information, (iv) battery charging state and (v) accelerometer data. We compare the performance of a Random Forest algorithm and two Support Vector Machines, one with an RBF kernel and one with a Pearson VII function based kernel, on a labelled dataset, and analyse the separate performances of the feature groups as well as promising combinations of feature groups. The winning combination of feature groups achieves an accuracy of 0.871 using a Random Forest algorithm on daily patterns and accelerometer data.

A detailed analysis reveals that daily patterns are the most discriminative feature group for the given semantic place labels. Combining daily patterns with WLAN information, battery charging state or accelerometer data further improves the performance. The classifiers using these selected combinations perform better than the classifiers using all feature groups. This is especially encouraging for mobile computing, as fewer features mean that less computational power is required for classification.

1 Introduction

Smartphones currently hold a handheld market share of over 30% - and this market share is rising[1]. Because of their built-in sensors, smartphones are a particularly suitable tool for capturing people's activities in a physical environment as opposed to people's interactions with electronic devices or interactions within virtual environments. Such mobile sensor data can be used to analyse behavioural patterns, or within user- and context-adaptive systems. Given the wide spread of smartphones, such systems have the potential to reach an incredible amount of users. In this paper, we describe how to use mobile sensor data to predict a mobile phone user's semantic place, i.e. *home, work, restaurant* etc.

---

[1] http://mobithinking.com/mobile-marketing-tools/latest-mobile-stats/a#smartphone-shipments

K. Zheng, M. Li, and H. Jiang (Eds.): MOBIQUITOUS 2012, LNICST 120, pp. 64–75, 2013.

Semantic place information exceeds geographic location information in that it gives a meaning to a user's location. Location-aware systems that exploit the geographic location or just the uniqueness of places (e.g., based on WLAN IDs) are state-of-the-art. Recommender systems like Yelp for restaurants or Friends for finding friends in the vicinity use geographic location information. The Llama App executes location-specific rules w.r.t. device system settings, and uses cell tower information to identify locations. In such Apps, semantic categories are assigned to places by users, but not exploited by the system. Systems that exploit place semantics are now cutting edge. Only recently, a recommender system for advertisements has been described that depends on geographic locations, identified via WLAN ID, but distinguishes places also via their semantics, e.g., fashion shop, restaurant, cinema etc. [8]. The mapping between geographic location and place semantics is not automated, but used by the system.

2   Dataset

The work described in this paper was carried out in the context of the Nokia Mobile Data Challenge 2012. The challenge provided a data set, the MDC dataset, collected by the NRC/Lausanne Data Collection Campaign 2009-2010 [9]. Smartphone data has been collected by almost 200 participants in the course of at least one year [10]. For each user, data about telephone usage, media usage, motion (accelerometer data), telephone status (bluetooth, battery charging) etc. has been collected [9].

In the MDC dataset, each data record contains the data of a sensor (e.g., battery charging status) and a timestamp. Each record has been collected by a single user, and is assigned to a place ID p_{ID} that defines a geographic location. However, it cannot be related back to geographic coordinates, and it corresponds to a circle of $100m$ radius. Each place ID p_{ID} is associated to a single user. Since geographic coordinates of place IDs p_{ID} are unknown, it is unknown whether place IDs $p_{ID}s$ from different users correspond to the same geographic location. A subset of records in the MDC dataset has been labelled with one of the predefined semantic place labels as ground truth. The full list of predefined semantic place labels is given below in Table 1.

Discussion. The MDC dataset is very unbalanced, in that much more labelled records exist for instance for the semantic place label *Home* than for *Holiday resort or vacation spot*. We do not know whether the distribution of labels is representative, and as we will discuss below, labelling behaviour may have influenced the classification results.

The classification problem that we tackle based on the MDC dataset is based on unique, but in terms of geographic location, unknown place IDs which define circles of $100m$ radius. Such an accuracy is plausible, if for instance cell tower triangulation is used, whilst with GPS or assisted GPS the location information should be more accurate [2]. However, in a scenario of real application, any semantic place prediction algorithm would probably have access to geographic location

---

[2] http://technowizz.wordpress.com/2010/01/03/lbs-technologies-part-1/

Table 1. Semantic place labels

1	Home
2	Home of a friend, relative or colleague
3	My workplace or school
4	Location related to transportation (e.g., bus stop, metro stop, train station, parking lot, airport)
5	Workplace or school of a friend, relative or colleague
6	Place for outdoor sports (e.g., walking, hiking, skiing)
7	Place for indoor sports (e.g., gym)
8	Restaurant or bar
9	Shop or shopping center
10	Holiday resort or vacation spot

information. This would be an important piece of complementary information that could be used for instance in map lookups.

3   Problem Statement

In this work, we tackle the following problem:

Given an unlabeled place p_{ID} that has a number of features (computed from the data records associated with p_{ID}), predict the semantics of p_{ID} out of a list of predefined semantic place labels.

We consider this task as a supervised classification problem in combination with resampling to address the unbalanced nature of the dataset, and feature selection. As classifier, we used the Weka [5] implementation of a Random Forest algorithm [1] and of a Support Vector Machine (SVM) with the Pearson VII function (PuK) kernel [15] and as well as of an SVM with an Radial Basis Function (RBF) kernel.

4   Features

We used five feature groups: (i) daily patterns, (ii) weekly patterns, (iii) WLAN information, (iv) battery charging state, and (v) accelerometer information. Each feature group consists of multiple features described in more detail below.

4.1   Daily and Weekly Patterns

A daily pattern is a behavioural pattern that changes with the time of the day. We use the term "weekly pattern" in analogy to denote patterns of behaviour that change with the day of the week.

In the MDC dataset, we found strong evidence for daily and weekly patterns of users. The strongest evidence exists for the semantic place labels "Home", "Home of a friend, relative or colleague", "My workplace or school" and "Workplace or school of a friend, relative or colleague" for daily patterns and "Place for outdoor sports" and "Place for indoor sports" for weekly patterns. Based on these insights, we used daily and weekly patterns as features.

For instance, between $1am$ and $4am$, people are most often at home or at the home of a friend, relative or colleague (cf. Fig. 1 for "Home"). Figure 1 depicts the probability that the visited place is "Home" or "My workplace or school" on the time of the day. The probability is calculated as follows:

$$p_s = (\frac{\#records(s,t_1)}{\#records(t_1)} \cdots, \frac{\#records(s,t_{24})}{\#records(t_{24})}) \quad (1)$$

where s is a semantic place label, t_i with $i = 0 \ldots 23$ is the timespan of an hour starting at the time denoted by t_i, $\#records(s,t_1)$ is the number of records in the timespan t_i that are labelled with the semantic place label s in the MDC dataset and $\#records(t_1)$ is the number of records in the timespan t_1 for which a semantic place label exists in the MDC dataset.

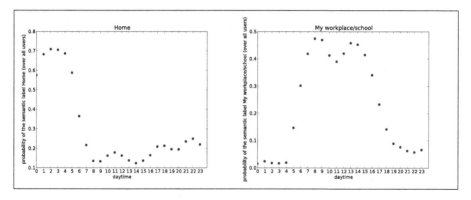

Fig. 1. Daily pattern for the semantic place label "Home" (left) and "My Workplace or school" (right)

Given a place ID p_{ID} and all data records associated with p_{ID}, the daily pattern feature group consists of 24 features, each for a timespan $t_i, i = 0 \ldots 23$ such that t_0 corresponds to the interval between midnight and $1am$, t_1 corresponds to the interval between $1am$ and $2am$ etc. Each of the 24 features is computed as follows:

$$\frac{\#records(p_{ID},t_i)}{\#records(t_i)} \quad (2)$$

where $\#records(p_{ID},t_i)$ is the number of records at place p_{ID} in the timespan t_i, and $\#records(t_i)$ is the number of records taken in the timespan t_i by the user associated with p_{ID}.

The weekly pattern feature group consists of 3 features: The number of records taken at place ID p_{ID} on weekdays (wd), the number of records taken at place ID p_{ID} on weekend days (we), and the ratio $\frac{we}{we+wd}$.

4.2 Accelerometer Data

We hypothesized that information about users' movements would be discriminative for the given semantic place labels, e.g., to identify sports and transportation related places. In the MDC dataset, such information could be derived from accelerometer data.

The MDC dataset was collected from Nokia N95 phones which have an accelerometer with a sensitivity of $\pm$ 2G and a bandwidth of 35Hz [17]. The main challenge for using accelerometer data from the MDC dataset was how to compute velocity information without orientation and position information. In smartphones newer than the N95, a gyroscope is used to deliver orientation information. With accelerometer data from N95 smartphones, a normalization of the coordinate system is necessary to calculate average velocity given accelerometer data only. However, in [16], it has been shown that such a normalization is subject to errors which lead to an inaccurately computed direction of velocity. Therefore we do not normalize accelerometer data w.r.t. gravity at all, but simply integrate acceleration information to get average, approximate, velocity. We hypothesized that for the very short time intervals over which we integrate this approximation is sufficient to distinguish between semantic place labels.

In the MDC dataset, an accelerometer record is an array that consists of single accelerometer measurements within a timeframe. Each accelerometer measurement consists of the x, y, z acceleration in mG ($10^{-3}G$) and the time difference to the start of the timeframe. Each accelerometer record is also associated with a unique place ID p_{ID}.

We computed the average velocity within a time frame (i.e. for one $record$) by first integrating the x, y, z values separately. This gives us the velocity in the x, y, z direction of the accelerometer within the time frame of the $record$:

$$v_x(record) = \int_x record * dt \tag{3}$$

$$v_y(record) = \int_y record * dt \tag{4}$$

$$v_z(record) = \int_z record * dt \tag{5}$$

The Euclidean distance gives the velocity within the timeframe of the record:

$$v(record) = \sqrt[2]{v_x(record)^2 + v_y(record)^2 + v_z(record)^2} \tag{6}$$

All velocities, computed over timeframes, are aggregated to give the average velocity and its standard deviation at a unique place p_{ID}. Both values are normalised to values between 0 and 1 with a min-max normalization.

$$av(p_{ID}) = \frac{\sum_i v(record_i(p_{ID}))}{\#records(p_{ID})} \qquad (7)$$

is the average velocity at place p_{ID}, and $i = 1 \ldots \#records(p_{ID})$.

$$std_v(p_{ID}) = \sqrt{\frac{1}{\#records(p_{ID})} \sum_i (v(record_i(p_{ID})) - av(p_{ID}))^2} \qquad (8)$$

is the standard deviation of the average velocity with $i = 1 \ldots \#records(p_{ID})$.

The accelerometer data feature group for p_{ID} consists of two features, namely the min-max normalised average velocity (min-max normalised Eq. 7) and the min-max normalised standard deviation of velocity (min-max normalised Eq. 8).

4.3   WLAN Information

We assumed that users connect to WLAN more frequently at some semantic places than at others. We therefore defined a feature that indicates the frequency of WLAN usage at a unique place p_{ID}:

$$\vec{fv}_{p_k} = \frac{\#connections(place_k)}{\sum\limits_{i=0}^{n} \#connections(place_i)} \qquad (9)$$

Given the fact that the N55 mobile phones that have been used to record the dataset, deactivate the WLAN connection when not currently used [12], the number of connections resembles the intensity of the WLAN usage.

The WLAN feature group consists of this single feature.

4.4   Battery Charging State

We assume that users charge their phones at selected semantic places. The MDC dataset provides four different charging states: (i) charger not connected (s_0), (ii) device is charging (s_1), (iii) charging completed (s_2), and (iv) charging continued after brief interruption (s_3). The feature vector for a unique place ID p_{ID} has four dimensions, i.e. one dimension for each charging state. Each dimension has a value between 0 and 1, denoting the number of records with the corresponding charging state at p_{ID} divided by the number of all charging state records of the user associated with p_{ID}:

$$\frac{|\{records(p_{ID})|record(p_{ID}) = s_i\}|}{|\{records(p_{ID})\}|} \qquad (10)$$

for $i = 0 \ldots 3$ where $record(p_{ID})$ is a charging state record at place p_{ID}.

The battery charging state feature group thus consists of four features.

5   Experiments and Results

The Random Forest (RF) algorithm is an ensemble classifier consisting of multiple randomized decision trees that are combined using bagging [14]. We used it since it is known to be a highly accurate and fast classification algorithm [2]. Besides, the algorithm is not very sensitive to outliers, is able to deal with missing values, and, as stated in [1], avoids overfitting. Due to their wide use for classification problems we also evaluated the performance of Support Vector Machines on the problem at hand. We used two Support Vector Machines with two different kernels. Both SVMs implement John C. Platt's sequential minimal optimization algorithm for training a support vector classifier using polynomial or RBF kernels[3]. The first SVM has a Radial Basis Function kernel (RBF-SVM). The second SVM has an SVM with the Pearson VII [15] function as a universal kernel function (PuK-SVM). The Pearson VII function is an alternative to the standard SVM kernels for which studies in the field of remote sensing suggest that it outperforms standard kernels [13].

To extract the best performing features from each feature group, we applied *feature selection* with a CfsSubsetEval[4] filter from Weka. This filter evaluates features with respect to their individual predictive ability along with the degree of redundancy between the features [6]. Since the training data is unbalanced, we applied a *resampling filter* from Weka to introduce a bias towards a uniform class distribution. If features, for instance WLAN information, are not available, we treat them as missing values. All evaluation results have been computed with a *10-fold cross validation* on the MDC dataset.

5.1   All Feature Groups for All Semantic Place Labels

We evaluated the performance of the Random Forest algorithm and both types of Support Vector Machines, the SVM with an RBF kernel and the SVM with the PuK kernel with all feature groups for all semantic place labels, which gives a 10 class multi-class problem with 5 feature groups and 32 single features. This experiment resulted in an average f-measure of 0.854 for the Random Forest, an average f-measure of 0.764 for the SVM with PuK kernel, and an average f-measure of 0.366 for the SVM with RBF kernel. Detailed results for each semantic place label are given in the next section.

5.2   All Feature Groups for Each Semantic Place Label

We evaluated both the Random Forest algorithm and the SVM with all features for each semantic place label separately. Their performances are given in terms of the F-Measure in Table 2 next to each other.

---

[3] http://weka.sourceforge.net/doc/weka/classifiers/SMO.html
[4] http://wiki.pentaho.com/display/DATAMINING/CfsSubsetEval

Table 2. F-measure of the Random Forest (RF) algorithm and the SVM using the Pearson VII function kernel (PuK-SVM) and the SVM using the RBF kernel (RBF-SVM). All three algorithms used all feature groups and classified each semantic place label separately.

Semantic Place Label	RF	PuK-SVM	RBF-SVM
1: Home	.766	.714	.769
2: Home of friend, relative or colleague	.566	.638	.364
3: My workplace or school	.8	.659	.737
4: Place related to transportation	.825	.538	.105
5: Workplace or school of a friend, relative or colleague	.875	.793	.305
6: Place related to outdoor sports	.871	.712	.061
7: Place related to indoor sports	.866	.788	.103
8: Restaurant or bar	.962	.938	.354
9: Shop or shopping center	.918	.857	.449
10: Holiday resort or vacation spot	.966	.894	.425

Discussion. The SVMs underperformed the Random Forest algorithm for all semantic place labels except *Home of a friend, relative or colleague*. Therefore we carry out further analyses only with the Random Forest algorithm. The performance of the last three classes (8-10) is deceivingly high. This is an artefact of the MDC dataset, which contains only few examples for these classes. Therefore we cannot assume a good generalisation ability of the classifiers for these classes (semantic place labels). This also holds true for all experiments below.

5.3   Single Feature Groups for Each Semantic Place Label

Next, we created Random Forest classifiers such that each classifier detects only one semantic place label and uses only one feature group (results shown in Table 3 on the next page). Such experiments lead to insights on the relevance of a particular feature group for different semantic places.

Discussion From Table 3 we can see that daily patterns perform very well on nearly all semantic place labels, except *Home of a friend, relative or colleague* and *Place related to transportation*. Especially the latter is surprising. One might assume that people travel very regularly for instance to and from work. In [3,4], strong daily patterns have been found in transportation networks. One possible solution for this discrepancy of results lies in the unknown labelling behaviour of the study participants who created the MDC labels within the MDC dataset. Did they tend to label places related to transportation maybe rather for unusual transportation paths and not for their daily routes to and from work, to and from supermarkets etc? The confusion matrix supports this interpretation as it shows that based on daily patterns, the class *Place related to transportation* is often confused with the class *Holiday resort or vacation spot*. We also expected

Table 3. F-measure of Random Forest classifiers that detect a single semantic place label using a single feature group. In the table below, Daily P. abbreviates Daily Patterns, Weekly P. abbreviates Weekly Patterns, Charging abbreviates Battery Charging State, and Accel. abbreviates Accelerometer Data.

Semantic Place Label	Daily P.	Weekly P.	Charging	WLAN	Accel.
1: Home	0.776	0.826	0.72	0.627	0.4
2: Home of a friend, relative or colleague	0.536	0.68	0.582	0.593	0.431
3: My workplace or school	0.836	0.737	0.698	0.485	0.426
4: Place related to transportation	0.646	0.468	0.794	0.806	0.889
5: Workplace or school of a friend, relative or colleague	0.966	0.655	0.889	0.918	0.903
6: Place related to outdoor sports	0.862	0.566	0.867	0.746	0.813
7: Place related to indoor sports	0.875	0.787	0.866	0.828	0.907
8: Restaurant or bar	0.883	0.763	0.949	0.95	0.884
9: Shop or shopping center	0.881	0.75	0.897	0.833	0.907
10: Holiday resort or vacation spot	0.785	0.672	0.977	0.966	0.966

the daily pattern feature group to perform better on the class *Home*. The main class of confusion is *Home of a friend, relative or collague*.

Weekly patterns perform worse overall compared to daily patterns. However, they outperform all feature groups with respect to the *Home* and the *Home of a friend, relative or colleague* class.

The typical mobile sensor data, i.e. battery charging state, WLAN information and accelerometer data serve very well to predict the semantic place labels 4-10. The battery charging state feature group for instance performs exceptionally well on the classes *Restaurant or bar* and *Holiday resort or vacation spot*.

5.4 Feature Group Combinations for Each Semantic Place Label

We evaluated combinations of the winning feature group of daily patterns with the battery charging state, WLAN information and accelerometer data feature groups. The results are shown in Table 4, next to the results of the daily pattern feature group.

Discussion. Combining the daily pattern feature group with other feature groups improves the classification performance, except for the classes *My workplace or school* and *Workplace or school of a friend, relative or colleague*. However, even

Table 4. F-measure of the Random Forest classifiers that detect a single semantic place label using a combination of feature groups. In the table below, DP abbreviates Daily Patterns, Charging abbreviates Battery Charging State, and Accel. abbreviates Accelerometer Data. The last column repeats the results when using only the daily pattern feature group.

Semantic Place Label	DP + Charging	DP + WLAN	DP + Accel.	DP
1: Home	.826	.783	.8	.776
2: Home of a friend, relative or colleague	.667	.604	.667	.536
3: My workplace or school	.75	.825	.743	.836
4: Place related to transportation	.836	.794	.844	.646
5: Workplace or school of a friend, relative or colleague	.935	.889	.935	.966
6: Place related to outdoor sports	.867	.844	.871	.862
7: Place related to indoor sports	.862	.892	.879	.875
8: Restaurant or bar	.916	.962	.962	.883
9: Shop or shopping center	.93	.876	.941	.881
10: Holiday resort or vacation spot	.988	.966	.955	.785

here, the differences in performance are very small. The different combinations of feature groups perform approximately equally well, with the combination "Daily Patterns and Accelerometer" slightly in the lead. The results shown in Table 4 for combinations of the daily pattern feature group with the battery charging state, WLAN or accelerometer feature group are even better than when using all feature groups (results shown in Table 2).

6   Comparison with Other Work on the MDC Dataset

Other authors, such as [7,11,18] have also worked on the MDC dataset but used different machine-learning approaches.

In [11], the authors develop one binary classifier for each semantic place label, and binary classifiers are either k-Nearest Neighbour or Support Vector Machines, using very similar features than the ones used within this paper. Results given within the paper are derived using a 2-fold cross-validation. The relevance of this paper lies in a newly developed multi-coded class based multiclass evaluation rule that combines classification results of the binary classifiers. However, the overall accuracy of the developed multi-class classifier is, with 73.26% significantly lower than what we show can be achieved within this paper.

In [7], the authors use a multi-level classification approach to address the fact that the dataset is unbalanced, and that the semantic place labels form sub-groups of semantic places that are distinguishable by different features. The authors use multiple classification algorithms like SVM, J48, etc. and combine diverging results of different algorithms by a fusion model. The authors have evaluated a very broad range of features (54) and identified movement behaviour, phone usage behaviour, communication behaviour as well as temporal behaviour of users and WLAN- and bluetooth information as good features. Using a 10-fold cross-validation, the authors reach an accuracy of 65.77%.

In [18], the authors compare the performance of Logistic Regression, SVMs, Gradient Boosted Trees, and Random Forests; the latter corresponds to our approach. The authors selected features automatically from the space of all combinations of all possible features. While many features correspond to raw sensor data, some are also preprocessed sensor data such as variance of accelerometer data etc. The best achieved result, with 10-fold cross validation, lies at 65.3%, achieved with the gradient boosted tree algorithm.

In terms of accuracy, our approach thus compares extremely favourable with algorithmically more complex approaches.

7   Conclusion

We have shown that for the problem of predicting semantic places based on mobile sensor data, a Random Forest algorithm outperforms both an SVM with an RBF kernel and an SVM with a Pearson VII function kernel, as well as other algorithmically more complex approaches. The performance of different feature groups, daily patterns, weekly patterns, WLAN information, battery charging state and accelerometer data, was analysed for the Random Forest algorithm. The single best performing feature group however was the daily pattern feature group. Its performance could be further improved by combining it with WLAN, battery charging state or accelerometer data. These combined feature groups result in a better performing classifier than even the classifier that uses all feature groups. This is highly encouraging for mobile computing, as fewer features mean that less computational power is needed to perform the classification.

Acknowledgements. The Know-Center is funded within the Austrian COMET Program under the auspices of the Austrian Ministry of Transport, Innovation and Technology, the Austrian Ministry of Economics and Labor and by the State of Styria. COMET is managed by the Austrian Research Promotion Agency FFG.

References

1. Breiman, L.: Random forests. Machine Learning 45, 5–32 (2001)
2. Caruana, R., Karampatziakis, N., Yessenalina, A.: An empirical evaluation of supervised learning in high dimensions. In: Proceedings of the 25th International Conference on Machine Learning, ICML 2008, pp. 96–103. ACM (2008)
3. Chen, C., Chen, J., Barry, J.: Diurnal pattern of transit ridership: a case study of the new york city subway system. Journal of Transport Geography 17(3), 176–186 (2009)
4. Grieco, M., Urry, J.: Mobilities: new perspectives on transport and society. Ashgate (January 2012)
5. Hall, M., Frank, E., Holmes, G., Pfahringer, B., Reutemann, P., Witten, I.H.: The WEKA data mining software: An update. SIGKDD Explor. Newsl. 11(1), 10–18 (2009)
6. Hall, M.A.: Correlation-based Feature Subset Selection for Machine Learning. PhD thesis, University of Waikato, Hamilton, New Zealand (1998)
7. Huang, C.-M., Ying, J.J.-C., Tseng, V.S.: Mining Users Behaviors and Environments for Semantic Place Prediction. In: Proceedings of the Mobile Data Challenge by Nokia Workshop, Co-Located with Pervasive 2012 (2012)
8. Kim, B., Ha, J.-Y., Lee, S., Kang, S., Lee, Y., Rhee, Y., Nachman, L., Song, J.: Adnext: a visit-pattern-aware mobile advertising system for urban commercial complexes. In: Proceedings of the 12th Workshop on Mobile Computing Systems and Applications, HotMobile 2011, pp. 7–12. ACM, New York (2011)
9. Kiukkonen, N., Blom, J., Dousse, O., Gatica-Perez, D., Laurila, J.: Towards rich mobile phone datasets: Lausanne data collection campaign. In: Proceedings of the ACM International Conference on Pervasive Services, ICPS (2010)
10. Laurila, J.K., Gatica-Perez, D., Aad, I., Bornet, B.J.O., Do, T.-M.-T., Dousse, O., Eberle, J., Miettinen, M.: The mobile data challenge: Big data for mobile computing research. In: Pervasive Computing (2012)
11. Montoliu, R., Martnez-Uso, A., Martnez Sotoca, J.: Semantic place prediction by combining smart binary classifiers. In: Proceedings of the Mobile Data Challenge by Nokia Workshop, Co-Located with Pervasive 2012 (2012)
12. Oliver, E.: A survey of platforms for mobile networks research. SIGMOBILE Mob. Comput. Commun. Rev. 12(4), 56–63 (2009)
13. Pal, M.: Kernel methods in remote sensing: a review. ISH. J. Hydraulic Eng. (Special Issue), 194–215 (2009)
14. Saffari, A., Leistner, C., Santner, J., Godec, M., Bischof, H.: On-line random forests. In: 2009 IEEE 12th International Conference on Computer Vision Workshops (ICCV Workshops), September 27-October 4, pp. 1393–1400 (2009)
15. Üstün, B., Melssen, W.J., Buydens, L.M.C.: Facilitating the application of Support Vector Regression by using a universal Pearson VII function based kernel. Chemometrics and Intelligent Laboratory Systems 81(1), 29–40 (2006)
16. Wang, S., Chen, C., Ma, J.: Accelerometer Based Transportation Mode Recognition on Mobile Phones. In: Proceedings of the 2010 Asia-Pacific Conference on Wearable Computing Systems, APWCS 2010, pp. 44–46. IEEE Computer Society, Washington, DC (2010)
17. Yang, J.: Toward physical activity diary: Motion recognition using simple acceleration features with mobile phones. Data Processing, 1–9 (2009)
18. Zhu, Y., Zhong, E., Lu, Z., Yang, Q.: Feature Engineering for Place Category Classification. In: Proceedings of the Mobile Data Challenge by Nokia Workshop, Co-Located with Pervasive 2012 (2012)

Recognizing a Mobile Phone's Storing Position as a Context of a Device and a User

Kaori Fujinami and Satoshi Kouchi

Department of Computer and Information Sciences
Tokyo University of Agriculture and Technology
Tokyo, Japan
fujinami@cc.tuat.ac.jp

Abstract. A mobile phone is getting smarter by employing a sensor and awareness of various contexts about a user and the terminal itself. In this paper, we deal with 9 storing positions of a smartphone on the body as a context of a device itself and a user: 1) around the neck (hanging), 2) chest pocket, 3) jacket pocket (side), 4) front pocket of trousers, 5) back pocket of trousers, 6) backpack, 7) handbag, 8) messenger bag, and 9) shoulder bag. We propose a method of recognizing the 9 positions by machine learning algorithms with 60 features that characterize specific movements of a terminal at the position during walking. The result of offline experiment showed that an overall accuracy was 74.6% in a strict condition of *Leave-One-Subject-Out* (LOSO) test, where a support vector machine (SVM) classifier was trained with dataset from other subjects.

1 Introduction

A mobile phone terminal is getting smarter due to the advancement of technologies such as Micro Electro Mechanical Systems (MEMS), high performance and low power computation. Various sensors are embedded into or attached to a mobile phone terminal and a wide variety of contextual information can be extracted, which is about a user, a device and/or environment. These sensors are (or will) not only utilized for explicit usage of the terminal's functionalities like user authentication [17], display orientation change and backlight intensity control [7], but also for activitiy recognition [18], indoor location [2], the state of a device [8], pedestrian identification [21], environment [20], etc. In this paper, we focus on the position of a smartphone on the human body as a context. The position is not an exact 3D coordinate, but parts of our body or clothes such as "hanging from the neck" and "inside a chest pocket".

According to a study of phone carrying, 17% of people determine the position of storing a smartphone based on *contextual restrictions*, e.g. no pocket in the T-shirt, too large phone size for a pants pocket, comfort for an ongoing activity [5]. These factors are variable throughout the day, and thus smartphone users change their positions in a day. This suggests that a context, *on-body placement*, has great potentials in improving the usability of a terminal and the quality of

K. Zheng, M. Li, and H. Jiang (Eds.): MOBIQUITOUS 2012, LNICST 120, pp. 76–88, 2013.

sensor-dependent services, facilitating human-human communication, and the reduction of unnecessary energy consumption.

On-body position sensing is getting attention to researchers in machine learning and ubiquitous computing communities [6][19][22], which starts from the work of Kunze et al. [11]. Vahdatpour et al. recently proposed a method to identify 6 regions on the body, e.g. head, upper arm, for health and medical monitoring systems [22]. In their case, a sensor was attached directly on the skin or on the clothes, and the recognition process were conducted in an offline manner. A preliminary work by Shi et al. seeks a method of on-body positioning of a mobile device into typical *containers* such as a trousers' pocket. Inertial sensors, i.e. accelerometer and gyroscope, are utilized in these work. By contrast, Miluzzo et al. proposes a framework of recognizing the position of a mobile phone on the body using multiple sensors [15]. In their initial stage, a simple placement, i.e. inside or outside pocket, is subject to detect using an embedded microphone. In this paper, we deal with nine storing positions including bags. Recognizing a situation in which a terminal is in a bag is challenging because of the diverse shape of a container and the carrying style. We attempt to find a set of features that can characterize and discriminate the motion of a smartphone terminal in a periodic motion, e.g. walking, using an embedded accelerometer. To the best of our knowledge, this is the first attempt to recognize a wide variety of a bag as a storing position.

The rest of the paper is organized as follows: Section 2 describes our approach. The performance of the algorithm is evaluated in Section 3. Then, the results are analyzed in Section 4. Section 5 describes implementation on an Android platform as a shareable component. Possible application scenarios are presented in Section 6 with validation of the results. Finally, Section 7 concludes the paper with future work.

2   On-Body Placement Detection Method

We describe the approach of the placement-detection and recognition features.

2.1   Target Positions and Sensing Modality

Nine popular positions shown in Fig. 1 are selected as the targets of recognition: 1) around the neck (hanging), 2) chest pocket, 3) jacket pocket (side), 4) front pocket of trousers, 5) back pocket of trousers, 6) backpack, 7) handbag, 8) messenger bag, and 9) shoulder bag.

Including a *bag* as a storing position is technically challenging due to its diverse shape of a container, e.g. a side pocket, and carrying style; however, as the survey [5] shows, a bag is a major location for storing a mobile phone for especially women (about 60%), and about 50% of them do not notice incoming call/message in their bags, which motivated us to detect a situation of carrying a mobile phone in a bag. If a mobile phone knows that it is inside a bag, it may ring louder or respond to the caller that the callee may take some time to answer the call [7]. Although Kawahara et al. utilized a heuristic that the variance of acceleration signals in a certain window is nearly zero when a mobile phone is in a bag [10], it is obviously not applicable while a person is moving. The four types of bags were specified as popular ones based on a pilot study on the street. We determined to recognize these types separately, rather than handle as one single type *bag*. This is because the movement patterns that we utilize in recognizing a storing position are so different from each other. Note that the type of a bag is not determined by the name and the shape, but by the relationship with the body, as shown in Table 1. So, a mobile phone inside a "handbag" (upper-right corner of Fig. 1) that is being slung like a shoulder bag (lower-right corner) is classified into "shoulder bag".

We have adopted an accelerometer to obtain signals that can characterize movement patterns generated by dedicated storing positions while a person is in a periodic motion, e.g. walking. The utilization of an accelerometer makes the placement detection feasible on today's smartphones because of the popularity. A feature vector is obtained from three-axes accelerometer readings, and our system classifies it into one of the nine positions.

Fig. 1. Target Storing Positions

Table 1. Characteristics of the four types of bags

Type	Way of sling	Relationship with body
backpack	over both shoulders	on the back
handbag	holding with hand	in the hand
messenger bag	on the shoulder opposite to the bag	around the waist
shoulder bag	on the same side of the shoulder as the bag	side of the body

2.2   Storing Position Recognition Process

Fig. 2 illustrates a flow of data processing from sensor readings to an event of placement change. A data processing (recognition) window is generated every 8 samples, i.e. the length of sliding from raw acceleration signals sampled at 25Hz. The effect of the window size on the recognition performance is discussed later.

As described above, the recognition is carried out while a person is in a periodic motion, e.g. walking, in which specific periodic movement patterns of a phone terminal are subject to recognize. Non-periodic motions such as jumping and sitting can be included in a stream of acceleration signal. So, a period of *walking* needs to be determined prior to position recognition, which is based on the constancy of acceleration signal proposed in [16]. Note that a person may change the storing position of a phone terminal while she is standing still. An action of storing(removing) a mobile phone terminal into(from) a certain storage position, e.g. a chest pocket, is also considered as a non-periodic motion. In [6], we proposed a method to recognize a specific gesture for each position. In the future, the result of the constancy decision is utilized to call appropriate recognition process: periodic movement patterns or storing gestures.

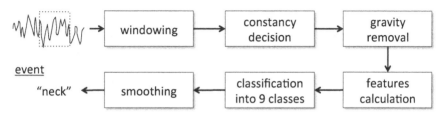

Fig. 2. Position Recognition Process

In the next stage, the acceleration of gravity is removed from the sensor readings and obtain force component for each axis. We adopted a method proposed by Cho et al. [4], in which the gravity components are approximately removed by subtracting the mean of accelerations at each time. Here, the mean is obtained per window. The approximate movement force is then normalized by the mean of the norm of three-axes components. A window of acceleration signal that is determined as what is obtained during walking in the previous stage is then given to a nine-class classifier. Since an output of the classifier is window-basis, *temporal smoothing* is carried out to reject a pulsed different output. Here, a majority voting is applied among successive 11 outputs. In this way, one position recognition is performed. In case of a change in the storing position, an event is generated so that an application could adapt to the change.

2.3   Recognition Features

Initially, we listed candidates of features by taking into account the independency on the direction of a terminal and the complexity of calculation, which was 130 features in total. Then, a machine learning-based feature selection (a forward searching) is applied to collected dataset using Weka [13]. Table 2 shows the selected 60 features for window size of 256. Note that x, y, and z axes of the accelerometer of NexusOne are set to the direction of *width*, *height* and *thickness* in a portrait mode, respectively.

Table 2. Selected Features (window size = 256; 60 features in total)

No.	Description	axis
1	S.D of amplitude	y, z
2	Max. amplitude of frequency spectrum	z
3	Frequency that gives the max. frequency amplitude	x, y
4	Max. of S.Ds of amplitude in frequency-windows (Max SDF)	y, z
5	Index in a frequency-window that gives the Max SDF	y
6	Max. amplitude in the low-frequency range	x, y, z
7	Max. amplitude in the mid-frequency range	y
8	Max. amplitude in the high-frequency range	y
9	S.D of amplitude in the mid-frequency range	y
10	S.D of amplitude in the high-frequency range	x, y
11	Min. amplitude of absolute value	x, y
12	Max. amplitude of absolute value	y, z
13	Inter-quartile range of amplitude in the time domain	z
14	Correlation coefficient between two axes	x-y, x-z
15	2nd max amplitude in the frequency domain	x, y, z
16	Frequency that gives the 2nd max amplitude	x, y
17	75 percentile of frequency amplitude	x, y, z
18	Inter-quartile range of amplitude in the frequency domain	y
19	Correlation coefficient in the entire frequency range	x-y, x-z, y-z
20	Correlation coefficient in the low-frequency range	x-y, x-z, y-z
21	Correlation coefficient in the mid-frequency range	x-y
22	FFT entropy in the entire range	x, y, z
23	FFT entropy in the low-range	x, y, z
24	FFT energy in the mid-range	x, y, z
25	FFT entropy in the mid-range	z
26	FFT energy in the high-range	x, y, z
27	Binned distribution of time domain values	x_2, x_6, x_9, y_4, y_9 z_4, z_5, z_6

S.D.: Standard Deviation, $axis_i$: i-th bin of binned distribution ($i = 1..10$)

The term "frequency-window" is a 2.93Hz window slid by 0.1Hz in frequency spectra. These window size and sliding-width were heuristically determined. The frequency spectra are divided into three "frequency ranges", in which *low*, *medium*, and *high* correspond to 0-4.2Hz, 4.2-8.4Hz and 8.4-12.5Hz, respectively. The FFT energy is calculated as the sum of squared values of frequency components, which is normalized by dividing by the window size [1]. The FFT entropy is then calculated as the normalized information entropy of FFT component values of acceleration signals, which represents the distribution of frequency components in the frequency domain [1]. The Binned Distribution is defined as follows: 1) the *range* of values for each axis is determined by subtracting minimum value from maximum one; 2) the range is equally divided into 10 bins; and 3) the number of values that fell within each of the bins is counted [12].

3   Evaluation on the Basic Performance of the Classifier

We describe the experiments on the classifier from the aspects of 1) window size, 2) types of classifier, 3) generalization, and 4) specialization. Note that *smoothing* process is not applied to the decisions of the classifiers.

3.1   Data Collection

Data were collected from 20 graduate/undergraduate students (2 females). They were asked to walk about 5 minutes (30 seconds x 10 times) for each storing position. To collect data from naturalistic condition, we asked participants to walk as usual, and there was no special instruction about the orientation of the device. Also, they wore their own clothes; we only lent them clothes in case that they did not have clothes with pockets. As for bags, we utilized one particular bag for each type of the category of a bag, and we asked the participants to carry bags as designed. That is, for example, carrying handbag with one hand, not slinging over a shoulder like a "shoulder bag". Totally, we obtained about 150,000 samples per position.

3.2   Experiment 1: The Effect of Window Size and Classifiers

As a first step, we evaluated the effect of the window size for feature calculation and various classifiers. We tested with three classes of window size, i.e. 128, 256 and 512 (5.12, 10.24 and 20.48 seconds, respectively). The categories of classifiers that we compared with are 1) an ensemble leaning method (Random Subspace method [9]), 2) a decision tree method (J48), 3) a Bayes method (Naive Bayes), 4) a support vector machine (SVM) classifier and 5) an artificial neural network-based method (Multilayer Perceptron (MLP)). After recognition features were calculated for each window size and stored in text files, we ran 10-fold cross validation (CV) tests on the Weka machine learning toolkit[13].

Fig. 3 shows the relationship between the window size and the accuracy of 10-fold CV, in which SVM performed best with all size of the windows (98.6, 99.4 and 99.7 %, respectively). We determined to utilize the size of 256 for the upcoming experiments although the accuracies increase as the size of the window grows. This is because a window of 512 samples takes 20.48 seconds to be available, which indicates that a window is usable only if a person is walking for more than 20.48 seconds, otherwise a window might be rejected at the constancy decision phase or lead to incorrect recognition. Additionally, the accuracy is being saturated with the size of 256.

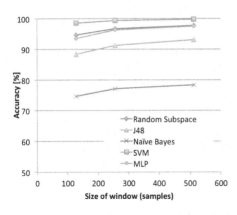 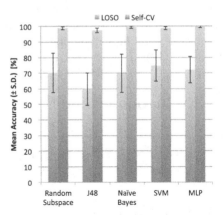

Fig. 3. Accuracy with different size of window and classifiers (10-folds CV)

Fig. 4. Mean accuracy with different classifiers in LOSO and Self-CV test (window size = 256, average number of instances per person = 701)

3.3 Experiment 2: Leave-One-Subject-Out Test

To see the capability of the generalization of the recognition system, we carried out Leave-One-Subject-Out (LOSO) test with the same dataset as Experiment 1. In a LOSO test, dataset from one person is utilized as a test set, while the others are utilized as training sets. A LOSO test can measure the performance on a realistic situation such that a person purchases an on-body placement-aware functionality from a third-party, because the data from a particular person are not utilized to train a classifier. Here, we iterated one test process for all (20) the persons in the dataset and calculated statistics.

In Fig. 4, the mean accuracies for various classifiers is presented as the bar on the left. The accuracies degraded 8 (Naive Bayes) to 32 (J48) points from CV-test. SVM also performed best, where the mean, the lowest and the highest accuracy are 74.6 %, 55.9 % and 89.8 %, respectively.

3.4 Experiment 3: Self-Cross Validation Test

Finally, a self-cross validation (Self-CV) was carried out to investigate the capability of specialization. Here, a 10-folds CV was conducted with dataset obtained from a particular person. On the right bar in Fig. 4, the mean accuracies were presented. All the mean accuracies were more than 97.0 % with small standard deviations, in which MLP performed best (99.7 %).

4 Analysis

The 10-folds CV (experiment 1) showed high accuracy (99.4 % with SVM); however, the performance in the LOSO test (experiment 2) was degraded and diverse in individuals ranging from 55.9 % to 89.8 %. Table 3 shows an aggregated confusion matrix of the LOSO test, in which each person's confusion matrix was accumulated to see the overall mis-recognition.

The recognition of "neck" performed very well in both recall (97.3 %) and precision (94.2 %). We consider that the moving pattern of an object hanging from the neck is quite different from the others. This might be applicable for a class of applications that monitor environmental conditions such as temperature and humidity since the measurement from the neck often differs from trousers pockets due to the effect of body heat and sweat [24]. An application can take an appropriate action, e.g. correction to the value measured outside and alerting a user, when a monitoring device (smartphone) is inside a trousers' pocket.

The low recall (65.1%) and precision (57.0%) of the recognition of "jacket's pocket". was due to relatively high heterogeneity of the shape of the pocket. The mis-recognitions of "jacket's pocket" from "shoulder bag" (192), "chest pocket" (186) and "messenger bag" (157) are reasonable because the three positions also have the diversity compared to the other positions. Also, the carrying positions of "shoulder bag" and "messenger bag" are close to a "jacket's pocket", which generate similar movement patterns. The data that belong to "messenger bag" are often mis-classified into "trousers' back pocket" (187), "backpack" (160) and "jacket's pocket" (157). We consider that this is because "messenger bag", "backpack" and "jacket's pocket" have enough room to move around. Also, the relationships with the body are similar in "messenger bag", "trousers' pocket" and "backpack" as shown in Table 1.

Table 3. Aggregated Confusion Matrix of LOSO test

	1	2	3	4	5	6	7	8	9	Recall
1	1504	4	14	1	2	0	1	0	20	97.3%
2	4	1183	186	4	13	0	16	81	36	77.7%
3	53	143	985	39	24	53	21	66	129	65.1%
4	7	1	93	1042	156	0	13	181	35	68.2%
5	1	49	34	92	1311	0	4	57	20	83.6%
6	0	44	17	0	0	1281	118	41	74	81.3%
7	2	58	51	0	0	95	1304	0	76	82.2%
8	9	94	157	95	187	160	51	706	143	44.1%
9	17	13	192	1	2	10	140	37	1168	73.9%
Precision	94.2%	74.4%	57.0%	81.8%	77.3%	80.1%	78.2%	60.4%	68.7%	74.8%

Row: original class, Column: predicted class.
Class label: 1=neck ,2=chest, 3=jacket's pocket, 4=trousers' front pocket,
5=trousers' back pocket, 6=backpack, 7=handbag, 8=messenger bag, 9=shoulder bag

Table 4. Recall and Precision with Aggregated Positions

	1	2	3	4+5	6+7+8+9
Recall	97.3%	77.7%	65.1%	84.0%	87.8%
Precision	94.2%	74.4%	57.0%	93.6%	88.1%

Class labels are the same as in Table 3.

By taking into account the semantic similarity of trousers' front and back pockets, they can be merged into one class "trousers' pocket". Similarly, the four types of bags can be considered as "bag". Table 4 shows the recall and the precision of the merged classes, in which the new classes are recognized well.

The accuracies in Self-CV were high (more than 97.0 %) because the complexity in the operating environment decreases. Even the worst classifier in the LOSO test (J48) got the accuracy of 97.5 %. We consider that it is necessary to investigate not only *stronger* features or classifiers but also a mechanism to adjust to an individual user in a post hoc manner. This can be addressed by integrating a sophisticated HCI technique with a semi-supervised machine learning technique. The method should be designed to motivate a user to make a personal belongings smarter by herself, which we are currently under investigation.

5   Implementation

The storing position recognition should be provided as a shareable component to allow application developers to focus on the application logic development as well as to maintain the consistency of various applications' behavior. Thus, we have selected the Google's Android platform because it allows an application to run background. We developed a software framework to bridge the proposed functionality with user applications, which is realized by Android inter-process communication (IPC) framework and our original Java interfaces and classes.

A compact version of Weka [14] and a support vector machine library (LIB-SVM [3]) are utilized to run a SVM model trained by Weka on a PC. The elapsed times of the feature calculation and the net classification on Samsung Galaxy Nexus platform (OS: Android 4.0.4, CPU: Texas Instruments OMAP4460 1.2GHz Dual Core, RAM: 1 GB) are about 100 msec and 7 msec, respectively. As described in Section 2.2, a window is generated every 8 samples (= 320 msec). So, we consider that the current processing speed is enough for completing one cycle of recognition until the next window creation.

6   Applications of On-Body Position Recognition

We discuss applications to emphasize the relevance of the placement-awareness of a mobile device, which is classified into three categories: smart notification, annotation for sensor readings and functionality control.

6.1   Smart Call/Message Notification

In our preliminary study, we found that the ease of perceiving an audio alarm and vibration of a mobile phone differs among the storing positions: "hanging from the neck" allowed notification with significantly smaller audio volume than the others. Moreover, "inside a chest pocket" and "hanging from the neck" were the fastest and the latest in the notification with the vibration, respectively [23].

This suggests that the notification should be adaptive to the storing position to save energy while allowing prompt and effective communication. The current high recognition performance of "hanging from the neck" might at least allow notification to a user with minimal audio volume when a terminal is there. Also, a caller can be notified of the possible delay in case a terminal is "not hanging from the neck", which is suggested by Cui et al. [5] and Gellersen et al. [7] to make communication smoother.

6.2   Assuring Sensor-Dependent System's Behavior

A sensor-augmented mobile phone is suitable for recognizing activity and physiological states of a user as well as monitoring environmental states around her in an implicit and continuous manner [12,15]. An issue is that people may change the storing position for some reasons as described before. This implies that an application would not perform as designed if the prerequisite is not upheld. We propose to utilize the storing position as *meta-data* that are attached to primary information processed by an application to assure reliable application's behavior.

In the activity recognition using wearable sensors, the sensors are basically assumed to be at an intended position [1,18]. In [18], an accelerometer hanging from the neck contributed to capture certain kind of movement of the upper body. In this case, our method can ask a user to keep hanging a mobile phone from the neck or turn the sensing component off to avoid noisy measurement based on application requirements.

In the paradigm of human-centric sensing, where a sensor-augmented mobile phone is utilized to capture environmental information throughout daily lives, the storing position of a mobile phone terminal is considered as a key element of reliable measurement because the measurements is affected by storing positions [15,20], especially "outside a container". We actually found a difference in the readings from a relative humidity sensor and a thermometer due to the effect of body heat propagation [24]. The fact not only has an impact on the correctness of environmental data collection, but also on the estimation of a risk from an environmental state such as heatstroke and influenza. The correctness of the risk estimation relates to the physiological condition of a user and the trust of a user on the device due to under- and over-estimation, respectively. We have developed a placement-aware heatstroke alert device that provides a message of possible under- (over-) estimate of the estimated risk level based on the relationship between the data from outside, i.e. "hanging from neck", and that of other positions [24]. We consider that the aggregated performance (Table 4) is promising for this application.

6.3   On-Body Placement-Aware Functionality Control

A mobile phone can control its functionality based on the placement. Harrison et al. specify a couple of application in this category: screen component would be switched off when a mobile phone is not visible, and keypads would be locked to avoid accidental input, e.g. in a pocket with keys [8]. These applications just like to know if a device is inside a storage container such as a pocket and a bag, which is not hanging from the neck (=outside) in our system's sense. As shown in Table 3, both the recall and the precision of "neck" are high (97.3 % and 94.2 %, respectively), which makes the scenario practical with our system.

In terms of functionality controlling for energy saving of a device itself, a mechanism of handling inaccurate placement of a mobile phone, *suspending*, can be classified into this category; an application would turn itself off to save energy after alerting to a user for a while without response from her.

7　Conclusion and Future Work

In this paper, we proposed a method to recognize a storing position of a mobile phone while it is being carried. To recognize nine positions, we specified sixty features obtained from a 3-axes accelerometer. The processing window size of 256 were chosen by taking into account the continuity of motion, i.e. walking, as well as the accuracy of recognition. Five types of classifiers were tested.

The results of offline experiment showed that an overall accuracy of identifying the nine positions with SVM classifier was 74.6% in a strict condition of LOSO test, which was the best in the other classifiers. Aggregations of positions (trousers' pockets and bags) showed better and promising performance in recall and precision. The results of Self-CV showed almost perfect recognition performance, which implies the necessity of on-the-fly or post-hoc personalization of a classifier for practical use. The proposed method was implemented on an Android platform as a shareable service, and we confirmed that one cycle of recognition finishes within sliding interval (320 msec).

We will incorporate a method of detecting the change of a storing position while a person is not walking, which is under investigation, in order to keep track of the position of a mobile phone all the time. Currently, the recognition process is repeated every 320 msec, which we consider can be optimized by changing the duty cycle while taking into account the delay to wake-up acceptable for an application. An application case study with a heatstroke alert is also planned to have deep understanding of the new idea of on-body placement-awareness of a smartphone from the perspective of human-sensor interaction.

Acknowledgments. This work was supported by MEXT Grants-in-Aid for Scientific Research (A) No. 23240014 and Kayamori Foundation of Information Science Advancement.

References

1. Bao, L., Intille, S.S.: Activity recognition from user-annotated acceleration data. In: Ferscha, A., Mattern, F. (eds.) PERVASIVE 2004. LNCS, vol. 3001, pp. 1–17. Springer, Heidelberg (2004)
2. Blanke, U., Schiele, B.: Sensing Location in the Pocket. In: Adjunct Proceedings of the 10th International Conference on Ubiquitous Computing (Ubicomp 2008), pp. 2–3 (September 2008)

3. Chang, C.-C., Lin, C.-J.: LIBSVM: A library for support vector machines. ACM Trans. Intell. Syst. Technol. 2(3), 27:1–27:27 (2011)
4. Cho, S.-J., et al.: Two-stage Recognition of Raw Acceleration Signals for 3-D Gesture-Understanding Cell Phones. In: Proc. of the Tenth International Workshop on Frontiers in Handwriting Recognition (2006)
5. Cui, Y., Chipchase, J., Ichikawa, F.: A Cross Culture Study on Phone Carrying and Physical Personalization. In: Aykin, N. (ed.) HCII 2007. LNCS, vol. 4559, pp. 483–492. Springer, Heidelberg (2007)
6. Fujinami, K., Jin, C., Kouchi, S.: Tracking on-body location of a mobile phone. In: Proc. of the 14th Annual IEEE International Symposium on Wearable Computers, ISWC 2010, pp. 190–197 (2010)
7. Gellersen, H., Schmidt, A., Beigl, M.: Multi-Sensor Context-Awareness in Mobile Devices and Smart Artifacts. Journal on Mobile Networks and Applications (MONET) 7(5), 341–351 (2002)
8. Harrison, C., Hudson, S.E.: Lightweight material detection for placement-aware mobile computing. In: Proc. of the 21st Annual ACM Symposium on User Interface Software and Technology, UIST 2008, pp. 279–282. ACM, New York (2008)
9. Ho, T.K.: The Random Subspace Method for Constructing Decision Forests. IEEE Trans. Pattern Anal. Mach. Intell. 20(8), 832–844 (1998)
10. Kawahara, Y., Kurasawa, H., Morikawa, H.: Recognizing user context using mobile handsets with acceleration sensors. In: IEEE International Conference on Portable Information Devices (Portable 2007), pp. 1–5 (2007)
11. Kunze, K.S., Lukowicz, P., Junker, H., Tröster, G.: Where am I: Recognizing On-body Positions of Wearable Sensors. In: Strang, T., Linnhoff-Popien, C. (eds.) LoCA 2005. LNCS, vol. 3479, pp. 264–275. Springer, Heidelberg (2005)
12. Kwapisz, J.R., Weiss, G.M., Moore, S.A.: Activity recognition using cell phone accelerometers. SIGKDD Explor. Newsl. 12(2), 74–82 (2011)
13. Machine Learning Group at University of Waikato. Weka 3 - Data Mining with Open Source Machine Learning Software in Java,
    `http://www.cs.waikato.ac.nz/ml/weka/`
14. Marsan, R.J.: Weka for Android,
    `http://rjmarsan.com/Research/WekaforAndroid`
15. Miluzzo, E., et al.: Pocket, Bag, Hand, etc.-Automatically Detecting Phone Context through Discovery. In: Proc. of the First International Workshop on Sensing for App. Phones, PhoneSense 2010 (2010)
16. Murao, K., Terada, T.: A motion recognition method by constancy-decision. In: Proceedings of the 14th International Symposium on Wearable Computers, ISWC 2010, pp. 69–72 (October 2010)
17. Okumura, F., et al.: A Study on Biometric Authentication based on Arm Sweep Action with Acceleration Sensor. In: Proc. of International Symposium on Intelligent Signal Processing and Communications (ISPACS 2006), pp. 219–222 (2006)
18. Pirttikangas, S., Fujinami, K., Nakajima, T.: Feature Selection and Activity Recognition from Wearable Sensors. In: Youn, H.Y., Kim, M., Morikawa, H. (eds.) UCS 2006. LNCS, vol. 4239, pp. 516–527. Springer, Heidelberg (2006)
19. Shi, Y., Shi, Y., Liu, J.: A Rotation based Method for Detecting On-body Positions of Mobile Devices. In: Proc. of the 13th International Conference on Ubiquitous Computing, UbiComp 2011, pp. 559–560. ACM (2011)

20. Stevens, M., D'Hondt, E.: Crowdsourcing of Pollution Data using Smartphones. In: 1st Ubiquitous Crowdsourcing Workshop at UbiComp (2010)
21. Sugimori, D., Iwamoto, T., Matsumoto, M.: A Study about Identification of Pedestrian by Using 3-Axis Accelerometer. In: Proc. of the 17th International Conference on Embedded and Real-Time Computing Systems and Applications (RTCSA 2011), pp. 134–137 (2011)
22. Vahdatpour, A., et al.: On-body Device Localization for Health and Medical Monitoring Applications. In: Proc. of the 2011 IEEE International Conference on Pervasive Computing and Communications, PERCOM 2011, pp. 37–44. IEEE Computer Society (2011)
23. Xue, Y.: A Study on Reliable Environmental Sensing and Alerting by an On-Body Placement-Aware Device. Master's thesis, Departent of Computer and Information Sciences, Tokyo University of Agriculture and Technology (2012) (in Japanese)
24. Xue, Y., et al.: A Trustworthy Heatstroke Risk Alert on a Smartphone. In: Adj. Proc. of the 10th Asia-Pacific Conference on Human-Computer Interaction (APCHI 2012), pp. 621–622 (August 2012)

Privacy Preserving Social Mobile Applications

Venkatraman Ramakrishna, Apurva Kumar, and Sougata Mukherjea

IBM India Research Laboratory,
ISID Campus, Institutional Area, Vasant Kunj, New Delhi - 110070, India
{vramakr2,kapurva,smukherj}@in.ibm.com

Abstract. Mobile users can obtain a wide range of services by maintaining associations, and sharing location and social context, with service providers. But multiple associations are cumbersome to maintain, and sharing private information with untrusted providers is risky. Using a trusted broker to mediate interactions by managing interfaces, user identities, context, social network links, policies, and enabling cross-domain associations, results in more privacy and reduced management burden for users, as we show in this paper. We also describe the prototype implementations of two practically useful applications that require awareness of participants' location and social context: (i) targeted advertising, and (ii) social network-assisted online purchases.

Keywords: Privacy, Multi-Domain, Social Network, Policy Management, Middleware, Identity Management, Online Advertising, Online Payment.

1   Introduction

Ubiquitous data communication infrastructure enables mobile device users to access web services on the go. It is common for users to maintain long term associations with multiple service providers, such as online merchants. These providers attempt to customize their services to be relevant to a user's context, which primarily includes location and social associations. The active involvement of a user's social network often results in applications that provide benefits to a service consumer, his social network friends, and service providers. With social networks like Facebook and Google+ being always available to a connected user, richer application scenarios can be realized [22]. We refer to these applications as *social mobile applications*, and they have the following in common: (i) remote service providers, (ii) mobile users, and (iii) social networks. Take online shopping for example, in which relevance of product information and advertisements plays a huge part. Service providers can send more relevant advertisements to a mobile user if that user's context and activities are known to them. In addition, a user's social network links can be used to determine shared interests, and to send relevant ads to multiple people. Mobile shoppers will benefit from this, as will providers who get to expand their target advertisement base. A different example involves payments using mobile devices, either at Point-of-Sale terminals or to online service providers. Though multiple payment systems have been devised in recent years [1][5][7], they force the payer to rely on his personal financial

K. Zheng, M. Li, and H. Jiang (Eds.): MOBIQUITOUS 2012, LNICST 120, pp. 89–102, 2013.

accounts, which may occasionally run out of funds. It would be useful to offer the payer a backup option of obtaining money from his social network friends as part of the payment protocol. These advertising and payment examples seem straightforward on their own, yet they face common issues that must be resolved before practical applications can be realized. First is the issue of privacy. Though the mobile device must itself possess location and social *awareness*, a user may feel uncomfortable sharing such private information with untrusted service providers for fear of misuse, and also for fear of violating his social network friends' privacy [12]. To realize the payment scenario, the payer may need to know his friends' financial state and willingness to pay, which those friends would justifiably like to keep private. The second major issue is the fact that it may become cumbersome for both users and service providers to maintain long term associations in the face of change and heterogeneity. The provider's service interface may change over time, and so may a user's domain affiliations (e.g., social network account, financial account, etc.).

In this paper, we present the design of infrastructure to handle the common requirements of such social mobile applications, thereby making it easier to build and maintain them. Our system (i) protects users' privacy from each other, and from service providers, and (ii) manages changes in user identities, affiliations, and service characteristics, which would otherwise be a burden on users and service providers. The fulcrum of our system is a *broker* that mediates interactions amongst users and providers. This broker is hosted by a trustworthy infrastructure provider with a large subscriber base, like a telecom operator or Google, and is relied upon by providers and consumers to relay messages without leaking a user's private information. It is aware of the identities a user assumes with service providers and in domains like social networks and financial organizations. The broker associates a unique *mobile identity* with every user, and maintains links among social network members. It discovers and updates user context, and uses it to guide interactions and information flow. Using a third party authorization framework such as OAuth [10], it can obtain limited user identity and context information from another domain. Users can register with it through a web service interface, and providers can register their service descriptions. The broker implements generic and pluggable functions to parse and redirect messages in the course of an interaction. The broker also has a role in *policy management*. It maintains policies specified by users that govern message delivery and disclosure or manipulation of user information. Since policies governing such behavior might also be set by other domains a user belongs to, and which are involved in the interaction (e.g., social network), the broker must resolve these different sets of policies. It does so by dynamically configuring a multi-domain policy enforcement workflow based on the assumption that all participating domains manage policies using the standard policy management architecture consisting of *decision* and *enforcement points* [21]. Individual domains may keep their autonomy by revoking the broker's access to them at any time. To summarize, our original contribution in this paper is a centralized architecture that enables a large number of users with possible social network links to obtain services from each other and from untrusted providers without violating their privacy and their desired behavioral policies.

We describe motivating examples in Section 2, and present our solution architecture in Section 3. In Section 4 we describe prototype implementations of two applications, and analyze our system in Section 5. We conclude the paper with a related work survey in Section 6, and thoughts on future work in Section 7.

2   Motivating Scenarios

Described below are two idealized scenarios from a mobile user's perspective.

2.1   Social- and Location-Aware Advertising

Alice enters a *My Style* store in a shopping mall and makes purchases. At checkout, she registers herself with the store using her mobile device, which uses the *MyTel* telecom data network, and opts to receive product updates. Subsequently, she receives an option to sign up for reward points in exchange for sharing and/or recommending relevant store advertisements and product information with her Facebook friends. When Alice receives an ad on her mobile phone, she indicates the names of friends who may find it interesting and relevant. One of those friends, Bob, who happens to be in the mall premises, receives a text message (and a graphical notification, if he possesses a smart phone.) and walks toward the *My Style* store to examine its wares. Jack, who is sitting in a book store in the mall, does not receive a notification as his phone has a 'Do Not Disturb' policy applied to incoming messages. Another friend, Carol, is not in the vicinity, and therefore receives an email instead of a text message.

2.2   Social Network-Assisted Shared Payments

Alice uses her mobile phone to make a purchase at a store where she has an account, and subsequently receives the purchase details. Next, the phone prompts her to pay using one of her credit cards. Payment attempts fail because of insufficient card balances, and Alice is presented with an option to request money from her social network friends (including relatives). Some of these friends hold joint accounts with her, and withdrawals require multiple authorization. Others may be willing to loan money from their accounts to Alice's. Friends likely to agree to payment requests from Alice receive query messages if their phones are turned on, and if they possess sufficient funds to make the payment. If one or more friends see the message and agree to pay, the store receives the payment, and the purchase completes.

2.3   Discussion

The above applications involve interactions among mobile users, their social network friends, and service providers. Users have multiple affiliations, and messages are sent based on relevance and context. Similar characteristics are desirable in other settings, like (i) a museum that could serve its patrons and their friends better with more contextual knowledge, and (ii) a traffic monitoring and guidance service that could make better decisions with inputs from more commuters (i.e., by including social network friends). These scenarios can be generalized to a larger class of social mobile applications, which give mobile users access to context-sensitive services and enable them to perform useful tasks using their mobile devices. If users' identities, context, and social network associations were made publicly available to each other and to service providers, such applications could be built easily as the users and providers would have the information to make optimal decisions. Yet exposing location and social network relationships would be a violation of privacy, and subject users to undue risks [12]. A social network member with a lax privacy standard (e.g., Alice) may inadvertently compromise the privacy of a user with a stricter standard (e.g., Bob) by revealing their association to an untrusted service provider (e.g., advertiser). Such a provider may use this information for spam, or something more nefarious. Building applications with privacy protection is possible, but only if a trusted broker or mediator is employed, as we will see in the following section.

3   Social Mobile Application Middleware

We model social mobile applications using service providers, consumers, social networks, resources or accounts owned by consumers, and data communication infrastructure. Every consumer/user has a mobile device that is capable of data communication, and stores its owner's personal data, preferences, and credentials to access the domains a user belongs to. (Here we define a *domain*, or a *security domain*, as a group of computing entities that are centrally managed and which enforces desired behavior within its boundaries through policies. E.g., social network, financial organization, professional group, etc.) Providers offer web services through which other entities can interact with them. Telecom and wireless networks are used for data communication. To support these applications, we design infrastructure that will (i) mediate provider-consumer interactions, (ii) offer interfaces for users and providers to register and send messages, (iii) manage user identities and associations, (iv) maintain user context, (v) access resources across domain boundaries, and (vi) manage policies. Figure 1 illustrates the functional diagram of the infrastructure.

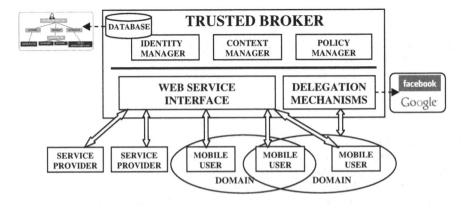

Fig. 1. Platform Architecture and Functions

Building an application that relies on the services provided by the broker involves creating client applications for mobile devices, creating web services a provider will offer, user-provider protocols, and policy rules. In some cases, new third party delegation mechanisms may be plugged into the broker. Messages among providers and users are processed and relayed by the broker, and are based on HTTP.

3.1   Interaction Mediation through a Trusted Broker

The infrastructure we envision is managed by a single entity to which multiple mobile users and service providers are subscribed. This entity mediates (or brokers) interactions amongst users, and between users and service providers, and is trusted to relay messages while maintaining integrity and confidentiality. Users trust the broker with the knowledge of their multiple identities and affiliations with various service providers and domains, and to protect their privacy. The broker itself interacts with users and providers through web services. It offers a service-based interface for users to subscribe and for providers to register their service offerings (e.g., using WSDL). Users register their affiliations with various service providers. They also register their identities as members of other domains (e.g., social network, a bank account holder, a professional organization). To realize a new application scenario, we must devise a new protocol, or a sequence of messages. These messages include service invocations (from user to provider), information requests and resource requests (user to another user or provider), or information dissemination (provider to users: e.g., ads). Every message is relayed by the broker as is, or after some semantically meaningful processing. If the message target is a group whose individuals are identified not through names but through attributes, it is the broker's function to determine the appropriate destinations and convey suitable messages to them. In the remainder of this section, we will discuss what information the broker needs to maintain in order to make suitable decisions in a given application and in a particular context.

In practice, the role of a broker can be played by a large trusted infrastructure provider, like a telecom/cellular network operator (e.g., Airtel, AT&T) or an IT services provider like Google or PayPal. Such providers may already have access to users' location context, and are reputed enough to be entrusted with other private information, especially if it makes applications easy to design and use. Telecom operators may be particularly suited to play this role in emerging markets as they are prominent entities with large subscriber volumes. Reputed cloud infrastructure providers like Amazon may also feasibly offer brokerage services.

3.2   Identity Management and Inter-domain Associations

The broker plays the role of an identity manager for mobile users. In this capacity, it maintains associations among multiple identities belonging to the same user (at multiple service providers, and in multiple domains) as well as associations among users with social network links. We refer to this unified, or federated [14], view as the *mobile identity* of the user. The mobile identity is used in conjunction with consent management protocols like OAuth [10] that provide web-based workflows for temporarily delegating privileges of a user account to the broker without explicitly sharing login credentials. Privileges could mean access to friend lists, contact information, or other private attributes. This enables the broker to act on behalf of the user and to acquire information from the user's account in another domain, such as a social network. Major social network providers like Facebook, Google and Twitter provide support for delegating privileges to third parties using OAuth.

3.3   Context Manager

The broker must be aware of a mobile user's contextual attributes for the purpose of guiding messages to appropriate entities. Users share their context with the broker and not with service providers (or even friends) because they trust the former to keep the information private. E.g., advertisements tagged with a certain location ("*in the mall*") in the scenario in Section 2.1 are relayed by the broker to only those users who are determined to be present at that location. The service provider need not know the identities or locations of the friends, but relevant ads must be sent only to the right people. Context includes location, information about a user's current activities, his organizational affiliations, his financial state, etc. Location can be detected using sensors on the mobile device or through cellular network triangulation by a telecom operator (if it plays the role of the broker). A user can set filter policies to prevent revelation of context information even to the broker based on his level of trust in it.

3.4   Multi-domain Policy Management

In our architecture, we assume that every domain enforces its policies in a centralized manner using a PAP, PIPs, PDPs, and PEPs [21]. But our scenarios involve the intersection of a user's multiple domains, which have policies framed independent of each other (e.g., the broker and the social network have different policies governing who may send messages to a user and at what times); hence a different workflow is necessary to resolve and apply the right policies. Inter-domain negotiation protocols are plausible candidates, but infeasible as they may run to arbitrary lengths [17].

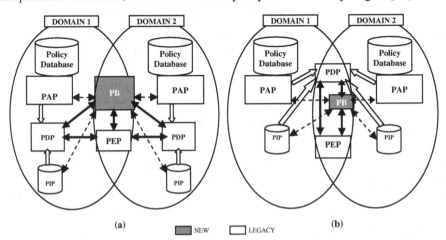

Fig. 2. Two-Domain Policy Management Dynamics using a Shared PEP and a Policy Broker

Instead, we extend the centralized policy management architecture to handle multi-domain intersections where a PEP (Policy Enforcement Point), represented by a user's mobile device, is shared by all the domains. To avoid changing the core nature of the PEP, our trusted broker also runs a module that we refer to as a **Policy Broker (PB)**; this is similar though not identical to the Policy Negotiation Point that has been proposed as a standard [9]. The PB can query the PAP and PIP modules, and mediates the PEP-PDP query-response protocol. It can work in either of two modes, illustrated in Figure 2 for a two-domain scenario. In the first mode, the PDPs of both domains are consulted independently by the PB, which obtains multiple decisions in response. The PB runs a reconciliation algorithm, which by default (but not mandated) is the Boolean AND (*conjunction*) and returns a final access decision to the PEP (Figure 2a). In the second mode, the PB selects a PDP from one of the domains and dynamically configures it to access policies and state information from the PAPs and PIPs of both domains. The PDP, having all the required information, now makes an access decision which is relayed by the PB to the PEP (Figure 2b).

4   Implementation: System and Application

We have implemented the core broker functions of identity, context and policy management, and built prototypes of the applications described in Sections 2.1 and 2.2 to demonstrate the utility and necessity of using a trusted broker. Users in our implementations were represented by Samsung Galaxy Ace S5830 phones running Android Linux v2.2 and v2.3. The broker was built as a Java application deployed on an IBM WebSphere Application Server 7.0 instance running on a SuSE Enterprise Linux 11 server. The IBM Tivoli Directory Server v6.3, which offers an LDAP User Registry and a DB2 database, was used to store user data. Services offered by providers were also implemented as Java applications exposing REST APIs that ran on similar WebSphere configurations. Mobile devices communicated with servers using WiFi. IBM Tivoli Security Policy Manager (TSPM) [3] instances were configured to protect the WebSphere applications, and used to store users' policies. For a social network, we used Facebook, as it provides an HTTP-based Graph API and delegation using OAuth, enabling us to build rapid prototypes. On the downside, Facebook does not run a policy manager based on our specification (or allows us to control its policies), thereby limiting the nature of applications we could build.

4.1   Social- and Location-Aware Advertising

An Android app enables a user representing Alice to register with a merchant, represented by a remote web service, and establish a customer account after providing identity and phone number and agreeing to the presented terms (Figures 3a and 3b). The merchant makes an offer to give reward points in exchange for allowing targeted ads to Alice's Facebook friends to the broker, which is hosted by the *MyTel* operator. *MyTel* can identify Alice by her phone number and associates it with her mobile identity (established earlier through a protocol that is out of scope of this paper). The

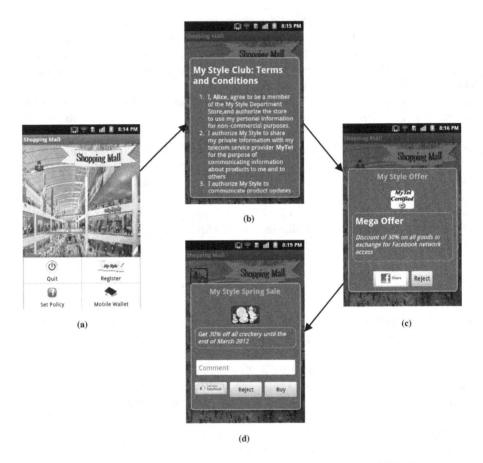

Fig. 3. Targeted Advertising Application Screenshots on an Android Device

broker, co-located with *MyTel*, relays the offer to Alice, who accepts the offer (Figure 3c). Under the covers, the OAuth protocol ensues among the client, broker and Facebook (through its Graph API) [18]. Using a Facebook app created for and hosted by the broker, a time-limited token to access Alice's friend list and post messages on her behalf is delegated to the broker after Alice signs in using her Facebook identity. The merchant is notified when this protocol completes.

Ads from the merchant are relayed by the broker to Alice's device (Figure 3d), who chooses to recommend it to her friends. The broker uses the Facebook access token to determine that Bob and Carol (who also have mobile identities) are on her friends' list. Based on its knowledge of their location contexts (which we simulated), the broker sends a text message to Bob's phone, as Bob is in the vicinity; whereas Carol, who is in a different location, gets a Facebook notification, which she sees the next time she logs into her Facebook account.

4.2   Social Network-Assisted Shared Payments

Our prototype of this scenario uses the relationship established among the parties in the advertising app. When Alice receives an ad notification, she has the option to '*Buy*' a product (Figure 4a) using a *mobile wallet* (money account) [5] she maintains with the broker. (Money can be credited to the wallet of a client from her bank accounts or credit cards using standard payment gateway protocols.) The broker is at first unable to authorize the purchase as the wallet has insufficient funds. Therefore it presents Alice with a list of payment options (Figure 4b). Alice selects the '*Facebook*' option, indicating that she wants to request her friends for money. The broker determines the list of her Facebook friends using its OAuth access token. This list is filtered through a variety of criteria. Alice may have specified a candidate list using a policy rule. The broker, using its delegated permissions, can mine Facebook information and activity to determine how close the friends are, whether they reside in the same city, etc. Knowing the mobile identities of the friends also helps the broker

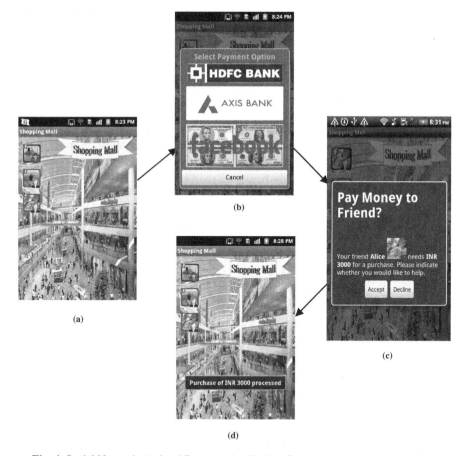

Fig. 4. Social Network-Assisted Payment Application Screenshots on an Android Device

determine whether they have sufficient funds in their wallets. Finally, a small (5-10) number of friends are selected, and query messages are sent to their personal devices in turn (Figure 4c). If a friend accepts, money is transferred from one wallet to another. If the requisite amount is collected, a payment is made to the merchant (Figure 4d).

4.3   Controlling Behavior through Policies

We show examples here of how different policy configurations can result in different behavior in our two scenarios. The policy rules are framed in XACML [20], but we describe them in plain English owing to lack of space.

1. In the advertising scenario, the user Bob frames a policy with the broker that has the effect of allowing advertisement notifications to be delivered to him only between 12 pm and 9 pm. Under normal operation, the ads will be displayed only if sent during that period. Subsequently, he adds a policy within his social network domain indicating that no more than 10 advertisements recommended by Alice should be displayed within a calendar day. The policy broker resolves the two policy rules, resulting in the blocking of ads recommended by Alice (even between 12 pm and 9 pm) when the count exceeds 10.

2. In the payment scenario, the default policy allows requests from one user to be sent to another user. But if Bob, as a social network member, frames a policy rule blocking payment requests from Alice, the broker will keep him off its list. In another variation, Bob frames a policy allowing any payment request of $50 or less to be automatically approved. In this case, the payment is automatically processed. Subsequently an email containing details of the payment is sent to Bob as per obligations associated with the policy.

5   Analysis

We analyze the security and privacy characteristics of our platform, using examples from the two applications. First, we want to ensure that participating entities are not susceptible to attacks by external entities. We do this by restricting all interactions to a service oriented model. Service providers, mobile users, and the broker interact through remote web service invocations. The broker itself does not allow direct access to its internal resources and offers a web service interface. Web services are *secure to the extent that they are implemented according to specification*; hence the security of the broker, service providers, or clients cannot be compromised through any process introduced by our platform. The broker's access to a user's domains is likewise service-oriented, limited in privilege, and can be revoked at any time. E.g., access to Facebook is limited by its Graph API. Getting a Facebook access token using OAuth is provably secure [10], and therefore does not create a new attack vector.

We examine our system based on two modes of privacy:

i. *Entity privacy*: entity A is considered to keep its privacy from entity B if B cannot identify A or communicate directly with A using any available mechanism.

ii.*Information privacy*: entity A keeps information X private from entity B if B cannot determine X through any communication channel with A, and cannot link X with A if it were to determine X through some other available mechanism.

We assert that these properties are maintained if the broker does not abuse the trust invested in it. In our two applications, only one mobile user (Alice) can be explicitly identified by a service provider, and this association was explicitly made by Alice. The identities of her friends remain unknown to the service provider even though they receive ads and payment requests; this is because the broker acts as a relay. Hence our system ensures *entity privacy*. *Information privacy* is also ensured by our system as follows. Bob's location is known to and used by the broker, and remains unknown to the service provider. Similarly, only the identity of the final payer is revealed to Alice, who does not get to know which of her friends rejected her request and how much money they have in their wallets. Also, allowing clients to set, enforce, and dynamically change policies within their domains allows them to keep control of their privacy irrespective of the motivations and actions of the service providers or the broker. Resolving policies on the basis of least privilege ensures that clients' wishes are respected in the most privacy-preserving manner. For example, if a client, or the social network she belongs to, chooses not to reveal friends' lists, the broker will be unable to obtain that information even if it possesses a valid access token.

The caveat is that an untrustworthy and unreliable broker could harm users by using delegated permissions to access user accounts for nefarious purposes, or collude with service providers to reveal private client information. Our entire system is based on the premise that the broker is a large and public entity that cannot escape legal bounds and obligations, and can be held accountable for any transgressions. In the future, we will attempt to increase the trustworthiness of this entity, by using frameworks like the Open ID Trust Framework [23]. We will also investigate the feasibility of distributing broker functionality among multiple agencies to limit the potential harm caused by a single centralized broker that abuses its power.

6   Related Work

To the best of our knowledge, no existing system mediates service interactions while protecting user privacy. The integration of identity, context, and policy management into a unified brokerage service that enables a range of social mobile applications is our original contribution. Research relevant to our work has focused exclusively on (i) areas like identity management or policy resolution, (ii) social network privacy [12], (iii) applications: e.g., targeted advertising, online payments, (iv) service composition.

Google is the closest approximation of our trusted broker in practice. It provides social networking services through Google+, mobile payment services using Google Wallet [7], and tracks user movements through Google Latitude. Possessing a Google account is very similar to possessing a mobile identity. Yet, though Google could plausibly play the role of a mediator, its primary aim is to be a service provider itself and provide better search results by gathering and mining data.

The MobiSoC middleware manages location and social context, and provides a development platform for mobile social applications [22]. It supports a different set of applications than our system does; also, it focuses only on interactions among users and does not consider service providers. MobiSoC enforces privacy constraints using policies, and the authors assert that a trusted centralized middleware provides better privacy guarantees than a distributed middleware. Related to this is a distributed privacy-conscious data sharing model of *personal networks* and *agents*, proposed by Connect.Me [24], though no working system has yet been produced.

Mediating access to heterogeneous web services in a *Service-Oriented Architecture* (SOA) is also a well-researched subject. Mediators can dynamically discover and compose web services [4], or match and translate data flowing from one web service to another [6]. Mashup services can be realized using a location service broker that enables service providers to access user context through lightweight APIs [13]. The Open Group's SOA specification [11] uses an integration layer to mediate interactions by relaying and routing messages. All these solutions conceive of the mediator as just a layer of indirection, whereas our design adds privacy protection, identity management, and policy management to the functions performed by the broker.

Research in the area of online advertising is relevant, but cannot be generalized to other application scenarios. The Privad system uses a mediator to convey ads from publishers to clients and to report click feedback to the publishers [8]. The mediator itself is not privy to much information about the client, and offers a higher level of privacy than our system does, but it does not handle social network associations. In the social networking world, advertising strategy is often ad hoc, such as Facebook allowing a user's activities on an external website to be displayed to his friends without their consent via the Beacon app. Needless to say, Facebook was forced to add stringent controls to Beacon following a popular outburst[1]. In contrast, our advertising app allows users to frame policies, which the broker must enforce.

Much research has been done to enable mobile financial transactions, both in academia [5] and industry. A number of solutions have sprung up in both developed and emerging markets to enable a user to make cardless payments at a PoS terminal using his mobile device. Boku [2], Airtel Money [1], and M-PESA [15] are based on mobile wallets maintained by the telecom operator who provides the data communication channel, whereas Google Wallet [7], Square [19], and Mobile Pay USA [16] rely on a user's existing bank and credit card accounts. All of these systems rely on mediation or infrastructure provided by an IT giant like Google (or Amazon or PayPal) or telecom operators like Airtel or Verizon. Yet these solutions focus only on ease of use, and do not provide privacy preservation or social awareness.

7   Conclusion and Future Work

Though increased physical and social awareness in mobile applications benefit service providers and consumers, the latter have legitimate concerns about untrusted

---

[1] Thoughts on Beacon, http://blog.facebook.com/blog.php?post=7584397130

providers misusing their private information. In this paper, we have presented a solution architecture based on a trusted broker that manages user identity, context, and policy. Interaction mediation by this broker enables mobile users to keep their privacy while interacting with other users and service providers. Relying on the broker to associate identities, manage context and policies, relay messages, and access cross-domain information using authorization delegation enables the rapid creation and deployment of a variety of social mobile applications, like targeted advertising and collaborative online payment. In the future, we intend to conduct user studies and run large scale experiments with our system. We will measure the broker's scaling properties with respect to the number of clients, and make suitable improvements. Enhancing the broker's functionality to support service discovery is another promising line of research. Also, our assumption of a single broker who is trusted by all mobile users and service providers must be tested in the real world. We may instead employ multiple brokers to serve disjoint sets of users, and configure these brokers to interoperate and establish trust relationships. We will also investigate and build more application scenarios that rely on our system. Lastly, we will explore ways to prevent the broker from abusing user trust and becoming a single point of failure.

References

1. Airtel Money, `http://airtelmoney.in`
2. Boku, `http://www.boku.com`
3. Buecker, A., et al.: Flexible Policy Management for IT Security Services Using IBM Tivoli Security Policy Manager. IBM Red Paper Publication REDP-451200 (March 17, 2009)
4. Cimpian, E., Mocan, A., Stollberg, M.: Mediation Enabled Semantic Web Services Usage. In: Mizoguchi, R., Shi, Z.-Z., Giunchiglia, F. (eds.) ASWC 2006. LNCS, vol. 4185, pp. 459–473. Springer, Heidelberg (2006)
5. Dahlberg, T., Mallat, N., Ondrus, J., Zmijewska, A.: Past, Present and Future of Mobile Payments Research: A Literature Review. Journal: Electronic Commerce Research and Applications 7(2), 165–181 (2008)
6. Fauvet, M.C., Aït-Bachir, A.: An Automaton-based Approach for Web Service Mediation. In: Proceedings of the 13th ISPE International Conference on Concurrent Engineering (ISPE CE 2006), Antibes, France, September 18-22 (2006)
7. Google Wallet, `http://www.google.com/wallet`
8. Guha, S., Cheng, B., Francis, P.: Privad: Practical Privacy in Online Advertising. In: 8th Usenix Conf. on Network Systems Design and Implementation (NSDI), Boston, MA (March 2011)
9. Haidar, D.A., Cuppens-Boulahia, N., Cuppens, F., Debar, H.: Access Negotiation within XACML Architecture. In: Proceedings of the Second Joint Conference on Security in Networks Architectures and Security of Information Systems (SARSSI), Annecy, France (June 2007)
10. Hammer-Lahav, E., et al.: The Oauth 2.0 Authorization Protocol (January 2011), `http://tools.ietf.org/pdf/draft-ietf-oauth-v2-12.pdf`
11. Integration Layer, `http://www.opengroup.org/soa/source-book/soa_refarch/integration.htm`

12. Krishnamurthy, B., Wills, C.E.: On the Leakage of Personally Identifiable Information via Online Social Networks. SIGCOMM Comput. Comm. Rev. 40(1), 112–117 (2010)
13. Loreto, S., Mecklin, T., Opsenica, M., Rissanen, H.M.: Service Broker Architecture: Location Business Case and Mashups. Comm. Mag. 47(4), 97–103 (2009)
14. Maler, R., Reed, D.: The Venn of Identity: Options and Issues in Federated Identity Management. IEEE Security and Privacy 6(2), 16–23 (2008)
15. Mas, I., Morawczynski, O.: Designing Mobile Money Services: Lessons from M-PESA. Innovations 4(2), 77–92 (2009)
16. Mobile Pay USA, http://www.mobilepayusa.com
17. Ramakrishna, V., Reiher, P., Kleinrock, L.: Distributed Policy Resolution Through Negotiation in Ubiquitous Computing Environments. In: Proceedings of IEEE PerCom 2009, Galveston, TX (March 2009)
18. Server-Side Authentication, http://developers.facebook.com/docs/authentication/server-side/
19. Square Inc. (US), https://squareup.com
20. Verma, M.: XML Security: Control Information Access with XACML, http://www.ibm.com/developerworks/xml/library/x-xacml/
21. Westerinen, A., et al.: RFC 3198: Terminology for Policy-Based Management (November 2001), http://www.ietf.org/rfc/rfc3198
22. Gupta, A., Kalra, A., Boston, D., Borcea, C.: MobiSoC: A Middleware for Mobile Social Computing Applications. Mobile Networks and Applications Journal 14(1), 35–52 (2009)
23. Open Identity Exchange, http://openidentityexchange.org/what-is-a-trust-framework
24. Conect.Me Trust Framework, https://connect.me/trust

Fine-Grained Transportation Mode Recognition Using Mobile Phones and Foot Force Sensors

Zelun Zhang and Stefan Poslad

School of Electronic Engineering and Computer Science, Queen Mary University of London,
London, United Kingdom
{zelun.zhang,stefan}@eecs.qmul.ac.uk

Abstract. Transportation or travel mode recognition plays an important role in enabling us to derive transportation profiles, e.g., to assess how eco-friendly our travel is, and to adapt travel information services such as maps to the travel mode. However, current methods have two key limitations: low transportation mode recognition accuracy and coarse-grained transportation mode recognition capability. In this paper, we propose a new method which leverages a set of wearable foot force sensors in combination with the use of a mobile phone's GPS (FF+GPS) to address these limitations. The transportation modes recognised include walking, cycling, bus passenger, car passenger, and car driver. The novelty of our approach is that it provides a more fine-grained transportation mode recognition capability in terms of reliably differentiating bus passenger, car passenger and car driver for the first time. Result shows that compared to a typical accelerometer-based method with an average accuracy of 70%, the FF+GPS based method achieves a substantial improvement with an average accuracy of 95% when evaluated using ten individuals.

Keywords: Transportation Mode Recognition, Foot force sensor, GPS, Accelerometer.

1 Introduction

According to a survey of world urbanization, 80% of the EU population lives in cities and this number is still rising [1]. Transportation mode is an important type of urban user context that facilitates several transport context adaptation applications such as maps and navigation that adapt to travel modes and user mobility profiling [2]. Transportation mode recognition in people's daily life can contribute to implicit human computer interaction in terms of reducing the user cognitive load when interacting with services during travel, and can help to enable the hidden computer part of the vision of ubiquitous computing. Automatic transportation mode recognition could also facilitate a range of applications as follows:

➢ *Physical Activity Monitoring*: The transportation modes of individuals are logged and mapped to locations to enable individuals to plan travel based on physical activity goals and health monitoring [3]. In addition to health-related applications, activity-profiling systems can play a fundamental role in ubiquitous computing

K. Zheng, M. Li, and H. Jiang (Eds.): MOBIQUITOUS 2012, LNICST 120, pp. 103–114, 2013.

scenarios [4]. In such applications, information from a variety of sensors is used to determine a mobility context for possible information service adaptation. For example, a mobile phone can detect when a person is driving or involved in vigorous physical activity, and automatically divert a call for safety consideration [5].

> *Individual Environmental Impact Monitoring*: Inferences of the transportation mode and location of an individual are used to provide a personalized environmental scorecard for tracking the hazard exposure and environmental impact of one's activities. Examples include Personal Environment Impact Report (PEIR) and UbiGreen [6, 7] along with commercial offerings such as Ecorio and Carbon Diem [8, 9].

> *User Mobility Profiling*: Transportation annotated mobility profiles (time, location, transportation mode traces) are created for profile based recruitment for gathering distributed user context and for group context awareness [10].

The confluence of advanced wearable sensor technology and widely available portable computing devices offers the opportunity for automatic recognition of a person's activities and transportation modes in daily living [11]. A mobile phone with integrated GPS can provide user spatial contexts (e.g. speed) in an outdoor environment [12, 13]. Wearable foot force (FF) sensors can capture a person's foot force variations from different postures (e.g. between standing and sitting) and activities (e.g. between cycling and driving) in real time [14]. Different transportation modes differ in terms of both the average movement speed (e.g. between walking and taking a bus) and foot activities (e.g. between cycling and driving). The combination of foot force sensors and mobile phone GPS could potentially be useful in enabling more fine-grained transportation mode recognition such as subdividing motorized transportation modes into bus-passenger, car-passenger and car-driver.

The primary aim of this pilot study is to assess how well a combination of mobile phone GPS and wearable foot force sensors can be used to recognise different transportation modes, compared with a more typical accelerometer-based method, i.e., as used in [15].

The main contributions of this paper are: i) we conducted a thorough survey of transportation mode recognition, which exposes two main limitations of current work; ii) we proposed a novel method combining foot force sensors and mobile phone GPS for improved transportation mode recognition; iii) we illustrated substantial improvements of our method through comparing it with an accelerometer-based method.

2   Related Work

Much related work exists to recognise transportation mode by sensing modalities that are viable or available to be used on mobile phones. The related work can be grouped based upon the type of sensors used, mainly the accelerometer and GPS.

-Accelerometer

In [16], Mizzel and his colleagues showed that the accelerometer signal can produce a good estimate of its vertical and horizontal components. The vector in turn holds an estimation of the magnitude of the dynamic acceleration caused by the phone carrying user.

Different human-powered transportation modes, such as walking and cycling, can generate different acceleration components. Dynamic acceleration patterns can be sensed by an accelerometer. A 3D-accelerometer can be used to classify different human daily activities. In [17], Juha utilised a wireless motion band attached to the user ankle to sense the acceleration generated by the ankle. This work has successfully differentiated different human-powered transportation modes such as walking, running and cycling through using a binary decision tree classification method. A personalised classification method also increases the accuracy of detection. In [18], Ravi also found that activities can be recognised with a fairly high accuracy through wearing a single 3D-accelerometer near the pelvic region. The results also showed that the pelvic region placement can recognise everyday activities with an overall accuracy rate of 84%. Similar work has also been done by Brezmes [19].

Accelerometer-based methods can achieve an increased accuracy when people carry their smart phones in a fixed place. However, many people tend to carry their mobile phones more freely, such as near the waist, in a front pocket, in a knee-high pocket, by hand, and so on. These on-body placement variations greatly change the nature of the acceleration signal (which is also impacted by different body motions such as bending, swaying and twitching) during user movement [2]. In [15], Wang et al. have also considered this issue and attempted to differentiate transportation modes without any placement restrictions for accelerometers. They used a smart phone embedded accelerometer to recognise six kinds of transportation modes, but the accuracy is relatively low (at 62% on average).

-GPS

GPS, as a global-wide positioning system, has already been integrated into mobile phones. The potential usability of GPS in profiling user daily outdoor activities has been widely presented, such as in [20] and [21].

In [20], Lin Liao et al. have developed a probabilistic temporal model that can extract high-level human activities from a sequence of GPS readings. Two main types of transportation mode (human powered and motorised) are inferred, based on the Conditional Random Fields model. Though they achieved over an 80% in accuracy, the range of the transportation modes is coarse, as it can only detect two main types of transportation modes: human powered and motorised.

In contrast to [20], Zheng et al. used a supervised learning based approach to infer more fine-grained transportation modes using the raw GPS data [21]. They proposed a change point (between different transportation modes) based upon a segmentation method. The results show that change point based segmentation achieved a better accuracy compared with uniform-duration based segmentation and uniform-length based segmentation. However, GPS information alone cannot detect change points precisely, since on many occasions, a person could take a taxi immediately after he/she gets off a bus and this very short change segment between two transportation modes is easy to be neglected using GPS.

The existing GPS work exposes an inherent limitation. GPS information alone is too coarse to enable fine-grained transport recognition with a good accuracy. For example, GPS performs poorly in the recognition of different transportation modes with similar speeds, e.g., with fast walking, cycling, and slow motorized traveling.

Table 1. Related work for transportation mode recognition

Ref No.	Sensor Type	Classifiers	Feature Used	Transportation Mode	Mobile Placement	Accuracy
[19]	Accelerometer	K-Nearest Neighbours	Raw three-axis vector readings from the Accelerometer	Stationary, Walk, Run	Jacket, chest, and trousers, Pockets	60%
[15]	Accelerometer	Decision tree (J48), K-Nearest Neighbour, SVM	Mean, standard deviation, mean-crossing rate, third-quartile, sum and standard deviation of frequency components between 0~4 HZ, ratio of frequency components (0~4 Hz) to all components, spectrum peak position.	Stationary, Walk, Bike, Bus, Car	Free	62%
[22]	Accelerometer, GPS, and Audio Sensor	Decision Tree (J48)	Mean, standard deviation, and number of peaks of the accelerometer readings ; mean and standard deviation of the DFT power of audio sensor readings	Stationary, Walk, Run	Pocket	78%
[20]	GPS	Hierarchical Conditional Random Fields	Mean GPS speed, Temporal information (time of the day),	Stationary, Walk, Motorised Modes	In-Hand	83%
[21]	GPS	Bayesian Net, Decision Tree, Conditional Random Field, SVM	Mean, maximum, and standard deviation of the velocity, Length of trips	Stationary, Walk, Bike, Motorised Modes	In-Hand	76%

Table 1 shows that the average accuracy for current transportation mode recognition methods is comparatively low, 70%, i.e., only a little over 2/3 of trips are recognised correctly. In addition, most current methods have restrictions with respect to how users should carry their mobile devices, except [15]. Moreover, much of the surveyed work does not support differentiating sub-motorised transportation modes, i.e., into car passenger, bus passenger, and driver. Only [15] has more sub-classes of motorised transportation modes (bus passenger, car passenger) and is closest to one of our aims in this paper - more fine-grained transportation mode recognition. Hence, we decide to reproduce the accelerometer-based method used in [15] as a baseline to evaluate our new method.

3 Method Design and System Overview

In order to solve the limitations of both low accuracy and coarse-grained recognition capability, we propose a novel method that leverages both mobile phone GPS and a set of foot force sensors. The rationale for choosing these two types of sensors is because of the obvious variations in GPS speed and foot force pattern in different transportation modes. Based on our observations (as table 2 shows), given different transportation modes, when the GPS mean speed is similar, the foot force patterns are different, and vice versa.

Table 2. Variations in GPS speed (mean ± standard deviation) and foot force patterns for different transportation modes

	Walking	Cycling	Bus Passenger	Car Passenger	Car Driver
GPS Speed (m/s)	1.3±0.2	2.5±1.2	5.2±2.0	8.5±5.2	7.8±4.9
Left Foot Force (Percentage of user weight)	67%±51%	18%±11%	53%±5%	21%±3%	35%±12%
Left Foot Force Patterns in Time Domain (5 min duration for each mode)					

Based on table 2, we hypothesise that our new method should be able to achieve more fine-grained transportation mode recognition with a higher accuracy compared with a typical accelerometer-based method. In addition, to variations in mean and variance, our new method also relies on basic time-domain features such as mean and standard deviation for transportation mode recognition. Time-domain features tend to consume less computational resources compared with frequency-domain features [23], e.g. those used in [15].

To the best of our knowledge, the potential benefits of using mobile phone GPS in combination with foot force sensors to improve transportation recognition has not been proposed or examined to date. Therefore, we propose the following system architecture to examine whether or not foot force sensors combined with mobile phone GPS can

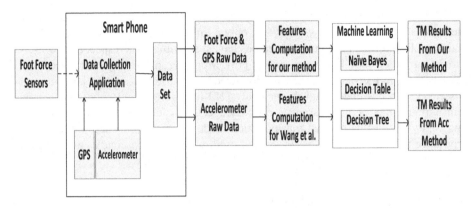

Fig. 1. Architecture of the FF+GPS transportation mode (TM) recognition system

discriminate between the five different transportation modes (walking, cycling, bus-passenger, car-passenger, and car-driver) that are most often used for commute purpose. The following system may answer our primary research question: does the addition of foot force monitoring to GPS improve the recognition of transportation mode beyond which is achieved by using accelerometer data alone.

In order to show the usefulness of our new method, we designed our new transportation modes recognition system using both foot force sensors and GPS as shown in figure 1. In order to evaluate our new FF+GPS based method and to compare it with the accelerometer-based method used in [15], our new transportation mode recognition system also collects the accelerometer data simultaneously with foot force sensor data and GPS data. This simultaneous sensor data collection scheme can minimize the effect of variability from different instances of sample which may affect the comparison results. No noise filtering is carried out on the raw sensor data. Any sensor errors arising via typical daily living environment, e.g., occasional GPS data interruption, are presented to the feature computation phase.

In the feature computation phase, the data window segmentation method used in [15] is applied to both the accelerometer-based and FF+GPS based methods. Eleven different features are extracted from our accelerometer data as used in [15]. For the FF+GPS based method, the following time-domain features are extracted: mean, max and standard deviation of GPS speed; mean, max and standard deviation of foot force readings from both feet.

In the transportation mode recognition phase, three commonly used machine learning schemes: Naïve Bayes (NB), Decision Tree (DT) J48, and Decision Table provided by WEKA toolkit [24] are used to compare the performance of these two methods. A 10-fold cross validation mechanism is used for evaluation.

4   Experiments and Results Evaluation

4.1   Participants

All study procedures were approved by the Research Ethics Committee at Queen Mary, University of London, and all participants signed a written informed consent form.

Data collection took place over a 6-month period from Dec, 2011 to June, 2012. Five transportation modes (walking, cycling, bus passenger, car passenger, and car driver) were performed by 10 volunteers (6 male; 4 female) with an age range from 24 to 56.

During data collection, volunteers had the liberty of carrying the mobile phone device in any orientation and position that was desired, such as near the waist, in a knee-high pocket, in a back-pack, in the top jacket, by hand, and so on. The collected data totals 2023 samples, which is equivalent to more than 7.5 hours of samples.

4.2   Equipment

During the data collection procedures, each participant carried a Samsung Galaxy II smart phone, and wore a pair of special insoles. The special insoles were instrumented by a set of Flexiforce sensors[1]. Four Flexiforce sensors have been mounted on each insole in order to cover the force reaction area of both forefoot and heel for each foot as shown in figure 2. The rationale for choosing heel and forefoot as the focused area of foot force monitoring is stated in [25]. All Flexiforce sensors are interfaced to the smart phone wirelessly but via a wired USB hub that connected to a portable laptop for power, as Flexiforce sensors need to be powered and cannot be powered by a smart-phone. Flexiforce sensor readings are set to 35 Hz, and mobile phone embedded GPS is set to 1 Hz for the Android 2.3.3 OS platform. The smart phone embedded accelerometer[2] frequency is set to 35 Hz according to settings used in [15].

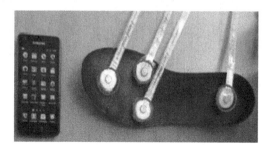

Fig. 2. Experimental equipment

4.3   Results and Evaluation

For each kind of transportation mode, we define true positive, true negative, false positive, and false negative as follows (The walking transportation mode has been chosen as an example to illustrate the point):

➢   **A true positive** occurs when a sample from a particular kind of transportation mode is classified as the same kind of transportation mode. For example, a sample from walking classified as walking is a true positive.

---

[1]   The sensitive range of each Flexiforce sensor is from 0kg to 45 kg with a linearity error less than±3%. The response time is less than 5 microseconds.

[2]   This is a 3-D accelerometer, whose sensitivity is programmed from -2g to +2g (g=9.8).

> **A true negative** occurs when a sample from one other kind of transportation mode is classified as not in this particular kind of transportation mode. For example, a sample from cycling classified as not walking is a true negative for walking.

> **A false positive** occurs when a sample from other kinds of transportation mode is classified as this particular kind of transportation mode. For example, a sample from cycling classified as walking is a false positive for walking.

> **A false negative** occurs when a sample from a particular kind of transportation mode is classified as other kind of transportation mode. For example, a sample from walking classified as cycling is a false negative for walking.

We present the accuracy for each classifier we chose in figure 3 and figure 4. The accuracy is the sum of true positives and true negatives over the total number of classifications. The accuracy tells us overall how good a method is at classifying different kinds of transportation mode.

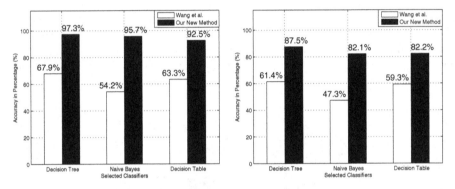

Fig. 3. Comparison of Recognition Results for All Five Transportation Modes   **Fig. 4.** Comparison of Recognition Results for Three Motorized Modes

The experimental results for all five transportation modes recognition using the different classifiers are listed in figure 3. It is noted that the FF+GPS based method obtains a much higher recognition accuracy than the accelerometer-based method as used in [15]. On average, FF+GPS based method achieves 95% which is 33% higher than that of [15]. In addition, the use of a decision tree (J48) classifier obtains the highest recognition accuracy for both methods.

The experimental results for more fine-grained recognition of three motorized transportation modes (bus passenger, car passenger, and car driver) using different classifiers are listed in figure 4. The FF+GPS based method obtains a substantially higher accuracy than the accelerometer-based method used in [15]. On average, our method achieves an accuracy of 84% which is 28% higher than [15]. This result illustrates that the FF+GPS based method compared to an accelerometer-based method can provide more fine-grained transportation mode recognition in terms of reliably differentiating bus passenger, car passenger, and car drivers.

Since the decision tree (J48) classifier outperforms other classifiers, the precision and recall for each transportation mode from the decision tree classifier are presented in figure 5 and figure 6. Precision is the number of true positives over the total number of true positives and false positives and tells us how well a method is able to discriminate between true and false positives. Recall is the number of true positives over the sum of true positives and false negatives and tells us how well a method is able to recognise one particular transportation mode given all samples from this kind of transportation mode.

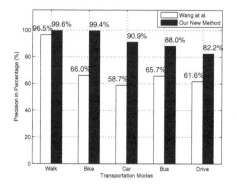 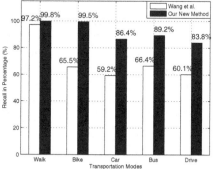

Fig. 5. Precision Results from the Decision Tree Classifier

Fig. 6. Recall Results from Decision Tree Classifier

With respect to the precision and recall results, the FF+GPS based method outperforms the typical accelerometer-based method in all aspects, especially in recognising cycling and in sub-differentiating motorised transportation modes into car-passenger, bus-passenger, and car-driver.

It is also noted that both methods perform equally well in detecting walking. This is because there are three stances in a normal human walking motion: which are heel strike, mid-stance, and toe-off [26]. Accelerometer-based method can detect the acceleration generated from these three stances, which differs from other transportation modes in terms of variance. The FF+GPS based method can also detect foot force patterns variations generated when walking, the patterns of which are quite unique in terms of both mean and variance as table 2 shows.

From figure 5 and figure 6, it is also found that our new FF+GPS based method can detect cycling to a very high accuracy (99%) compared with accelerometer-based method (65%). This is because the cycling apparently differs from other transportation modes in terms of both mean GPS speed and foot force patterns. The average speed for cycling is about 2.5m/s which is quite different from both walking (about 1.3 m/s) and motorised transportation modes (about 6.8m/s), see table 2. Besides, as people need to power the bike by pedalling regularly when cycling, the foot force patterns generated are also distinct from other transportation modes (as shown in table 2). For the case of accelerometer, the acceleration during cycling is mainly affected by the road conditions and is sometimes quite similar to those of motorised transportation instances. This introduces errors from false negatives for a typical accelerometer-based method.

For the case of sub-classifying motorised transportation modes using accelerometer, it is noted that the instances from one particular motorised mode are easily misclassified as those of other motorised mode, or even as cycling, using a typical accelerometer-based method. These motorised modes were mistaken as cycling since coasting on a bike is similar with low speed vehicles in terms of acceleration. Moreover, since the acceleration mainly depends on the vehicle and road conditions, the acceleration patterns of the samples from car-driver and car-passenger are almost identical, which can hardly be differentiated by any typical classifiers.

Our new FF+GPS based method in this case achieved an overall 84% accuracy on average. This is mainly because foot force patterns in different sub motorised modes tend to be very different. As in the driving case, people need to step on both the accelerator pedal and the brake pedal regularly in order to control the car. In the bus-passenger case, people may stand and move inside the bus, which would never happen when being a car passenger. Moreover, the GPS speed patterns from bus is also different from samples of private car, since buses need to stop more regularly at bus stops and move slower than private cars for safety consideration.

It is also noted that some instances of driving from the FF+GPS based method have been mistaken as being bus-passenger. This is because in some cases, when passengers move around in a bus, foot force patterns tend to be similar to the patterns of stepping on pedals when driving. Some instances from driving have also been mistaken as being car-passenger. These errors occurred during slow speeds or after stopping for a period of time. In these cases, foot force patterns tend to be similar as drivers were stationary and were not operating the vehicle foot control pedals.

5   Discussion and Future Work

Use of the FF+GPS based method achieves a substantial accuracy improvement and a more fine-grained transportation recognition capability, compared with a typical accelerometer-based method. In a practical system, one must also consider computational and energy costs. A mobile devices cannot dedicate its full computing resources to such (location-based) auxiliary applications given its primary roles are more for user interaction and communication. The FF+GPS transportation recognition method is only based upon an analysis of time-domain features. It can achieve an improved transportation mode recognition capability at a relatively low computation cost (compared to frequency-domain based methods). More specific testing involving computational load analysis will be included in a future study.

With regard to energy efficiency, the FF+GPS based method also showed that foot force sensors also perform very well in recognising human powered transportation modes (such as walking and cycling) without GPS. This means that foot force sensors can be used to reduce the usage of GPS (the most energy consuming sensor in most location determination systems) and its consequent energy consumption. We leave exploring the delicate balance between extendability, computability, and energy efficiency as future work.

6   Conclusion

In this work, the potential benefits of using mobile phone GPS in combination with a set foot force sensors to improve transportation mode recognition have been examined for the first time. Five fine-grained transportation modes, including walking, cycling, bus passenger, car passenger, and car driver, have been performed by ten different users. The results have been investigated in detail, evaluated (by comparing with a more typical accelerometer-based method in [15]), and fully discussed.

Given the sample size of this pilot, and based on the classification algorithms employed, our new FF+GPS based method has improved the transportation mode recognition accuracy from 62% to 95% on average. The key contribution of our work is that the FF+GPS based method provides more fine-grained transportation mode recognition capability in terms of differentiating between bus passenger, car passenger and car driver with an accuracy of 84% on average.

Acknowledgments. This work was made possible thanks to the financial support of the scholarship from Queen Mary, University of London, and equipment funded from the SUNSET[3] Project.

References

1. U. N. D. o. Economic and P. D. Social Affairs.: World Urbanization Prospects: The 2009 Revision, United Nations (2010),
   http://esa.un.org/unpd/wup/Documents/
   WUP2009_Highlights_Final.pdf
2. Liu, J., Goraczko, M., Kansal, A., et al.: Subjective Sensing. In: NSF Workshop on Future Directions in Networked Sensing Systems: Fundamentals and Applications, NSF (2009)
3. Consolvo, S., Klasnja, P., McDonald, D.W., et al.: Flowers or a robot army?: encouraging awareness & activity with personal, mobile displays. In: 10th Int.Conf. on Ubiquitous Computing, pp. 54–63. ACM (2008)
4. Streitz, N., Nixon, P.: The disappearing computer. In: Communications of the ACM, vol. 48, pp. 32–35. ACM (2005)
5. Preece, S.J., Goulermas, J.Y., Kenney, L.P.J., et al.: Activity identification using body-mounted sensors—a review of classification techniques. Physiological Measurement 30(4), R1 (2009)
6. Mun, M., Reddy, S., Shilton, K., et al.: PEIR, the personal environmental impact report, as a platform for participatory sensing systems research. In: 7th Int. Conf. on Mobile Systems, Applications, and Services, pp. 55–68. ACM (2009)
7. Froehlich, J., Dillahunt, T., Klasnja, P., et al.: UbiGreen: investigating a mobile tool for tracking and supporting green transportation habits. In: 27th Int.Conf. on Human Factors in Computing Systems, pp. 1043–1052. ACM (2009)
8. CarbonHero, Carbon diem - Is that knowledge now? (2011),
   http://www.carbondiem.com

---

[3] http://www.sunset-project.eu

9. Kao, J., Lam, R., Pong, G., Talukdar, T., Wong, J.: Ecorio - Track Your Mobile Carbon Footprint (2008), http://ecorio.org

10. Agapie, E., Chen, G., Houston, D., Howard, E., Kim, J., Mun, M., Mondschein, A., Reddy, S., Rosario, R., Ryder, J.: Seeing Our Signals: Combining location traces and web-based models for personal discovery. In: 9th Workshop on Mobile Computing Systems and Applications, pp. 6–10. ACM (2008)

11. Subramanya, A., Raj, A., Bilmes, J., Fox, D.: Recognizing activities and spatial context using wearable sensors. In: 21st Conf. on Uncertainty in Artificial Intelligence, pp. 494–502. AUAI Press (2006)

12. Schutz, Y., Herren, R.: Assessment of speed of human locomotion using a differential satellite global positioning system. Medicine & Science in Sports & Exercise 32(3), 642–646 (2000)

13. Witte, T., Wilson, A.: Accuracy of non-differential GPS for the determination of speed over ground. J. of Biomechanics 37, 1891–1898 (2004)

14. Zhang, K., Sun, M., Kevin Lester, D., Xavier Pi-Sunyer, F., Boozer, C.N., Longman, R.W.: Assessment of human locomotion by using an insole measurement system and artificial neural networks. J. of Biomechanics 38, 2276–2287 (2005)

15. Wang, S., Chen, C., Ma, J.: Accelerometer based transportation mode recognition on mobile phones. In: Asia-pacific Conf. on Wearable Computing Systems, pp. 44–46. IEEE (2010)

16. Mizell, D.: Using gravity to estimate accelerometer orientation. In: 7th Int. Symposium on Wearable Computers, pp. 252–253. IEEE (2003)

17. Parkka, J., Cluitmans, L., Ermes, M.: Personalization algorithm for real-time activity recognition using PDA, wireless motion bands, and binary decision tree. IEEE Transactions on Information Technology in Biomedicine 14, 1211–1215 (2010)

18. Ravi, N., Dandekar, N., Mysore, P., Littman, M.L.: Activity recognition from accelerometer data. In: American Association for Artificial Intelligence, pp. 1541–1546. AAAI (2005)

19. Brezmes, T., Gorricho, J.-L., Cotrina, J.: Activity recognition from accelerometer data on a mobile phone. In: Omatu, S., Rocha, M.P., Bravo, J., Fernández, F., Corchado, E., Bustillo, A., Corchado, J.M. (eds.) IWANN 2009, Part II. LNCS, vol. 5518, pp. 796–799. Springer, Heidelberg (2009)

20. Liao, L., Fox, D., Kautz, H.: Extracting places and activities from gps traces using hierarchical conditional random fields. Int. J. of Robotics Research 26, 119–134 (2007)

21. Zheng, Y., Liu, L., Wang, L., Xie, X.: Learning transportation mode from raw gps data for geographic applications on the web. In: 17th Int.Conf. on World Wide Web, pp. 247–256. IW3C2 (2008)

22. Miluzzo, E., Lane, N.D., Fodor, K., Peterson, R., Lu, H., Musolesi, M., Eisenman, S.B., Zheng, X., Campbell, A.T.: Sensing meets mobile social networks: the design, implementation and evaluation of the cenceme application. In: 6th Int.Conf. on Embedded Network Sensor Systems, pp. 337–350. ACM (2008)

23. Martín, H., Bernardos, A.M., Iglesias, J., Casar, J.R.: Activity logging using lightweight classification techniques in mobile devices. Personal and Ubiquitous Computing 16, 1–21 (2012)

24. Witten, I.H., Frank, E., Hall, M.A.: Data Mining: Practical machine learning tools and techniques. Morgan Kaufmann (2011)

25. Veltink, P.H., Liedtke, C., Droog, E., van der Kooij, H.: Ambulatory measurement of ground reaction forces. IEEE Transactions on Neural Systems and Rehabilitation Engineering 13, 423–427 (2005)

26. Yeh, S., Chang, K.H., Wu, C.I., Chu, H., Hsu, J.Y.: GETA sandals: a footstep location tracking system. Personal and Ubiquitous Computing 11, 451–463 (2007)

Towards In-network Aggregation for People-Centric Sensing

Christin Groba and Siobhán Clarke*

Lero Graduate School of Software Engineering
Distributed Systems Group
School of Computer Science and Statistics
Trinity College Dublin, Ireland
{grobac,Siobhan.Clarke}@scss.tcd.ie

Abstract. Technological advances in the smartphone sector give rise to people-centric sensing that uses the sensing capabilities of mobile devices and the movement of their human carriers to satisfy the ever increasing demand for context information. The quick adoption of such pervasive and mobile services, however, increases the number of contributors, strains the device-to-server connections, and challenges the system's scalability. Strategies that postpone load balancing to fixed infrastructure nodes miss the potential of mobile devices interconnecting to preprocess sensor data. This paper explores opportunistic service composition to coordinate in-network aggregation among autonomous mobile data providers. The composition protocol defers interaction with peers to the latest possible moment to accommodate for the dynamics in the operating environment. In simulations such an approach achieves a higher composition success ratio at similar or less delay and communication effort than an existing conventional composition solution.

1 Introduction

Mobile devices have evolved from special purpose equipment to smart entities that can sense their environment and communicate with servers on the Internet. People-centric sensing projects, as presented in [8], use these technological advances and the movement of human carriers to improve the micro- and macroscopic view on today's and future cities. Bubble-sensing [10], for example, affixes a sensing task to a certain location and entrusts mobile devices in vicinity to upload sensor data to a server as a basis for deriving higher level context-information.

However, for sensing tasks that require multiple independent readings from different sensors, the number of individual data uploads increases. In addition, the growing demand for context information creates many of such complex sensing tasks that further strain the device-to-server connection. Targeting the scalability issues of such centralised architectures, research has recently explored ways to balance the load for data processing [2,12].

---

* Partially supported by Science Foundation Ireland grant 03/CE2/I303_1 to Lero - the Irish Software Engineering Research Centre (http://www.lero.ie).

K. Zheng, M. Li, and H. Jiang (Eds.): MOBIQUITOUS 2012, LNICST 120, pp. 115–126, 2013.

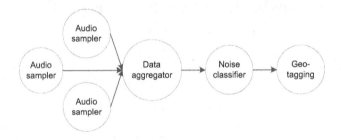

Fig. 1. In-network aggregation request phrased as service composite

In line with these efforts, this work investigates the application of service-oriented principles, namely dynamic service composition, to support in-network aggregation among mobile devices. In-network aggregation is well-studied in wireless sensor networks [1], however, people-centric sensing introduces participation autonomy and mobility that, traditionally not part of those networks, changes the system topology frequently. Dynamic service composition creates new value-added services from existing ones by discovering, allocating, and invoking service providers only at runtime to accommodate for the dynamics in the operating environment. Imagine, for example, a cloud service that provides a noise map of the city. For each geographic area it requires multiple independent audio samples to improve its quality. Instead of transmitting small data packets via multiple individual connections, co-located mobile devices collaborate to aggregate their recordings, add noise classifications and geo-tags, and upload one big data packet from one device. The cloud service posts its complex query and leaves the management of such a service composite (Figure 1) entirely to the ad hoc network of mobile nodes. This way, the query flexibly adjusts to currently available providers, their interconnections and localised knowledge about classification patterns.

This paper proposes opportunistic service composition, a composition protocol that defers all interactions with peers to the latest possible moment. In contrast to our previous work [3,4], it explores service composition from the perspective of autonomous service providers and how on-demand discovery, just in time release, and observation of the composition progress enables them to cooperatively control their availability. Focusing on the composition management within the ad hoc network, the paper leaves the integration with the cloud service to future work. With the analysis of dynamic service composition in mobile ad hoc environments, we hope to contribute to a better understanding of how complex tasks, such as in-network data aggregation, can be coordinated among autonomous and transiently available providers of sensor data.

2   Related Work

Scalability issues of centralised, single-server systems have led to alternative architectures that support load balancing in people-centric sensing. In G-sense [12],

Internet servers create a peer-to-peer sensing overlay to manage the distributed collection and aggregation of sensor data. An alternative approach [2] leverages existing cluster or cloud infrastructure to evaluate different tree-based aggregation strategies. Sensor and context cloudlets [9] use computers with Internet connection, deployed on local business premises and in the vicinity of mobile device to pool sensory data and to provide data fusion and context reasoning. Mobile devices in these solutions are sole data sources that connect to fixed infrastructure to trigger data processing there. In contrast, this work investigates the possibility of mobile devices interconnecting to process complex data queries within their ad hoc network.

CountTorrent [6] devises aggregation techniques for sensor networks whose topology, in contrast to traditional wireless sensor networks, is continuously evolving. While efficient and accurate, the solution assumes simple queries that include all currently available nodes. Queries phrased as abstract service composites, on the other hand, allow for more complex and selective specifications. However, their enactment, in particular the discovery and allocation of resources, remains challenging in mobile ad hoc environments [9].

The willingness of service providers to participate in sensing compositions depends on local resources, their current load, and individual objectives. Probing techniques [5,11], primarily used for optimal provider selection, enable service providers to actively commit to a composition rather than allocating them without their confirmation and risking their later refusal. Alternatively, proactive discovery solutions explicitly ask for participation [14]. Both such approaches, however, require additional communication on top of establishing knowledge about available services. Binding and releasing services just in time is crucial to maintain good service availability and to mitigate overload situations. Composition approaches that start the execution only after the selection is complete [15][14][5][16], allocate all required services even those that do not get executed due to conditional paths or premature termination. They block providers unnecessarily and possibly make them unavailable for other compositions. Timeouts are a way to release those providers [5] but are difficult to configure. Further, the time a service must be blocked depends on its position in the request because it must wait on its predecessors to execute. Execution solutions that allow for interleaving selection and execution [17][18], as proposed in this work, do not target mobile ad hoc environments and the need for reducing communication over an unreliable network.

3   On-Demand and Just in Time Service Composition

Mobile ad hoc networks come with their own set of challenges, namely unreliable communication links, autonomous providers, and loalised service bottlenecks. Wireless communication in mobile environments is prone to interference, collision, and topology changes that can cause the composition to fail. Reducing network traffic is key to utilise scarce bandwidth effectively. Further, potential providers may hesitate to announce their services if they have little knowledge

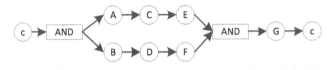

Merge service: S$_G$
Synchronisation partners: S$_E$, S$_F$
Service router for sync partners: S$_A$, S$_B$, S$_C$, S$_D$

Fig. 2. Composition request with parallel execution paths

about the composition and the extent to which they will be involved. One could argue that service providers are still in full control after they have announced themselves because they can always refuse to deliver their services or simply drop out. A composition, however, will notice such unexpected behaviour only after it invokes the service and used up scarce bandwidth. In addition, compositions seek providers that are in close proximity to satisfy locality needs of their clients. Where there is high demand in one location, however, compositions compete for the same services because the resource-constraints of mobile devices limit the number of requests they can process simultaneously. A complex service request can be modelled as an abstract directed graph that defines the nature and order of required services. A request for in-network aggregation may contain parallel execution paths that deliver data from different sensors and merge for aggregation before the result reaches the client c (cp. Figure 2). For the request to become executable, suitable service providers must be discovered and selected.

3.1 Design Decisions

The service composition remains more flexible towards changes if it postpones the discovery and allocation of service providers to the time when the composite is actually invoked because then it has the most up to date view of available services. Further, due to the lack of a centralised composition entity with global system view, we choose a decentralised approach similar to a product line in which service providers receive a composite description, execute part of it, and forward it to the next provider. In the proposed composition protocol, assigned service providers act in a decentralised interleaved manner: They search, allocate, and invoke their successors after they executed their own service[1]. Such hop-by-hop processing pursues only paths that are actually required and reduces the time a provider is blocked. The composition request contains the entire composite including its current status to facilitate a provider's decision whether to block local resources and to announce its participation. Despite its high effort for finding distant services, we choose request-based service discovery because it creates network traffic only on demand, localises the use of bandwidth to the

---

[1] Typically, all providers get allocated before the execution of the composite starts.

area where the request is issued, and permits providers to voice their commitment selectively per composition request. Blocking local resources already when responding to a discovery request avoids overload but at the same time locks more providers than needed because only one of them will get the service assigned. For this reason, all known candidates receive a release message as soon as an allocation decision has been made to free them just in time for other requests. In wireless multihop networks, messages rely on being forwarded until they reach their destination and can be received by anyone who is in range of the forwarding node. Service providers thus receive messages for which they may not be the primary addressee. Instead of dropping these messages unseen, they infer what progress a composition has made and whether they should act. Listening to by-passing traffic allows for proactive behaviour and complementary to targeted messaging may reduce the composite's communication overhead.

3.2   Protocol

The protocol for opportunistic service composition runs on each service provider and is modelled as a finite state machine (cp. Figure 3). The following description refers to providers that have only enough resources to handle one composition at a time. Transitions between protocol states occur upon the arrival of a composition message. A composite request contains the composite description and shows with the service that is required next which parts of the request still need to be allocated and executed. A token message transfers the composition control and indicates which service and corresponding provider execute next.

Each provider is initially in the listening state. If a listener receives a composition request and offers a service that is immediately required, it responds with an advertisement and changes its state to applying (A). Otherwise, if it provides any other required service, the provider remains silent and switches to observing (B). Checking for local objectives is not explicitly modelled, however, the protocol defines state transitions only on basis of a positive attitude towards participating in a composition.

An observing provider infers from an arriving token message and the request message heard earlier whether to announce its services to the token's primary recipient (C_1) or to transition to pre-finish (D_1). The choice depends on the conditions stated in Table 3b. Upon receiving a composition request it either keeps observing (D_2) or switches composites and applies for a different one (C_2).

A provider in applying state derives from a token whether it got selected to execute a service (E). If not, the applicant can decide to immediately apply for the next required service (G_1), observe the composite further to issue a new application at a later stage (F_1), or to finish its participation (H_1). In terms of a composite request, applicants generally do not respond except from two cases: First, if the request searches for a service for which the provider has already applied, then the provider resends the ad as the earlier one must have gotten lost (G_2). Second, the composition has made progress and the request reveals that all applications of the applicant are obsolete. then the applicant is free to apply (G_3), observe (F_2), or pre-finish (H_2).

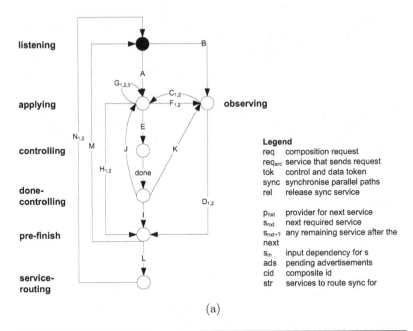

(a)

State	Message	Condition	Transition
listening	req	$\text{offer}(s_{nxt})$	A
	req	$\neg\text{offer}(s_{nxt}) \wedge \text{offer}(s_{nxt+?})$	B
observing	tok	$cid_{tok} == cid_{local} \wedge \text{offer}(s_{nxt})$	C_1
	tok	$cid_{tok} == cid_{local} \wedge \neg\text{offer}(s_{nxt}) \wedge \neg\text{offer}(s_{nxt+?})$	D_1
	req	$cid_{req} == cid_{local} \wedge \neg\text{offer}(s_{nxt}) \wedge \neg\text{offer}(s_{nxt+?})$	D_2
	req	$\text{offer}(s_{nxt})$	C_2
applying	tok	$cid_{tok} == cid_{local} \wedge \text{this}==p_{nxt}$	E
	tok	$cid_{tok} == cid_{local} \wedge \neg(\text{this}==p_{nxt}) \wedge \text{ads}==\emptyset \wedge \neg\text{offer}(s_{nxt+1}) \wedge \text{offer}(s_{nxt+1+?})$	F_1
	tok	$cid_{tok} == cid_{local} \wedge \neg(\text{this}==p_{nxt}) \wedge \text{ads}==\emptyset \wedge \text{offer}(s_{nxt+1}) \wedge \text{inrange}(p_{nxt})$	G_1
	tok	$cid_{tok} == cid_{local} \wedge \neg(\text{this}==p_{nxt}) \wedge \text{ads}==\emptyset \wedge \neg\text{offer}(s_{nxt+?})$	H_1
	req	$cid_{tok} == cid_{local} \wedge \exists s : req_{src} == s_{in} \wedge s \in \text{ads}$	G_2
	req	$\text{ads}==\emptyset \wedge \text{offer}(s_{nxt})$	G_3
	req	$\text{ads}==\emptyset \wedge \neg\text{offer}(s_{nxt}) \wedge \text{offer}(s_{nxt+?})$	F_2
	req	$\text{ads}==\emptyset \wedge \neg\text{offer}(s_{nxt}) \wedge \neg\text{offer}(s_{nxt+?})$	H_2
done-controlling		$\neg\text{offer}(s_{nxt}) \wedge \neg\text{offer}(s_{nxt+?})$	I
		$\neg\text{offer}(s_{nxt}) \wedge \text{offer}(s_{nxt+1})$	J
		$\neg\text{offer}(s_{nxt}) \wedge \neg\text{offer}(s_{nxt+1}) \wedge \text{offer}(s_{nxt+1+?})$	K
pre-finish		$\neg(str==\emptyset)$	L
		$str==\emptyset$	M
service-routing	sync	$str==\emptyset$	N_1
	rel	$str==\emptyset$	N_2

(b)

Fig. 3. Protocol for on-demand and just in time service composition

In the controlling state the service provider executes its assigned service, searches for a successor and when both these tasks are completed hands over the composition control to its successor. Controllers generate composition requests, token messages, and release redundant resources. Once done with controlling, the provider knows the composite status first hand and has again the choice to apply (J), observe (K), or pre-finish (I).

Pre-finishing determines whether the provider is a service router. The role of a service router was introduced by our synchronisation protocol [4] to handle requests with parallel execution paths. Service routers use the structure of the composite and the observed allocation history to route synchronisation messages between mutually unknown synchronisation partners that must agree on a common provider for the merge service. For example in Figure 2, the provider for S_B is a service router for S_E and S_F to route their synchronisation messages and help them decide on a common provider for S_G. If the provider is not a service router, it returns to listening (M), otherwise to service-routing (L). A provider exits service routing on receiving a release or sync message that indicates all routing responsibilities have been completed (N_1, N_2).

In the protocol, observers, applicants, and service routers block local resources and must be released in time to increase service availability. Observers may unblock any time to respond to more urgent service demand in different composite requests (C_2). Applicants are free as soon as they have no pending ads and are not assigned to provide a service. The list of pending ads is updated each time a token message or composite request signals that the relevant service has been allocated elsewhere. The allocator sends the token to all known advertisers. If the unreliable network looses ads, the allocator is not aware of these blocked candidates and does not release them. By-passing composition messages may indicate the progress of the composition. If this fails, too, a timeout is the last resort to unblock these resources. Service routers analyse all synchronisation messages which they forward to update and reduce their services-to-route list. Synchronisation messages, however, may find shortcuts in the network and do not follow the exact composite structure to reach their destination. In this case, a service router sends a release message back in its branch to enable other service routers to unblock.

3.3   Implementation

We implemented the opportunistic composition protocol on the discrete event simulator Jist/SWANS Ulm edition[2] by extending `ducks.driver.GenericNode` with a composite initiator and a composite provider. Both these types of composition entities require messages to be observable such that they receive and analyse any message issued in their transmission range. Lower layer network protocols typically discard messages if the node is not the primary addressee and let only broadcasts pass. Ordinary broadcasts, however, are not recovered and solely used imply high composite failure in unreliable networks. As a solution the

---

[2] `http://vanet.info/jist-swans/download.html`

protocol sends all composition messages as *directed broadcasts*, i.e., broadcasts with a primary addressee who acknowledges the receipt to ensure recovery and which can be received without acknowledgement by any other node in range. Further, a composition message may have multiple recipients. For example, a token message must be delivered to the next controller and all redundant applicants to unblock them. Instead of sending multiple messages, the directed broadcast includes a list of primary addressees and specifies for each destination the next hop. This way a single message is sufficient to inform all next hops. The management of directed broadcasts currently resides on the simulator's application layer to ensure the network layer passes messages directly to the MAC layer without consulting the routing protocols implemented in the simulator.

4   Simulation-Based Evaluation

The following study explores the impact of on-demand and just in time composition on the success and communication effort of complex service requests in multi-client scenarios.

4.1   Experimental Setup

The Jist/SWANS simulator configuration (Table 1) reflects a medium dense network of walking service providers. This setup was chosen based on the analysis in [7] to ensure zero percent partition and short routes (three hops on average) to reduce the effect of the particular routing protocol. The ratio of clients determines the number of composite requests that, scattered in the network, are issued at the same time. The study uses CiAN*, an adapted version of CiAN [15], as baseline that dispatches all messages with AODV [13] instead of the original publish-subscribe mechanism because of its otherwise higher message overhead. Just like the original, CiAN* implements ad-based discovery, client-controlled all-at-once service allocation, and decentralised service invocation. Opportunistic service composition implements on-demand request-based discovery with situational advertising, interleaved hop-by-hop allocation and invocation of services, and directed broadcasting. Any options for route repair and collision avoidance are disabled to analyse the failure probability of service composition prior to any recovery measures. Both composition models use the same non-standard description of the test composite in Figure 2 and select most recent neighbours first for required services. For each client ratio and composition model the simulation repeats 100 times with different randomised initial settings. Each such setting is used in both models. We test the most dynamic behaviour in which each required service must be bound to a unique provider. Autonomous node movement and the restriction to one composite at a time per node provides enough variance such that the willingness to participate is not modelled and assumed to be positive at all times.

Table 1. Simulation configuration

General		Random	
Simulation type	terminating	Node movement	Random Waypoint
Field ($m \times m$)	500×500	Node speed (m/s)	1-2
Radio range (m)	100	Service exec time (ms)	10-100
Nodes in total	150	**Controlled**	
MAC	802.11 non-promisc	Clients from total (%)	1, 5, 10, 15, 20

4.2   Results

Composition Success. A composition request is successful if all required services have executed and the client receives the final composition result.The left graph in figure 4 depicts the number of successful clients relative to the total number of clients in the simulation study. Opportunistic service composition achieves a higher success ratio than CiAN*, most notably, for five percent clients where the difference is 45 percent points. The success ratio degrades in both approaches as the demand for complex services increases. Opportunistic service composition grows more prone to service allocation failure because an increasing number of clients competes for the same service providers and soon reaches the maximum search radius unable to find unblocked resources. Blocking service routers contribute substantially to provider depletion in a search area. In the test composite (cp. Figure 2), service routers S_A, S_B, S_C, and S_D do not respond to other composites until they can be sure the synchronisation partners S_E and S_F know each other. In the worst case (when no by-passing traffic accidentally introduces parallel branch providers) all these six services block. CiAN* fails mainly due to provider overload since clients allocate services in isolation and providers handle only one composite at a time, silently dropping any other allocation. A service provider may resolve this conflict but only after it has detected the overload. Recovery strategies are out of scope and not implemented in either of the two approaches to study the original composition behaviour. Network failure due to collision and stale routes occur in both approaches, but at a lower percentage than their main failure source.

Response Time. The response time is the delay on the client from sending the first allocation or composition request to receiving the final result. The right graph in figure 4 depicts the average response time of compositions that completed successfully. CiAN* takes around four seconds to respond and is less affected by number of clients. The opportunistic approach responds in scenarios with one and five percent clients quicker than CiAN* because services and routing information is available in close proximity. Completing a composite quickly, releases bound service providers early and make them available for other requests. With an increase in clients, however, opportunistic composition faces service discovery delays as well as the same route finding problems as CiAN* such that both approaches respond after similar time.

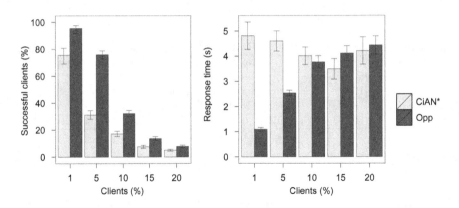

Fig. 4. Composition success and response time

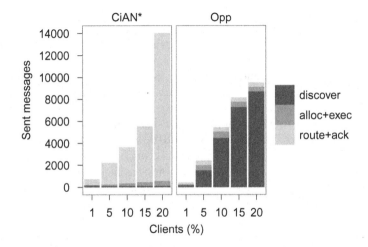

Fig. 5. Communication effort

Communication Effort. Composition and routing messages sent from the MAC layer determine the communication effort for handling complex service requests. These messages are counted until each of the started compositions either completes successfully or stops due to failure. Figure 5 shows the network load regardless of the final composition status. Starting with fewer messages, the opportunistic approach gradually exceeds CiAN*'s communication effort mainly because it completes more composite requests successfully than the baseline for which message counting stops early after a failure. In particular, the test cases with one and five percent clients indicate that opportunistic composition reduces network traffic. In contrast to CiAN*, routing layer messages in the opportunistic approach are rare demonstrating the benefit of directed broadcast. Service discovery messages dominate the message exchange and their increasing proportion with the increasing number of clients shows again the difficulty of finding unblocked service providers.

5   Discussion

The simulation study shows that opportunistic service composition is more successful at less or similar communication effort and delay than a conventional composition solution. In particular, for moderate client densities it outperforms the baseline. Stress testing the approach with many clients that issue the exact same request and the exact same time, the requests compete for the same service providers and extent their search for alternatives. Thereby they consume more time and bandwidth, and eventually fail due to provider depletion in the search area, making recovery strategies (that have not been considered in this study) indispensable for actual deployments.

The strength of opportunistic service composition is at the same time its weakness: Immediately executing partial composites reduces the impact of system changes but also leads to inconsistency if required services are not available in the network. The notion of standard services hosted on every mobile device would ease the problem as the existence of an ad hoc network would then imply the availability of such services. In comparison, composition approaches like the baseline that verify availability in advance, may fail nonetheless as the dynamics of the environment render earlier verifications invalid.

Opportunistic service composition is a promising approach toward in-network aggregation for participatory sensing as it overall shows an advantage over conventional composition approaches when it comes to managing complex service requests in unreliable networks. This work focused on how service composition could be used to coordinate the collective effort of autonomous mobile nodes to achieve a complex task. It did not touch on the technical realisation of ad hoc communication and radio broadcast with state-of-the-art smartphones as well as related security and routing issues. Future work will also have to investigate how the composition effort in an ad hoc network compares to the overhead of uploading sensor data individually. Each device may experience delays, losses, and energy costs when transferring small data packets to the distant cloud or to consecutive service providers.

References

1. Fasolo, E., Rossi, M., Widmer, J., Zorzi, M.: In-network aggregation techniques for wireless sensor networks: a survey. IEEE Wireless Communications 14(2), 70–87 (2007)
2. Ferreira, H., Duarte, S., Preguiça, N., Navalho, D.: Scalable data processing for community sensing applications. In: Puiatti, A., Gu, T. (eds.) MobiQuitous 2011. LNICST, vol. 104, pp. 75–87. Springer, Heidelberg (2012)
3. Groba, C., Clarke, S.: Opportunistic composition of sequentially-connected services in mobile computing environments. In: International Conference on Web Services (ICWS), pp. 17–24. IEEE (2011)
4. Groba, C., Clarke, S.: Synchronising service compositions in dynamic ad hoc environments. In: International Conference on Mobile Services, pp. 56–63. IEEE (2012)

5. Gu, X., Nahrstedt, K., Yu, B.: Spidernet: An integrated peer-to-peer service composition framework. In: International Symposium on High performance Distributed Computing (HPDC), pp. 110–119. IEEE (2004)

6. Kamra, A., Misra, V., Rubenstein, D.: Counttorrent: ubiquitous access to query aggregates in dynamic and mobile sensor networks. In: International Conference on Embedded Networked Sensor Systems (SenSys), pp. 43–57. ACM (2007)

7. Kurkowski, S., Camp, T., Navidi, W.: Two standards for rigorous manet routing protocol evaluation. In: International Conference on Mobile Adhoc and Sensor Systems (MASS), pp. 256–266. IEEE (October 2006)

8. Lane, N., Miluzzo, E., Lu, H., Peebles, D., Choudhury, T., Campbell, A.: A survey of mobile phone sensing. IEEE Communications Magazine 48(9), 140–150 (2010)

9. Loke, S.W.: Supporting ubiquitous sensor-cloudlets and context-cloudlets: Programming compositions of context-aware systems for mobile users. Future Generation Computer Systems 28(4), 619–632 (2012)

10. Lu, H., Lane, N.D., Eisenman, S.B., Campbell, A.T.: Fast track article: Bubblesensing: Binding sensing tasks to the physical world. Pervasive and Mobile Computing 6(1), 58–71 (2010)

11. Park, E., Shin, H.: Recon gurable service composition and categorization for power-aware mobile computing. Transactions on Parallel and Distributed Systems 19(11), 1553–1564 (2008)

12. Perez, A., Labrador, M., Barbeau, S.: G-sense: a scalable architecture for global sensing and monitoring. IEEE Network 24(4), 57–64 (2010)

13. Perkins, C.E., Belding-Royer, E.M., Das, S.: Ad hoc on-demand distance vector (aodv) routing, http://www.ietf.org/rfc/rfc3561.txt

14. Prinz, V., Fuchs, F., Ruppel, P., Gerdes, C., Southall, A.: Adaptive and fault-tolerant service composition in peer-to-peer systems. In: Meier, R., Terzis, S. (eds.) DAIS 2008. LNCS, vol. 5053, pp. 30–43. Springer, Heidelberg (2008)

15. Sen, R., Roman, G.-C., Gill, C.: CiAN: A workflow engine for manets. In: Lea, D., Zavattaro, G. (eds.) COORDINATION 2008. LNCS, vol. 5052, pp. 280–295. Springer, Heidelberg (2008)

16. Wang, M., Li, B., Li, Z.: sflow: Towards resource-efficient and agile service federation in service overlay networks. In: International Conference on Distributed Computing Systems (ICDCS), pp. 628–635. IEEE (2004)

17. Yu, W.: Decentralized orchestration of BPEL processes with execution consistency. In: Li, Q., Feng, L., Pei, J., Wang, S.X., Zhou, X., Zhu, Q.-M. (eds.) APWeb/WAIM 2009. LNCS, vol. 5446, pp. 665–670. Springer, Heidelberg (2009)

18. Zaplata, S., Hamann, K., Kottke, K., Lamersdorf, W.: Flexible execution of distributed business processes based on process instance migration. Journal of Systems Integration 1(3), 3–16 (2010)

Smartphone Sensor Reliability
for Augmented Reality Applications

Jeffrey R. Blum, Daniel G. Greencorn, and Jeremy R. Cooperstock

McGill University, Montréal, Québec, Canada
{jeffbl,dangreencorn,jer}@cim.mcgill.ca

Abstract. With increasing reliance on the location and orientation sensors in smartphones for not only augmented reality applications, but also for meeting government-mandated emergency response requirements, the reliability of these sensors is a matter of great importance. Previous studies measure the accuracy of the location sensing, typically GPS, in handheld devices including smartphones, but few studies do the same for the compass or gyroscope (gyro) sensors, especially in real-world augmented reality situations. In this study, we measure the reliability of both the location and orientation capabilities of three current generation smartphones: Apple iPhone 4 and iPhone 4s (iOS) phones, as well as a Samsung Galaxy Nexus (Android). Each is tested in three different orientation/body position combinations, and in varying environmental conditions, in order to obtain quantifiable information useful for understanding the practical limits of these sensors when designing applications that rely on them. Results show mean location errors of 10–30 m and mean compass errors around 10–30°, but with high standard deviations for both making them unreliable in many settings.

Keywords: GPS, location, compass, magnetometer, augmented reality, sensor fusion, smartphones.

1 Introduction

Smartphone augmented reality applications typically require the user's location (latitude, longitude) and orientation (relative to north) within certain bounds of accuracy. Some applications may require only relative device orientation, such as that produced by a gyroscope, which can determine changes in device orientation, albeit not relative to north. For example, our In Situ Audio Services application [2], which renders points of interest via spatialized audio to blind users, relies on both the location of the device and its orientation relative to north. Due to the unreliability of the sensors, the scene was frequently misrendered, with points of interest in the wrong direction and/or at the incorrect distance. The study described in this paper was motivated by these issues arising from smartphone sensor unreliability. Specifically, we needed to determine when and by how much these sensors failed to provide accurate GPS, orientation, and gyro data. To do so, we walked two separate areas in Montreal 18 times each,

K. Zheng, M. Li, and H. Jiang (Eds.): MOBIQUITOUS 2012, LNICST 120, pp. 127–138, 2013.

with three smartphones in different body position and device orientation combinations, resulting in a total of 108 device logs for analysis. Based on the results, we are able to offer several recommendations for designers of other augmented reality smartphone applications. By way of example, we describe how we revised one of the rendering techniques of our application to take into account the high degree of sensor unreliability.

2   Previous Work

Accuracy has significant impact on real-world usability of mobile devices, e.g., for transit tracking systems [12], and there has thus been considerable work in evaluating the accuracy of smartphone sensors. Most such studies find that the GPS accuracy of a smartphone is considerably less than that of a dedicated GPS device designed solely for navigation purposes. These findings hold true for devices such as the Apple iPhone, which augments the standard GPS with WiFi and cellular tower information, as well as an online database of satellite locations, to implement augmented GPS (A-GPS) [16]. Accuracy is often measured by maintaining the device in a stationary position over a given sampling duration. This scenario is common in domains such as forestry, where the GPS unit can be left in position for an extended period to obtain a better fix, but is of limited relevance to an augmented reality application. For such tests in ideal open-sky conditions in a forest, even the best consumer-grade dedicated GPS systems yield average errors on the order of 2 m [15]. In more typical augmented reality application conditions, on-body location of the GPS receiver has been found to impact accuracy [13], as does the manner in which a smartphone is held [3]. Studies that examine the accuracy of various location sensors while the device is in motion often use one, presumably more accurate, device, such as a higher-end GPS unit, as the reference, although this can only establish relative error. This may be a reasonable approach in areas without tall buildings in good weather conditions, and when evaluating devices and approaches that are expected to have significantly higher error than the "reference" unit [4]. Other reports do not appear to use ground truth measurements, but instead rely solely on location accuracy estimates reported by the device itself [14]. To save power, the GPS sensor can be turned off between readings, although this may further decrease accuracy [7].

A tradeoff between cost of components, power and accuracy is also evident for the three-axis magnetometers, commonly used to determine the orientation of a device relative to north [6]. Again, the often poor accuracy of the compass headings produced by the magnetometer can be a critical issue for augmented reality (AR) applications [1]. Body position, how the phone is held, and the effects of device movement when carried while walking can all impact compass readings [4]. Filtering the raw magnetometer data in order to remove sensor noise has been proposed [5,8], but such solutions do not measure or improve the accuracy of the compass when it is subjected to distortions of the local magnetic field. One measure of the compass accuracy of a Nokia phone, taken while walking in an indoor corridor, found a mean error of 18.1°, with a standard deviation of 12.3° [10]. In such indoor spaces, attempts to use a built-in smartphone camera to better detect motion or location have been tried, coupled with sensor fusion via a Kalman filter [11]. However, such camera-based solutions have the practical problem of greatly reduced battery life due to their power requirements. In addition, they require maintaining the device in a position that provides sufficient viewing area to compute optical flow, which is impossible, for example, if the smartphone is kept in a pocket. Another effort to overcome limitations of the compass sensor involves indoor uses of ultrasound signals with multiple receivers on the device to determine orientation. However, this solution requires the introduction of new infrastructure in the environment [9], which may be impractical for general deployment.

The results of the previous studies notwithstanding, there exists very limited quantitative data on the performance of current smartphone location and orientation sensors. In particular, there is a notable lack of such data for dynamic urban environments and under realistic conditions relevant to augmented reality applications. For these reasons, we undertook the experiment described in the remainder of this paper.

3   Experiment Design

An undergraduate student (the *walker*) walked the same path repeatedly under different conditions to log compass, orientation (particularly yaw) and location data under a variety of conditions. Each of two different paths, termed *Downtown* and *Commercial*, was walked half the time in a clockwise (CW) direction, and half in a counterclockwise (CCW) direction. Three smartphones (iPhone 4, iPhone 4s and Google Galaxy Nexus) were carried on each walk, each in one of three body positions: attached to a belt, hanging on the chest, or resting flat on the head, as shown in Figure 1. Each combination was repeated three times. This resulted in 2 walking locations × 2 directions × 3 carrying positions/orientations × 3 repetitions = 36 data logs for each of the three devices.

The first two body positions were chosen to test the devices in the most practical carrying positions in real-world situations. The head position was included, regardless of practicality, since this exposes the device maximally to the sky, which we expected to result in the best location performance. In this case, we could determine whether the other two body positions further compromise location accuracy.

3.1   Walking Locations

The two areas walked are described in Figure 2. Each leg of each walk is analyzed independently in Section 4 to provide a comparison of the different conditions. Before each walk, the walker noted the weather conditions for the upcoming walk, shut down and restarted the application, and recalibrated the system to start with reasonably good initial sensor readings. Data plans and WiFi were enabled

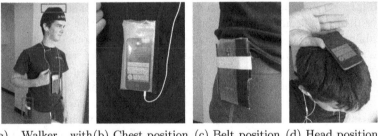

(a) Walker with three phones (b) Chest position (c) Belt position (d) Head position, under hat

Fig. 1. The three device positions/orientations. To avoid magnetic interference, the only metal used in the carriers was a belt buckle on the opposite side of the waist from the belt position.

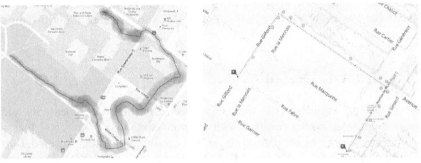

(a) Reported data from one downtown walk, including McGill campus and downtown skyscrapers. Error estimates are shown in purple.

(b) Commercial walk, outside downtown Montreal, with mostly with mostly sub-three story buildings nearby. Orange circles are ground truth points.

Fig. 2. The two areas walked during testing

on all phones used in this study, and were thus using A-GPS and potentially WiFi triangulation. This implies that we were not testing the GPS in isolation, but rather, the full location hardware and software stack of each device.

3.2 Ground Truth

To facilitate data analysis, the walker clicked a button on the headphone cable upon reaching each of the location ground truth waypoints, and at the start and end of each leg. This helped exclude corners and intersections, which require head movement to cross safely. All three device clocks were tightly synchronized, which allows us to capture these clicks on one device as an accurate timestamp reference for all three. With the system's clock synchronization setting enabled on each device, the log files generated during a laboratory test indicated that the timestamps associated with simultaneous button presses on the two iPhones occurred within 250 ms. When verifying manually before each walk in the Commercial set, we did not see differences greater than 1 s between any of the devices.

Compass ground truth was established by using a map screenshot of the area being walked and measuring the angle of each straight-line leg relative to north. For all of the data gathering and analysis, true north, as corrected from magnetic north via the magnetic declination, was used.

Distance error was calculated by comparing the most recently reported GPS location to the ground truth value at each waypoint. We used commercial online mapping systems to determine the ground truth waypoint locations along the path. Comparison against known survey points yielded accuracy for the manually selected map locations of within 1 m. This avoids experimental bias that could be introduced by comparing one GPS against another, especially knowing that even high-end units can have difficulty with limited view of the sky.

3.3   Sources of Error

There are several sources of potential error that result from our choice of using real-world conditions for these tests. First, the walker could not hit every waypoint exactly, but reported being within approximately 1 m of the ground truth targets. Second, as the walker moves, he sways from side-to-side. Similarly, to avoid other pedestrians and maintain his safety around traffic, some changes in direction were inevitable, although he endeavoured to keep his body as straight as possible. Judging from the local minimum and maximum gyro values manually measured from the graphs of several iPhone walks, it appears that the walker typically swayed by roughly 8-17°to each side for the Belt and Chest positions, but only roughly 5°for the Head position. Third, especially in the chest position, where the phone is hanging in a pouch around the neck, we expect more motion due to the device swaying on its lanyard. In the Head and Belt positions as well, we expect some error in the manual alignment process at the beginning of the walk. A cursory examination of the data indicated that compass error can be consistently positive in one leg, and consistently negative in the next. This precludes the possibility of estimating device alignment error from an assumption of a zero-mean error distribution. A more rigid apparatus for holding the devices may reduce these errors, but would also make the test significantly less realistic.

4   Results

4.1   Individual Log Results

Before discussing the aggregate data across all walks, an explanation of the data from a single walk, illustrated in Figure 2a, may prove helpful.[1]

---

[1] Our data, along with additional figures not shown here for space reasons, are available for review from `isas.cim.mcgill.ca/Sensors/`.

In addition to the location path, we can also plot various heading values over time, visualizing where the sensors deteriorate, and how they perform relative to each other. Figure 3 indicates compass values (cyan) against ground truth (black), the latter of which is constant (horizontal) for each straight-line leg of the walk. Actual compass error (red) is calculated as the absolute difference between these two, whereas reported compass error (grey) is an estimate of error magnitude by the sensor itself. As can be seen, the actual error fluctuates above and below the estimate. Gaps in the plot represent transitions between legs of the walk, during which we have no ground truth heading information.

Yaw (green), obtained from the gyro sensor, is not calibrated to north, so only represents relative variation. This data is generally expected to be flat, excepting body sway while walking. Slope in yaw indicates drift, observed in all legs of this walk. The reported course (purple) is derived from the direction of travel based on previous location updates. Both the iPhone and Android devices report course and speed based on location changes, but these appear to be of limited use even in the constrained straight-line testing we performed.

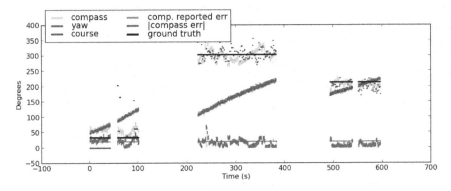

Fig. 3. Sensor values over time for a single device log file. Values are compass heading (cyan), heading ground truth (black), compass error estimate reported by the system (grey), yaw (green), course (purple), and |ground truth - compass reading| (red).

Aggregating the data across walks and segmenting it into the legs (for headings) or individual measured ground truth waypoints (for locations), allows us to discern general trends in the sensor performance.

4.2 Heading Accuracy

The only sensor on a smartphone with any knowledge of north is the magnetometer. However, large metal objects such as cars, electric power lines, and other interference can cause distorted readings. In early testing, we noted a 30°change in an iPhone 4's heading information when walking near a large vehicle.

To summarize our data, we pooled all of the values for a given condition, then calculated the mean and sample standard deviation, shown as error bars.

For heading data, since the samples did not arrive on a regular period, we re-sampled the data at 25 samples/sec to make the sets consistently sampled per unit time. Without this, a single sample, valid for more than a second due to lack of device motion, would be weighted far less in the analysis than a series of samples within the same second on another device. Due to differences in walking speed across walks, we also subsampled the compass updates in order to balance the number of samples in each set for analysis. On Android, we simply regis-tered for TYPE_ROTATION_VECTOR updates, which is north aligned, with no parameter for their frequency. Separate yaw values are not provided. On both platforms, compass or yaw changes greater than 0.2°were logged, which resulted in anywhere from less than one to over 30 unique samples/s, depending on the amount of motion. Most notably, the Head position appears to be more stable than Chest or Belt, and on the iPhone devices has dramatically fewer compass values, in some cases, well under one sample / second. For the two iPhone de-vices, the yaw value was updated on a timer, at a maximum of 10 samples/s in the Downtown walks, and 20 samples/s in the Commercial walks.

Aggregate data for the Downtown walks (omitted for space) indicate compass errors with a mean near 10°in the open area in the middle of McGill's campus, rising to nearly 30°near large skyscrapers. Compass errors in the Commercial walk (Figure 4) had means more consistently around or below 15°.

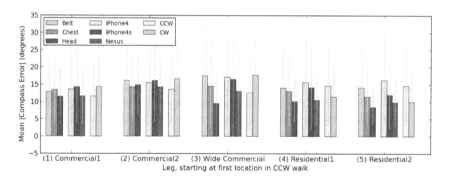

Fig. 4. Commercial walks compass error

Given natural body sway and alignment deviations from a straight-line path, these error means may seem tolerable for many purposes. However, the standard deviations raise questions as to their reliability. Thus, it is useful to determine whether the devices' estimates of their own accuracy are generally correct, as this would allow us to warn the user when values should not be trusted.

Reported Error Estimate Accuracy. iPhone devices provide an estimate of compass error in degrees, whereas Android devices only provide coarse levels of sensor reliability and are thus excluded from this evaluation. Figure 5 allows us to comment on the accuracy of the error estimates, e.g., if the compass indicates it is within 30°of the actual value, is the reading actually within 30°? If not, how often does this happen, and how far off is it? Bar values represent the mean number of degrees by which the actual error exceeds (positive bars) or is within (negative bars) the estimated error. The numbers below each set of bars represent the percentage of samples within the reported error. For example, in the first bar, 83% of the samples were within the reported error estimate, and under that estimated error by a mean of approximately 13°. The remaining 17% of the samples exceeded the estimated error by a mean of approximately 9°.

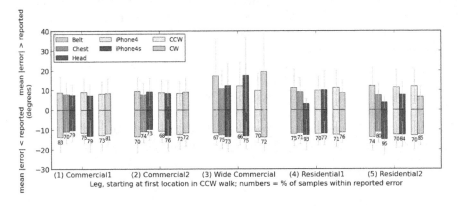

Fig. 5. Commercial walks: compass ground truth accuracy vs. reported error estimates

Although the 10-20°by which the actual error is seen to exceed the estimates may well be within the achievable tolerance of our experimental setup, the large standard deviations in some areas imply that there will be frequent cases with larger errors. Note that in some legs (e.g., leg 3), the compass error exceeds its estimate 25% or more of the time. The Downtown walks (not shown for reasons of space) performed more poorly outside of the central campus location, with periods where less than 50% of the samples were within the reported error, as well as error exceeding the estimate by more than 50°in some cases.

Yaw Drift. We had originally hoped that we could use the orientation sensors, primarily the gyro, to obtain better heading estimates by fusing them with the compass (magnetometer) data. We thus implemented a sensor fusion algorithm that recalibrated the gyro to north whenever a compass update was received with reported accuracy at 30°or less. When the compass error exceeded this threshold, we simply ignored further compass readings until the reported error returned below 30°. The hope was that the gyro would be sufficiently accurate to provide interim values. However, the observed yaw drift, which seems to accelerate in each leg, as seen in Figure 6, makes this futile. Downtown drifts range up to almost 3°/s, and up to over 4°in the Commercial walks. Downtown walks were roughly 6.5 minutes each, and Commercial walks were approximately 9 minutes from the time the walker clicked the button to begin the walk, up until the final click at the end. Due to initial calibration time, the sensors may have been started earlier. Even worse, Figure 7a illustrates that gyro drift progressively increases with time. At least on iPhone, shutting down the application allows the gyro to be turned off, and we speculate that it recalibrates on restart. We believe that as a result, yaw drift is typically minimal in the first leg.

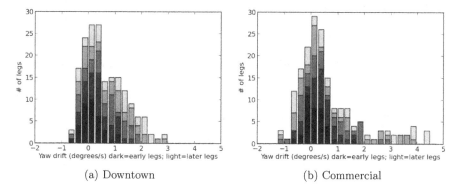

|(a) Downtown | (b) Commercial|

Fig. 6. Histogram of yaw drifts for the two iPhone devices, calculated by a linear regression of the yaw values within each leg. If the yaw sensor behaved perfectly, the drift would always be zero. Note that in both sets, drifts tend to be biased in a clockwise direction (to the right of zero), for which we have no explanation.

We suspect that Google's Android API only provides device orientation data fused with the magnetometer to better correct for gyro drift. Since the Nexus heading does not seem to perform appreciably better than the iPhones, the benefit of this fusion may be marginal when trying to find a north-calibrated reading. However, such fusion may indeed stabilize the gyro values significantly, useful for applications where only a relative yaw value is needed, not calibrated to north. Apple offers the same option of a fused gyro/compass orientation relative to north starting in iOS5, possibly because they came to the same realization.

4.3 Location Accuracy

Unlike heading, location data (Figure 8) was only sampled at 11 and 15 specific ground truth locations for the Downtown and Commercial walks respectively. In good conditions, we generally received updates separated by 1–3 m once the values had stabilized, although they sometimes rise higher. We also noted a "caterpillaring" effect in which an iPhone device would deliver a series of sparser location updates, then cluster a number more closely together, despite the walker moving at a consistent speed. These may be due to some sort of smoothing algorithm, with the system giving a series of more sparse points as

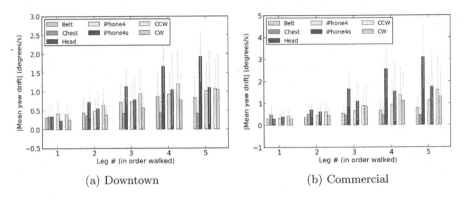

(a) Downtown   (b) Commercial

Fig. 7. Yaw drift for the two iPhones. Note that these graphs are arranged by leg in the *order walked* instead of by physical location, since the primary effect of yaw drift is associated with time rather than location. Thus, leg 1 is the first location walked in either CW or CCW direction, with the results averaged over the different corresponding segments. Interestingly, head position performs worse than the other positions/orientations, for which we do not have an explanation.

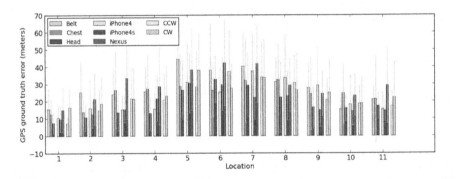

Fig. 8. Downtown walks: location ground truth errors

it tries to "catch up" to a new position, since we see this frequently with the reported location often lagging behind the walker's actual position.

As with heading, areas with taller buildings unsurprisingly cause the most difficulty for location accuracy. In these cases, locations may exhibit mean errors in the 30 m range, with maximum error values beyond 60 m in the vicinity of tall skyscrapers. The Commercial walks (not shown for reasons of space), with buildings generally no taller than three stories, exhibit mean error more consistently around 10–15 m, apart from location 10, which was particularly troublesome for all of the devices. As expected, the Head position tended to outperform the Chest and Belt positions.

Given the relatively large standard deviations, it is crucial to inform the user when the location sensors are having difficulty. Alternatively, such knowledge would allow the application to render information in a more appropriate manner. As before, we evaluate reliability of the location sensing by comparing actual ground truth error with the reported error estimate from the device. Disappointingly, the actual error frequently exceeds the estimated error. For the Downtown walks, the location was within the reported error only 20.4% of the time, and still less than half the time at 46.3% for the Commercial walks.

5   Conclusions

The results of our experiment demonstrate important accuracy issues for the location and orientation sensors found in current smartphones. Their location sensors (using A-GPS) exhibit errors with means of 10–30 m, depending on the surrounding buildings. Compass error frequently exhibits a mean around 10°of ground truth, which is quite good given the other sources of error in our experiment, but in some areas, increases to approximately 30°. The relatively large standard deviations around these means will result in frequently poorer performance experienced by users, e.g., with location errors of 60 m within the standard deviation when walking near skyscrapers. Compounding these problems, reported error is frequently underestimated, reducing trustworthiness. Improving the results with sensor fusion, e.g., by leveraging the gyro to improve heading estimates, is problematic due to difficulty in determining a "good" initial compass reading. In addition, we observed significant gyro drift over time, accelerating to over 4°/s in some cases. Practically, we conclude that augmented reality applications that rely on better location or heading accuracy than indicated by these results will be difficult at best to realize on current smartphone hardware if relying on raw sensor values. Further mining across our data set may also reveal additional correlations that would help point to the specific conditions under which the sensors are inaccurate.

Until smartphone sensors improve, we are exploring alternative rendering methods that can cope with poor accuracy and error estimation, as well as algorithms such as "snapping" the user to a nearest street to overcome location errors. In many cases, these subjectively appear to improve accuracy, but formal testing is required. Although such methods show promise, they also generate new failure cases, such as worsening the location error by snapping to an incorrect street when nearing an intersection. Snapping can be effective for those location errors lateral to the street, but not for errors in the direction of travel, which appear to occur more frequently, often with the reported location lagging the user's actual position. In terms of implications to our own research we are now aware of the importance of carefully picking the areas in which we test our application, and treat the error estimates for both orientation and location sensors with a dose of skepticism.

Acknowledgements. This work was possible thanks to the financial support of the Québec Secrétariat du Conseil du trésor through the *Appui au passage à la société de l'information* program, as well as additional funding from a Google

Faculty Research Award. We gratefully acknowledge Mathieu Bouchard's Android work, as well numerous discussions with him and other Shared Reality Lab members concerning experiment design, implementation and analysis.

References

1. Azenkot, S., Ladner, R.E., Wobbrock, J.O.: Smartphone haptic feedback for non-visual wayfinding. In: Computers and Accessibility, pp. 281–282. ACM (2011)
2. Blum, J.R., Bouchard, M., Cooperstock, J.R.: What's around me? Spatialized audio augmented reality for blind users with a smartphone. In: Puiatti, A., Gu, T. (eds.) MobiQuitous 2011. LNICST, vol. 104, pp. 49–62. Springer, Heidelberg (2012)
3. Blunck, H., Kjærgaard, M.B., Toftegaard, T.S.: Sensing and Classifying Impairments of GPS Reception on Mobile Devices. In: Lyons, K., Hightower, J., Huang, E.M. (eds.) Pervasive 2011. LNCS, vol. 6696, pp. 350–367. Springer, Heidelberg (2011)
4. Constandache, I., Choudhury, R., Rhee, I.: Towards mobile phone localization without war-driving. In: INFOCOM, pp. 2321–2329. IEEE (2010)
5. Gotow, J.B., Zienkiewicz, K., White, J., Schmidt, D.C.: Addressing Challenges with Augmented Reality Applications on Smartphones. In: Cai, Y., Magedanz, T., Li, M., Xia, J., Giannelli, C. (eds.) Mobilware 2010. LNICST, vol. 48, pp. 129–143. Springer, Heidelberg (2010)
6. Jones, W.: A compass in every smartphone. IEEE Spectrum 47(2), 12–13 (2010)
7. Kjærgaard, M., Langdal, J., Godsk, T., Toftkjær, T.: EnTracked: energy-efficient robust position tracking for mobile devices. In: Mobisys, pp. 221–234. ACM Press, NY (2009)
8. Ozcan, R., Orhan, F., Demirci, M.F., Abul, O.: An Adaptive Smoothing Method for Sensor Noise in Augmented Reality Applications on Smartphones. In: Venkatasubramanian, N., Getov, V., Steglich, S. (eds.) Mobilware 2011. LNICST, vol. 93, pp. 209–218. Springer, Heidelberg (2012)
9. Priyantha, N., Miu, A., Balakrishnan, H., Teller, S.: The cricket compass for context-aware mobile applications. In: MobiCom, pp. 1–14. ACM, NY (2001)
10. Ruotsalainen, L., Kuusniemi, H., Chen, R.: Heading change detection for indoor navigation with a Smartphone camera. In: Indoor Positioning and Indoor Navigation, pp. 1–7. IEEE (September 2011)
11. Ruotsalainen, L., Kuusniemi, H., Chen, R.: Visual-aided Two-dimensional Pedestrian Indoor Navigation with a Smartphone. Global Positioning Systems 10(1), 11–18 (2011)
12. Thiagarajan, A., Biagioni, J., Gerlich, T., Eriksson, J.: Cooperative transit tracking using smart-phones. In: Embedded Networked Sensor Systems, pp. 85–98. ACM, New York (2010)
13. Vaitl, C., Kunze, K., Lukowicz, P.: Does On-body Location of a GPS Receiver Matter? In: Body Sensor Networks, pp. 219–221. IEEE (June 2010)
14. von Watzdorf, S., Michahelles, F.: Accuracy of positioning data on smartphones. In: Workshop on Location and the Web, pp. 2:1–2:4. ACM, New York (2010)
15. Wing, M.: Consumer-Grade GPS Receiver Measurement Accuracy in Varying Forest Conditions. Research Journal of Forestry 5(2), 78–88 (2011)
16. Zandbergen, P.: Accuracy of iPhone Locations: A Comparison of Assisted GPS, WiFi and Cellular Positioning. Transactions in GIS 13, 5–25 (2009)

Differential Private Trajectory Obfuscation

Roland Assam, Marwan Hassani, and Thomas Seidl

RWTH Aachen University, Germany
{assam,hassani,seidl}@cs.rwth-aachen.de

Abstract. We propose a novel technique to ensure location privacy for mobility data using differential privacy. Privacy is guaranteed through path perturbation by injecting noise to both the space and time domain of a spatio-temporal data. In addition, we present to the best of our knowledge, the first context aware differential private algorithm. We conducted numerous experiments on real and synthetic datasets, and show that our approach produces superior privacy results when compared to state-of-the-art techniques.

Keywords: Spatial Database, LBS, Differential Privacy.

1 Introduction

The widespread usage of pervasive devices has made it easier to track humans and moving objects. This has garnered huge research interest on how to ensure location privacy when storing mobility data into Moving Object Databases (MOD) or Location Based Services (LBS). Recent revelation that an A-list company like Apple stored location information without its smart phone customers' knowledge highlights the elevated and immediate need to address mobility privacy. Gartner Research and its Research VP William Clark[1] are heralding Context Aware Computing as the future of computing. Sophisticated context aware data mining techniques without strong privacy guarantees will scare users from using location aware applications. The situation gets even grimmer, because some extremely good existing privacy solutions[2], [5] did not take into consideration the context of the location when anonymizing or obfuscation data. New location privacy research has the obligations to address and ensure privacy without losing the context of the original location. As a result of this, in this paper, we employ a privacy paradigm called differential privacy [3] and introduce a new privacy notion called context aware differential privacy. Providing privacy with a *very strong* privacy paradigm like *differential privacy* in context aware applications will have a profound impact w.r.t. user acceptance, or usage of context aware systems in areas such as mobile social networking, national security and trend analysis. To the best of our knowledge, this is the first location privacy work that provides a context aware location privacy using *differential privacy*.

---

[1] http://www.gartner.com/technology/research/context-aware-computing/

K. Zheng, M. Li, and H. Jiang (Eds.): MOBIQUITOUS 2012, LNICST 120, pp. 139–151, 2013.
© Institute for Computer Sciences, Social Informatics and Telecommunications Engineering 2013

1.1 Our Contributions

Although the theoretical strength of differential privacy has been highly and widely applauded, it is quite difficult and challenging to practically apply it in different domains as mentioned in [4], partly due to the problems that might be encountered during the derivation of the sensitivity of a metric space. In this paper, we address this challenge, and provide a differential private solution for location privacy using the exponential mechanism. In addition, we present a differential private context aware location privacy technique for moving objects. Here is a summary of our contributions:

- we derive the sensitivity of a trajectory metric space by introducing notions like Burst and Obfuscation Region (OBRegions).
- we propose a novel technique to achieve differential privacy for spatio-temporal trajectory data.
- we present to the best of our knowledge the first differential private context aware location privacy technique.

1.2 System Setup

The setup consists of a single user or multiple users carrying a GPS-enabled device and a central server that performs data perturbation. As a user or object moves, its current spatio-temporal location data is perturbed and sent to the MOD or LBS via a randomization mechanism located at the central server. Our system employs non-interactive data publishing. That is, the data is first perturbed and then published, so that any data miner can have a copy of the published perturbed data. Throughout this work, we utilize the term *Trace* to refer to a single spatio-temporal GPS point.

In many trajectory models [1], [14] significant or important locations are extracted from raw GPS data by considering only locations where an object stays for at least a given threshold time (usually termed "Stay Time"). Stay Time is the time interval between two successive traces of an object's trajectory. In this paper, any location where an object stays above a threshold stay time is called a stay point. Formally,

Definition 1. (Stay Point): *is the spatio-temporal data point of an object at a given location when its duration at that location is greater or equal to a Threshold Stay Time T_{st}.*

Definition 2. (Differential Private Context Aware Location (DP-CAL)): *is an obfuscated location that fulfills differential privacy and has a similar semantic location context as the true location from which it was derived from.*

Definition 3. (Problem Definition 1): *Given that an (outlier) object $\mathcal{M}$ sends raw spatio-temporal GPS data which consists of a sequence of stay points to an LBS or MOD through a trusted server, obfuscate the significant locations (stay points) of the GPS data using differential privacy at the trusted server.*

Definition 4. (PROBLEM DEFINITION 2): *Given the same object $\mathcal{M}$ and the assumptions used in Definition 3, determine a Differential Private Context Aware obfuscated trace.*

As a summary, this paper has two main goals. These include the use of differential privacy at a central server to ensure: 1) Non-context aware (or Random) obfuscation and 2) Context aware location obfuscation of the stay points of outliers or multiple moving objects.

Paper Organization. The rest of this paper is organized as follows. Section 1.3 focuses on relevant related works. In Section 2, some basic concepts of differential privacy and location obfuscation are explained. Section 3 discusses data pre-processing for differential privacy. In Section 4, we present our differential private techniques to ensure non-context and context aware differential privacy.

1.3   Related Works

Trajectory Anonymization and Location Privacy. Techniques such as [5], [6] use the spatial k-Anonymity paradigm. The topography of this paradigm typically comprises of users who send their request through a trusted server to the LBS. Anonymization is accomplished in the trusted server. This is done by selecting an area called cloaking region (CR) and for a given object's request, it ensures that at least *k-1* other object requests in that CR are sent to the LBS. Our approach is similar to these techniques only from the setup point of view. k-Anonymity is achieved in [7] by suppression, which depends on the probability of an adversary to correctly determine a trajectory sequence. [2] used inherent GPS error to propose a (k, δ)-Anonymity algorithm called Never Walk Alone (NWA) where δ represents the error radius. Our technique differs from [2] since we utilize the differential privacy paradigm while [2] is based on k-Anonymity.

Differential Privacy. Fundamental theories of differential privacy are provided in [3], [8]. We also employ some important guidelines and theories from [9] to derive a sensitivity function for the trajectory metric space which is pivotal during the derivation of noise. The data access interface of PINQ [10] and [4] are used for interactive data publishing, while ours is geared towards non-interactive publishing.

2   Background

2.1   Basics of Differential Privacy

Differential privacy is a privacy paradigm proposed by Dwork [3] that ensures privacy through data perturbation. It is based on the core principle that for any two datasets that differ in only one entry, the ratio of the probability of their outputs generated by a randomized mechanism is bounded. Specifically, this is formally given as follows.

Definition 5. (ϵ-DIFFERENTIAL PRIVACY [9]): *A randomization mechanism $\mathcal{A}$ (x) provides ϵ-differential privacy if for any two datasets $\mathcal{D}_1$ and $\mathcal{D}_2$ that differ on at most one element, and all output $\mathcal{S} \subseteq Range(\mathcal{A})$,*

$$Pr[\mathcal{A}(\mathcal{D}_1) \in S] \leq \exp(\epsilon) * Pr[\mathcal{A}(\mathcal{D}_2) \in \mathcal{S}]$$

where ϵ is the privacy parameter called privacy budget or privacy level.

Sensitivity. Sensitivity is defined as the maximum change that occurs, if one record is added or removed from a dataset.

Definition 6. ($\mathcal{L}_1$ SENSITIVITY [9]): *The $\mathcal{L}_1$ sensitivity of a function $f : D^n \to \mathbb{R}^d$ is the smallest number $S(f)$ such that for all x and x' which differ in a single entry,*

$$\|f(x) - f(x')\| \leq S(f)$$

Exponential Mechanism. Differential privacy is achieved by adding noise to data. This study uses the Exponential Mechanism[8] to add noise to data. The exponential mechanism guarantees differential privacy by approximating the true value of a data with the help of a quality or utility function . Specifically, it takes in several input data and maps them to some outputs. It then uses the utility function to assign scores to all the mappings. The output whose mapping has the best score is chosen and sampled with a given probability such that differential privacy is guaranteed. This is formally given as follows.

Theorem 1. *[8] For a given input $\mathcal{X}$ and a function $u : (\mathcal{X} \times y) \to \mathbb{R}$, an algorithm that chooses an output y with a probability $\propto \exp(-\epsilon \frac{u(\mathcal{X},y)}{2\Delta u})$ is ϵ-differential private.*

Composition. [10] mentioned that there are basically two types of compositions. These include, *Sequential Composition* and *Parallel Composition*. Sequential composition is exhibited when a sequence of computations provides differential privacy in isolation. The final privacy guarantee is said to be the sum of each ϵ-differential privacy.

2.2   Location Obfuscation

Location obfuscation can be achieved by 1)Hiding Locations 2)Inserting Dummy Regions 3)Merging Regions 4) *Perturbation*. In this work, location obfuscation is accomplished by *perturbation* (using differential privacy). Location obfuscation techniques generally ensure privacy by degrading the true geographic location of an object. Most techniques [11], [12] usually define beforehand a region where the degraded location can lie on. This is then followed by the distortion of the true geographic location to any position inside the latter defined region.

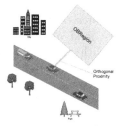

Fig. 1. An OBRegion hosts several candidate traces

3 Pre-processing Data for Privacy

3.1 Burst

The movement of an object is characterized by a sequence of stay points and points that are not stay points. Since stay points depict interesting and important locations, they are naturally the type of locations that are targeted by an adversary. Hence, they need to be properly protected. In this work, we utilize the notion of stay points to portray the mobility of an object as differential privacy problem as follows. A sequence of raw GPS data is partitioned into different data slots. Each data slot is called a Burst. Each Burst consists of one or more stay points and a trip entails one or more Bursts.

Definition 7. (BURST): *is a data slot that comprises of a finite amount of stay points.*

In terms of differential privacy, the goal is that, for any given Burst which consists of a sequence of stay points, the removal or addition of a stay point within a Burst should not reveal any information about another stay point in the Burst.

Notations. Let $\mathbf{T}$ be a trajectory or a trip consisting of a set of GPS points. The GPS points in $\mathbf{T}$ are partitioned into several Bursts $\mathbf{B}_j$ where $j \in \{1, 2, 3, ...m\}$. Let $\mathbf{p}_j$ denotes a stay point in $\mathbf{B}_j$ and each stay point $\mathbf{p}_j$ given by (x_j, y_j, t_j) corresponds to a geographic position (x_j, y_j) at time t_j.

3.2 Trajectory Obfuscation

In Section 2.2, we mentioned that in existing location obfuscation techniques, the region on which the perturbed location can fall must be defined before hand. In this work, such a region is termed the *Obfuscation Region*.

Obfuscation Region. [12] used circles to determine obfuscation regions. Our OBfuscation Region (OBRegion) is a square grid depicted in Figure 1 whose grid radius is denoted by r_o. It is connected to an arm that spans from the latter grid to the moving object. Moreover, the perpendicular distance between a moving object and the obfuscation region is called the *Orthogonal Proximity* (ρ). Using such a structure ensures higher coverage for small grid radius. The trusted server is responsible for the determination of obfuscation regions and the obfuscation of traces as follows. Once a trace arrives at the trusted server, it uses some user specified distance parameters (r_o and ρ) to determine an obfuscation region. Then, it populates this region with a finite number of *candidate obfuscation traces*. Each of these candidate traces could be chosen to replace the *stay point* of the object, thereby ensuring trace obfuscation.

Candidate Trace Generation. There are two ways by which the server can generate candidate traces. 1) By randomly picking a finite number of locations within the obfuscation region (non-context aware location obfuscation). 2) By choosing only locations within the obfuscation region that have the same location context as the true location of the object. Formally,

Definition 8. (OBFUSCATION REGION (OBREGION)): *is a square grid region that is determined by the trusted server with the use of a user defined radius. It is also home to the **k** candidate traces generated by the trusted server. The radius of the obfuscation region is denoted by r_o.*

4   Trajectory Differential Privacy

4.1   Linking Differential Privacy to Trajectory

As aforementioned in Section 2, the exponential mechanism requires at its input among others 1) *input dataset* 2) *output range* and 3) *utility function*.

Input Dataset. The dataset of a Burst is used as the exponential mechanism's dataset. For example, assume that the dataset $\mathcal{T}_1$ corresponds to a collection of stay points within a given Burst. Adding or removing one stay point from that Burst forms a new dataset $\mathcal{T}_2$ such that $\mathcal{T}_1$ and $\mathcal{T}_2$ differ in just one single entry. $\mathcal{T}_1$ and $\mathcal{T}_2$ are sent as input dataset to a randomized mechanism $\mathcal{A}(x)$.

Output Range. Like other location obfuscation privacy techniques [11], [12], an obfuscation region that comprises of a set of locations is defined beforehand as described in Section 3.2. In addition, we indicated that the trusted server determines an OBRegion and populates it with k finite candidate obfuscation traces. An obfuscated trace is destined to fall on an OBRegion. Since the theoretical concept dictates that an output range has to be made up of a finite set of elements, we partition the OBRegion into sub regions.

The subdivision of the OBRegion is performed by the central server as follows. The grid square of an OBRegion is (vertically) divided into N equidistance sub-regions. Each of the sub-region is called *Sub-Obfuscation Region (Sub-OBRegion)* and it is denoted by S_i. Intuitively, after this division, the candidate traces are distributed into the N Sub-OBRegions as illustrated in Figure 2. In this paper, the output range of the exponential mechanism is given by the finite set of Sub-OBRegions that contain candidate traces. In order to prevent that no element in the output range should have a zero probability of being chosen, we have to ensure that no Sub-OBRegion is empty. Hence, Sub-OBRegions which do not contain candidate traces are discarded and the size of N is reduced. For

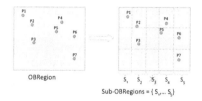

Fig. 2. Sub-OBRegion formed from an OBRegion

example, the output range R for the OBRegion in Figure 2 is given by $R = \{S_1, S_2, S_3, S_4, S_5\}$. The k candidate traces are distributed within the different Sub-OBRegions. The Sub-OBRegion S_3 is discarded since no trace is found in it and N is updated to 4.

Quality or Utility Function. As previously alluded, we intend to make the stay points private. Intuitively, the closeness between a stay point and a given Sub-OBRegion of the output range can be used to measure the quality of an obfuscated trace. Hence, the utility function for our trajectory metric space is the Euclidean distance between the stay point and the *center* of a Sub-OBRegion as formalized in Equation 1.

$$U = -dist(p_j - S_i^c) \tag{1}$$

where $dist$ denotes the Euclidean distance, p_j the stay point and S_i^c is the center of the ith Sub-OBRegion. Each Sub-OBRegion is given a score based on its distance from the stay point by using this utility function. The goal is to obtain a Sub-OBRegion that is closest to the stay point. Hence, the smaller the distance, the higher the score.

Exponential Mechanism. The exponential mechanism will now map each stay point in a Burst (input dataset) to a given Sub-OBRegion (output range) and use the defined utility function to choose the optimum location which it can output as a good approximation of the original stay point. We should note that the input dataset variables (stay points from a GPS Device) are *independent* from the output range variables (traces generated by Server) since the former is retrieved from GPS readers while the latter is generated by the trusted server without any knowledge of the former.

4.2 Sensitivity Function

The utility function $U(\overline{\mathbf{p}}_j, f(\mathcal{T}_1))$ reflects how good the output obfuscated trace $\overline{\mathbf{p}}_j \in S_i$ is w.r.t. a stay point which belongs to a dataset $\mathcal{T}_1$ at a given Burst. The sensitivity of the utility function measures the maximum possible change that will occur in a trajectory metric space when one GPS stay point is added or removed from the dataset $\mathcal{T}_1$ to form a dataset $\mathcal{T}_2$ within a Burst. This sensitivity is given by :

$$S(f) = \max_{\overline{\mathbf{p}}_j \in S_i, \mathcal{T}_1, \mathcal{T}_2} |U\left(\overline{\mathbf{p}}_j, f(\mathcal{T}_1)\right) - U\left(\overline{\mathbf{p}}_j, f(\mathcal{T}_2)\right)| \tag{2}$$

Since we are dealing with geographical positions, the bounds of the sensitivity function is finite, and are defined.

4.3 Differential Private Trajectory Algorithm

Noise Addition. Algorithm 1 shows the differential private obfuscation algorithm, including the input parameters. Stay points are separated into Bursts (Line 1). Besides, the server determines the output range of the exponential mechanism by populating and computing the Sub-OBRegions with candidate traces in Line 2. Non-context aware or context aware candidate traces (Section 4.4) can be generated in Line 2 depending on the candidate trace type C_t. Non-context aware candidate traces are generated by default. The utility function in Line 3 computes the score of each Sub-OBRegion, and all candidate traces within a given Sub-OBRegion are assigned *the same score*.

The most profound step of our algorithm (Line 5) is the selection of a Sub-OBRegion based on the scores from the utility function. The exponential mechanism chooses the Sub-OBRegion using the best score with a probability proportional to $\exp\left(\frac{\epsilon}{2S(f)}.\mathbf{U}\left(\overline{\mathbf{p}}_j, f(\mathcal{T})\right)\right)$. Thus, the likelihood for a Sub-OBRegion with a better score to be selected is of an exponential magnitude. Finally, a trace within the chosen Sub-OBRegion is sampled and sent to the MOD or LBS as a differential private obfuscated trace in Line 6.

Analysis of Privacy Guarantee. Differential privacy is guaranteed for all obfuscated traces emanating from the trusted server.

Theorem 2. *Algorithm 1 is ϵ-differential private.*

Proof. In Line 5 of algorithm 1, the probability of the exponential mechanism to choose a Sub-OBRegion is given by

$$\frac{\exp\left(\frac{\epsilon}{2S(f)}.\mathbf{U}\left(\overline{\mathbf{p}}_j, f(\mathcal{T}_1)\right)\right).|S_i|}{\sum_i \exp\left(\frac{\epsilon}{2S(f)}.\mathbf{U}\left(\overline{\mathbf{p}}_j, f(\mathcal{T}_2)\right)\right) d\overline{\mathbf{p}}_j.|S_i|}$$

where $|S_i|$ is the number of Sub-OBRegions. When the best Sub-OBRegion has been chosen, a trace within the selected Sub-OBRegion is uniformly sampled with a probability.

$\propto \exp\left(\frac{\epsilon}{2S(f)}.\mathbf{U}\left(\overline{\mathbf{p}}_j, f(\mathcal{T})\right)\right)$. Since obfuscation occurs within a Burst, we utilize the longitudes, latitudes and time values of points in the Burst to extract prior knowledge about the lower and upper bounds of the sensitivity function, this means integrating $\exp\left(\frac{\epsilon}{2S(f)}.\mathbf{U}\left(\overline{\mathbf{p}}_j, f(\mathcal{T})\right)\right)$ delivers finite values. Hence sampling is being performed such that:
$Pr\left[\mathcal{A}(\mathcal{T}_1) = \overline{\mathbf{p}}_j\right] =$

$$\frac{\exp\left(\frac{\epsilon}{2S(f)}.\mathbf{U}\left(\overline{\mathbf{p}}_j, f(\mathcal{T}_1)\right)\right)}{\int_{\overline{\mathbf{p}}_j \in S_i} \exp\left(\frac{\epsilon}{2S(f)}.\mathbf{U}\left(\overline{\mathbf{p}}_j, f(\mathcal{T}_2)\right)\right) d\overline{\mathbf{p}}_j}$$

Line 5 is performed only once for a given Burst. Hence according to Theorem 1, Line 5 guarantees $1 \times \alpha$-differential privacy. However, because a stay point is a spatio-temporal data which contains three dimensions, namely the X-position, Y-position and the time domain, the privacy budget needs to be carefully managed to control the cost of privacy. Using the Sequential Composition [10] described in Section 2, the total cost of privacy within a Burst to obfuscate the different dimensions is $\alpha.|D|$, where $|D|$ is the number of dimensions and $2 \leq |D| \leq 3$. This means, if all domains of the original stay point are obfuscated (i.e. $|D| = 3$) then each Burst is 3α-differential private. On the other hand, if only the spatial domains of a stay point are obfuscated, then each Burst will be 2α-differential private. Thus, for a given Burst dataset and its corresponding output range, each obfuscated trace sent to the MOD or LBS after selection by the exponential mechanism is $\alpha.|D|$-differential private.

Therefore, if an overall privacy budget ϵ is provided by the data miner, for $\alpha = \frac{\epsilon}{|D|}$, Algorithm 1 is ϵ-differential private.

Algorithm 1. Differential Private Trace Obfuscation

Input: *Dataset* $\mathcal{T}_1$, *privacy budget* ϵ, *size of Burst* n, OBRegion Radius r_o, N, *Orthogonal Proximity* ρ, *Candidate Trace Type* C_t

Output: differential private obfuscated Trace

1 **Partition**: *Partition and group* n *stay points into Bursts*

2 **Get Output Range**: *Use* r_o *and* ρ *to determine the OBRegion. Populate OBRegion w.r.t.* C_t *and divide OBRegion into* N *Sub-OBRegions*

3 **Utility Function**: *Allocate scores to each Sub-OBRegion using the stay point and the utility function in Equation 1*

4 **Sensitivity**: *Get the sensitivity* $S(f)$ *of the trajectory metric space using Equation 2,* $\mathcal{T}_1$ *and* $\mathcal{T}_2$*; where* $\mathcal{T}_2$ *is formed by adding or removing a stay point from* $\mathcal{T}_1$ *for each Burst*

5 **Perturbation**: *Select an Sub-OBRegion and then choose a candidate trace within the latter region by sampling with noise whose probability is*

$$\propto \exp\left(\frac{\epsilon}{2S(f)}.\mathbf{U}\left(\overline{\mathbf{p}}_j, f(\mathcal{T})\right) \right)$$

6 **return**: *the sampled trace and send to MOD or LBS*

4.4   Context Aware Location Privacy

Context Aware computing motivations were described in Section 1. The second problem definition (Definition 4) requires the guarantee of DPCAL. As a recap, the main goal of DPCAL is to add more contextual meaning to noisy differential private traces. This is achieved using the notion of **Location Privacy Context Resolution Utility** (LPCRU).

LPCRU is a utility found at the trusted server that generates a resource pool based on the user's current location. This is used in Algorithm 1 to output a differential private context aware location. The resource pool generated by LPCRU is basically a list of location coordinates mapped to some categories. These categories have similar semantic location context to the original location.

LPCRU Candidate Traces. The LPCRU is needed to nourish Algorithm 1 with context-aware locations. The latter locations are employed by Algorithm 1 at Line 2 to populate the OBRegion with context aware locations, if the candidate trace type C_t is specified as *Context Aware Location Privacy*. The context-aware candidate traces generated by the LPCRU are used in the main algorithm (Algorithm 1 at Line 3 to 6) to produce a context aware differential private trace. In real life, there are scenarios where by an object can be found in a very sparely populated area (e.g. a desert) and there is no neighboring location which has the same location category or semantic context as the object. If LPCRU returns no candidate context-aware traces, the OBRegion which it has to populate will be empty, and this will lead to zero probability of chosen elements in the output range. This violates differential privacy. To address this problem, we stress that if no location with similar context could be found, the LPCRU will return non-context aware candidate traces to prevent zero probabilities a the output range. However, this rarely occurs in urban areas.

5 Case Study and Empirical Evaluation

The implementations were done in Java. We based our evaluations on two criteria. 1) Quantifying Privacy obtained by the user. 2) Quality and Utility of the obfuscated trace to databases and data mining. In each of these criteria, we compared our technique with that of two state-of-the-art works. They include the Never Walk Alone (NWA) algorithm [2] and the Path Confusion (PPC) algorithm [13]. Throughout this section, we will refer to these previous works as NWA and PPC, respectively.

Experimental Dataset. We conducted our experiments with one synthetic dataset and two real datasets. The Brinkhoff[2] Oldenburg synthetic dataset was used. We generated 101,070 traces for 19 objects. Besides, we utilized 90,104 traces from the GeoLife [14] real dataset. In addition, the Athens Truck[3] real dataset that entails 276 GPS trajectories of 50 moving trucks in Athens and a total of 112203 location traces was used.

5.1 Quantifying User's Privacy

We utilized two location privacy metrics to analyze the privacy obtained by a user during obfuscation. They include 1) Expectation of Distance Error and Quality of Service (QoS) 2) Location Entropy.

Expectation of Distance Error and QoS. These privacy metrics were proposed by [13]. Expectation of Distance Error measures the accuracy by which an adversary can estimate the true position of a moving object. It is given by:

$$E[d] = \frac{1}{NT} \sum_{t=1}^{T} \sum_{i=1}^{I} p_i(t) d_i(t) \tag{3}$$

---

[2] http://iapg.jade-hs.de/personen/brinkhoff/generator/
[3] http://www.rtreeportal.org

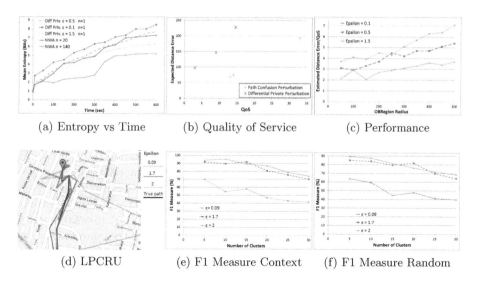

(a) Entropy vs Time   (b) Quality of Service   (c) Performance

(d) LPCRU   (e) F1 Measure Context   (f) F1 Measure Random

Fig. 3. Evaluation of differential private trace obfuscation

where N is the number of objects, d_i denotes the total distance error between the true and obfuscated location, T the total observation time and $p_i(t)$ is the probability to track a user. On the other hand, **QoS** is given by:

$$QoS = \frac{1}{NT} \sum_{n=1}^{N} \sum_{t=1}^{T} \sqrt{\sum_{j=1}^{J} (\widetilde{a_n}(t) - a_n(t))^2} \qquad (4)$$

where a is the domain, $a_n(t)$ is the true trace and $\widetilde{a_n}(t)$ the obfuscated trace of user n at step t.

We passed the Geolife dataset which has a GPS sampling rate of 2 to 4 seconds into the randomized mechanism. The stay point GPS data for each trajectory was partitioned into blocks of 15 stay points per Burst.We considered the movement of a user with the GeoLife dataset and perturbed the traces using our technique with an OBRegion radius of 300, 500 and 700. We computed $E[d]$ and QoS, and compared our results with that of PPC. Figure 3b illustrates these results; our technique delivers a better QoS than the PPC technique. Figure 3b orchestrates that for an OBRegion radius of 300, an adversary is expected to make an additional 18m error when comparing our method with PPC. This error distance increases as the size of the OBRegion increases.

In [13], Performance is given by the ratio of $E[d]$ to QoS. We analyzed the interplay between this ratio and ϵ for OBRegion radius $r_o \leq 500$. Figure 3c shows that for a given r_o, as ϵ decreases, the the overall performance increases. This can be explained by the fact that for each domain of the trace, smaller values of ϵ leads to greater distortion, hence causing the $E[d]$ to increase.

Entropy. Location entropy captures the uncertainty of the adversary during the inference of the correct location. Location entropy is given by:

$$H_l = -\sum P(x, y) \log_2 (P(x, y)) \tag{5}$$

where $P(x, y)$ is the probability that an object is located at position (x,y). We compared our method with the NWA technique for $\delta = 1000$. Since NWA does not anonymize the time domain, we left out the time domain of traces. We used the Geolife dataset to determine the uncertainty of the adversary for $r_o = 1000$ and $\epsilon = 0.1, 0.5, 1.5$. Figure 3a depicts the results of the experiment. Our technique produced superior entropy results when compared to the NWA, despite the fact that our technique uses just a single object while NWA uses 20 moving objects. It is important to point out that our technique insert uncertainty to each stay point of a trajectory and does not depend on neighboring objects (like in k-Anonymity). Thus, if stay points of an outlier object are passed through our randomized mechanism with low ϵ values, a very strong privacy is guaranteed.

5.2   Quality and Utility of Obfuscated Trace

LPCRU Evaluation. We conducted several experiments to evaluate the LPCRU. Figure 3d shows the map obtained when LPCRU is used for the Athens dataset with 9 stay points per Burst. The map shows distortions for ϵ values ranging from 0.09 to 2 for two categories (shops and roads). The graphical illustration shows a much larger distortion as ϵ increases. To evaluate the benefits of context aware obfuscated traces for data mining, we compared the utility of context aware and non-context aware (or random) obfuscated traces produced by Algorithm 1. We clustered each set of obfuscated trace separately using KMeans and evaluated the quality of the cluster. Figure 3e and Figure 3f shows the F1 measure results of the context aware trace and the non-context aware trace, respectively. It can be seen that the F1 Measure for context aware obfuscated trace is better.

Runtime. The time required to obfuscate traces depends on the obfuscation mode. Context aware obfuscation requires a longer time than its counterpart. For non-stream datasets, the server requires minutes to obfuscate 87K traces.

6   Conclusions

We presented a novel technique to achieve differential privacy for trajectories. Our technique extracts significant locations called stay points from raw GPS data and then obfuscates these stay points using a differential private randomized mechanism. We provide to the best of our knowledge, the first differential private context aware privacy technique and showed that our technique protects outliers.

Acknowledgments. This research was funded by the cluster of excellence on Ultra-high speed Mobile Information and Communication (UMIC) of the DFG (German Research Foundation grant EXC 89).

References

1. Ashbrook, D., Starner, T.: Using GPS to learn significant locations and predict movement across multiple users. UbiComp (2003)
2. Osman, A., Francesco, B., Mirco, N.: Never walk alone: Uncertainty for anonymity in moving objects databases. In: ICDE (2008)
3. Dwork, C.: Differential privacy. In: Bugliesi, M., Preneel, B., Sassone, V., Wegener, I. (eds.) ICALP 2006. LNCS, vol. 4052, pp. 1–12. Springer, Heidelberg (2006)
4. Friedman, A., Schuster, A.: Data mining with differential privacy. In: KDD (2010)
5. Kalnis, P., Ghinita, G., Mouratidis, K., Papadias, D.: Preventing Location-Based Identity Inference in Anonymous Spatial Queries. IEEE Trans. on Knowl. and Data Eng. (2007)
6. Mohamed, F.: Query processing for location services without compromising privacy. In: VLDB (2006)
7. Manolis, T., Nikos, M.: Privacy Preservation in the Publication of Trajectories. In: MDM (2008)
8. Mcsherry, F., Talwar, K.: Mechanism design via differential privacy. In: FOC (2007)
9. Dwork, C., McSherry, F., Nissim, K., Smith, A.: Calibrating noise to sensitivity in private data analysis. In: Halevi, S., Rabin, T. (eds.) TCC 2006. LNCS, vol. 3876, pp. 265–284. Springer, Heidelberg (2006)
10. Mcsherry, F.: Privacy integrated queries. In: SIGMOD (2009)
11. Duckham, M., Kulik, L.: A Formal Model of Obfuscation and Negotiation for Location Privacy. In: Gellersen, H.-W., Want, R., Schmidt, A. (eds.) PERVASIVE 2005. LNCS, vol. 3468, pp. 152–170. Springer, Heidelberg (2005)
12. Ardagna, C.A., Cremonini, M., Damiani, E., De Capitani di Vimercati, S., Samarati, P.: Location Privacy Protection Through Obfuscation-Based Techniques. In: Barker, S., Ahn, G.-J. (eds.) Data and Applications Security 2007. LNCS, vol. 4602, pp. 47–60. Springer, Heidelberg (2007)
13. Hoh, B., Gruteser, M.: Protecting Location Privacy Through Path Confusion. In: SECURECOMM (2005)
14. Yu, Z., Li, Q., Chen, Y., Xie, X.: Understanding Mobility Based on GPS Data. In: UbiComp (2008)

CooS: Coordination Support for Mobile Collaborative Applications

Mario Henrique Cruz Torres, Robrecht Haesevoets, and Tom Holvoet

iMinds-DistriNet, KU Leuven, 3001 Leuven, Belgium
{MarioHenrique.CruzTorres,Robrecht.Haesevoets,
Tom.Holvoet}@cs.kuleuven.be

Abstract. The advent of mobile devices, such as smartphones and tablets, and their integration with cloud computing is turning ubiquitous computing into reality. This ubiquity opens doors to innovative applications, where mobile devices collaborate on behalf of their users. Applications that leverage this new paradigm, however, have yet to reach the market. One of the reasons is due to the inherent complexity of developing such collaborative applications on mobile devices.

In this paper, we present a middleware that enables coordination on mobile devices. Our middleware frees applications from directly managing the interaction between collaboration partners. It also uses contextual information, such as location, to dynamically determine possible collaboration partners. We focus on a particular class of applications in which mobile devices have to collaborate to allocate tasks (e.g., picking up passengers) to physically distributed resources (e.g., taxis). The technical feasibility of our middleware is shown by the implementation of our middleware architecture, a deployment of our middleware on a real cloud environment and operating it with over 800 clients.

1 Introduction

Every day, developers create dozens of new applications for smartphones and other mobile devices. Two important trends are making mobile devices the platform of the future. First, they provide a hardware platform, filled with technology, that is getting cheaper everyday. Modern devices come with communication technologies, like Bluetooth, GPRS, EDGE, and WiFi, and an abundance of sensors, such as accelerometers, compasses, altimeters, and GPS (Global Positioning System). Second, with the advent of cloud computing, it is possible to create applications that scale to serve hundreds of thousands of clients, while providing minimum delays, needed for near real-time mobile collaborative applications. In fact, cloud computing is changing the way computing is offered. Computing power has become a utility that applications can consume at will, facilitating the deployment of large scale mobile collaborative applications. Ubiquitous computing [17] is finally reality due to the advent of mobile devices and cloud computing, opening doors to innovative applications.

One particularly promising type of applications, are applications where mobile devices closely collaborate, on behalf of their users. These applications include crowd sourcing internet connections [9], collaborative traffic routing [1], collaborative scheduling of resources (e.g., cars) [7, 11], search and rescue systems [8], or allocating

K. Zheng, M. Li, and H. Jiang (Eds.): MOBIQUITOUS 2012, LNICST 120, pp. 152–163, 2013.

taxis to passengers in a dial-a-ride problem [6]. In the resource sharing problem, users can use the location information from their mobile devices to collaborate with other users in their vicinity, to organize on-the-spot car pools, for instance. Another very useful application is for improving public transportation with the use of autonomous vehicles, that could collaborate to find the best way to pick passengers [11].

Despite today's pervasiveness of mobile devices and the challenging problems that could be addressed using collaborations, applications that truly leverage the power of collaboration on mobile devices are still missing. One of the main reasons for this lack of applications is due to the inherent complexity of developing such applications. Mobile collaboration may also require users coordination. Existing coordination mechanisms, such as ContractNet [15], or MASCOT [12], require specific interaction flows involving large amounts of messages between coordination partners. Ensuring the correct implementation and execution of such mechanisms can be time consuming and error prone. Another problem is that collaboration partners are often not known in advance, but have to be determined dynamically, for example, based on their location. In addition, all these problems take place in a very dynamic environment, where everybody is moving, and where disconnections and changes in commitment are widespread.

To stimulate the future development of mobile collaborative applications, we need good middleware support that relieves developers of such complexities. In this paper, we present CooS[1], a middleware that operates providing common-middleware services [14] that enable the creation of decentralized collaboration of mobile devices. CooS targets a particular class of applications in which mobile devices have to collaborate to allocate tasks (e.g., picking up passengers), to physically distributed resources (e.g., taxis, autonomous cars). CooS addresses three key challenges:

1. dynamically determining collaboration partners (e.g., based on their location),
2. achieving scalable collaborations,
3. managing the interactions between collaboration partners.

The main contribution of this paper is a middleware to enable the creation of large-scale mobile collaborative applications. The novelty of our approach is to integrate location-based participant selection with coordination mechanisms, and offering this functionality as a reusable middleware service. The middleware service is designed to be deployed on any cloud computing provider.

Overview. The remainder of this paper is organized as follows: Section 2 describes the challenges faced to create mobile collaborative applications. Section 3 details the design goals and Section 4 the architecture of our middleware. We describe experiments of an application developed on top of CooS, and analyze their results, at Section 5. Section 6 discusses related work. Finally, in Section 7 we present our conclusions.

2   Problem Statement

Our goal is to provide a middleware that supports the development of collaborative applications on mobile devices. Such applications typically require coordination of mobile devices to set up and execute the required collaborations. To illustrate the type

---

[1] CooS: Coordination on Clouds.

of applications we want to address, we focus on the dial-a-ride problem for taxis. In this problem mobile devices have to collaborate to allocate tasks (i.e., picking up and dropping off passengers), to physically distributed resources (i.e., taxis).

The dial-a-ride problem has been extensively studied due to its applicability in various domains. The problem is computationally demanding, even for small scale instances [10], and can involve various stakeholders with opposing goals. In the taxi problem, for example, taxi companies want to maximize their profit, typically at the expense of competing companies, and are even willing to compromise their quality of service (e.g., picking up a passenger on time). Passengers, however, want to be picked on time and reach their destination as soon as possible. The goal of the dial-a-ride problem is to pick up passengers in time, while maximizing the profit of all taxi companies.

Resources have a physical location and are mobile. Tasks are also location-based. Resources can commit to tasks (e.g., a taxi agreeing to pick up a passenger), de-commit to tasks (e.g., a taxi taking an alternate route), and can break down (e.g., a taxi breaking down). The number of involved resources and tasks can vary dynamically and scale up to thousands, for large collaborations.

In the rest of this section, we elaborate some key challenges in building mobile collaborative applications.

2.1 Key Challenges

Dynamically Determining Collaboration Partners Based on Location. Classic coordination mechanisms, such as ContractNet or auctions, do not take location into account when determining possible collaboration partners. In our taxi problem, this would result in mobile devices of passengers interacting with the devices of all taxis in the system to find a possible resource. This leads to our first challenge.

> **Challenge 1.** A device should only collaborate with those devices whose location fits within the solution space of the underlying problem.

In our taxi problem, the mobile device of a passenger should only collaborate with the devices of taxis that are within a feasible range to pick up the passenger. Since both taxis and passengers are mobile, collaboration partners can change dynamically.

Scalable Collaboration. Each mobile device, active in the system, will have a communication overhead. This overhead can be related to the actual collaborations a device is involved in, but also to the process of finding the right collaboration partners. While a device may only have to collaborate with a few dozen of other devices, there can be thousands of devices that are all potential collaboration partners. Finding the relevant collaboration partners may induce a communication overhead that is disproportionate to the overhead induced by the actual collaboration. This defines our second challenge.

> **Challenge 2.** The communication overhead of a device in the system, related to finding relevant collaboration partners, should be independent of the total number of devices in the system.

The communication overhead of each device in the system is only dependent on the number of devices it directly collaborates with.

Managing the Interactions between Collaboration Parters. Coordination mechanisms tend to get complex, requiring asynchronous interactions with complex message flows. Current technologies, such as GCMA (Google Cloud Messaging for Android) [2], only provide a basic messaging mechanism for the interaction of cloud services and mobile devices. Managing these interactions can be time consuming and error-prone. Reuse existing coordination mechanisms could greatly improve these problems. Achieving such reuse, however, requires a clean separation between application logic and coordination logic, which poses an even bigger problem. This leads to our final challenge.

> **Challenge 3.** Coordination mechanisms and their required interactions should be easy to manage, allowing developers to separate application logic from coordination logic, while promoting reuse of existing coordination mechanisms.

2.2 Requirements for the CooS Middleware

Given the challenges for developing mobile collaborative applications, we can derive a set of functional and non-functional requirements for the CooS middleware. There are two main functional requirements for the CooS middleware:

1. **Dynamic Partner Selection.** The middleware dynamically selects the relevant collaboration partners based on their location.
2. **Managing Interactions between Collaboration Partners.** The middleware enforces the coordination mechanisms, chosen by the application developer, ensuring the required interactions take place without violating message flows or timing constraints.

We can also derive two non-functional requirements for the CooS middleware:

1. **Scalable Partner Selection.** The middleware ensures that communication overhead, of each device, related to participant selection is independent of the number of devices in the system.
2. **Encapsulation of Coordination Mechanisms.** The middleware encapsulates the coordination mechanisms and related interactions as reusable middleware services. The middleware provides an API to application developers that allows to separate application logic from coordination logic.

3 Design of the CooS Middleware

Before explaining the CooS Middleware architecture in detail, we provide a high-level overview of its design and motivate the most important design decisions.

---

[2] http://developer.android.com/guide/google/gcm/

Providing Coordination Mechanisms as a Reusable Middleware Service. A key requirement of the CooS middleware is to manage the interactions between collaboration participants, relieving application developers from the related complexities. To do so, the middleware provides a set of predefined coordination mechanisms as reusable middleware services. Applications can then choose the proper coordination mechanisms according to their needs.

Using an Event-Driven Architecture to Enforce Coordination Mechanisms. To provide the coordination mechanisms, the middleware needs to enforce the required interactions between the collaboration partners. To do so, the CooS middleware relies on an event-driven architecture. Each coordination mechanism is defined as a set of interaction events (i.e., sending and receiving messages) that have to take place in a specific order and within particular timing constraints.

The event-driven architecture is particularly suited to handle the continuous internet connections and disconnections of mobile devices. It also allows to create a thin middleware layer to be deployed on mobile devices, which are typically computational constrained.

Using Location-Based Publish/Subscribe to Select Partners. Another key requirement of the CooS middleware is to dynamically select coordination partners based on their location. This avoids interaction with irrelevant participants, such as taxis in other cities. To achieve this dynamic partner selection, the CooS middleware employs a location-based Publish/Subscribe mechanism [2]. The location-based Pub/Sub system allows to subscribe to events, based on the location or region in which an event occurs. Every time a new event is created in a location, the subscribers to that location or region receive a notification. Publishers of events attach location information to their events, so this information can be used to match interested subscribers.

Using the location-based Pub/Sub system, the middleware notifies the relevant applications whenever a new collaboration is triggered within their regions of interest. To do so, the CooS middleware maintains the location of each mobile device active in the system.

Offloading Coordination-Specific Functionality to Mobile Devices. Providing coordination mechanisms and dynamically selecting coordination partners requires functionality such as determining the location of mobile devices, or calculating the shortest path from a passenger to a taxi. The CooS middleware relies on the capabilities of modern devices to offload these tasks to the devices themselves. The CooS middleware uses the GPS of the device, for example, to determine the location of taxis or passengers, and the locally available routing software to calculate possible paths.

Using a Cloud-Based Infrastructure. While mobile-devices can be used to offload some of the coordination-specific functionality, the actual enforcement of coordination mechanisms and selection of collaboration partners can put a heavy burden on the mobile devices, if done locally. To relieve the mobile devices, the CooS middleware relies on a cloud-based infrastructure to enforce the coordination mechanisms and to determine the possible collaboration participants.

The cloud-based infrastructure also provides a more uniform communication channel. Many times, mobile devices cannot communicate directly with each other, because they are situated behind proxies or firewalls. The cloud, however, is able to provide a uniform messaging layer to all mobile devices.

To provide additional scalability to applications, middleware services deployed on the cloud can easily be replicated to more computers. This allows to scale applications to match the current number of users.

4   CooS Architecture

The runtime architecture of the CooS middleware consists of two main components: the CooS Client Component, deployed on each mobile device, and the CooS Middleware Component, deployed on a cloud provider.

The CooS Middleware Component has two main responsibilities: (1) dynamically selecting relevant collaboration partners based on their location, and (2) enforcing a particular coordination mechanism, chosen by the application developer, among the selected partners.

The CooS Client Component serves as a mediator between the CooS Middleware Component and the application. It provides an API that allows the application use the coordination mechanisms provided by the CooS Middleware Component. A user has two possible ways of collaborating with other users, as an initiator, triggering a collaboration, or as a participant, waiting for collaboration requests, the CooS Client Component allows applications to play two possible roles: the initiator role or the participant role. In the taxi application, for example, the application plays the initiator role at the passenger's device, and the participant role at the taxi driver's device.

We illustrate the middleware architecture with ContractNet as coordination mechanism (Sect. 4.3), and briefly discuss the implementation of the CooS middleware architecture (Sect. 4.4).

4.1   CooS Middleware Component

The CooS Middleware Component uses an event-driven architecture to enforce its coordination mechanisms, and relies on a location-based Publish/Subscribe mechanism [2] to dynamically select the collaboration participants. The internal architecture of the CooS Middleware Component consists of four components: a Coordination Component a Location-Based Publish/Subscribe Component, a Location Store, and an Event Dispatcher (Fig. 1).

The Coordination Component is responsible for enforcing the selected coordination mechanisms among the active participants. This includes making sure that interaction events (i.e., sending or receiving message) take place in the right order without violating any timing constraints. The Coordination Component is also responsible for maintaining the state the ongoing coordinations. Coordination mechanisms can define constraints based on location information. The Coordination Component is a publisher and a subscriber of events from the Location-Based Publish/Subscribe Component.

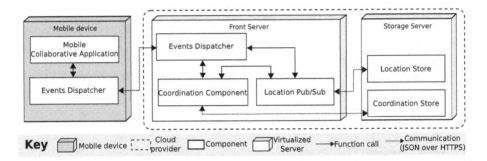

Fig. 1. Deployment view of CooS middleware on a cloud provider

The Location-Based Publish/Subscribe Component provides the functionality for location-based participant selection. Active devices publish their location information using the CooS Client Component. The location information is processed by the Location-Based Publish/Subscribe Component and persisted on secondary storage.

The Event Dispatcher is responsible for receiving events and dispatching events from and to the CooS Client Components. The Event Dispatcher relies on a unique *DeviceID* to identify each CooS Client Component, allowing to have asynchronous interactions between CooS Client Component and CooS Middleware Component. Interaction between the Event Dispatcher and the CooS Client Components is based on stateless protocols, such as HTTP.

4.2   CooS Client Component

The CooS Client Component acts as a mediator between the CooS Middleware Component and the application. It provides an asynchronous API to applications to use the coordination mechanisms provided by the CooS Middleware Component. The main API operations are illustrated below:

```
requestCollaboration(DeviceID device,
  Coordinates location,
  Payload payload,
  InitiatorCallback cb)

registerAsParticipant(LocationCallback lcb,
  ParticipantCallback pcb)
```

To start a collaboration the application uses the *requestCollaboration* operation of the CooS Client Component. The CooS Client Component, in turn, creates an event including the *DeviceID*, the location of the device, and an application-specific payload. The CooS Client Component then dispatches this event to the CooS Middleware Component. When invoking the *requestCollaboration*, the application needs to pass an *InitiatorCallback*. This callback is specific to the coordination mechanism, and provides the actual functionality of the application to be the initiator of the coordination. For example, when using the ContractNet coordination mechanism, the callback should provide the functionality to inform the application with the outcome of the ContractNet protocol. The *Payload* is application specific data not inspected by the middleware. The middleware only passes this data back to the application.

To participate in collaborations, applications have to register two callbacks, using the *registerAsParticipant* operation of the CooS Client Component. The first callback is the *LocationCallback*. This callback is responsible for providing the middleware with the proper location information, required by the location-based participant selection of the CooS Middleware Component. The second callback is the *ParticipantCallback*. Like the *InitiatorCallback*, this callback is specific to the coordination mechanism, and provides the actual functionality of the application to be a participant in the coordination.

4.3   Illustration of the CooS Middleware Architecture

To illustrate the CooS middleware architecture, we show how applications can register as participant and how applications can request collaborations. To register as participant, applications call the *registerAsParticipant* operation on the CooS Client Component (Fig. 2). The local CooS Client Component then starts a process that will retrieve the application-specific location on regular intervals from the application, and send location updates to the CooS Middleware Component. The CooS Middleware Component stores these locations in its location store. Once registered as a participant, the CooS middleware will take these applications into account when selecting the relevant collaboration partners for each new collaboration.

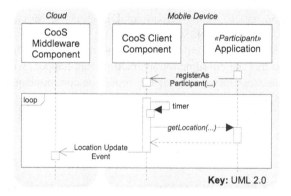

Fig. 2. A sequence diagram showing how the CooS middleware maintains the location of each potential collaboration participant

When an application starts a collaboration, it calls the *requestCollaboration* operation on the CooS Client Component (Fig. 3). The CooS Client Component sends this request to the CooS Middleware Component, which selects the relevant participants, among the registered applications, based on their stored location. The CooS Client Component of each selected participant is then informed about the collaboration request. These CooS Client Components will then start a coordination-specific interaction with their local application (in Fig. 3, this interaction is shown as generic *collaborationCalls* and *Coordination Events*). All interaction events between participants pass through the CooS Middleware Component, which uses the context of active coordination sessions to act as an interaction hub.

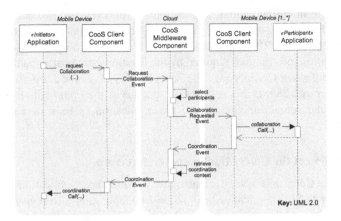

Fig. 3. A sequence diagram showing how an application can initiate a collaboration

4.4   Implementation

The CooS prototype uses off-the-shelf technologies. The CooS Middleware Component uses Node.js[3], a high-performance event-driven application server for networked
applications. The CooS Middleware Component maintains location and on-going coordination information, which is stored on a mongoDB[4] database. MongoDB is a scalable,
high-performance, open-source NoSQL database.

The CooS Client Component and CooS Middleware Component have bi-directional
communication, so that the coordination interactions can happen, with the cloud notifying the mobile devices and vice-versa. The prototype communication is made using
the WebSockets [3] protocol.

5   Evaluation

5.1   Case Study: Using Smartphones for Coordinating Taxis in Brussels

We performed a case study in order to evaluate the technical implications of using our
middleware in a more realistic setting. We implemented a coordination application to
coordinate all the taxis in Brussels on their task of picking passenger and delivering
them at the requested locations.

Our goal with this case study was to check the technical feasibility of using our
middleware for such problem. Coordinating taxis consists in allocating the taxi that can
pick a passenger in the shortest time, that way minimizing the passenger waiting time.
Passengers have the application installed on their mobile phones. When a passenger
wants a ride, he simply indicates when he will need a taxi and where he wants to go. This
information, together with the location information given by the GPS of the passenger's
mobile device, is sent to all taxis that are interested in picking passenger and delivering
them in a particular region.

---

[3] http://nodejs.org/
[4] http://www.mongodb.org/

5.2   Evaluation System Model

We have implemented a prototype version of our middleware, and deployed the **EventSignaling** part of our middleware on the Heroku[5] cloud provider.

We setup 80 computers to participate in the emulation, executing the taxi application. Every computer having 10 instances of the taxi application running as independent processes. Besides the taxi applications, we also setup 8 computers to simulate the passengers. Every computer executing 10 instances of the **PassengerApp**.

Hence, in our emulation we executed 880 instances of an application using our middleware. Each instance had a very simple simulator, responsible for issuing commands to the application. The commands consisted in simulating a taxi driver driving a taxi following a particular route and in passengers asking rides on their mobile phones.

We developed two simple components to simulate the behavior of a passenger and a taxi driver using our application. The simulators have the following behavior:

- **Passenger Simulator**, reads a location from the destinations list and asks a new ride to the *PassengerApp*. When the *PassengerApp* indicates the ride is done, the *Passenger Simulator* requests a new ride. Otherwise, if the *PassengerApp* indicates there is no taxi available, the *Passenger Simulator* chooses the following location from the destinations list and issues a new ride.
- **Driver Simulator**, simulates a taxi moving into the location of a passenger. It does this by virtually following a route given by the *TaxiApp*.

On a real world deployment of our application it would be possible to configure the location updates issued by the middleware to one update every few seconds, or more. However in our emulation we configured the middleware to issue a location update every 100 ms. What in our experiments lead to 8800 requests per second without any delay due to the number of requests. The application showed delays when handling more than 14.000 requests per second. The operation of the middleware at the client side is negligible, while the operations at the CooS Middleware Componentheavily relies on the performance of the cloud provider. The main shortcoming can be the response time due to the internet connection of the mobile devices.

Regarding the implementation of the taxi application, we learned that using the GPS (Global Positioning System) of mobile devices has to be done carefully in order to avoid draining the device's battery. Another lesson we learned from implementing the taxi client application is that delegating the communication complexity to the CooS middleware facilitated the application development, however it was still complex to manage all the callback functions needed by CooS.

6   Related Work

Our middleware does not deal with low level communication issues, instead it facilitates to coordinate the task allocation between several entities participating in an application. [14] proposes a layered view to position the different types of middleware

---

[5] http://www.heroku.com

available. Our work fits into the **Common Middleware Services** layer, since our middleware provides a higher-level domain-independent component that allows application developers to concentrate on programming application logic, rather than focusing on low level hurdles specific to the coordination protocol in use.

The work [5] adds quality-of-service guarantees to middleware which works upon the elastic resources from cloud computing. It shows a technique to guarantee a specified quality-of-service even on a changing cloud environment. In our evaluation we linearly increased the available cloud resources used by our middleware, in order to guarantee that all messages were properly delivered. Our middleware could integrate the results from [5] and become apt to work on more dynamic environments with sudden changes in usage.

There are several works exploiting middleware as a way mitigate different challenges associated with the application development for mobile devices [4], [13], [16], to cite a few.

The work [13] provides a number of abstractions to deal with mobile applications. The main goal of that work is to encapsulate the protocol behavior on well defined abstractions and to facilitate group formation of entities whom want to collaborate on a certain protocol. Our work does not deal with group formation, since we assume that service requests are sent to any device subscribed to the content of the service request. Our work focuses on facilitating the allocation of tasks between a number of mobile devices.

The development of mobile applications that leverage the cloud infrastructure is explored in [4]. [4] proposes a middleware capable of relocating specific parts of a application to be executed on the cloud, based on the quality criteria defined by the application developers. Our work also leverages from cloud computing, but we do not focus on optimizing the application execution. We focus on allowing the creation of collaborative applications on the mobile devices, leveraging the cloud as an infrastructure to interconnect the mobile devices.

7   Conclusion

In this paper, we presented CooS, a middleware that enables the creation of collaborative applications on mobile devices. CooS targets applications in which mobile devices have to collaborate to allocate tasks (e.g., picking-up passengers) to distributed physical resources (e.g., taxis). CooS addresses several key challenges for developing mobile collaborative applications. These challenges include dynamically determining collaboration partners, achieving scalable collaboration, and managing the interactions between collaboration partners.

We presented a middleware architecture for CooS that encapsulates coordination mechanism as a reusable middleware service for applications. This encapsulation provides a clear separation of concerns, freeing application developers from handling coordination-specific complexities. The evaluation of CooS showed the technical feasibility and scalability of the presented middleware architecture. As future work, we plan to perform an empirical study, with real software developers, to assess how CooS impacts the development of mobile collaborative applications.

Acknowledgments. This research is partially funded by the Interuniversity Attraction Poles Programme Belgian State, Belgian Science Policy, and by the Research Fund KU Leuven.

References

1. Bazzan, A.: A distributed approach for coordination of traffic signal agents. Autonomous Agents and Multi-Agent Systems 10(1), 131–164 (2005)
2. Eugster, P.T., Garbinato, B., Holzer, A.: Location-based publish/subscribe. In: Proceedings of the Fourth IEEE International Symposium on Network Computing and Applications, NCA 2005, pp. 279–282. IEEE Computer Society, Washington, DC (2005)
3. Fette, I., Melnikov, A.: The WebSocket Protocol. RFC 6455 (Proposed Standard) (December 2011), http://www.ietf.org/rfc/rfc6455.txt
4. Giurgiu, I., Riva, O., Juric, D., Krivulev, I., Alonso, G.: Calling the cloud: Enabling mobile phones as interfaces to cloud applications. In: Bacon, J.M., Cooper, B.F. (eds.) Middleware 2009. LNCS, vol. 5896, pp. 83–102. Springer, Heidelberg (2009)
5. Hoffert, J., Schmidt, D.C., Gokhale, A.: Adapting distributed real-time and embedded pub-/sub middleware for cloud computing environments. In: Gupta, I., Mascolo, C. (eds.) Middleware 2010. LNCS, vol. 6452, pp. 21–41. Springer, Heidelberg (2010)
6. Koźlak, J., Créput, J.C., Hilaire, V., Koukam, A.: Multi-agent approach to dynamic pick-up and delivery problem with uncertain knowledge about future transport demands. Fundam. Inf. 71(1), 27–36 (2006)
7. Kutanoglu, E., Wu, S.: On combinatorial auction and lagrangean relaxation for distributed resource scheduling. IIE Transactions 31(9), 813–826 (1999)
8. Luqman, F., Griss, M.: Overseer: a mobile context-aware collaboration and task management system for disaster response. In: Eighth International Conference on Creating, Connecting and Collaborating through Computing, UC San Diego, La Jolla CA, United States (2010) (2010)
9. Papadopouli, M., Schulzrinne, H.: Connection sharing in an ad hoc wireless network among collaborating hosts. In: Proc. International Workshop on Network and Operating System Support for Digital Audio and Video (NOSSDAV), pp. 169–185 (1999)
10. Parragh, S.N., Doerner, K.F., Hartl, R.F.: Variable neighborhood search for the dial-a-ride problem. Computers & Operations Research 37(6), 1129–1138 (2010)
11. Rocha, R., Cunha, A., Varandas, J., Dias, J.: Towards a new mobility concept for cities: architecture and programming of semi-autonomous electric vehicles. Industrial Robot: An International Journal 34(2), 142–149 (2007)
12. Sadeh, N., Hildum, D., Kjenstad, D., Tseng, A.: Mascot: an agent-based architecture for dynamic supply chain creation and coordination in the internet economy. Production Planning & Control 12(3), 212–223 (2001)
13. Schelfthout, K., Weyns, D., Holvoet, T.: Middleware for protocol-based coordination in mobile applications. IEEE Distributed Systems Online 7(8), 1–18 (2006)
14. Schmidt, D.C.: Middleware for real-timeand embedded systems. Communications of the ACM (2002)
15. Specification, F.: http://www.fipa.org/specs/fipa00029.SC00029H.html (2003)
16. Ueyama, J., Pinto, V.P.V., Madeira, E.R.M., Grace, P., Jonhson, T.M.M., Camargo, R.Y.: Exploiting a generic approach for constructing mobile device applications. In: COMSWARE 2009, pp. 12:1–12:12. ACM, New York (2009)
17. Weiser, M.: Some computer science issues in ubiquitous computing. Communications of the ACM 36(7), 75–84 (1993)

Spitty Bifs are Spiffy Bits: Interest-Based Context Dissemination Using Spatiotemporal Bloom Filters*

Evan Grim and Christine Julien

Mobile and Pervasive Computing Lab
The University of Texas at Austin
{evangrim,c.julien}@mail.utexas.edu
http://mpc.ece.utexas.edu/

Abstract. Acquiring accurate context information is crucial to mobile and pervasive computing, and *sharing* context among nodes enables unique applications. As context information and the applications that consume it become increasingly diverse, they will need an efficient means to indicate tailored interest in this context information. This paper proposes a new probabilistic data structure, spatiotemporal Bloom filters (SpTBF) or "spitty bifs," which allow nodes to efficiently store and share their context interests. SpTBF provide both spatiotemporal locality and a fine-grained ability to control how context interests are disseminated. SpTBF are evaluated by modifying the Grapevine context sharing framework to inform its context dissemination capabilities, and the benefits are characterized in a variety of network scenarios.

Keywords: context awareness, publish/subscribe, mobile computing, bloom filters.

1 Introduction

Mobile and pervasive computing applications are strongly influenced by their environments, and this has driven research to seek effective and efficient means for sensing, characterizing, and acting upon this valuable context information. Many approaches focus on purely egocentric notions of context, which limit the information a node can directly collect or otherwise infer about its surroundings. Mechanisms that allow nodes to efficiently *share* context information with nearby nodes enhance local notions of context, enabling applications to better react to their environments and allowing applications to leverage the shared context of groups to stretch beyond solely egocentric approaches. For example, a group of nodes that can individually only sense the direction in which an object of interest lies can triangulate that information into a shared notion of *where* the object is.

* This work was funded in part by the National Science Foundation (NSF), Grant #CNS-0844850 and Grant #OCI-0753360. The views and conclusions herein are those of the authors and do not necessarily reflect the views of the sponsoring agencies.

K. Zheng, M. Li, and H. Jiang (Eds.): MOBIQUITOUS 2012, LNICST 120, pp. 164–175, 2013.

Simple context dissemination approaches work well in networks where every node is interested in the same context information throughout the system's lifetime. Efficiently sharing context becomes challenging when interests are less static, and scenarios with more diverse and dynamic context needs abound. Many smart phones run applications that have widely varying interests in available context information. Even within a single application context needs may change over time. For example, a vehicular application providing localized traffic and safety information may find information from cars beside or near the interstate of no interest to vehicles speeding by. Furthermore, individual users may have differing interests. For instance, an application facilitating social interaction among park patrons need not enumerate all the capabilities of a multi-sport athlete if all nearby patrons are interested in quieter games like chess.

Efforts that ignore these dynamics and heterogeneities will either share too much context information, resulting in wasted network resources, or share too little information, missing opportunities for providing valuable context. These scenarios suffer when distribution relies on the *producer* of context information to know what information is desired by nearby nodes, when it is the *consumers* who are best suited to provide this information. What is needed is a lightweight means for nodes to communicate consumers' context *interests* to nearby producers.

This paper's novel contribution is a means for applications to efficiently maintain an awareness of what context information is of interest to other nearby nodes and a demonstration that this awareness improves the use of network resources significantly. We introduce a Bloom filter variant, spatiotemporal Bloom filters (SpTBF or "spitty bifs" for short), that allow a node to efficiently communicate, acquire, and maintain information about others' context interests within the node's spatiotemporal region of a mobile network. Our approach is rooted in the *publish/subscribe* paradigm, which has demonstrated efficiency improvement in the heterogeneous and dynamic network systems we target. The SpTBF approach can represent generic types of context and provides consumers the flexibility to control the scope in space and time within which their individual interest is distributed. In this paper, we introduce the SpTBF data structure, demonstrate it in practice by applying it to the Grapevine context dissemination framework [9], and evaluate its performance.

2   Related Work

Our task is to track context interests within a spatiotemporal region; our approach is informed by the domain of publish/subscribe (pubsub) mechanisms. We survey these predecessors, first examining more generic approaches that build an overlay to aid in the distribution and matching of publications and subscriptions. We then focus on approaches that leverage spatial and/or temporal properties for distribution, and discuss how they do not sufficiently address our challenges.

Many approaches provide pubsub capabilities by constructing overlay routing structures that hierarchically organize the network. The content based approach of [11] eschews address based routing entirely, opting instead to route only based on content and leveraging Bloom filters to compress the routing information required to inform forwarding decisions. Other efforts maintain traditional addressing but cluster nodes in tree structures based on shared interests [2,10,12,18]. These approaches provide interest-based distribution but require a relatively high communication burden to maintain the overlay, especially in dynamic networks. We strive to reduce this burden by recognizing that many applications involve context information that is most useful to nodes that are *here* and interested *now* and thus are served best by pubsub mechanisms that use inherent spatial and temporal locality to quickly and efficiently identify interested consumers.

Other efforts have investigated pubsub informed by spatial and temporal properties. TACO-DTN [19], B-SUB [21], and ZigZag [22] subscribe to information using specified timing conditions, while [6] enriches subscriptions with location. These approaches provide improved efficiency through more granular subscription specifications that prevent unnecessary use of network resources. Other work leverages location to guide information to "bazaars" [17] or provide informed guesses as to where in the network information is most likely to be useful [5,6,14,15,16]. Many of these lessons are synthesized in the abstract context pubsub model in [8], which provides an expressive and generic system for spatially and temporally guided subscriptions. Our work diverges from these approaches by leveraging the fact that interest in context information will often be concentrated near where that information is generated. This allows us to simplify the distribution of interest information by enabling nodes to indicate interests that automatically decay over distance and time, i.e., a subscription is concentrated in space and time around its originator.

As in other approaches [10,11], SpTBF leverage the efficiencies made possible by probabilistic data structures. We introduce a variant of the Bloom filter [3], which has enjoyed recent popularity in network-centric applications due to its ability to encode large amounts of information within very small space requirements [4]. The original Bloom filter allows set membership to be encoded in an array of m bits using k hash functions to transform a potential set member into addresses within the bit array. To insert an element, each of the k addressed locations in the array is set to 1. Querying whether or not a value is in the set involves hashing the value using the same k functions and checking to see if all the bits addressed by the hash values are set. If any of the bits are 0, then it is certain that the value was never added to the set. If all the bits are 1, then the item is *probably* in the set. Applications use this functionality to solve varying problems (e.g., quick cached value checks [4], privacy-preserving algorithms [13]).

One downside to Bloom filters is that there is no way to reliably remove an element from the set. The Counting Bloom Filter (CBF) [7] replaces the array of bits with an array of counters. Instead of setting a bit to 1 upon insertion, a CBF increments the k associated counters; removal decrements the counters. The ability to remove comes at the cost of additional space requirements and introduces the possibility of a false negative (there is a small chance the associated counters may all have been decremented by unrelated remove operations [4]).

B-SUB proposes a further extension, the Temporal Counting Bloom Filter (TCBF) [21,22], which modifies the semantics of the counters in CBF so that entries are set to a time value representing the length of time the entry should remain in the structure. As time passes, maintenance operations decrement all counter values by the amount of time elapsed[1]. When any of the k counter values for an entry reaches 0, the entry is no longer in the set. This allows entries to automatically expire after a given amount of time and thus provides a subscription mechanism with a temporal component; however, the TCBF has no notion of spatial proximity.

3   SpittyBifs

This paper proposes a Bloom filter variant that provides the spatial component. We call this variant a *spatiotemporal bloom filter* (SpTBF), or "spitty bif" for short. It uses a construction similar to that found in TCBF involving k hash functions (h_i from $1 \leq i \leq k$) but replaces the array of timer values with an array a of m 2-tuples, each containing a hop limiter and a timer. Fig. 1 shows an example of a small SpTBF populated with values. The hop limiter is decremented each time the structure is passed from one node to another[2]. Timer values are all relative to a specific point in time, so each SpTBF also includes a timebase t_b that records this time value, allowing operations to decay values relative to the current time (as in TCBF). Entries are automatically removed from a SpTBF when any of the tuple value components reaches zero, indicating that *either* the structure has traveled a specified number of hops from its origin *or* a given amount of time has elapsed.

hops	time
4	6
0	0
1	21
0	0
1	21
0	0
4	6
4	21

timebase = 42

Fig. 1. SpTBF

Operations

A SpTBF supports the typical Bloom filter operations, allowing *insert*, *query*, and *merge* [3]. Two housekeeping operations are also required (*decrementHops* and *adjustTime*); these decay the tuple components in space and time.

Table 1. Operation signatures

$insert\,(label, hopLimit, timeLimit, currentTime)$
$query\,(label, currentTime)$
$merge\,(currentTime)$
$decrementHops\,()$
$adjustTime\,(currentTime)$

These operations are similar to those found in TCBF, however the use of a tuple requires a slightly different approach than that employed when the underlying array holds a single value.

---

[1] This restores the perfect false negative properties lost in CBF, since counter values are all decremented simultaneously.

[2] For simplicity we use "hops" (number of node traversals) as a spatial metric. Future work could add additional tuple entries to encode more precise notions of location.

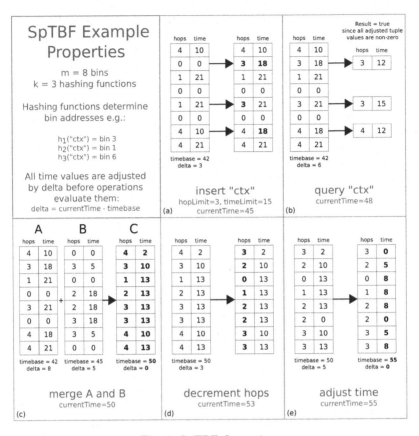

Fig. 2. SpTBF Operations

Insertion. To insert an item with label l, we use the k hash functions that each map l into one of the m addresses in the SpTBF's array a of tuples. The spatial and temporal components from each tuple are compared with l's specified limits, and the maximum of each forms the new tuple, which is returned to the same location in the array. This results in the following operation:

$$\forall i \in \{1, \ldots, k\} \left\{ \begin{array}{l} a\left[h_i\left(l\right)\right].hop = max\left(a\left[h_i\left(l\right)\right].hop, hopLimit\right) \\ a\left[h_i\left(l\right)\right].time = max\left(a\left[h_i\left(l\right)\right].time, timeLimit + \delta\right) \end{array} \right\}$$

The $timeLimit$ is adjusted by δ, the difference between the current time and the timebase used for all the temporal components in the SpTBF. Fig. 2(a) shows an example, where the starting SpTBF is shown on the left (which already contains context interest elements). The label "ctx" is inserted with a $hopLimit$ of 3, and a $timeLimit$ of 5, resulting in the updated SpTBF on the right.

Query. Querying whether an item with label l exists in a SpTBF again uses the k hash functions to retrieve k tuples from the array a. Iterating through these tuples, both the spatial and temporal components are checked. If either component from any of the tuples is zero, l is not in the set—either it was never inserted in the set or at least one of its components has decayed to zero. If all the tuples' components have non-zero values, then the item is likely to be in the set, and the query result is true. This operation can be expressed as:

$$\begin{cases} true & \text{if for } \forall i \in \{1, \ldots k\} \; a\,[h_i\,(l)]\,.hop \neq 0 \land a\,[h_i\,(l)]\,.time - \delta > 0 \\ false & \text{otherwise} \end{cases}$$

Again, the temporal component is adjusted by the difference between the current time and the structure's timebase. Fig. 2(b), shows that the newly inserted item labeled "ctx" will result in an affirmative query because all of the bins chosen by the hashing functions hold non-zero tuple elements.

Merge. Multiple SpTBF can be merged into a single structure by choosing the dominant tuple values from each to create a space efficient representation of the consolidated set memberships. Both structures must have the same underlying array a size of m; merging involves iterating over *all* the tuples in each, comparing their spatial and temporal components and storing the maximum of each in the new array at the same location. Merging A and B to create C is as follows:

$$\forall i \in \{1 \ldots m\} \left\{ \begin{array}{c} a_C\,[i]\,.hop = max\,(a_A\,[i]\,.hop, a_B m\,[i]\,.hop) \\ a_C\,[i]\,.time = max\,(a_A\,[i]\,.time - \delta_A, a_B\,[i]\,.time - \delta_B) \end{array} \right\}$$

$$t_{b_C} = current\,time$$

Each temporal component is adjusted by its timebase's difference from the current time. The temporal components are then relative to the current time, and as such the new SpTBF uses the current time as its own timebase. Fig. 2(c) shows an example. The new structure may end up using the spatial component from one structure and the temporal component from another. For example, imagine a SpTBF entry has existed locally for long enough that its temporal component(s) are on the cusp of expiring, but since the structure has stayed local, its hop count is still strong. If it is merged with a SpTBF with a more recent entry that shares an array slot, but one that has come from several hops away, then the resulting array entry would use the first spatial component and the second temporal component. In these scenarios an entry will persist beyond its originally intended spatiotemporal components if all of its array entries fall prey to this situation. The likelihood of these collisions is determined by the underlying array size m and the number of hashing functions used [4]; applications can control this likelihood by appropriately tuning these parameters.

Housekeeping. Two additional operations support the decay of spatial and temporal components, facilitating automatic removal of elements.

Spatial. Used whenever the SpTBF travels a network hop (i.e., is transmitted from one node to another), spatial decay is accomplished by a simple decrement of all the non-zero spatial components within each of the m tuples in the array a, as seen in Fig. 2(d), and defined in the *decrementHops* operation:

$$\forall i \in \{1 \ldots m\} \ a\,[i]\,.hop = max\,\{a\,[i]\,.hop - 1, 0\}$$

Temporal. Decay in time involves adjusting the temporal tuple component values and the timebase to which they are relative to match the current time. Periodically performing this operation minimizes the amount of space required to represent the temporal tuple component and is also useful when sharing with external entities that may not use the same reference clock (e.g., preparing to transmit a SpTBF over a network connection). This adjustment is accomplished by calculating the difference between each temporal component's timebase-adjusted value and the current time, and then subtracting this value from each temporal entry, as seen in Fig. 2(e). The structure's timebase is set to the current time:

$$\forall i \in \{1 \ldots m\} \ a\,[i]\,.time = max\,\{a\,[i]\,.time - \delta, 0\}$$

$$t_b = current\,time$$

Application

SpTBF allow nodes to maintain an awareness of interest in context information unique to their location in the network; nodes can use this awareness to share only context information known to be of interest to nearby nodes. Tracking this interest requires each node to store a single SpTBF, which is initially empty (all tuple values initialized to zero) and is populated upon encountering other nodes. When such an encounter occurs, a node creates a copy of its SpTBF, *adjusts* its timebase to the current time, *decrements* the spatial components, and then *inserts*

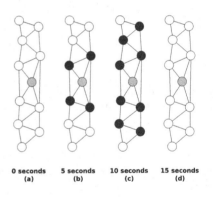

0 seconds   5 seconds   10 seconds   15 seconds
(a)   (b)   (c)   (d)

Fig. 3. Interest Lifecycle

labels for each context item it is interested in receiving before sharing the newly constructed SpTBF with its neighbor. Upon receiving a SpTBF, a node sets the timebase for the received SpTBF to its current timeand *merges* the received SpTBF with its own. The node can then *query* its SpTBF to determine whether nearby nodes are interested in receiving context information it has available. Sharing the context of interest is outside the purview of the SpTBF structure; it can be handled by a variety of existing techniques [9].

Fig. 3 shows an example of a lifecycle of interest awareness for a single context interest. In (a), the center node determines that it will be interested in a given item of context from neighbors up to 2 hops away and for the next 15 seconds. It informs its neighbors of this interest by *inserting* the context item's label into outgoing SpTBF with a spatial component of 2 hops and a temporal component of 15 seconds. Within the next 5 seconds, as seen in (b), the node has shared this interest with its direct neighbors. After another 5 seconds, each of these neighbors has shared their interest awareness with their own neighbors and the central node's interest has propagated to the limit of its spatial component. After another 5 seconds, the temporal component has decayed to zero, and the central node's interest in the context information will expire from each node's SpTBF. The potential *consumer* of context can specify the spatial and temporal lifetimes of each of their interests individually, allowing fine grained control over how wide a net to cast for desired context information on an item-by-item basis.

4   Evaluation

To evaluate the usefulness of SpTBF, we augmented the Grapevine context dissemination framework [9] to use SpTBF to track interest awareness and to improve context information sharing efficiency. Grapevine provides programmers a simple and efficient library for sharing context and collaboratively forming groups based on that shared context. Grapevine shares context by encoding it into space-efficient *context summaries* that are piggybacked onto outgoing traffic. In Grapevine, the onus of determining what context information to share rests on the producers of that information. With a few simple modifications to the existing framework, Grapevine can leverage SpTBF to send an *interest summary* in addition to context summaries. Nodes do not include context information in their context summaries until they know (via a received interest summary) that a nearby node indicated interest in that context label.

The SpTBF interest summaries pack the spatial and temporal tuple components into 1 byte. Each spatial component uses 2 bits, allowing up to 3 hops to be specified, and each temporal component uses 6 bits, allowing just over a minute (64 seconds) to elapse[3]. In total, an interest summary requires one byte per array entry and an additional four bytes for the baseline timestamp.

We evaluated Grapevine with SpTBF interest summaries using OMNet++ [20] and INET-MANET [1] to realistically simulate the communications of mobile *ad hoc* networks. Our goal is to characterize when an interest-enabled context dissemination mechanism outperforms an interest-agnostic approach and gives rise to two important questions: (1) how heterogeneous does context interest need to be to benefit from tracking interest; and (2) how much space should be allocated to the interest summary?

How heterogeneous does context interest need to be to benefit from tracking interest? Interest-based dissemination requires additional bytes to be transmitted; the goal is that this overhead can be reclaimed in savings from context information that does not need to be shared. If all the nodes are interested in all the available context, then the overhead of the interest communication is wasted.

To examine this question, we used 100 interest tracking Grapevine nodes using INET-MANET's IEEE 802.11b network layer and mass mobility profiles to

---

[3] These choices are specific to our particular evaluation and can easily be adapted for different spatial and temporal scopes.

simulate nodes traveling at a natural human walking speed and with realistic mobility. We evaluated their network resource use in a variety of scenarios, varying node density, interest allocation, and the number of hops over which interest and context information were shared to determine the savings that interest tracking provided over Grapevine's previous resource consumption. Each scenario was run for a simulated period of 20 minutes. We collected data using two different arena sizes, one which provided a 5 km by 5 km square area, simulating a sparse node density where nodes would encounter new neighbors relatively infrequently (approximating a neighborhood), and a smaller arena of 1 km by 1 km, simulating a more densely populated area (approximating a popular park).

We allocated interests node in two different ways. In the first, each node randomly selects a percentage of the available context labels for which they indicate interest. In the second, we divide the context labels among a set of applications and assign those applications to nodes in equal proportions. These allocations are evaluated using the sparse and dense configurations and with a handful of hop limits that determine how many hops both interest and context summaries are forwarded. For each scenario, we compare the total number of bytes sent by the nodes; the results are reported as percent savings of the SpTBF approach over the interest-agnostic approach in the same scenario.

Figs. 4 and 5 show that savings can be significant for sparse networks with diverse context interests. The savings are strongest in sparse scenarios with more heterogeneous interest, where each node is interested in only a small portion of available context ($< 30\%$ of the available contexts, as shown in Fig. 4) or when more applications are present (> 3 applications, as shown in Fig. 5). As the network density increases, so does the likelihood that a neighbor is interested in the context a node has to share; it becomes increasingly likely that all context information is shared from every node. As a result, savings are clearly less compelling in denser networks, but there is very little penalty in adding the SpTBF interest summaries (averaging at approximately five percent overhead) making interest dissemination potentially beneficial in networks with varying needs.

How much space should be allocated to the interest summary? The amount of space allocated to the interest summary can be chosen arbitrarily by using different values of m (the number of bins into which the tuples can be placed). However, smaller values of m will result in false positive rates that negate the benefits of interest tracking. To characterize the effects of this choice on false positive rates, we allocated a variety of sizes for the interest summaries and measured how much unnecessary context information was shared due to false positives indicating there was interest when if fact there was not. The results are reported in additional percentage of savings that could have been achieved had these false positives not occurred. Fig. 6 shows the savings missed due to false positives for various percent interest allocations (using the first scheme for interest allocation in which each node is assigned a random set of the available context types). We used a hop limit of three for all interest disseminations[4].

---

[4] Graphs for other configurations are similar and are omitted for brevity.

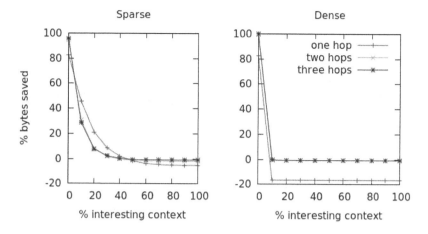

Fig. 4. Percent Allocation

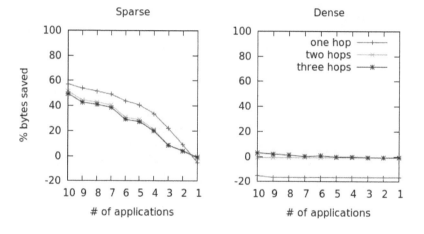

Fig. 5. Application Allocation

Additional space allocated for interest summaries are important in systems with heterogeneous interest, where the extra space provides significant benefit. However, allocating space for bins beyond the number of context items available (100 in this case) is unlikely to provide additional benefit. Furthermore, systems with largely homogeneous interest can safely reduce their allocations without significantly impacting the amount of context sent. This may allow the more heterogeneous parts of context sharing systems to benefit from interest-based context dissemination, while minimizing the negative impacts on more clustered or homogeneous parts of the network.

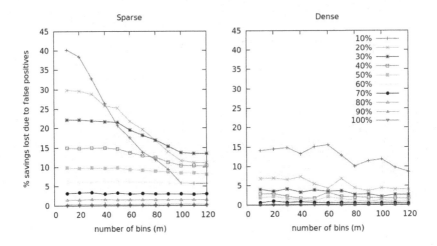

Fig. 6. Lost Savings Due to False Positives

5 Reflection

Sharing context information in mobile and pervasive computing environments is necessary to supporting expressive and flexible application behavior. While many approaches like the Grapevine context dissemination framework support sharing context information, they traditionally accomplish context dissemination while ignoring what interest nearby nodes have in context information. In this paper, we clearly demonstrated that the efficiency of Grapevine's context dissemination can be improved by enabling nodes to share their interests in available context information. Specifically, we explored using a novel probabilistic data structure (the spatiotemporal Bloom filter, SpTBF, or "spitty bif") to provide this interest awareness with a minimum impact on network resources. The SpTBF ensures that context information shared among network nodes is useful.

Reflecting on the results in this paper, we have opened several potential avenues for future work. First, in situations when nodes' overlap in context interest is high (e.g., > 30%), the benefit of the SpTBF data structure is limited. Future work should investigate how and when the benefits of SpTBF can be achieved in these additional situations (e.g., in more diverse network scenarios). As described earlier, incorporating additional definitions of *space* in addition to network hops is also an item of future work.

Longer term, the traditional Bloom filter concept as we apply it in SpTBF is binary—a value is either (probably) in the structure or it is not. The SpTBF structure contains additional semantic information that could, for example, provide information about the *strength* of interest in a particular context label. Not only could this information be used to influence future context information dissemination, but applications might use it in other ways as well, for example influencing node movement (e.g., nodes may move towards where interests lie) or setting up interest *gradients* that can direct context information flows.

The presented SpTBF represents a promising new tool that aids in efficient and expressive sharing of context information that is relevant *locally* in space and time. This has potential to be useful in many application and network scenarios.

References

1. The INET-MANET Framework for OMNeT++
2. Balakrishnan, D., Nayak, A.: CSON-D: Context dissemination in autonomous systems using overlays. In: Proc. of IE (2008)
3. Bloom, B.H.: Space/time trade-offs in hash coding with allowable errors. Comm. of the ACM 13(7), 422–426 (1970)
4. Broder, A., Mitzenmacher, M.: Network Applications of Bloom Filters: A Survey. Internet Mathematics 1(4), 485–509 (2004)
5. Carreras, I., De Pellegrini, F., Miorandi, D., Tacconi, D., Chlamtac, I.: Why neighbourhood matters: interests-driven opportunistic data diffusion schemes. In: Proc. of CHANTS, p. 81 (2008)
6. Eugster, P., Garbinato, B., Holzer, A.: Location-based Publish/Subscribe. In: Proc. of NCA, pp. 279–282 (2005)
7. Fan, L., Cao, P., Almeida, J., Broder, A.Z.: Summary cache: a scalable wide-area Web cache sharing protocol. IEEE/ACM Trans. on Networking 8(3), 281–293 (2000)
8. Frey, D., Roman, G.-C.: Context-Aware Publish Subscribe in Mobile Ad Hoc Networks. In: Murphy, A.L., Vitek, J. (eds.) COORDINATION 2007. LNCS, vol. 4467, pp. 37–55. Springer, Heidelberg (2007)
9. Grim, E., Fok, C.-L., Julien, C.: Grapevine: Efficient situational awareness in pervasive computing environments. In: Proc. of Percom Workshops (2012)
10. Hebden, P., Pearce, A.R.: Data-Centric Routing using Bloom Filters in Wireless Sensor Networks. In: Proc. of ICISIP, pp. 72–77 (December 2006)
11. Jerzak, Z., Fetzer, C.: Bloom filter based routing for content-based publish/subscribe. In: Proc. of DEBS, vol. 71 (2008)
12. Khambatti, M., Ryu, K.D., Dasgupta, P.: Structuring peer-to-peer networks using interest-based communities. In: Aberer, K., Koubarakis, M., Kalogeraki, V. (eds.) DBISP2P 2003. LNCS, vol. 2944, pp. 48–63. Springer, Heidelberg (2004)
13. Korkmaz, T., Sarac, K.: Single packet IP traceback in AS-level partial deployment scenario. In: Proc. of GLOBECOM, p. 5 (2005)
14. Leontiadis, I.: Publish/subscribe notification middleware for vehicular networks. In: Proc. of Middleware Doctoral Symposium, pp. 1–6 (2007)
15. Leontiadis, I., Costa, P., Mascolo, C.: Persistent content-based information dissemination in hybrid vehicular networks. In: Proc. of Percom, pp. 1–10 (2009)
16. Leontiadis, I., Mascolo, C.: Opportunistic spatio-temporal dissemination system for vehicular networks. In: Proc. of MobiOpp, p. 39 (2007)
17. Motani, M., Srinivasan, V., Nuggehalli, P.S.: PeopleNet: engineering a wireless social network. In: Proc. of MobiCom (2005)
18. Patel, J.A., Rivière, É., Gupta, I., Kermarrec, A.-M.: Rappel: Exploiting interest and network locality to improve fairness in publish-subscribe systems. Computer Networks 53(13), 2304–2320 (2009)
19. Sollazzo, G., Musolesi, M., Mascolo, C.: TACO-DTN: a time-aware content-based dissemination system for delay tolerant networks. In: Proc. of MobiOpp (2007)
20. Vargas, A.: OMNeT++ Web Page
21. Zhao, Y., Wu, J.: B-SUB: A Practical Bloom-Filter-Based Publish-Subscribe System for Human Networks. In: Proc. of ICDCS, pp. 634–643 (2010)
22. Zhao, Y., Wu, J.: ZigZag: A Content-Based Publish/Subscribe Architecture for Human Networks. In: Proc. of ICCCN, pp. 1–6 (July 2011)

Trust Evaluation for Participatory Sensing

Atif Manzoor, Mikael Asplund, Mélanie Bouroche, Siobhán Clarke, and Vinny Cahill

School of Computer Science and Statistics, Trinity College Dublin, Ireland
`firstname.lastname@scss.tcd.ie`

Abstract. Participatory sensing, combining the power of crowd and the ubiquitously available smart phones, plays an important role to sense the urban environment and develop many exciting smart city applications to improve the quality of life and enable sustainability. The knowledge of the participatory sensing participants' competence to collect data is vital for any effective urban data collection campaign and the success of these applications. In this paper, we present a methodology to compute the trustworthiness of the participatory sensing participants as the belief on their competence to collect high quality data. In our experiments, we evaluate trust on the sensing participants of BusWatch, a participatory sensing based bus arrival time prediction application. Our results show that our system effectively computes the sensing participants' trustworthiness as the belief on their competence to collect high quality data and detect their dynamically varying sensing behavior.

Keywords: Trust evaluation, participatory sensing, mobile and ubiquitous computing.

1 Introduction

Participatory sensing, a novel sensing technique that enables citizens to use ubiquitously available smart phones and high speed Internet to share data, is enabling many exciting applications for transportation and planning, environmental monitoring, and health-care [1,8]. The performance and the efficacy of these applications is heavily dependent on the quality of data contributed by the sensing participants [3]. However, the data collection may not be the primary task of the sensing participants and they may also have different capabilities to collect data, depending on their context, familiarity with data collection application and task, and demographics [9,12]. Consequently, they may submit low-quality, misleading, or even malicious data that can threaten the usefulness of the applications [6,12]. Available sensing participants contributing high quality data may opt out of a sensing campaign due to a lack of motivation [10]. A trust evaluation system that associates a trust score to sensing participants as the belief on their competence to collect high quality data enables the applications, using participatory sensing to collect data, to dynamically identify and select sensing participants contributing high quality data [2,10]. However,

K. Zheng, M. Li, and H. Jiang (Eds.): MOBIQUITOUS 2012, LNICST 120, pp. 176–187, 2013.
© Institute for Computer Sciences, Social Informatics and Telecommunications Engineering 2013

existing research work lacks a system that evaluates trust on the participatory sensing participants using aforementioned criteria.

In this paper we define and evaluate trust in participatory sensing participants considering their competence to collect high quality data. We use system predictions derived from contributed data and system user feedback about those predictions as input to the trust evaluation system to first estimate the quality of contributed data and later use the data quality score to compute the trustworthiness of sensing participants. Our system bootstraps the trust score of the newly arrived participants, contributing data for the first time and continuously refines the trust score of the existing participants on every new interaction with the application. The trust score presents the evidence of the quality of sensing participants' contribution to the application.

In our experiments, we compute the trust in the sensing participants of BusWatch, an application that uses the bus sighting reports from sensing participants to predict bus arrival times. Our dataset, provided by Dublin Bus, consists of ten days of bus arrival times. We simulate different user behaviors, such as trusted users, malicious users, and users changing their behavior from trusted to malicious and evaluate their trustworthiness. Our results show that the trust evaluation system successfully estimates the data quality of sensing participants' contributions and keeps track of the historical evidence of the trustworthiness of different sensing participants to identify their data contribution behavior pattern to an application. Our paper has the following contributions.

- Definition of trust in participatory sensing participants
- Methodology to evaluate the quality of sensing participants' contributed data
- Novel approach to compute participatory sensing participants' trust score
- Strategy to bootstrap sensing participants trust score
- Methodology to dynamically evolve trust score to depict varying quality of sensing participants' data contributions

The rest of the paper is organized as follows: Section 2 illustrates a motivational scenario. Section 3 discusses our trust evaluation system. Section 4 describes the data set, provided by Dublin Bus that we use in our experiments. Section 5 presents the experiments to evaluate our approach. Section 6 compares existing works and our approach. Section 7 summarizes this work and discusses future directions.

2   Motivational Scenario: BusWatch

Figure 1 shows a participatory sensing based bus arrival time perdition system - *BusWatch*. In this system, the *Data Manager* collects and manages bus sighting reports from *BusWatch* users. The *Bus Time Predictor* uses the bus sighting reports with already trained and tested machine learning algorithms to predict bus arrival time. When a *BusWatch* user makes a bus arrival time query, the *Data Manager* selects and provides bus sighting reports to the *Bus Time Predictor* to predict bus arrival time for that specific user. Before leaving the office

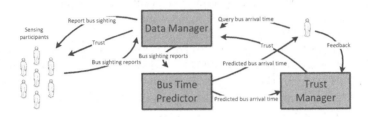

Report bus sighting   Data Manager   Query bus arrival time

Sensing participants

Trust   Feedback

Bus sighting reports   Bus sighting reports   Predicted bus arrival time

Bus Time Predictor   Predicted bus arrival time   Trust Manager

Fig. 1. Participatory sensing based bus arrival time prediction system-BusWatch

this evening Bob uses *BusWatch* to check the bus arrival time on his usual bus stop. The *Data Manager* selects the bus sighting reports and the *Bus Time Predictor* uses these reports to predict the bus arrival time and conveys it to Bob. Bob leaves office in time to catch the bus and reaches the bus stop before the expected bus arrival time. However, he waits for the bus longer than expected, considering the BusWatch prediction. Once he boards the bus, the *Trust Manager* requests Bob's feedback about the *BusWatch* prediction. The *Trust Manager* combines the *BusWatch* prediction with Bob's feedback and correlates it with participants' bus sighting reports to find the quality score of each participants' data contribution and transform quality score to trust on corresponding participants as the belief on their competence to contribute high quality data. The *Trust Manager* keeps record of the scores for future transactions. The *Data Manager* uses participants' trust score to select trustworthy bus sighting reports from available bus sighting reports. Evaluating, managing, and using the sensing participants' trust helps *BusWatch* to improve *BusWatch* prediction accuracy.

3   System Details

Trust is commonly defined as the belief in the competence of an entity to act reliably to perform her functionality [5]. As the participatory sensing based applications expect from a sensing participant entity to collect high quality data we define trust in a participatory sensing participant entity *as the belief in the competence of an entity to collect high quality data*. The *Trust Manager*, as shown in Figure 2, is a trust evaluation system that takes predictions, based on the sensing participants' data contributions and user feedback as its input and evaluates trust on the sensing participants considering this definition. *Error Analyzer*, *Quality Evaluator*, and *Trust Evaluator* are the main components of the *Trust Manager*. In this section we describe these components.

3.1   Error Analyzer

The *Error Analyzer* takes predictions and user feedback as input and outputs error analysis, consisting of prediction residuals and mean value of prediction

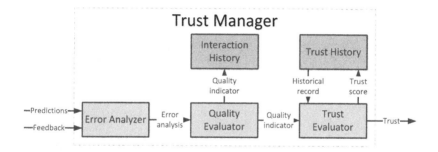

Fig. 2. Trust evaluation system for participatory sensing - Trust Manager

residuals. The *Error Analyzer* computes prediction residuals as the difference between the predictions, made on the basis of sensing participants' data contribution and real values, based on the user feedback. For example, if sensing participant i contributes data x_i, bus arrival time prediction system predicts bus arrival time t_{pi} on the basis of x_i, and user gives his feedback about real bus arrival time as t, prediction residual r_i for user i is calculated as the difference between predicted time and real time as follows.

$$r_i = t - t_{pi}$$

We further calculate mean value of error residual $\bar{r}$ for n users as follows

$$\bar{r} = \begin{cases} \frac{\sum_{i=1}^{n} r_i}{n} & \text{if } n > 1 \\ mean\ prediction\ residual\ during\ testing\ phase & \text{otherwise} \end{cases}$$

The equation shows that if more than one sensing participants contribute data to predict the bus arrival time, we calculate $\bar{r}$ as the mean value of the prediction residuals. Otherwise we take the mean value of the prediction residuals that we calculate during the bus arrival time predictor testing phase as $\bar{r}$. We discuss more about the bus arrival time predictor testing phase in Section 5.1.

3.2   Quality Evaluator

Quality Evaluator takes error analysis report, consisting of prediction residual for a specific sensing participant's data contribution and mean value of prediction residuals as the input of the function and outputs data quality indicator in the range $[0 .. 1]$. *Quality Evaluator* uses the Gaussian membership function for that purpose. Gaussian membership function is a real-valued function that depends upon the distance of a point from origin, so that $\phi(x) = \phi(|x|)$. It means that quality indicator will only depend upon the absolute value of prediction residual. Positive and negative prediction residuals having same absolute value will have same quality indicator value. We set the origin of the curve as mean value of the prediction residual. We use the following equation to transform prediction residual to reputation measure.

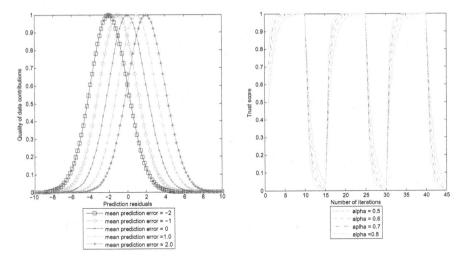

Fig. 3. Quality evaluator computing quality of data contributions with different mean prediction error values

Fig. 4. Trust evaluator computing trust score with different values of α and quality indicator score

$$Q(r) = \frac{e^{(r-\bar{r})^2}}{2\sigma^2}$$

Where e is Euler's number, approximately equal to 2.71828, r is the prediction residual, and $\bar{r}$ is man prediction residual. Mean prediction residual set the center of the Gaussian curve as shown in Figure 3 that shows Gaussian membership function curves mapping prediction error to quality indicator using different mean prediction error values. Quality is maximum at the mean prediction error and then it starts to decrease smoothly in both directions. We can also set the width of curve with change in value of σ. These attributes of Gaussian membership function make it very suitable to transfer prediction residual to quality indicator value.

3.3   Trust Evaluator

Trust Evaluator combines the quality indicator value of the sensing participant's data contribution derived by *Quality Evaluator* for current interaction with sensing participant's historical trust score based on her previous interactions to evaluate sensing participants' trustworthiness. If the sensing participant is contributing data for the first time then her historical trust score will be 0 and *Trust Evaluator* only uses quality score to transform it to trust score. *Trust Evaluator* uses the following equation to combine current quality indicator score and historical trust scores.

$$Trust = \alpha Q + (1 - \alpha)T^h$$

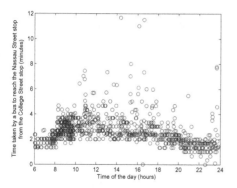
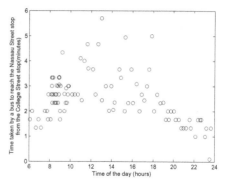

(a) Nine days Dublin Bus data for route 25B used to train prediction algorithm

(b) One day Dublin Bus data for route 25B used to test prediction algorithm

Fig. 5. DublinBus data for route 25B used for training and testing predictor

Where Q is the current quality indicator score, T^h is the historical trust score, and α decides the proportion of the current quality score and historical trust scores in the trust value. A higher value of α means that trust depends more upon the value of data quality indicator for last interaction, while a lower value of α means that current value of trust depends more upon historical trust value. Applications using participatory sensing data may choose the value of α depending upon their requirements for trust evaluation system.

Figure 4 shows trust evaluator function combines current quality indicator score and historical trust value of a sensing participant with increase in number of iterations with different values of α. Sensing participants current quality indicator score fluctuates as 1 for first ten interactions and 0.5 for next five interactions. This cycle is repeated for three times. Different graphs show that how smoothly trust is shifted with change in data quality indicator with different values of α.

4   Data Description

We use Dublin Bus bus arrival time data at different bus stops on route 25B. Dublin Bus uses a combination of Global Positioning System (GPS) and an estimation system to track their buses in the city and records their arrival time at different bus stops from the Dublin Bus control center. In our experiments, we use ten days of data for all the bus journeys of route 25B between bus stops College Street and Nassau Street. These bus stops are situated in the Dublin city center and the bus travel time between them varies considerably depending on the time of the day and the volume of traffic, as shown in Figure 5. We divide the data in two parts. We use nine days of data, as shown in Figure 5a, to train the bus arrival time prediction system and one day of data, as shown in Figure 5b, to test the system and simulate sensing participants in our experiments.

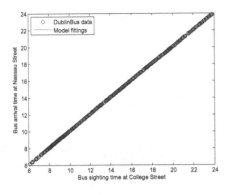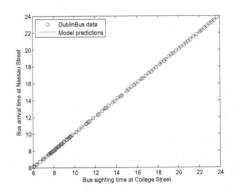

(a) Training phase data and predicitons   (b) Testing phase data and predictions

Fig. 6. Ten days Dublin Bus data showing the real bus arrival time and predicted bus arrival time at bus stop Nassau Street against bus sighted times at bus stop College Street for bus route 25B for predictor training and testing phase

5   Experiments and Evaluation

We evaluate our trust computation system on the basis of the motivational scenario discussed in Section 2. For that purpose we developed a prototype participatory sensing based bus arrival time prediction system. In our experiments, we evaluate the quality of the sensing participants' data contribution We further compute the trustworthiness of the sensing participants by combining the quality score of the sensing participants' data contribution with their historical trust score. We imitate different sensing behaviors of the sensing participants over their multiple interactions with the bus arrival time prediction system. The subsequent section discusses our experiments in detail.

5.1   Experiment 1: Bus Time Prediction and Error Analysis

The bus time predictor takes bus sighting reports at one stop as an input to the system and predicts the bus arrival time at the other stop. We use a data set provided by Dublin Bus. The dataset consists of bus sighting times at College Street bus stop and bus arrival times at Nassau street bus stop. As shown in Figure 5a, we use nine days of dataset to train the bus arrival time predictor. We use a first degree linear regression model to fit the training data. Figure 6a shows the fitting of the prediction model to training data. The prediction model has a mean absolute prediction residual of 37.72 seconds during the training phase.

To test the prediction accuracy of the bus arrival time prediction system on unseen data, we use one day Dublin Bus data, as shown in Figure 5b. Figure 6b shows the predicted bus arrival times the Nassau Street bus stop. We have a mean absolute prediction residual of 35.29 seconds during the testing phase. Figure 7 also shows that most of the instances in the testing phase have a prediction residual of less than half a minute. Considering the variability of bus

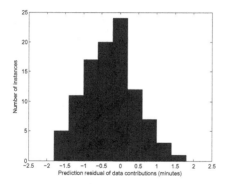
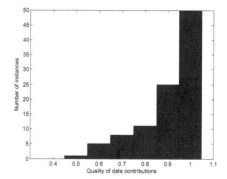

Fig. 7. Prediction residual distribution over time for bus sighting reports

Fig. 8. Quality score distribution for bus sighting reports

traveling times during the different hours of the day, as shown in Figure 5, the mean absolute prediction residual of about half minute proves that if we get accurate bus sighting reports at one stop we can predict the bus arrival times at subsequent stops with a high accuracy. We use this prototype implementation of the participatory sensing based bus arrival time prediction system to evaluate the trust evaluation system.

5.2 Experiment 2: Quality Evaluation

In this experiment we use the one day data designated for testing purpose, as described in Section 4. We simulate sensing participants' data contributions and user feedback with the data. We use the bus arrival time at the College Street as the sensing participants bus sighting reports and the bus arrival times at Nassau Street as user feedback about the exact bus arrival time. Sensing participants send the bus sighting reports at College Street to the bus arrival time prediction system that predicts the bus arrival time at Nassau Street. User gives feedback in terms of the exact bus arrival time. We calculate the prediction residuals as the difference between bus arrival time predictions and the user feedback as described in Section 3.1. Figure 7 shows the prediction residuals distribution. Figure 9 shows the prediction residuals for each bus sighting report.

We further evaluate the quality score for each instance of a bus sighting report as discussed in Section 3.2. We set the width of the function as 1.5 and its center at 0 to fit the prediction residual distribution. We provide prediction residuals as an input to the quality evaluation function to get a data quality score for each interaction. Figure 8 shows the quality score distribution. Figure 10 shows the quality score for each instance of bus sighting reports.

We observe that bus sighting reports number 5, 55, and 92 have prediction residual of about −1.48 , 1.66, and −1.52 minutes respectively and corresponding quality scores of about 0.61, 0.54, and 0.59, as evident from their values enclosed in circles in Figure 9 and Figure 10 respectively. We find out that we almost have

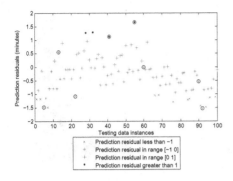
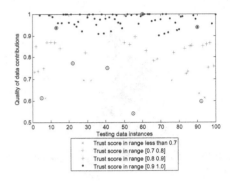

Fig. 9. Prediction residuals for each bus sighting report instance

Fig. 10. Quality score for each bus sighting report instance

the same quality score independent of the sign of prediction residual. It means that the quality evaluation function is independent of whether the predicted time is before or after the real bus arrival time.

We further observe that the bus sighting reports number 22, 41, 13, 90, and 60 have prediction residuals of $-1.08, 1.13, 0.54, -0.53, 0$ and corresponding quality scores of $0.77, 0.75, 0.93, 0.93$, and 1, as evident from their values enclosed in circles in Figure 9 and Figure 10 respectively. Looking at these values we validate that the quality score for a single interaction is dependent on the absolute score of the prediction residual. We also observe that the quality score increases with decrease in the absolute value of the prediction residual and hence increase in the quality of contribution. These facts establish that our quality evaluation function evaluates quality score for a single interaction as the significance of contribution from the sensing participants.

5.3   Experiment 3: Trust Evaluation

In this experiment we imitate different sensing behaviors of the sensing participants over multiple interactions by adding or subtracting an offset value to the Dublin Bus data. For the first interaction, the system does not have any historical value of the trust score and hence bootstraps the trust score using the data quality score as described in Section 3.3. For every subsequent interaction, we combine its data quality score with the historical trust score of that participant. Figure 11 shows data quality scores for every single interaction and evolved trust scores with every subsequent interaction for six users.

Figure 11(a) shows a user that is very trustworthy and always contributes high quality data as evident from the data quality score of each interaction close to 1. We find that their trust score also evolves close to single interaction score and stays there for subsequent interactions. Conversely, our second user is a malicious user and always contributes low quality data as depicted by Figure 11(b). Consequently, the trust score also always stays at its minimum value. Figure 11(c) shows a user that starts with contributing good quality and hence

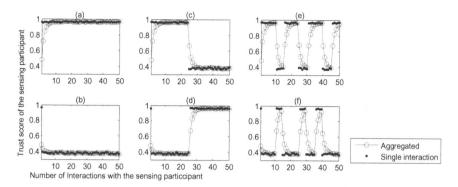

Fig. 11. Evolution of sensing participants trust score over multiple interactions

earned high trust score. However, afterwards the user started to contribute low quality data. The evolution of the trust value also shows the same behavior.

Conversely, Figure 11(d) shows a user that starts by contributing low quality data while ending up contributing high quality data. Figure 11(e) and Figure 11(f) show careless users that alternatively contribute high and low quality data for a few interactions and then change their behavior. In these illustrations, we can observe that sensing participants' trust scores evolve with respect to a change in their sensing behavior. We can also observe that sensing participants trust score successfully depict the quality of sensing participants data contributions.

6   Related Work

Trust evaluation is the subject of research efforts in different computer science domains, such as commercial and on-line applications [7], mobile adhoc networks [4], and wireless communications [13]. In those domains, systems compute the trust on an entity as the belief that the entity will act cooperatively and reliably to accomplish a collective objective [5]. However, different domains may have different objectives and hence different criteria to measure the cooperativeness and reliability of an entity. In participatory sensing, we define cooperativeness and reliability of an entity as the belief on the competence of the entity to collect and contribute high quality data. In this section, we discuss existing approaches that compute trust on the participants of sensing campaigns and compare them with our approach.

Saroiu, et al. present their approach at preventing untrusted software and malicious users interfering with sensor readings on a mobile phone[11]. In their approach they sign each sensor reading with a private key specific to a mobile device. They proposed using a trusted platform module for this purpose. However, participatory sensing participants may contribute their observations, such as bus sighting reports, to collectively perform a task. Huang, et al. quantify the reputation of mobile phone sensors, such as a noise sensor, based on their cooperativeness to collect data [6]. They use a consensus-based technique to combine different sensor readings, such as taking the average of all the sensor readings, to find the cooperativeness of a specific sensor and map it to a reputation score. Census-based technique may not be suitable in the case of sensors contributing text data or a single available sensor. Their approach that concentrates only on mobile phone sensors and does not consider human contributed data is not suitable to participatory sensing scenarios.

Reddy, et al. presented a directed sensing campaign model to gather data [10]. Although they emphasized that data timeliness, relevance, and quality are significant for a participant's trust computation, they only used sensing participants likelihood to capture a sample to compute their reputation. Yang, et al. discussed the potential of participatory sensing to realize different applications and proposed to use the sensing participants' demographic information to evaluate the trust on their contributed data [12]. As compared to these work we evaluate trust on sensing participants as the belief on their competence to collect and contribute high quality data.

Mashhadi, et al. propose to calculate trust on sensing participants using their mobility pattern and the quality of their contribution history [9]. They proposed to rate the contribution of a sensing participants by comparing it to the contribution of a trusted sensing participants or explicitly asking the sensing participants to rate each others' contributions. As compared to their proposed system, our approach involves system user feedback to evaluate trust on sensing participants and does not require a trusted sensing participants contributing data from the same vicinity. Our system also keeps historical evidence the participants' contribution to imitate their behavior over large number of transactions.

7 Summary

Participatory sensing is an important tool to sense the cities and enable many useful urban applications. Trust computed as the belief on the capabilities of the sensing participants to collect and contribute high quality data may help to dynamically identify and connect to the competent sensing participants and collect high quality data. In this paper, we present trust computation system to compute trust on the participatory sensing participants as the belief on their competence to collect high quality data. Our experiments show that the trust score computed by our system successfully depicts sensing participants' capabilities to collect and contribute high-quality data during their interaction with the participatory sensing based application.

For future work we plan to investigate if the sensing participants' context, such as their location or current activity, demographics, such as age and education, and experience of using data collection applications and smart phone devices affect their capabilities to collect data. We plan to devise a model to correlate different users' data contributions to find their plausibility. We also plan to evaluate our strategies with publicly available data sets.

Acknowledgment. This work was supported by Science Foundation Ireland under the Principal Investigator research program 10/IN.1/I2980 "Self-organizing Architectures for Autonomic Management of Smart Cities" The authors also would like to thank Dublin Bus for sharing bus arrival times data with us.

References

1. Burke, J., Estrin, D., Hansen, M., Parker, A., Ramanathan, N., Reddy, S., Srivastava, M.B.: Participatory sensing. In: Workshop on World-Sensor-Web: Mobile Device Centric Sensor Networks and Applications (WSW 2006), pp. 117–134 (2006)
2. Christin, D., Rosskopf, C., Hollick, M., Martucci, L.A., Kanhere, S.S.: Incognisense: An anonymity-preserving reputation framework for participatory sensing applications. In: Proceedings of the IEEE Pervasive Computing and Comunication (PerCom), pp. 117–134 (2012)
3. Gilbert, P., Jung, J., Lee, K., Qin, H., Sharkey, D., Sheth, A., Cox, L.P.: Youprove: authenticity and fidelity in mobile sensing. In: Proceedings of the 9th ACM Conference on Embedded Networked Sensor Systems, SenSys 2011, pp. 176–189 (2011)
4. Govindan, K., Mohapatra, P.: Trust computations and trust dynamics in mobile adhoc networks: A survey. IEEE Communications Surveys Tutorials 14(2), 279–298 (2012)
5. Grandison, T., Sloman, M.: A survey of trust in internet applications. IEEE Communications Surveys Tutorials 3(4), 2–16 (2000)
6. Huang, K.L., Kanhere, S.S., Hu, W.: On the need for a reputation system in mobile phone based sensing. Ad Hoc Networks (2012)
7. Jøsang, A., Ismail, R., Boyd, C.: A survey of trust and reputation systems for online service provision. Decision Support Systems 43(2), 618–644 (2007)
8. Lane, N., Miluzzo, E., Lu, H., Peebles, D., Choudhury, T., Campbell, A.: A survey of mobile phone sensing. IEEE Communications Magazine 48(9), 140–150 (2010)
9. Mashhadi, A.J., Capra, L.: Quality control for real-time ubiquitous crowdsourcing. In: Proceedings of the 2nd International Workshop on Ubiquitous Crowdsouring, UbiCrowd 2011, pp. 5–8. ACM (2011)
10. Reddy, S., Estrin, D., Srivastava, M.: Recruitment framework for participatory sensing data collections. In: Floréen, P., Krüger, A., Spasojevic, M. (eds.) Pervasive 2010. LNCS, vol. 6030, pp. 138–155. Springer, Heidelberg (2010)
11. Saroiu, S., Wolman, A.: I am a sensor, and i approve this message. In: Proceedings of the Eleventh Workshop on Mobile Computing Systems & Applications, HotMobile 2010, pp. 37–42. ACM (2010)
12. Yang, H., Zhang, J., Roe, P.: Using reputation management in participatory sensing for data classification. Procedia Computer Science 5, 190–197 (2011)
13. Yu, H., Shen, Z., Miao, C., Leung, C., Niyato, D.: A survey of trust and reputation management systems in wireless communications. Proceedings of the IEEE 98(10), 1755–1772 (2010)

HealthyLife: An Activity Recognition System with Smartphone Using Logic-Based Stream Reasoning

Thang M. Do, Seng W. Loke, and Fei Liu

Department of CSCE La Trobe University, Bundoora, VIC, 3086, Australia

Abstract. This paper introduces a prototype we named *HealthyLife* which uses Answer set programming based Stream Reasoning (ASR) in combination with Artificial Neural Network (ANN) to automatically recognize users activities. HealthyLife aims to provide statistics about user habits and provide suggestions and alerts to the user to help the user maintain a healthy lifestyle. The advantages of HealthyLife over other projects are: (i) no restriction on how to carry the phone (such as in hand bag), (ii) detect complex activities and give recommendations, (iii) deal well with ambiguity when recognizing situations, and (iv) no additional devices are required.

Keywords: health promotion, Answer Set Programming, stream reasoning, sensors, smart phone, activity recognition.

1 Introduction

Using smartphones for health support and health-associated activity recognition has been receiving much attention from researchers and end users. However, most projects have one or more of the following limitations.

The first limitation is the way users carry a smartphone. To maintain accuracy, most projects require users to carry their phones at a fixed position on their bodies or carry additional equipment. The most flexible prototype requires the phone was put in users' pants pocket [1]. This position may not be practical for many women who often keep their phone in their hand bag. The second issue is the automation; some commercial products (e.g., sports tracker of Nokia [2]) can provide useful statistics information about fitness activities but requires users to manually label start, stop times and name the activity.

The third issue is the usefulness of provided information; many projects can automatically detect only users' "basic" activities like walking, standing and running and do not use this information to give further useful suggestions, or infer higher level complex activities. Also, once activities are recognized, reasoning is needed to then provide the right suggestions to users.

To fill the above gaps, we are working on *HealthyLife*, a prototype system which focuses on using available smartphone sensors to automatically recognize user's basic, and complex activities, and give useful health-related suggestions

K. Zheng, M. Li, and H. Jiang (Eds.): MOBIQUITOUS 2012, LNICST 120, pp. 188–199, 2013.
© Institute for Computer Sciences, Social Informatics and Telecommunications Engineering 2013

and alerts. *HealthyLife* virtually requires no restriction on how users carry a smartphone (users can put it in pants pockets, jacket pockets, belly belt, handbag, shoulder bag, or backpack). We don't require user to wear any additional devices, and explore what is possible without such devices.

Our methodology is to use an ASR (Answer Set Programming based Stream Reasoning) logic framework (first briefly introduced in [8], and will be extended here) as the reasoning engine. ASR allows dealing with ambiguity in a logic-based framework when reasoning about situations (or *ambiguity reasoning* (§3)), decomposing complex activities into simpler ones, querying long-term data history for inferring complex activities, as well as integration with different reasoning techniques such as machine learning to process different types of sensor data (e.g., accelerometer, sound, image, etc).

The rest of this paper is organized as follows: section 2 provides a brief review of related work; section 3 introduces the concept of the ASR logic framework; section 4 discusses the design and implementation of *HealthyLife*; section 5 evaluates the prototype; and section 6 concludes.

2   Related Work

In this section we review related work which focuses on using smartphone to support users' health, more compreihensive surveys can be found in [14,13].

The applications which were deployed commercially and obtained much attention from users are the Nokia sports tracker. This application provide rich statistics of users' fitness information such as total running time, cycling time, approximate energy burned, etc. However, users still have to manually label the activity they are doing with start and stop times. Even with this limitation, the number of users are very high across more than 200 countries [2]. This number shows the huge market for this kind of application. Apple also has a similar product name Run Keeper which keeps track of user workouts.

The project in [3] uses a special fitness equipment pedometer attached to the user's waistband to detect the number of steps of a user and transmit data to the mobile phone wirelessly. The project in [4] requires users to wear a paper-sized wearable sensing device on the waist for automatically detecting user activities.

In [5], a Nike+iPod kit was put in the shoes and an iPhone in a pants pocket. This solution still has limitations as additional equipment is needed. Users in [6] are required to wear many sensors at fixed positions on their body. The prototype in [1] seems to be the most flexible in how users carry the phone but still requires putting the mobile phone in the front pants pocket.

Projects surveyed above detect simple physical activities such as walking, running, biking, lying down, or being stationary, and requires different levels of restrictions in the way users carry the smart phone and may need additional devices sometimes. Therefore, we see the necessity to have a prototype which requires no additional equipment, no limitation in carrying the phone and automatically recognize user activities (basic and complex).

3   The ASR Reasoning Framework

This section briefly introduces the ASR Programming Framework[1] which is proposed for stream reasoning [7] tailored for activity recognition.

An ASR program is a 7-tuple: $\Pi = (\alpha, \beta, \gamma, \delta, \varepsilon, \zeta, \eta)$ where: α is a set of facts, β is a set of predicates to query external resources, γ is a set of basic activity models which may use weak constraints (discussed later), δ is a set of complex activity models, ε is a set of functional reasoners (such as an ambiguity reasoner, discussed later), ζ is a set of control commands (loop control, registration), and η are other auxiliary rules, such as converting data and performing calculations.

Among them, $\alpha, \gamma, \delta, \eta$ components are built from the ASR Core Language which is based on Answer Set Programming (ASP [9]) theory and the *dlv* solver[2]. Other components facilitate stream reasoning (or continuous reasoning). In the rest of this section, we introduce our definition of basic and complex activity models, and discuss our ambiguity reasoning feature.

Activity Complexity. A *data predicate* is one which holds sensor data values.

If a rule r defining an activity and its body $B(r)$ contains only data predicate(s) then predicates in the head $H(r)$ represent *basic activities*.

If a rule r defining an activity and its body $B(r)$ do not contain any data predicate(s) (but contain predicates representing basic or complex activities), then predicates in the head $H(r)$ represent *complex activities*.

(For well-defined semantics, at the moment, ASR assumes that the program Π has only basic and complex models of activities and doesn't have any model in which the body has a mixture of basic activities and data predicates.)

For example, we have a model defining two activities: "running while late" and "running while early":

```
1. accelerometer(3). time(17). % 17 is 5PM
2. running :- accelerometer(X),#int(X), X > 2.
3. runningWhileLate :- running, time(T), #int(T), T > 18.
4. early :- time(T), #int(T), T < 8.
5. runningWhileEarly :- running, early.
```

In this program, `accelerometer` and `time` are data predicates as they hold sensor data values (line 1). `running` and `early` are basic activities[3] as there are only data predicates in the rules' body (lines 2 and 4). `runningWhileEarly` is a complex activity as there is no data predicate in the rule body (line 5); `runningWhileLate` have both a basic activity and data predicates in the body (line 3) - which we call "middle complex" and will be considered further in future work, but middle complex rules can be easily avoided by having a rule called `late` as a basic activity.

---

[1] ASR language was proposed by us in another paper which is under review process.

[2] http://www.dlvsystem.com/dlvsystem/index.php/Home

[3] We can think of being "early" as a situation rather than an activity, as we have in mind the condition of the user getting there early.

Ambiguity Reasoning in ASR. Sensor data for activity recognition is normally ambiguous. Two activities (such as staying still and sitting on train) can have similar sensor data patterns. *Ambiguity reasoning* is applying a process (as below) in trying to find out the right activity in this situation.

Using normal rules and (strong) constraints (conditions which are not allowed to happend) gives only the right answer which is 100 percent true, according to the knowledge base of a logic program. However, using weak constraints (conditions which can happend with a violation cost), besides the the right answer, we keep potential answers (called the *best models*) with their violation degrees (or costs). The right answer will have violation cost = 0.

Each weak constraint has a weight which is defined based on how important the constraint is. In general, the more important a weak constraint is the more weight it has. The violation cost of a best model is the sum of the weight of all weak constraints which the best model violates.

ASR ambiguity reasoning observes sequences of the best models over a period of time to discover which activity seems to be the most likely answer.

For example, a program (*dlv* syntax) uses weak constraints (marked with ":~", [1:1] is [violation cost:priority level]) to recognize activities based on accelerometer data and GPS-acquired speeds as follows:

```
1. running :- acce(A), A >= 13.
2. walking :- acce(A), A < 13, A > 10.
3. :~ running, speed(S), S <= 2. [1:1] % 2m/s
4. :~ walking, speed(S), S > 2. [1:1]
5. talk :- noise(N), N >= 3.
6. quiet :- noise(N), N < 3.
```

This program processes a data window of sensor data (say, from t1 to t4) and gives best models with costs as follows:

```
t1: A=13, S=3, N=3 -> Best model: {running, talking}, cost: 0
t2: A=12, S=2, N=4 -> Best model: {walking, talking}, cost: 1
t3: A=10, S=2, N=3 -> Best model: {walking, talking}, cost: 1
t4: A=11, S=2, N=2 -> Best model: {walking, quiet},   cost: 1
```

Among activities in this window, we see that running and walking (also talk and quiet) can not happen at the same time (we say they are in a *mutually exclusive* relationship) and we have to choose which activity is the more likely. The first result is *running* with zero violation but all the others are *walking* with "small" violation. This may imply that the real activity (over the period from t1 to t4) can be walking.

We use a weight function to calculate how "right" a best model is in comparison to all others. In other words, the bigger cost the less value weight function has. For example, a weight function f_w can be defined as: $f_w = (MinTop - Cost)$, where $MinTop$ is the smallest number which is greater than any cost that may appear in a program Π. in the example above, we can set $MinTop = 3$ and $f_{w_1} = 3 - 0 = 3$, and $f_{w_2} = 3 - 1 = 2$ and so on, where f_{w_i} is the weight function value of best model at time t_i.

The violation cost and weight function value (or *weight*) of a best model is also the cost and weight of each activity in that model. In the above example, the violation cost of the best model at time t_1 is 0 and the weight is 3, and so, each activity *running* and *talking* in that model has cost 0 and a weight of 3.

We then use a membership function to estimate which activity has the best chance of being the right answer. For a given activity, the membership function f_m calculates the division of (i) the sum of the weights of the activity in every best model, and (ii) the sum of the weights of all activities in every best model. The activity having the highest membership value is chosen as the answer. For example, $f_m(running) = 3/(3 + 2 + 2 + 2) = 0.33$, $f_m(walking) = (2 + 2 + 2)/(3 + 2 + 2 + 2) = 0.67$. So *walking* is the more likely activity over the time period from t1 to t4. In similar way, *talking* is the more likely over *quiet*.

4   *HealthyLife*: Design and Implementation

HealthyLife automatically detect users' daily activities for recording, making statistics and providing useful suggestions. *HealthyLife* aims to support office workers who normally work indoors and need to keep their life balance between being stationary and physically active, between working and relaxing, between spending time indoors and outdoors, and between being isolated and social.

Design. The architecture of *HealthyLife* is illustrated in Figure 1 and has four main components: (i) Client, which is installed on users' mobile phones, (ii) Web Server, which manages data transmission between the mobile phone and server, (iii) Data stream Manager System (DSMS), which stores and manages collected data, and (iv) Reasoning Server, which performs logical inference.

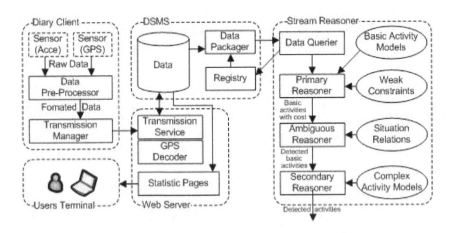

Fig. 1. Components Diagram

(i) Client: collects 3D accelerometer data, GPS data and performs pre-processing to reduce the amount of data transmitted to the server over the mobile network (and wifi in the next version). The pre-processor is a trained Artificial Neural Network (ANN) to recognize basic activities such as walking, running, driving, and staying still (when the phone is stationary).

(ii) WebServer: has a servlet for receiving data from the client and does reverse geocoding with the Google API to find out the place and address where the user is. After that, all the data is passed to the DSMS.

(iii) DSMS: stores data coming from the client through the WebServer and prepares data as requested by the reasoner. DSMS also stores streams of results from the reasoner.

(iv) Stream Reasoner: is an ASR program (§3) which has four main components as follows:

- Data Querier β: gathers four possible basic activities detected by the pre-processor and the GPS data from the DSMS stored in the form of data predicates.
- Primary Reasoner γ: uses basic activity models and weak constraints to detect all basic activities with violation cost, if any.
- Ambiguous Reasoners ε: perform ambiguity reasoning (§3) to choose the most likely user activity, periodically, over predefined periods.
- Secondary Reasoner δ: uses detected basic activities with other data (GPS at the moment) to recognize complex activities which normally happen over a longer period of time such as "user is wondering around". The secondary reasoner also gives predictions and suggestions to the user such as "user needs to exercise".

At the moment, since there is no standard ontology for activities, the decision regarding which activities are basic and which are complex is application-dependent. Also, in the set of rules used in the reasoner, we leave up to the modeller to recognize which predicates are to model basic activities and which are to model complex activities, and which predicates do not define activities.

Another component of the *HealthyLife* is the user terminal which users use to review their lifestyle with a web browser. The user terminal can be a desktop, laptop, tablet, or the smartphone itself.

Ambiguity Reasoning. We implement ambiguity reasoning in a Java package named *reasoner* with main parameters as follows:
$|W| = 5$ (basic activities window size), and window slide is 2, this mean we observe five consecutive best models and repeat ambiguity reasoning after having every two new best models. $f_w = |W| - C$ is the weight function, where C is the violation cost,
f_m is the membership function, mentioned earlier, and more generally, it is:

$$f_m(a) = \frac{\displaystyle\sum_{P \in g(a)} P}{\displaystyle\sum_{(q,r) \in F} (q * r)}$$

Where: $BM^{t'} = (\{a_i^{t'}|1 \leq i \leq k_{t'}\}, f_w^{t'}) = (A^{t'}, f_w^{t'})$ is the best model at time t', a is an activity, $BM = \{(\{a_i^t|1 \leq i \leq k_t\}, f_w^t)|1 \leq t \leq |W|\}$, $F = \{(f_w^t, |A^t|)|BM^t = (A^t, f_w^t), 1 \leq t \leq |W|\}$, $g(a) = \{f_w^t|a \in A^t, BM^t = (A^t, f_w^t), 1 \leq t \leq |W|\}$.

ANN. Because developing an ANN network is not a research goal of this paper, we used sample structure in Encog[4] as follows.

Input data: The features extracted from 3D accelerometer data is the magnitude A [10] of the force vector of three values according to three directions acceX, acceY, and acceZ: $A = \sqrt{acceX^2 + acceY^2 + acceZ^2}$. For every window of five A, we calculate $Min(A)$ and $Max(A) - Min(A)$ to feed into the ANN.

ANN structure: The ANN we use has four layers which are input, output and two hidden layers. The input layer has two inputs: $Min(A)$ and $Max(A) - Min(A)$. The output layer has two bits which encode four activities: 00 - walking, 01 - running, 10 - driving, 11 - staying still. Each hidden layer has seven neurons. The activation function for hidden and output layers is the TANH, and the input layer is the Linear function.

Implementation. We developed the Client on a Samsung Galaxy S2 running Android 2.3 and the Client Repository for buffering transmitted data is SQLite. We use a HTTP client for Android to communicate with the WebServer. The database server is MySQL 5.1 DBMS. The reasoner uses the ASR logic framework. WebServer is the Apache Tomcat 7 and the reasoning server, WebServer, and Database Server are installed in Ubuntu 11.10 running as a guest OS in Virtual Box 4.1.6 (as software compatibility and quick experiment) on a Windows 7 x64 Desktop PC with Quad CPU Q9550 2.83 GHz and 4GB RAM.

5 Experimentation and Evaluation

In this section we describe how *HealthyLife* was used, and activities detected, and discuss the accuracy, system performance and the feasibility of the prototype. After being started, the Client component runs on the user's mobile phone silently and doesn't have obvious side effects on the usage of the phone. Every time the user wants to check their lifestyle activities inferred they just need to use any device having a web browser to view statistics (figure 2) and suggestions about their life style (though it is quite feasible to give suggestions and alerts on the users' mobile phone automatically).

Data Set and Training Data. Data from the 3D accelerometer, in the mobile phone, was taken at the sampling rate of 5Hz (this rate was chosen based on work in [11,12]), and GPS data is refreshed at the rate of 0.2Hz. Data for training and evaluating system was taken from 8 users with age from 6 to 67 (the app aims at office workers but we still use a variety of users' age, gender, and job to check the precision and generality of our approach), and the phone was carried in different

---

[4] http://www.heatonresearch.com/encog

Statistic 1 last hour

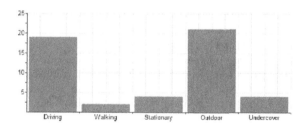

Fig. 2. Statistics information, x-axis is activities, y-axis is time in minutes

ways such as in tight/loose pants pocket, jacket high/low pocket, hand-held bag, and shoulder bag. When the data was collected, each user was encouraged to do different activities in different styles like walk with/without shoes, run slowly/quickly, run with high/low steps. We have 4 long-term users who used the prototype for 1 to 3 weeks and others used it for 20 minutes. Data collected from each user is marked with a unique id and we call them *original data*. For long term analysis where only short term data was available, the original data from all users were combined to create new data which simulates virtual long-term users. We used both original and simulated data to evaluate our prototype. When data was collected, users were required to take note in their diaries for labelling the data sets.

We selected, as ANN training data, a set of 6,850 "typical" accelerometer data samples which was collected when users continuously performed four basic activities walking, running, driving and putting the phone still on a table. The accelerometer data are packed in windows of size 5 samples to be fed into the trained ANN. The output of the ANN, which is recognized basic activities, is further processed by a window sliding technique with a size of 7 and slides of step size 5. The activity which appears most often in the window will be the final result of the recognition phase using the ANN. This process has a recognition rate of 0.2 Hz and was used in [15]. These window sizes are chosen based on the assumption that: A user is said to perform a basic activity if it lasts for more than 5 seconds; this time hurdle can vary with specific applications. We also define the *Activity time* is the sampling time of the last sample of the data window used for activity recognition.

In practice, our prototype can transmit all this data through a mobile network. But because mobile phone signals may drop at some times, in some areas, and optimizing transmission is not our goal here, to evaluate our prototype we store data in files and stream them to our system for reasoning. In next version, we will use compressed data such as in the approach in [15].

Recognized Activities and Accuracy. Basically, the human daily activities which can be detected by using a single accelerometer are: walking, running, driving (or in transportation), and staying still; so, we call them basic activities.

HealthyLife detects these basic activities and combine these with GPS data to infer the users' place (where users are) and to infer complex activities. To evaluate the accuracy, we compare the activities detected by *HealthyLife* with the diary which user noted manually. Then for each activity, we divide the total time *HealthyLife* detects correctly over the total time the real activities happen.

Basic Activities. Because one of the major design feature is to let users be free in the way they carry their phone, this is a source of ambiguity in activity recognition. For example, we say the user is *softwalking* when the user walks barefoot or puts the phone in their suitcase or handbag. Figure 3 shows that softwalking and driving have very similar sensor data patterns. To deal with this ambiguity, we combine accelerometer data and GPS data via weak constraints as follows and use ambiguity reasoning as implemented in section 4.

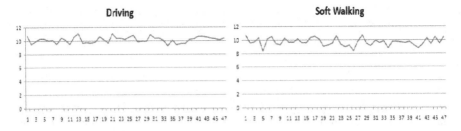

Fig. 3. Accelerometer patterns, x-axis is time, y-axis is A: force vector magnitude

```
:~ basicActivity(ActName), gps(GpsAccuracy, GpsSpeed),
   ActName = driving, GpsSpeed <= 2. [4:1]
:~ basicActivity(underCover), basicAct(driving). [4:1]
:~ basicActivity(stayingStill), gps(GpsAccuracy, GpsSpeed),
   #int(GpsSpeed), GpsSpeed > 1. [4:1]
```

In this code fragment, *underCover* means the user is staying indoor, or surrounded by high trees or buildings. [4 : 1] is the [*violation cost* : *priority level*] of the weak constraints which shouldn't happend.

The result of recognition without ambiguity reasoning is shown in tables 1, with ambiguity reasoning in table 2. Table 1 shows that, without ambiguity reasoning, when user was (soft) walking Healthy Life tends to recognize that user was driving. This is understandable as shown in figure 3. With ambiguity reasoning, the accuracy increased significantly from $\simeq 50\%$ to $\simeq 73\%$ for detecting (soft) walking. These two tables also show that ambiguity reasoning doesn't effect the accuracy of detecting activities which are not ambiguous (or don't have similar sensor data pattern) such as running and staying still.

Users' Current Place and Complex Activities. We detect users' location (their current place) and then combine that with detected basic activities to infer complex activities. To detect user's place (in a meaningful way as opposed to numerical coordinates), we use the Google API to find places (or Points of Interest) around the user and compare their addresses with the closest address from the user's position. The place which has a matching address is where the user is.

Table 1. Result without ambiguity reasoning

		Recognized			
		walk	run	drive	stay still
	walk	50%	0%	50%	0%
Actual	run	3%	97%	0%	0%
	drive	23%	0%	70%	7%
	stay still	0%	0%	0%	100%

Table 2. Result with ambiguity reasoning

		Recognized			
		walk	run	drive	stay still
	walk	73%	0%	27%	0%
Actual	run	2%	98%	0%	0%
	drive	7%	0%	88%	5%
	stay still	0%	0%	0%	100%

We use GPS data with a precision of $\leq 30m$ for detecting user places; a detected precision of > 30 implies that user is undercover like indoors or surrounded by tall buildings. A set of places which can be detected in *HealthyLife* is found in table 3. With big places (park, shopping mall) or well defined places (home, office), Healthy Life can recognize with high accuracy. For small area (bank, gym), the accuracy reduce quickly as there may be many other small places around. Note that with such knowledge, one can estimate how often the user goes to the gym as health related information, and also, when the user is at the gym, how active s/he was over that time s/he was there. We asked users to provide the address of their home and office to detect when the user is at home and at work and we realized the ability to detect these addresses automatically. The rules to detect user places have form as follows:

```
userAt(Place) :- closestAddress(Adress1,UserPosition),
place(Place, Address1), Address1 = Address2.
userAt(underCover,Time) :- gpsData(accuracy,Time), accuracy > 30.
```

Table 3. Detected User Places

Places	Accuracy
User at Home	100%
User at Work	100%
User at Gym	67%
User at Shop-ping mall	90% 90%
User at Park	100%
User at bank	51%

Table 4. Complex Activities & User Preference

Complex Activities	Users Preference
User active at work	Like stay indoor
User working late	Like stay at home
User working hard	Like shopping
User may be tired	Like nature
Need more workout	Like fitness
At risky activity	Driving much
Running at park	Seems to be fit

We can predict users' status based on a previous week's data and users' preferences (indicated in table 4) with rules of the form:

```
userWorkingHard :- userAtWork(Hours),avgWorkHours(AH),Hours > AH + 5.
userMayBeTired :- avgWorkHours(AH),userAtWork(Hours),Hours > AH + 10.
userWorkingLate :- userAtPlace(office,T),#int(T),lateWorkTime(T).
lateWorkTime(T) :- time(T), #int(T), T > 17. % 5pm.
runningAtPark :- userAtPlace(park), basicAct(running).
```

Transmission Feasibility. Optimizing bandwidth utilization was not our goal, but we examined the feasibility (not to compare with other algorithms) of transmitting *HealthyLife* data from the users' smart phone to our server. Every data record includes 2 characters of basic activity code, 10 of time stamp, 19x2 of latitude and longitude, 4 for accuracy, 3 for speed, 10 for GPS time, and 6 separators. To sum up, we need 73 characters/bytes to represent a data record.

If the system runs 24/7 at the data rate of 0.2Hz (one data record every 5 seconds) , everyday, *HealthyLife* needs to transmit 73 bytes x 0.2 Hz x 86,400 s/day = 1.2 MB/day or about 36 MB/month. Transmitting this amount of data is possible for a mobile phone network in Australia. For example, a $29 VirginMobile package has a quota of 250MB/month. If this amount of data becomes an issue, we could use the algorithm in [15] to optimize the transmission.

System Speed. After getting data from the user's smart phone (with the rate 0.2 Hz), our single ASR reasoner, as noted in 4, have a reasoning speed of 1Hz and so can service 5 users at the same time (this is easily scaled by having more reasoners and more machines).

Potential Applications. *HealthyLife* has potential for many applications for single users and groups of users - to infer group or collective activities from single users' activities. Single users can have statistics about their fitness status and daily activities automatically to organize their time and lifestyle better. This prototype also has the ability to connect to other smart systems such as smart house, smart office or a social network. If more users share their data (without any id information), people can become aware of community events (e.g., a community marathon) and friends' activities. For example, a user who wants to find a quiet area can avoid the park where there is a public event. *HealthyLife* can provides statistics data for health promotion bodies, a city council and businesses to service citizens and customers better. For example, local governments can invest more on sports infrastructure if there are more people doing exercise. More generally, companies can send advertisement messages to users, if allowed to, when users are stationary (say in a bus or train) where they are more likely to give attention.

6   Conclusion

HealthyLife differs from other work by automatically detecting users' basic and complex activities and also does ambiguity reasoning. We combine accelerometer data, GPS data (reverse geocoded into meaningful places) and weak constraints to perform ambiguity reasoning, and showed how this can improve real-life activity recognition performance. Besides detecting basic activities, *HealthyLife* is able to detect complex activities, which can be tracked for statistics for health-related purposes and rules can be used to map inferred activities and activity histories to suggestions for users, all within a logic-based rule framework.

References

1. Kwapisz, J.R., Weiss, G.M., Moore, S.A.: Activity recognition using cell phone accelerometers. In: SIGKDD Explor. Newsl., vol. 12(2), pp. 74–82. ACM, New York (2010)
2. Sport-Tracker, http://www.sports-tracker.com/blog/about/
3. Mattila, E., Parkka, J., Hermersdorf, M., Kaasinen, J., Vainio, J., Samposalo, K., Merilahti, J., Kolari, J., Kulju, M., Lappalainen, R., Korhonen, I.: Mobile Diary for Wellness Management–Results on Usage and Usability in Two User Studies. IEEE Transactions on Information Technology in Biomedicine 12(4), 501–512 (2008)
4. Sunny, C., David, W.M., Tammy, T., Mike, Y.C., Jon, F., Beverly, H., Predrag, K., Anthony, L., Louis, L., Ryan, L., Ian, S., James, A.L.: Activity sensing in the wild: a field trial of ubifit garden. In: Proceedings of the Twenty-Sixth Annual SIGCHI Conference on Human Factors in Computing Systems (CHI 2008), pp. 1797–1806. ACM, New York (2008)
5. Washington Education, https://dada.cs.washington.edu/research/projects/aiweb/main/media/papers/UW-CSE-08-04-02.pdf
6. Alhamid, M.F., Saboune, J., Alamri, A., El Saddik, A.: Hamon: An activity recognition framework for health monitoring support at home. In: 2011 IEEE Instrumentation and Measurement Technology Conference (I2MTC), pp. 1–5 (May 2011)
7. Della Valle, E., Ceri, S., Barbieri, D.F., Braga, D., Campi, A.: A first step towards stream reasoning. In: Domingue, J., Fensel, D., Traverso, P. (eds.) FIS 2008. LNCS, vol. 5468, pp. 72–81. Springer, Heidelberg (2009)
8. Do, T.M., Loke, S.W., Liu, F.: Answer set programming for stream reasoning. In: Butz, C., Lingras, P. (eds.) Canadian AI 2011. LNCS, vol. 6657, pp. 104–109. Springer, Heidelberg (2011)
9. Michael, G., Vladimir, L.: The stable model semantics for logic programming. In: Kowalski, R., Bowen, K. (eds.) Proceedings of International Logic Programming Conference and Symposium, pp. 1070–1080 (1988)
10. Reddy, S., Mun, M., Burke, J., Estrin, D., Hansen, M., Srivastava, M.: Using mobile phones to determine transportation modes. ACM Trans. Sen. Netw. 6, 13:1–13:27 (2010)
11. Bao, L., Intille, S.S.: Activity recognition from user-annotated acceleration data. In: Ferscha, A., Mattern, F. (eds.) PERVASIVE 2004. LNCS, vol. 3001, pp. 1–17. Springer, Heidelberg (2004)
12. Huynh, T., Schiele, B.: Analyzing features for activity recognition. In: Proceedings of the 2005 Joint Conference on Smart Objects and Ambient Intelligence: Innovative Context-Aware Services: Usages and Technologies, pp. 159–163. ACM (2005)
13. Ye, J., Dobson, S., McKeever, S.: Situation identification techniques in pervasive computing: A review. Pervasive and Mobile Computing 8, 36–66 (2012)
14. Predrag, K., Wanda, P.: Healthcare in the pocket: Mapping the space of mobile-phone health interventions. Journal of Biomedical Informatics 45(1), 184–198 (2012)
15. Jayaraman, P.P., Sinha, A., Sherchan, W., Krishnaswamy, S., Zaslavsky, A., Haghighi, P.D., Loke, S., Do, M.T.: Here-n-Now: A Framework for Context-Aware Mobile Crowdsensing. In: Proceedings of the Tenth International Conference on Pervasive Computing, UK (June 2012)

GroupMe: Supporting Group Formation with Mobile Sensing and Social Graph Mining

Bin Guo, Huilei He, Zhiwen Yu, Daqing Zhang, and Xingshe Zhou

Northwestern Polytechnical University, Xi'an, 710072, China
guobin.keio@gmail.com

Abstract. Nowadays, social activities in the real world (e.g., meetings, discussions, parties) are more and more popular and important to human life. As the number of contacts increases, the implicit social graph becomes increasingly complex, leading to a high cost on social activity organization and activity group formation. In order to promote the interaction among people and improve the efficiency of social activity organization, we propose a mobile social activity support system called GroupMe, which facilitates the activity group initiation based on mobile sensing and social graph mining. In GroupMe, user activities are automatically sensed and logged in the social activity logging (ACL) repository. By analyzing the historical ACL data through a series of group mining (group extraction, group abstraction) algorithms, we obtain implicit logical contact groups. We then use the sensed contexts and the computed user affinity to her logical groups to suggest highly relevant groups in social activity initiation. The experimental results verify the effectiveness of the proposed approach.

Keywords: Social graph mining, context-awareness, group formation and recommendation, mobile sensing, social activity organization.

1   Introduction

Forging social connections with others is the core of what makes us human. In modern life, people participate in various social activities each day. Depending on the distinct nature of a social activity, different crowds of people are involved. In this paper, we define the people participated in a social activity a *group* or a *clique*. For example, groups in a university can be project teams, dining partners, co-players, etc. The reason for the formation of distinct groups for different activities is that *people tend to be with a similar group of people to participate in certain activities*. Selecting members to form groups has thus become a significant step to organize social activities. This paper present our efforts for group formation in social activity organization, leveraging advanced mobile sensing and data mining techniques.

The design of a tool to facilitate social group formation is non-trivial. *The first challenge is how to accurately model and efficiently manage human groups.* For example, people usually participate in multiple groups with different roles, group size, and involved members. We use *social graph* to characterize the structure of a social activity participation network, which often consists of a set of overlapping and nested groups. For instance, *A* can be involved in both a sport team and a project team, the

K. Zheng, M. Li, and H. Jiang (Eds.): MOBIQUITOUS 2012, LNICST 120, pp. 200–211, 2013.
© Institute for Computer Sciences, Social Informatics and Telecommunications Engineering 2013

two relevant groups are thus overlapping); *A* has lunch with *B, C, D* one day and with *B, C* another day, the two activity groups are nested. This observation has prompted many social communication tools (e.g., Gmail Contact, friend manager in Facebook) that allow users to group their contacts. However, as investigated in previous studies [1, 2], group creation is time-consuming and tedious, and users of social communication tools rarely manually group their contacts. Furthermore, human relationships often evolve and groups change dynamically (e.g., having one member joined or removed). The creation of static social groups can thus quickly become stale. Supposing that implicit groups of a user can be extracted, *the second challenge becomes how to recommend highly relevant groups to the user when an activity is initiated.* It is affected by several factors, such as in-situ contexts (e.g., where the organizer locates, who is together with), adhesion of each group to the user, etc.

To lesson user effort on social activity organization and group management, it is beneficial to provide an intelligent application that can automatic category human groups and recommend relevant groups for a specific activity at hand (e.g., in terms of contexts). There have been recently several studies devoted to this (refer to Section 2 for details) [2, 3], which cluster and suggest contacts by virtue of analyzing historical interaction data among people. However, these systems are mainly focused on contact grouping and recommendation in online communities (e.g., emails, Facebook; typically used for formal or long-distance communication), they do not represent social activities in the real world, which are often formed in ad hoc, face-to-face manners. Comparing with online interactions, real-world interactions are more difficult to capture and record. For instance, there basically lacks a preexisting infrastructure (online interaction data can be maintained in mail servers or social web servers) for physical activity logging and mining. Furthermore, activity organization in the real world is often impacted by various social/personal contexts, which should be additionally considered when designing group recommendation algorithms.

To address the above issues, we have developed GroupMe, a group formation and recommendation tool that aims to facilitate social activity organization in the real world. Different from previous work that mainly works in online environments, we exploit sensor-enhanced mobile phones to capture human interactions and assist group formation in real world settings. Specifically, our contributions include:

- A social activity logging model, which depicts the major elements for real-world activities. We have also proposed the social graph, to characterize the social activity participation network at multiple granularities, e.g., raw/logical groups.
- A novel algorithm for automatic *group extraction* and *abstraction* from large-scale mobile sensing data, coupled with a user interface that can suggest contact groups, given the context of the user (e.g., user location, nearby people) and the estimated user affinity to the group.
- An evaluation of the quality and accuracy of our system. Results suggest that our algorithm models users' social activities sufficiently well, and can suggest contacts with high precision and recall.

The rest of this paper proceeds as follows: we first survey related work in Section 2; followed by the system architecture in Section 3; the activity logging and group models are described in Section 4; in Section 5, we present the core algorithms for group formation and recommendation; the prototype implementation and an evaluation of our system are described in Section 6; finally, we conclude the paper in Section 7.

2   Related Work

There are two closely related research areas of our work: *social interaction enhancement* and *group formation and management*.

2.1   Social Interaction Enhancement

Social interaction is important to human life and work. There have been numerous studies that aim to enhance human interaction and communication. One direction is to facilitate the management of the ever-increasing human contacts. For example, ContactMap provides an editable visualization of personal contacts, spatially organized and colored by group membership [4]. Our previous work, SCM (social contact manager) [5], is designed to automatically collect contact data and support efficient retrieval of human contacts based on associative cues. However, all these systems do not automatically group and suggest contacts, instead requiring manual layout and assignment of each contact.

Another direction is to enhance face-to-face human interactions. There have been studies that aim to improve social connectivity in physical communities by leveraging the information detected by mobile devices that contact. Social Serendipity is one of such studies, in which matching interests among nearby people who do not know one another are indicated as a cue for informal, face-to-face interactions [6]. The SOCKER application we developed is another example, which can build ad-hoc communities of like-minded people [7]. Though these systems can enhance the interaction among people with similar interests, they do not support mining and recommendation of groups to users based on their interaction history.

2.2   Group Formation and Management

Group formation and management is crucial for social activity organization and interpersonal communication. Researchers from Google have proposed a friend-suggestion algorithm, which can generate a recipient group when composing e-mails, given a small seed set of contacts [3]. MacLean et al. from Stanford University have developed a social group browser called SocialFlow [2], which can show social groups automatically mined from email data. These systems can extract social groups from online interactions and facilitate Web-based communication, but fail to address social activity initiation in real-world settings.

There have been quite few studies that devote to group formation in the physical world. For example, Flocks [8] is a system that supports dynamic group creation based on user profiles and physical proximity (e.g., forming a group with nearby badminton-lovers). MobilisGroups [9] is a location-based group creation service, which allows the user to initiate a social event on the map and recruit the ones using temporal and spatial filters (i.e., who is nearby at a given period of time). Though facilitating group formation in real-world settings, they mainly aim to group people who are already nearby and share certain commons, while not supporting the recommendation of contacts who are not yet gathered but should be, in terms of historical situations and in-situ contexts.

3   System Architecture

GroupMe aims to support social activity organization in the real world. There are two basic requirements: *(1) how to mine implicit groups from human interaction history in the physical world; (2) how to recommend highly relevant contact groups in terms of context.* We have designed a layered architecture to meet these requirements.

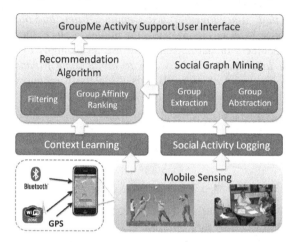

Fig. 1. GroupMe system architecture

The first layer is the *mobile sensing* layer, which consists of mobile phones enhanced by various sensors (e.g., Bluetooth, WiFi, GPS, accelerometers). Nowadays, mobile phones have become intimate "personal companions", which makes it possible to monitor human daily behaviors.

The second layer is the *data processing* layer, which involves two modules: context learning and social activity logging. The context learning module extracts *in-situ* user contexts from raw sensed data. The social activity logging module, nevertheless, transforms raw data to social activity logs and inserts into the SAL repository, according to the social activity logging model presented in Section 4.

In the third layer, the *group computing algorithm* layer, we have two components, *social group mining* and *recommendation*. The social group mining algorithm can extract and abstract logical groups from activity logging records. The recommendation algorithm can suggest highly relevant groups (mined from social group mining algorithm) to the user in terms of sensed contexts.

The fourth layer is *user interface*, which provides intelligent group formation and activity organization service with little manual effort.

4   Modeling Activity Organization and Group Formation

As shown in other studies, maintaining an interaction repository is the basis for group mining and suggestion. Distinct from online communication systems, where the interaction history has been kept in Web servers, social interaction in the real world should be captured and logged via a new way. In this section, we first present our definition of social activity; the social activity logging (SAL) model will then be presented; we finally describe the social graph and group model.

4.1   Social Activity Logging Model

Social activities can be held in physical, face-to-face or online/virtual manners. Here, we refer to traditional *meeting-based social activities (MSA)*, which can be defined as *a crowd of people that gather together at a preplanned time and place for a specific purpose*. Each activity MSA_i has its initiator, the initiation place, the activity venue, a group of activity members or participants. We use an example to illustrate it: *One day, Bob is in the laboratory and he wants to invite some friends to have dinner together in the Golf restaurant.* Here, Bob is the activity initiator; he initiates the activity in his laboratory; the activity venue is the Golf restaurant.

Fig. 2. The SAL model

According to the definition, we formulate the social activity logging (SAL) model, which describes how *MSAs* should be recorded in the data repository (we call it the SAL repository). It is illustrated in Fig. 2. The metadata are explained below.

- A_i: Activity index.
- *Tag:* Users may give one more tags for a activity, e.g., dinner, party, meeting.
- *Initiator:* The initiator of a social activity. We define the person who send out the activity invitation message as the initiator.
- *Time:* Activity initiation time.
- *I-Loc:* It refers to the location where the organizer initiates the social activity. For instance, the dinning activity may be initiated by Bob in his laboratory.
- *A-Place:* Place or venue of the social activity, e.g., the dinning activity may happen in the university restaurant.
- *MemList:* A list of members who participate the social activity. As group activities, we have: $Size[MemList] \geq 2$

Messaging and Logging. When an activity is initiazed, the initiator will send an invitation message (e.g., SMS) to a group of contacts. We category the message into two types: SA_{in} and SA_{out}. All the invitation messages will be kept in the initiator's SA_{out} box, the received activity requests will be kept in the SA_{in} box. For privacy, the *I-Loc* will be sent to empty to all the message receivers. People being invited (e.g., group members) can add new tags for incoming messages. All the logged messages (SA_{in} , SA_{out}) form the SAL repository.

4.2   Social Graph and Group Modeling

We use *social graph* to characterize the structure of a social activity participation network. Edges are formed by sending or receiving activity requests. We employ the egocentric network method used in [3], which considers a message sent from a user to a group of contacts as forming a single edge (a *hyperedge*). The edge is directed, represented as *in* and *out* edges (corresponding to SA_{in} and SA_{out}). We call each hyperedge an *explicit/raw group*. Figure 3 gives an example of *A*'s social graph, where three raw groups are involved (e.g., *G1* to *G3*). The directed edges are also illustrated in Fig. 3.

As presented in the introduction, the social graph of a person often consists of a set of overlapping (e.g., group *G1* and *G3*) and nested groups (e.g., group *G1* and *G2*). Here we also give a formulation of the two types of groups, as shown in Eq. (1), (2).

$$Overlap(G1, G2) = (G1 \cap G2 \neq \phi) \wedge (G1 \not\subset G2) \wedge (G2 \not\subset G1) \tag{1}$$

$$Nested(G1, G2) = (G1 \subset G2) \vee (G2 \subset G1) \tag{2}$$

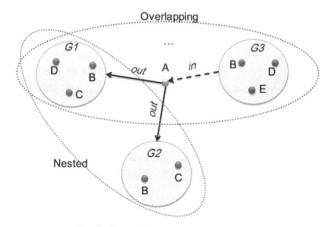

Fig. 3. Group formation and abstraction

People can participate in various social activities, and different social activities usually link different group instances. This will result in a large number of groups in the initial social graph. Different from the approach used in [3], which recommends groups based on the raw extracted groups. Our work introduces the *group abstraction* process, which can eliminate minor subsets of groups by merging highly nested or overlapping groups. For example, *A* has lunch with *B*, *C* and *D* each day, except for one day that *D* didn't come for some reason, this result in two different groups: *{A, B, C, D}* and *{A, B, C}*. In our approach, the two groups will be merged as the unique group: *{A, B, C, D}*. We call the groups after group abstraction *implicit/logical groups*.

5   Algorithms for Group Formation and Recommendation

Having described the approach for group modeling, in this section we first present the group abstraction process (i.e., *social graph mining*, distilling logical groups from raw extracted groups); the algorithm that can measure users' affinity to each logical group and support context-aware group recommendation will then be presented.

5.1   Group Abstraction

The group abstraction process is to merge highly nested/overlapping raw groups. We refer to the merging of nested groups as *group subsumption* and the merging of overlapping groups as *group integration*.

(A) Group Subsumption

Given two nested groups, *G1* and *G2* ($G1 \subset G2$). The two groups can be subsumed if they are highly nested. Here we refer to MacLean *et al.*'s *information leak* metric for group nesting evaluation [2]. The information leak value is determined by two factors: *similarity of the two groups*, and *the ratio of the number of social activities held by each group* (e.g., the number of records in SAL). We thus define a new parameter *subrate*, to measure if two groups can be subsumed. This is formulated in Eq. (3).

$$subtrate(G1, G2) = \frac{|G2| - |G1|}{|G2|} \times \frac{num(G1)}{num(G2)}, \quad when \ G1 \subset G2 \tag{3}$$

Where: $|Gi|$ refers to the number of members of group *Gi*, and $\dfrac{|G2| - |G1|}{|G2|}$ characterizes the similarity of two groups; *num(Gi)* refers to the number of social activities held by *Gi*. Suppose *G1= {A, B}*, *G2={A,B,C}*, and there are 5 and 100 records relevant to *G1* and *G2* in SAL, we have $subtrate(G1, G2) = \dfrac{3-2}{3} \times \dfrac{5}{100} = 1/60$. If the value is below a predefined threshold (*subThreshold*), the two groups can be subsumed.

(B) Group Integration

The two overlapping groups can be integrated if they are very similar. To measure the similarity between two groups, we use the *Jaccard* metric which is often used for similarity measurement [10, 11]. A new parameter called *intrate* is defined, formulated in Eq. (4). The two groups can be integrated if their similarity exceeds a threshold (*intThreshold*).

$$intrate(G1, G2) = \frac{|G1 \cap G2|}{|G1 \cup G2|}, \quad when \ overlap(G1, G2) \tag{4}$$

5.2   Group Recommendation

Having identified implicit groups, the next requirement is to recommend highly relevant groups to users in real-world settings. The recommendation is based on two major factors: *the context of the user*, and *the affinity between the user and his groups*.

The algorithm is thus designed by two major parts: *context-aware group filtering* and *group affinity ranking*.

(A) Context-Aware Group Filtering

One basic principle for group recommendation is to suggest relevant groups in terms of user needs with little human intervention. Various contexts that are obtained when users initialize activities are leveraged to filter irrelevant logical groups.

- *Time*: we divide the initiation time into four logical period of times, namely *morning* (6:00-11:00), *noon* (11:00-13:00), *afternoon* (13:00-18:00), *night* (18:00-6:00).
- *Location*: the location where the user initiates an activity (e.g., *I-Loc*). It can be obtained through *in-phone* GPS positioning or WiFi positioning.
- *WithWhom*: nearby friends are often co-initiators or members of an activity. We use *WithWhom (i)* to represent that a number of *i* contacts are together with the initiator. This context can be obtained through the Bluetooth ID of user mobile phones, and a user will keep the Bluetooth ID of her friends in her contact book.
- *Tag*: a tag given by the user often shows the type of an activity being organized.

The rule for group filtering is performed in this way: for each context Ci obtained when organizing a new activity, if a logical group Gj does not have any historical record (as depicted in Section 4.1, each logical group corresponds to a set of historical records in SAL) that matches Ci, Gj is considered irrelevant and thus will be filtered.

(B) Group Affinity Ranking

Group affinity ranking is to calculate the tie strength between a user and her logical groups. There have been numerous studies on tie-strength evaluation in social networks [12, 13, 3]. Here, we employ the method used in [3], which is originally used for contact tie-strength measurement in email networks. The tie strength between two entities is computed based on their interaction history. Besides interaction frequency, two other factors are considered:

- *Recency*. Human relationship is evolvable and dynamic over time.
- *User role*. The social activities that the user initiates (i.e., as the initiator) are considered more important than those he or she is merely a participant.

We define the affinity rank between user Ui and logical group Gj as *affrank(Ui, Gj)*, which can be computed by Eq. (5) :

$$affRank(Ui,Gj) = \omega_{out} \sum_{Ai \in SA_{out} \wedge G(Ai)=Gj} (\frac{1}{2})^{d_{now}-d(Ai)} + \omega_{in} \sum_{Ai \in SA_{in} \wedge G(Ai)=Gj} (\frac{1}{2})^{d_{now}-d(Ai)} \quad (5)$$

Where: ω_{out} and ω_{in} weight the user roles in social activities, the former one is bigger to represent the importance of initiator roles. We use empirically 1.5 and 1.0 in the current implementation.

SA_{out} and SA_{in} follow the definition in Section 4.1, indicating initiated activity records and being invited activity records; $Ai \in SA_{out} \wedge G(Ai) = Gj$ means that the activity record Ai is from SA_{out} and the corresponding group of Ai is Gj.

d_{now} and $d(Ai)$ refer to the current date and the initiation time of activity Ai.

Given Ui, the implicit group with the highest rank will finally be recommended.

6   Implementation and Evaluation

In this section, we first present a prototype implementation of GroupMe. The implementation of GroupMe is based on several key components, such as context-aware recommendation and group abstraction. We will then evaluate the affects of these components to the performance of GroupMe. An initial user study was also conducted to validate the usability of our system.

6.1   Prototype Implementation

We have implemented GroupMe on the Android platform. The SQLite was used as the database for activity data storage. The interface for activity organization is shown in Fig. 4 (a). The *location*, *initiation time*, and *WithWhom* context can be sensed automatically; tags and activity venue can be added by users for activities. Recommended friends are also listed. When pressing the 'SMS' button, an SMS message will be sent out to the selected contacts (Fig. 4b). The contact management interface is shown in Fig. 4 (c), where user profile can be managed.

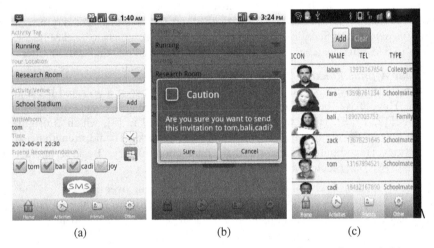

(a)   (b)   (c)

Fig. 4. User interfaces: (a) activity organization, (b) invitation sending, and (c) contact management

6.2   Data Collection

As an intelligent system based on social interaction history mining, data collection becomes the basis for system performance evaluation. In the current stage, a combination of two methods can be used for data collection: *mobile phone logging* and *online blogging*. The prior method automatically logs user activities when they initialize them using the GroupMe software (installed in sensor-enhanced mobile phones). The latter one asks users to manually record their daily social activities in an online blogging webpage.

Since it is not easy to equip a smart phone to each data contributor, the online blogging method was used chiefly in the data collection process. Twenty more students from our lab were recruited to contribute data, the data collection activity lasted for about one month during April-May, 2012. Almost four hundred activity records were collected, among which the five most popular activities recorded are *lunch (38.3%), lesson (16.8%), discussion (13.4%), sports (6.15%), meeting (5.6%).* The two most popular initiation places are *lab* and *student dormitory*. We plan to collect more data using mobile phone logging in the next stage.

6.3   Performance Evaluation

(A) Evaluation Metric and Parameter Setting
To validate the effectiveness of the recommendation algorithm, we employ two generic criteria — *Precision* and *Recall. Precision* is the ratio of the correct number of recommendations (*RightRecNum*) and the total number of recommendations (*TotalRecNum*). Recall is the ratio of *RightRecNum* and the number of people who are actually invited (*ActMemberNum*), i.e., the *ground truth*. The two criteria are formulated by Eq. (6) and (7).

$$precision = \frac{RightRecNum}{TotalRecNum} \qquad (6)$$

$$recall = \frac{RightRecNum}{ActMemberNum} \qquad (7)$$

For instance, suppose *A*, *B* and *C* participate an activity, the recommendation result of GroupMe is *A*, *B*, *D* and *E*. Here, the *RightRecNum, TotalRecNum,* and *ActMemberNum* are 2, 4, and 3, respectively. The *Precision* of the recommendation is thus 50% and the *Recall* is 67%. In the experiments, we choose 300 SAL records as the training set, and 50 as the test set. The *MemList* in the test records are used as the ground truth, and the training set is used for computing recommendations. In the experiments, the *subThreshold* and *intThreshold* are set empirically to 0.2 and 0.3.

Table 1. The effect of contexts

Context Groups	Precision	Recall
(Initiation) Time + I-Loc	58.2%	74.6%
Time + I-Loc + Tag	71.2%	80.7%
Time + I-Loc + WithWhom (1)	68.13%	94.7%
Time + I-Loc + WithWhom (2)	81.01%	98.66%

(B) The Effect of Contexts
One of the major differences between GroupMe and other group tools is that our work is to provide group suggestion in pervasive, real-world settings. Many contexts obtained through mobile sensing are leveraged to filter irrelevant groups and improve recommendation performance. To evaluate the effects of different contexts to group suggestion, we have chosen four different groups of contexts, with *Time* and *I-Loc* as the basic group, and *Tag, WithWhom(1), WithWhom(2)* as additional elements in the other three context groups. The experiment results are listed in Table 1, which shows that more contexts can enhance recommendation performance, and the *WithWhom* context performs better than the *Tag* context.

(C) The Effect of Group Abstraction

Group abstraction is another contribution to group formation and suggestion, which can eliminate noisy groups and merge relevant raw groups to logical units. We have conducted experiments to validate its effect to GroupMe, by comparing the *Precision* and *Recall* of the recommendation with and without group abstraction. Three contexts are used: *time*, *I-Loc*, and *WithWhom* (0, 1, 2). The experimental results are shown in Fig. 5, which indicates that group abstraction can better draw the social graph of a user and provide more effective support for activity organization.

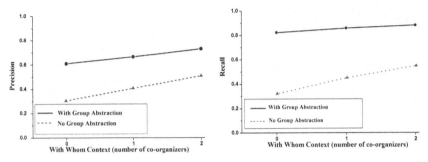

Fig. 5. The effect of group abstraction

(D) User Study

To understand the usability of our system, we have made a user study to compare the efficiency of activity organization in traditional flat contact lists and in GroupMe. Ten subjects who have contributed in the data collection process were recruited for this study. For each of them, we specified an "activity tag" (according to her activity records in the SAL repository), and asked the subject to invite the people who often participate this activity together with her. The flat contact list contains a list of 100 people. For GroupMe, three contexts were used for contact recommendation: *Time*, *I-Loc*, and *WithWhom(1)*. Once the subject specified the three contexts, the recommendations were given. The average time used for the two methods is 12s (for flat contact list) and 3s (for GroupMe), which illustrates that GroupMe can save much time on group formation.

7   Conclusion

We have presented our early efforts for social activity organization in real world settings. The activity logging and social graph model is proposed to characterize meeting-based social activities and complex, heterogeneous group structure in activity participation. A series of group computing algorithms are presented to extract logical groups from raw groups. To suggest highly relevant groups, the context and adhesiveness-aware algorithm are proposed. Experiments over the one-month activity logs collected from 20 more subjects show that, by using various contexts and the group abstraction process, the performance of group formation and suggestion can be improved. The user study indicates that our system greatly decreases the time cost on group formation than traditional ways. Social activities and human behaviors are difficult to model due to its complex nature. For instance, people sometimes want to have activities with close friends, and sometimes they intend to make new friends. As for future work, we intend to extend the system to involve more group formation methods (e.g., not only mining existing groups, but suggesting new contacts to join). We will leverage the opportunistic contact nature [14] and social network structure (e.g., triadic closure [15]) theories to achieve this.

Acknowledgement. This work was partially supported by the National Basic Research Program of China (No.2012CB316400), the National Natural Science Foundation of China (No. 61222209, 61103063), the Program for New Century Excellent Talents in University (No. NCET-12-0466), the Natural Science Basic Research Plan in Shaanxi Province of China (No. 2012JQ8028), and the Basic Research Foundation of NPU (No. JC20110267).

References

1. Kuhn, M., Wirz, M.: Cluestr: Mobile social networking for enhanced group communication. In: Proc. of the International Conference on Supporting Group Work, GROUP (2009)
2. MacLean, D., Hangal, S., Teh, S.K., Lam, M.S., Heer, J.: Groups without tears: mining social topologies from email. In: Proc. of IUI 2011, pp. 83–92 (2011)
3. Roth, M., et al.: Suggesting friends using the implicit social graph. In: Proc. of the 16th ACM SIGKDD International Conference on Knowledge Discovery and Data Mining (2010)
4. Whittaker, S., et al.: ContactMap: Organizing communication in a social desktop. ACM Transactions on Computer-Human Interaction (TOCHI) 11(4), 445–471 (2004)
5. Guo, B., Zhang, D., Yang, D.: "Read" More from Business Cards: Toward a Smart Social Contact Management System. In: Proc. of WI 2011, pp. 384–387 (2011)
6. Eagle, N., Pentland, A.: Social Serendipity: Mobilizing Social Software. IEEE Pervasive Computing 4(2), 28–34 (2005)
7. Zhang, D., Wang, Z., Guo, B., Raychoudhury, V., Zhou, X.: A Dynamic Community Creation Mechanism in Opportunistic Mobile Social Networks. In: Proc. of the Third IEEE International Conference on Social Computing (SocialCom 2011), pp. 509–514 (2011)
8. Boix, E.G., et al.: Flocks: enabling dynamic group interactions in mobile social networking applications. In: Proc. of SAC 2011, pp. 425–432 (2011)
9. Lubke, R., Schuster, D., Schill, A.: Mobilisgroups: Location-based group formation in mobile social networks. In: Proc. of PerCom Workshops, pp. 502–507 (2011)
10. Tan, P., Steinbach, M., Kumar, V.: Introduction to Data Mining. Addison Wesley (2005)
11. Liben, N.D., Kleinberg, J.: The link prediction problem for social networks. In: Proc. of CIKM 2003, pp. 556–559 (2003)
12. Gilbert, E., Karahalios, K.: Predicting tie strength with social media. In: Proc. of CHI 2009, pp. 211–220 (2009)
13. Xiang, R., Neville, J., Rogati, M.: Modeling relationship strength in online social networks. In: Proc. of WWW 2010, pp. 981–990 (2010)
14. Guo, B., et al.: Enhancing Spontaneous Interaction in Opportunistic Mobile Social Networks. Communications in Mobile Computing (ComC) 1(6) (2012)
15. Kleinberg, J., Easley, D.: Networks, Crowds, and Markets. Cambridge University Press (2010)

Locus: An Indoor Localization, Tracking and Navigation System for Multi-story Buildings Using Heuristics Derived from Wi-Fi Signal Strength

Preeti Bhargava[1], Shivsubramani Krishnamoorthy[1], Aditya Karkada Nakshathri[2], Matthew Mah[1], and Ashok Agrawala[1]

[1] Department of Computer Science
University of Maryland, College Park
{prbharga,shiv,mah,agrawala}@cs.umd.edu
[2] Department of Telecommunications
University of Maryland, College Park
anakshat@umd.edu

Abstract. The holy grail in indoor location technology is to achieve the milestone of combining minimal cost with accuracy, for general consumer applications. A low-cost system should be inexpensive both to install and maintain, requiring only available consumer hardware to operate and its accuracy should be room-level or better. To achieve this, current systems require either extensive calibration or expensive hardware. Moreover, very few systems built so far have addressed localization in multi-story buildings. We explain a heuristics based indoor localization, tracking and navigation system for multi-story buildings called Locus that determines floor and location by using the locations of infrastructure points, and without the need for radio maps or calibration. It is an inexpensive solution with minimum setup and maintenance expenses. Initial experimental results in an indoor space spanning 175,000 square feet, show that it can determine the floor with 99.97% accuracy and the location with an average location error of 7m.

Keywords: Indoor location, Localization, Tracking, Navigation, Context- and location-aware applications and services.

1 Introduction and Related Work

Location is increasingly important for mobile computing, providing the basis for services such as navigation and location-aware advertising. The most popular technology for localization is GPS, which provides worldwide coverage and accuracy of a few meters depending upon satellite geometry and receiver hardware. Its major shortcoming is that it is reliable only in outdoor and environments with direct visibility to at least four GPS satellites. For indoor environments, alternative technologies are required. The holy grail in indoor location technology is to achieve the

K. Zheng, M. Li, and H. Jiang (Eds.): MOBIQUITOUS 2012, LNICST 120, pp. 212–223, 2013.
© Institute for Computer Sciences, Social Informatics and Telecommunications Engineering 2013

milestone of combining minimal cost with accuracy, for general consumer applications. A low-cost system should be inexpensive both to install and maintain, requiring only available consumer hardware to operate and its accuracy should be room-level or better. To achieve this level of accuracy, current systems require either extensive calibration or expensive hardware. Most of them are based primarily on either time or signal strength information. A third alternative, angle-of-arrival information is useful in outdoor environments but is not generally helpful indoors due to obstructions and reflections. Time-based systems require hardware support for timestamping that is not available in consumer products.

The use of wireless received signal strength indicators or RSSI values for localization of mobile devices is a popular technique due to the widespread availability of wireless signals and the relatively low cost of implementation.(We use RSSI and signal strength interchangeably in the paper). Its simplest version involves the mobile device measuring the signal strengths of existing infrastructure points such as Wi-Fi access points (APs) or mobile phone base stations and reporting the origin of the strongest signal it can hear as its location. This technique may be applied both to short range communications technologies such as RFID or Bluetooth as well as longer range technologies such as Wi-Fi or mobile phones but its performance is directly linked to the density of reference points. The precision of signal strength approaches is improved to meter-level by fingerprinting techniques, such as those in RADAR [1] or Horus [10], that use pre-measured fingerprinting radio maps. There are commercial solutions available as well such as Ekahau [3] that achieves a high precision of 1 to 3 m but requires proprietary hardware. However, a major drawback of fingerprinting is the cost of recording the radio map; a large amount of human effort is required to record the signal strength at each desired location using a receiver. Also, if the infrastructure or environment changes significantly, for instance the locations of APs are changed, furniture is moved around, the number of people occupying the closed space increases dramatically, or the test site is changed; the radio map must be remeasured to maintain performance [2].

Systems that don't use fingerprinting techniques often suffer from very low precision. These include Active Campus [4], that uses an empirical propagation model and hillclimbing algorithm to compute location with a location error of about 10 meters, and a ratio based algorithm proposed by Li [5], which produces median errors of roughly 20 feet (6.1 m) by predictively computing a map of signal strength ratios. Lim et al [6] proposed an automated system for collection of RSSI values between APs and between a client and an AP to determine the client's location with an error of 3m. They do not create a radio map but require initial AP calibration and its modification for continuous data collection.

However, more important than the raw error in distance is the computation of the correct floor in indoor multi-story environments. Even a most modest error in altitude can result in an incorrect floor leading to a high location error as determined by human walking distance. Identifying the exact floor is also more difficult because there are multiple APs on each floor and a device can receive signals from APs across floors. To address this, we explain a heuristics based indoor localization, tracking and navigation system for multi-story buildings - Locus (Section 3), that determines a device's floor and location by using the locations of infrastructure points but without the need of radio maps. As explained in Section 5, it can enable indoor location based services and applications such as a smartphone application that automatically downloads a map of a building when a user enters it, tracks his approximate current position on a floor map, and provides indoor navigation directions for destinations such as restrooms, offices, or conference rooms. It is also essential for situations like search and rescue operations where knowledge of the exact floor and location of a device/person on that floor is crucial for timely assistance.

Our system is calibration-free and is an inexpensive solution suitable for localization with minimum setup, deployment or maintenance expenses. By avoiding the dependence on radio maps, it is readily deployable and robust to environmental change. It relies on existing infrastructure and mobile device capabilities, and requires no proprietary hardware to be installed. Initial experimental results (Section 4) with commercial tablet devices in an indoor space spanning 175,000 square feet across multiple floors, show that our system can determine the floor with 99.97% accuracy and the location with an average location error of 7m, and with very low computational requirements. Though our system has a higher location error as compared to fingerprinting techniques, we believe it still serves as a competitive alternative particularly in scenarios where extensive fingerprinting is not feasible or affordable or it is preferable to trade a little precision for saved human effort. To the best of our knowledge, our system is the first calibration-free system for floor as well as location determination in multi-story buildings. Active Campus [4] has options for user adjustments to correct the computed floor while in [5], the testbed is assumed to be on a single floor. Skyloc [8] uses GSM based fingerprinting for floor determination only and determines it correctly in 73 % of the cases while FTrack [9] uses an accelerometer to capture user motion data to determine floor but requires user input for initial floor.

2   Data and Experimental Setup

2.1   Signal Strength Data Gathering

The testbed for Locus is a four story academic office environment at the University of Maryland - the A.V. Williams Building. Figure 1 shows the floor maps with the location of the APs and test points where the RSSI values were recorded. The APs deployed in the building and used for Locus are of the Cisco AIR-LAP1142N-A-K9 model that can run multiple virtual APs. They are mounted on the ceiling and have an omnidirectional radiation pattern in the azimuth plane. Most of the APs are located in corridors rather than within offices, but are not at the same location on every floor. The indoor dimensions as of the four floors are shown in Table 1, covering a total of 175,000 square feet of deployment area. The number of APs for each floor are also shown.

The RSSI samples were taken in the corridors of each floor and a few accessible rooms. Two sets of samples were taken, the first set contained 500 samples

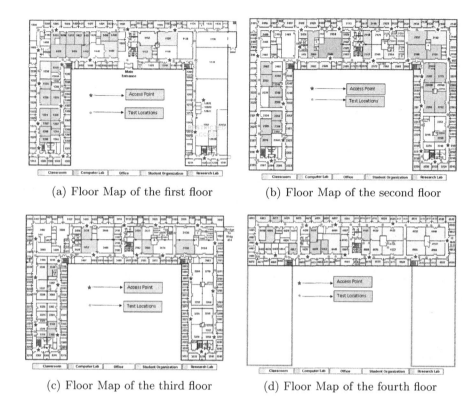

(a) Floor Map of the first floor　　　　(b) Floor Map of the second floor

(c) Floor Map of the third floor　　　　(d) Floor Map of the fourth floor

Fig. 1. Floor Maps

Table 1. Building Parameters

Floor	Dimensions (ft.)	Area (ft.^{2})	Number of APs
1	354 x 62, 2 x 182 x 80	51068	15
2	354 x 62, 2 x 182 x 80	51068	19
3	354 x 62, 2 x 182 x 80	51068	20
4	354 x 62	21948	10

from 120 test points and the second set contained 300 samples from 90 test points. Each sample contained the network name (SSID), MAC address, signal strength and frequency for each AP heard and was recorded with the (x, y, floor) coordinates for the test point.

2.2 Access Points Data

We have obtained a database of the 64 APs deployed in the A.V. Williams building, that includes their MAC addresses, AP IDs (the room number of the nearest room), and the floors and wings where they are installed. We have also added the (x,y) coordinates for each AP to the database.

3   Locus Floor and Location Determination System

3.1   Client Side Processing

The client application is an Android mobile application running on a tablet. The application scans the environment for Wi-Fi access points using the standard Android scan functionality. This data is then sent by the client to the Locus Location Server in XML format. On the server, we then lookup the database for every AP's (x,y) coordinates and floor.

In our experimental environment, each AP runs several virtual APs. The last hexadecimal digit for the base MAC address (for one physical AP) is 0, for instance 00:25:84:86:96:20 while for each virtual AP, it is varied as [1,9], for example 00:25:84:86:96:22, 00:25:84:86:96:24, etc. Some MAC addresses of virtual APs were seen to repeat for 802.11a and 802.11b/g/n networks.

3.2   Locus Floor and Location Determination Algorithm

The Locus system determines the location in two phases: the floor determination phase and the location determination phase for that floor.

Floor Determination. Locus uses four *properties*, of every sample of signal strength data that it receives from the client, to determine the floor. The values of the properties are basically floor number(s). The properties are :

1. *maxNumFloors*: Floors with maximum count of signals [1]
2. *maxSSFloor*: Floor with maximum signal strength
3. *maxAvgFloor*: Floor with maximum average signal strength
4. *maxVarFloor*: Floor with maximum signal strength variance

These properties were selected based on the fact that AP signals are attenuated when passing through ceilings and floors. As a result, a client is more likely to hear signals from its current floor than other floors, and those signals are likely to be stronger. Because of the same fact, both the average signal strength and variance of signal strengths of APs from the same floor will be higher on average. Signal strengths from a different floor will be weaker and hence their average signal strength will be less. In addition, since a large number of APs from a different floor are not heard, the signal strength variance is lower as well. There are exceptions to these heuristic, particularly for the floors below and above the true floor, but the combined use of the four properties yields the correct floor with very high probability ($> 99.9\%$), as we observed empirically.

A dataset of 500 samples was collected and pruned to remove all detected signals weaker than a threshold value of -90dBm.[2] This data was then used as a

---

[1] We saw several cases where two floors had the same count of signals and have handled this in our implementation.

[2] We selected a threshold value of -90 dBm because we observed the sensitivity of the android devices to be in the range of -20dBm to -95 dBm but all the signals less than -90dBm were very weak and inconsistent.

Table 2. Accuracy for individual properties and combination of properties

Combination/Property	Precision	Recall	F-Score/Accuracy
maxNumFloors = maxSSFloor= maxAvgFloor = maxVarFloor	1.0	0.67	0.802
maxNumFloors = maxSSFloor= maxAvgFloor	0.97	0.79	0.87
maxNumFloors= maxAvgFloor = maxVarFloor	1.0	0.725	0.84
maxNumFloors = maxSSFloor= maxVarFloor	0.975	0.727	0.833
maxSSFloor= maxAvgFloor = maxVarFloor	1.0	0.672	0.80
maxNumFloors = maxSSFloor, maxVarFloor = maxAvgFloor	1.0	0.7	0.824
maxNumFloors = maxAvgFloor, maxVarFloor = maxSSFloor	0.997	0.690	0.816
maxNumFloors = maxVarFloor, maxSSFloor = maxAvgFloor	0.997	0.678	0.807
maxNumFloors = maxSSFloor	0.97	0.866	0.915
maxAvgFloor = maxVarFloor	0.92	0.889	0.905
maxSSFloor = maxAvgFloor	0.948	0.812	0.874
maxNumFloors = maxAvgFloor	1.0	0.76	0.86
maxNumFloors = maxVarFloor	0.925	0.81	0.86
maxSSFloor= maxVarFloor	0.945	0.737	0.828
maxNumFloors	-	-	0.907
maxAvgFloor	-	-	0.848
maxSSFloor	-	-	0.857
maxVarFloor	-	-	0.816

training input to a classification algorithm which produced a label floor, based on heuristics derived from the four properties and their combinations, along with an accuracy measure for each heuristic. The combinations included taking two, three and all four properties together. The heuristics were:

1. If all four properties are equal, then the floor which matches all the four properties is the label floor.
2. If three properties are equal, then the floor which matches the three equal properties is the label floor.
3. If two properties are equal and the other two are not equal, then the floor which matches the two equal properties is the label floor.
4. If pairs of properties are equal, then the pair with the higher F-Score (explained next) is the label floor.

The accuracy measure for a heuristic is its F-Score which is the harmonic mean of precision and recall. Precision and recall are defined here as:

$$\text{Precision } p = \frac{\text{Number of test cases for a heuristic where the label floor matched with the ground truth floor}}{\text{Number of test cases that were valid for a heuristic}}$$

$$\text{Recall } r = \frac{\text{Number of test cases that were valid for a heuristic}}{\text{Total number of test cases in the test dataset}}$$

$$\text{F-Score } f = \frac{2 * p * r}{p + r}$$

Algorithm 1. Locus Floor and Location Determination Algorithm

---

Data: network name, mac address, and RSSI value for each AP heard
Result: client's estimated location
remove all APs with signal strength less than threshold;
while *not at end of data* **do**
| map mac to floor, x,y;
end
foreach *floor* **do**
| compute num of signals, average SS, max SS, variance of SS
end
Check the combinations and individual properties in the order they are
mentioned in Table 2 to determine label floor;
compute weights for every AP on label floor based on signal strength;
location ⟵ weighted average of locations of n APs heard from labelFloor;

The accuracy measure for every individual property is

$$\text{Accuracy a} = \frac{\text{Number of test cases where ground truth floor}}{\text{Total number of test cases in the test dataset}}$$

Based on these accuracy measures (shown in Table 2), we established an order for these heuristics in Locus Floor and Location Determination Algorithm
(Algorithm 1) to determine the label floor. Since the first heuristic involving a
combination of all four properties being equal encompasses all other combinations, it is tested first. Similarly, the heuristics of three properties being equal
are tested next as they include the combinations of two of the properties being
equal within them, and so on.

Location Determination. Once the algorithm determines the label floor of the
client, it uses a simplified radio propagation model and determines the client's
approximate location by normalizing the signal strength of each AP and taking a
weighted average of the location of the n strongest APs on the label floor, where
n is varied from 1 to the maximum number of APs heard from the label floor.[3]
The signal strength for each AP is essentially the average of the signal strength
of all the virtual APs running from it. The weights are calculated by converting
this averaged signal strength to power (mW) and normalizing it. This nullifies
the effect of location of APs that are far away and have weaker signal strengths,
as they will have a much lower weight as compared to APs that are closer and
have stronger signal strengths. Thus,

$$\text{Power } P_i = 10^{\frac{\text{signal strength of AP}_i \text{ in dBm}}{10}}$$

$$\text{Weight } w_i = \frac{P_i}{\sum_{i=1}^{n} P_i}$$

---

[3] When n =1, the location of the strongest AP is picked as the client's location.

Table 3. Average Location Error for n ∈ [1,7] (n = Number of strongest APs)

n	Average Location Error (in feet)	(in m)
1	30.86	9.4
2	24.15	7.36
3	23.66	7.21
4	23.66	7.21
5	23.83	7.26
6	23.92	7.29
7	23.90	7.28

4 Evaluation

4.1 Test Dataset

A test dataset containing 300 samples readings generated by Locus was collected using the methodology explained in Section 2.1.

4.2 Results

We evaluated our approach with respect to six performance measures: Floor Accuracy, Location Error, Complexity, Scalability, Robustness and Cost.

1. Floor Accuracy: Since our test site is a multi-story building, we have considered floor accuracy to be a measure of the percentage of correct floor estimations by Locus. We believe that it is an important performance measure especially for practical environments such as multi-story buildings, offices, hotels, or malls that have multiple APs on each floor. The floor accuracy of our system is 99.97 %.
2. Location Error: Once the floor is determined, we determine the client's location by calculating a weighted average of the locations of the n strongest APs being heard on that floor. Table 3 shows the average location error for n ∈ [1, 7]. [4] As seen in the table, the average location error settles around 24 feet (7.3 m) with n ≥ 3. This implies that localization can be done by Locus by using a minimum of 3 APs. The best average and median location errors are 23.71 feet (7.2 m) and 20.43 feet (6.2 m) for n=3. Figure 2(a) shows the CDF plots of location errors for n ∈ [1, 7] and Figures 2(b) and 2(c) show the PDF and histogram of the location errors for n= 3. 25 % of the errors lie within 12 feet, 50 % within 20 feet and 75% within 30 feet. Figure 2(d) shows a visualization of the locations of APs and the calculation of the client's location by Locus.
3. Complexity: Complexity can be measured in terms of software or hardware. Since our approach requires no proprietary hardware and is based solely on

---

[4] For n ≥ 7, the average location error did not change significantly.

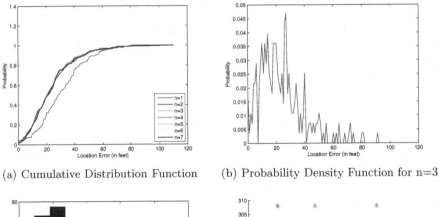

(a) Cumulative Distribution Function

(b) Probability Density Function for n=3

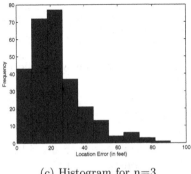

(c) Histogram for n=3

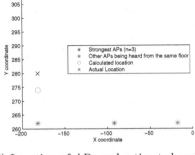

(d) Location of APs and estimated and actual locations of client for n=3

Fig. 2. Location Error

existing infrastructure, the hardware complexity is minimal. Also, the Locus system runs on a central server that has ample processing capability and power supply. The client side application is very lightweight and is restricted only to scanning and detecting the APs being heard, and then sending this information to the server.

4. Scalability: Scalability of a location system can be assessed in terms of Geographic scalability which means that the system will work even when area or volume covered is increased and Density scalability which means that as the number of units located per unit geographic area/space per time period, wireless signal channels may become congested, and hence more calculations or communication infrastructure may be required to perform localization. Another measure of scalability is the dimensional space of the system. Locus can be used in multi-story and 3D spaces as shown by the experimental studies. Since the density of APs is part of the infrastructure, we have tested Locus on different floors of the same building where the density varies. Also, the localization process in Locus is independent of the number of floors in the building and hence, it can be used for any multi-story building.

5. Robustness: Since Locus avoids any dependency on radio maps, it is robust to changes in the environment such as the time of the day, number of people in the closed space etc. Even if the positions of APs are changed, only the AP database will have to be updated. The deployed system and its underlying algorithm will remain unchanged unlike fingerprinting, where the radio map has to be calculated afresh.

6. Cost: One of the biggest advantages of Locus is that it has zero cost for deployment and maintenance as it relies solely on the existing infrastructure. The time cost of setting up is also minimal as it only requires setting up access to a database with the AP information.

5   Location-Aware Applications

5.1   Navigation

We present *Mye-Nav*, an indoor navigation tool that provides navigation instructions between rooms in a building. The application is being developed with the core modules functional. Based on the floor and location information obtained from Locus, the application displays the user's current location on the appropriate floor map of the building, tiled over an ArcGIS ESRI map. He/she can then select a particular point on the map to set the destination by a simple tap gesture. It could be a room or a point in hallway. The application immediately calculates a shortest path to the destination and reflects it on the map, as in Figure 3(a) and figure 3(b).

For accomplishing this, we maintain floor plan of every floor of the building divided into two segments - *room segment* and *walkable segment*. The room segments are defined bounded areas that have some information associated with them, such as room number, classroom/conference room/office room, occupant(s), phone number etc. The walkable segment area is where the user can move in order to reach the destination point. Our algorithm starts with the nearest point to the source in the walkable segment and tries to calculate successive points in the walkable segments towards the nearest walkable point to the destination point. We maintain a graph data structure associated with each floor, with vertices defined with respect to corners, rooms and other prominent landmarks in the hallways. The path is calculated in two phases - *Long hops* - wherein a shortest path between the source and destination is calculated in the graph. This path would be between two nodes, in the graph, that are at proximate distance from the source and destination points respectively; and *Short hops* - where the path is completed between the nearest graph nodes to the actual source/destination points at the location coordinates level.

We have tested Mye-Nav on the fourth floor of our test site (A.V Williams Building) successfully and intend to test it on the other floors and buildings. The main challenge we face is unavailability of readily usable building floor plans which makes the whole process tedious. We intend to discuss Mye-Nav and the experiments associated with it in detail in a follow-up paper.

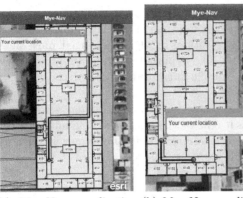
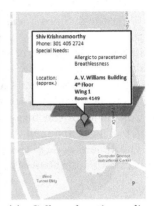

(a) Mye-Nav application screenshot

(b) Mye-Nav application screenshot

(c) Caller location displayed on the dispatcher console

Fig. 3. Screen shots of applications using Locus for indoor localization

5.2 Tracking

M-Urgency [7] is a public safety system that redefines how emergency calls are made to a Public Safety Answering Point (PSAP) like the 911 system and is designed to be context-aware of the situation in which it is used. M-Urgency enables mobile users to stream live audio and video from their devices to local PSAP along with the real time location. A precise information about the callers location will be extremely helpful for the responders to get to the location of emergency, avoiding confusions and delay. During a normal 911 call, the emergency personnel are able to locate the building where the call originates from, but often find it difficult to zero in on the actual floor and the location of the caller on that floor. A system like Locus is essential here.

As an M-Urgency call is made to the police department, the caller application makes a *location request* to the Locus. From the Wi-Fi information provided by the caller application, Locus resolves the floor and the approximate location of the caller with an error of few metres and makes it available to the dispatcher as shown in figure 3(c). We intend to incorporate this feature in the next release of the already deployed M-Urgency system at the UMD Police Department.

6   Conclusion and Future Directions

In this paper, we presented the Locus system and its underlying algorithm, for floor and location determination in multi-story buildings, that are solely based on heuristics derived from signal strengths. The system requires no calibration, fingerprinting or proprietary hardware. It is a low-cost solution suitable for location determination with minimum setup, deployment or maintenance. It is readily deployable and robust to environmental change. Initial experimental results in an indoor space spanning 175,000 square feet show that it can determine the floor with 99.97% accuracy and the location with an average location error of 7m. These results give us confidence that a calibration-free system can achieve a better precision if a more sophisticated radio propagation model is employed for calculating location. We also believe that the precision of the system can be greatly enhanced by taking into account, the building structure, floor plans as well as the AP locations and using this information to pinpoint the exact location of the client, and are working in this direction. Other factors that will come into play as part of this analysis is the number of APs not being heard and the substance through which signals pass. Though this may make the system less generic, we are in the process of analyzing this additional data in such a way that the system still retains its generality and flexibility. Meanwhile, we are also in the process of testing the system in other locations on our campus, by the means of crowdsourcing, to ensure its usability across test sites.

References

1. Bahl, P., Padmanabhan, V.N.: Radar: An in-building rf-based user location and tracking system. In: Proceedings of the IEEE Nineteenth Annual Joint Conference of the IEEE Computer and Communications Societies, INFOCOM 2000, vol. 2, pp. 775–784. IEEE (2000)
2. Bahl, P., Padmanabhan, V.N., Balachandran, A.: Enhancements to the radar user location and tracking system. Technical report, Microsoft Research (2000)
3. Ekahau, http://www.ekahau.com/
4. Griswold, W.G., Boyer, R., Brown, S.W., Truong, T.M., Bhasker, E., Jay, G.R., Shapiro, R.B.: Activecampus-sustaining educational communities through mobile technology. University of California, San Diego, Department of Computer Science and Engineering. Technical Report (2002)
5. Li, X.: Ratio-based zero-profiling indoor localization. In: IEEE 6th International Conference on Mobile Adhoc and Sensor Systems, MASS 2009., pp. 40–49. IEEE (2009)
6. Lim, H., Kung, L.C., Hou, J.C., Luo, H.: Zero-configuration indoor localization over ieee 802.11 wireless infrastructure. Wireless Networks 16(2), 405–420 (2010)
7. M-Urgency, http://m-urgency.umd.edu/
8. Varshavsky, A., LaMarca, A., Hightower, J., de Lara, E.: The skyloc floor localization system. In: Fifth Annual IEEE International Conference on Pervasive Computing and Communications, PerCom 2007, pp. 125–134. IEEE (2007)
9. Ye, H., Gu, T., Zhu, X., Xu, J., Tao, X., Lu, J., Jin, N.: Ftrack: Infrastructure-free floor localization via mobile phone sensing. In: 2012 Tenth Annual IEEE International Conference on Pervasive Computing and Communications. IEEE (2012)
10. Youssef, M.A., Agrawala, A., Udaya Shankar, A.: Wlan location determination via clustering and probability distributions. In: Proceedings of the First IEEE International Conference on Pervasive Computing and Communications (PerCom 2003), pp. 143–150. IEEE (2003)

Honeybee: A Programming Framework for Mobile Crowd Computing

Niroshinie Fernando, Seng W. Loke, and Wenny Rahayu

Department of Computer Science and Computer Engineering, La Trobe University,
Australia
tnfernando@students.latrobe.edu.au, {s.loke,w.rahayu}@latrobe.edu.au

Abstract. Although smartphones are increasingly becoming more and more powerful, enabling pervasiveness is severely hindered by the resource limitations of mobile devices. The combination of social interactions and mobile devices in the form of 'crowd computing' has the potential to surpass these limitations. In this paper, we introduce Honeybee; a crowd computing framework for mobile devices. Honeybee enables mobile devices to share work, utilize local resources and human collaboration in the mobile context. It employs 'work stealing' to effectively load balance tasks across nodes that are a priori unknown. We describe the design of Honeybee, and report initial experimental data from applications implemented using Honeybee.

Keywords: mobile crowd computing, mobile cloud computing, remote execution, offloading, crowd sourcing.

1 Introduction

Collaboration among mobile devices paves the way for greater computing opportunities in two ways; Firstly, it solves the inherent resource limitations of mobile devices [19]. Secondly, a mobile device is usually accompanied by a human user, who can use his/her 'human expertise' to crowd source problems that need a human element [12]. Increasing usage and capabilities of smartphones, combined with the potential of crowd computing [17] can provide a collaborative opportunistic resource pool. This paper aims to provide Honeybee, a programming framework that facilitates the development of mobile crowd computing applications exploiting such resources. We define 'mobile crowd computing' as a local 'mobile resource cloud' comprising a collection of mobile devices, and their users.

We build on previous work where we first investigated static job farming among a heterogeneous cluster of mobile devices in [8], and a more load balanced approach in [9] using 'work stealing' [5]. To our knowledge, no other work has used work stealing in the mobile computing domain, although it has been employed for job scheduling with load balancing in distributed environments such as Cilk ([4], [14]), and Parallel XML processing [15].

There exists a number of proposed systems on mobile clouds [10] and crowd computing [11,21,18]. The work on mobile clouds mainly focus on offloading

K. Zheng, M. Li, and H. Jiang (Eds.): MOBIQUITOUS 2012, LNICST 120, pp. 224–236, 2013.

machine computation to or with the support of a remote server, while crowd computing systems focus on either collecting data or coordinating human intelligence tasks, also using a remote server. To our knowledge, no single system supports both kinds of 'work sharing' mentioned above, i.e, machine computation tasks, and human computation tasks, using local neighbourhood resources.

Typical grid/distributed computing solutions are not applicable in mobile environments due to the following characteristics of mobile resources: less processing power, finite energy, high volatility of the resource pool resulting in inconsistent node availability, unknown devices a priori calling for opportunistic behaviour, and heterogeneity. Therefore, mobile crowd computing requires a dynamic load balancing method that is decentralized, proactive and self-adaptive instead of conventional master-slave static work farming.

The main contributions of this paper are, incorporating work stealing on a mobile resource pool to achieve load balancing without a prior knowledge of participating nodes, an API to support job sharing and crowd-sourcing among mobile devices, and evaluation of Honeybee using three different applications.

Outline. Key related work are discussed in §2, and the concepts and design principles of Honeybee in §3. An overview of implementation details are given in §4, and experiments conducted on three different applications are described in §5, with conclusions and future work outlined in §6.

2   Related Work

Opportunistic computing on mobile devices has been explored recently in a number of contexts. Job sharing via cyber foraging [20] in particular plays a main role. At the other end of the spectrum, Crowd-sourcing [12] utilizes the collective power of human expertise to solve problems. In Honeybee, we focus on a programming framework that provides an API to enable applications that cater to both ends in a mobile context.

In a large number of cases concerning mobile task offloading, a central server is essential to either co-ordinate the tasks among the mobile devices ([16]), or to offload the processing on to [6]. However, our focus is on local and decentralized job sharing owing to the issues in connecting to a remote server such as latency, bandwidth issues [20], network unavailability, battery drain when connecting via 3G, and data costs.

Crowd Computing is introduced in [17] which shows the potential of using mobile devices in a social context to perform large scaled distributed computations. They use message forwarding in opportunistic networks as basis and use a static task farming approach. We, however, show that work stealing can give better results compared to a static farming approach. In CrowdSearch, [21], image search on mobile devices is performed with human validation via the Amazon mechanical turk (AMT)[1]. CrowdSearch requires a backend server as well, since the processing is done on both local and remote resources. [11] is a query processing system that uses human expertise to answer queries that database systems and search engines find difficult. In Medusa [18], a crowd sensing framework for collecting sensor data from mobile phones, users are able to specify high level abstractions for sensing tasks, using AMT. Our work is different from these in terms of using only local mobile resources opportunistically. Furthermore, our focus is on a framework that can be used to implement a variety of tasks, not limited to query processing, sensing, or human validation. However, previous work showed us that user participation is at a considerable level, and 'micro tasking' is viable. WiFi or 3G has been the popular choice among many of these work, except in cases such as the MMPI framework [7], which is a mobile version of the standard MPI over Bluetooth, and in [3] where swarm intelligence techniques has been adopted for message propagation. We have only used Bluetooth in this implementation due to its widespread availability and low energy consumption. However, other protocols shall be implemented in future work.

3   Honeybee: Concept and Design

The objective of the Honeybee framework is twofold:

1. In case of human aided computation such as qualitative classification tasks, to enable collaboration of multiple human users using mobile devices. For example, conducting surveys, asking for opinions, image identification and comparison, audio transcribing, collecting data etc.
2. In case of machine computation, improve the efficiency of the execution by either giving a speedup gain, and/or conserving resources (eg: battery). For example, image processing, natural language processing, e-learning, and multimedia search.

Honeybee's work stealing algorithm for mobile devices was described in detail in our previous work [9], which will be briefly explained here using an example scenario that combines human and machine intelligence.

3.1   How Honeybee Works: Lost Child Scenario

Consider a carnival setting attended by hundreds of people. Among these attendees, a toddler goes missing and the security officials are notified. Charged with quickly locating the missing child among the throng of visitors, the authorities decide to use crowd computing. They broadcast a request, notifying the attendees of the situation, and send out a photograph of the child through opportunistic forwarding. Here, the initial 'task' is the request containing details about the child, his photograph, and whom to contact if seen. Instead of selecting a few worker nodes, the crowd computing system specifies that this is a message needing to be propagated to all encountering devices. People who receive the message go through their photo gallery and check if a child can be spotted in their photographs taken on the carnival. However, it is common for many of people to take many photographs at such an event. To go through all of them requires time and patience. Let us say John is such an attendee. He has taken over hundred photographs in the carnival and he chooses instead to first filter out photographs containing faces. However, facial detection is an expensive task. Therefore, he employs Honeybee to share the face detection work among other people, possibly employing an app similar to our prototype in Section 5.1. Here, John's mobile device is the 'delegator' and Honeybee will first identify available 'worker nodes' in the vicinity and then proceed to distribute the 'job pool' containing the images to be processed among them. Since there is no way to determine device capabilities a priori, Honeybee will initially distribute the job pool equally. As time progresses, the nodes who complete running the face detection on their share of jobs will attempt to 'steal' jobs from other nodes, ensuring that 'faster' nodes will receive more jobs, contributing to a higher speedup. John's device, which is the delegator, continues to do a part of the work as well, while listening for incoming 'result transmissions'. Once all the jobs results are collected, the delegator sends out a termination signal that notifies the workers that task is done. Once the face detection is done, John checks the filtered photographs manually to check for an appearance of the child.

There are several issues that arise considering such a scenario as above: What kind of tasks can be 'shared' using a mobile resource pool? Where would the job pool be stored? How does the delegator manage executing, stealing and distributing jobs? How does device mobility affect program execution? Why not distribute jobs one by that would ensure load balancing? What will motivates users to participate in such a scheme? These shall be addressed in the following section.

3.2   Design Considerations

We extensively focus on the concept of *busyness*, to keep participating devices busy as much as possible and minimize idling. Honeybee is catered for tasks that can be broken down into several independent jobs that can be executed in parallel, so that the complete task $J = \sum_{i=1}^{n} j_i$ where there are a total of n jobs. The delegator selects at random, a pool of f workers such that $f \leq n$. The sub task distribution is twofold: initial jobs and stolen jobs. Initial tasks are distributed by the delegator at time t_0 such that each participating device receives n/f jobs. The delegator also starts executing its share of jobs at time t_0, in parallel to the job distribution. The workers read the job parameters, and start the execution as

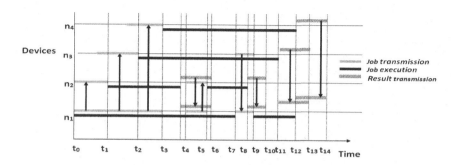

Fig. 1. Four nodes working in collaboration using work stealing

soon as they receive them. So, worker n_2 shall start execution at time t_1, n_3 at t_2, and so on. Depending on device capabilities, resources, start time of computation, and job size/complexity, some nodes are likely to finish their jobs before others. If this occurs, the finished nodes shall transmit their finished result back to the delegator, and attempt to 'steal' some jobs from another node.

This scenario is illustrated in Figure 1 where four nodes are collaborating together. In this example, the four nodes are of different capabilities. That is, while n_0 does 1 job in time t, n_1 might do 3 jobs. As can be seen in the figure, the delegator n_1 distributes the jobs in parallel with its own share of job execution, until time t_3, when it finishes transmitting. From thereon, n_1 carries out its computations until time t_7. However, before it reaches t_7, a couple of communication incidents have occurred: at time t_4, node n_2 finishes its jobs, and starts transmitting the results back to n_1. This transmission occurs until t_6. Meanwhile, node n_2 also steals some jobs from n_1, since it has finished its queue. This 'stealing' process occurs until t_5, where n_1 is seen transmitting some of its jobs to n_2. After finishing its jobs at t_7, n_1 also steals some jobs from the job queue of n_3. This cycle of job execution, result transmission and stealing continues until all jobs are finished, and collected, which occurs at time t_{14}. Note that the nodes are kept busy throughout.

Job Expiry. In a practical scenario, it is unrealistic to assume all nodes will be static, or at least be relatively static during the execution. What happens if a worker node moves out of proximity before it can transfer the results? To overcome this problem, a 'deadline' needs to be set by the delegator n_1. So if the delegator does not receive any result from a particular worker within this time, it will add those jobs back to its queue and either proceed to execute them itself, or have them 'stolen' eventually to be done by another worker.

Device Mobility. Three constraints must be taken into consideration; (a)the job distribution time must not exceed the time the devices are in contact with the delegator, (b)to enable work stealing, at least several devices must be in contact with each other for the duration of execution, and (c)worker devices must transmit the result/s before an 'expiration time'. It should be noted that for different classes of applications, different settings apply. For example, if the objective of using Honeybee is to gain a speedup, performance time is of great importance. In that case, a low entropy setting where a group of people are stationary relative to each other is most suitable. Some examples for this kind of topology are, a group of passengers in a train, a hiking group, and a group of people at a restaurant. A certain percentage of devices being out of range at times is acceptable however, and these can be handled via fault tolerance methods. If the objective is to conserve resources, or data collection, where the expiration time is greater, higher entropy topologies can be considered, and in some cases are even more suitable. In this setting, a larger number of nodes will be available, and will be moving around, within a specific area. Examples are, a shopping mall, a sporting event, and an airport. Worker nodes can pass their results either through direct encounters, or opportunistic forwarding.

Bundle Size. Bundle size refers to the number of jobs assigned to a participating device at a given time. Rather than maintaining a central job queue at the delegator, we have designed Honeybee to distribute the jobs among workers such that bundle size is ≥ 1. In most cases, bundle size is n/f. Unlike in a typical distributed system setting, a resource cloud of mobile devices need to be vary of limited battery, mobility and communication. If bundle size is 1, load balancing would be automatic, but worker devices would have to continuously poll the delegator for new jobs, and the delegator would have to maintain many connections simultaneously, causing heavy communication costs. Furthermore, devices are liable to move away from the delegator during the course of execution. By setting a bundle size that is ≥ 1, we limit the probability of workers starving of jobs if they are not in proximity to the delegator.

User Participation. As with all crowd sourcing apps, the success of Honeybee depends on device participation, and participation depends on the incentives. Experiences with other micro task frameworks such as AMT have given positive indications on monetary incentives, and Wikipedia is a good example of human collaboration for non-financial gain. Incentives could also be in the form of social contract such as in a group of friends, or common goals such as in [13]. Since users may hesitate to form connections with arbitrary devices due to privacy and security concerns, a crowd computing framework must ensure secure communications, possibly by granting anonymity as suggested in [18]. Although not yet implemented in Honeybee, this is an essential part of our future work.

3.3 Upper Bound for Speedup

We now give a theoretical upper bound for speedup using Honeybee, versus monolithic execution. It is useful to formulate an upper bound to evaluate and understand the best possible result for our practical implementation. We define a speedup as the time taken to complete a task using Honeybee divided by the time taken to complete the task on the delegating device alone. We make the following assumptions for the upper bound: a)the complete task is composed of l equal jobs, and there are a total of f' devices in the opportunistic network, b)communication costs are not considered, and c)there are no restrictions on number of connections per delegating device.

The delegating device shall be denoted as n_1, and others as n_i. The time to complete m jobs (where $m < l$) on device n_i is given as t_i. Therefore, the time to complete l jobs on n_1, and therefore the time for monolithic execution, is given as $\frac{t_1}{m}l$. Let us say there exists a non negative constant k_i for each n_i device such that $\frac{t_i}{t_1} = k_i$. Thus, total number of jobs done in t_1 time in the network is equal to $m[1 + \frac{1}{k_2} + \frac{1}{k_3} + ... \frac{1}{k_i} ... + + \frac{1}{k_f}]$. Therefore, the Speedup $S = \frac{t_1 l}{m} \times \frac{m[1+\frac{1}{k_2}+\frac{1}{k_3}+...\frac{1}{k_i}...++\frac{1}{k_f}]}{t_1 l}$, and so, $S = 1 + \frac{1}{k_2} + \frac{1}{k_3} + ... + \frac{1}{k_f}$. Due to non-negligible communication in actual scenarios, the actual speedup would be less than S.

4   System Implementation

The Honeybee framework is implemented on Android, using Bluetooth as the connection protocol. The framework contains interfaces and methods for developing mobile crowd applications. We have implemented three applications using Honeybee, which will be explained in the Applications section. Figure 2 shows the main components of the system from the delegator's perspective.

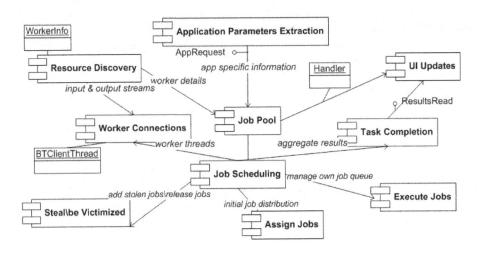

Fig. 2. Main components of Honeybee

Application Parameters. As the starting point of execution, the application passes app specific task parameters to the framework using interface *AppRequest*. In Figure 3, we show a snippet from the Face detection app (5.1), where the complete task is stored as a *FaceRequest* object, that has a list of subtasks (*FaceInfo* objects). When Honeybee processes a FaceRequest, it knows the job parameters are multiple files (from mode in FaceRequest), and each file is represented as a FaceInfo object.

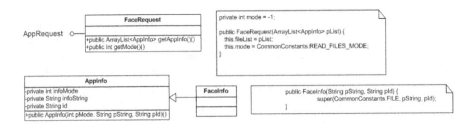

Fig. 3. Abstraction of jobs in the API

Resource Discovery and Worker Connections. Connecting to workers is achieved by calling the *ResourceDiscoveryActivity* class, which looks for available devices, connects, and creates threads for handling each connection. Each successful connection is registered with the system as a *WorkerInfo* instance.

Job Pool. The job pool is initiated by calling the *initJobPool(AppRequest pReq)* method of factory class *JobPool*, using the information passed in AppRequest. These jobs are then assigned to workers in individual threads. The 'mode' specified in AppRequest is needed when the delegator transmits the jobs to workers. The transmitting thread first writes the 'mode' of the parameters (eg: string, file, integer, etc), and then proceeds to transmit the actual parameters themselves. Constants defined in class *CommonConstants* are used to specify the modes.

UI Updates. UI Updates to the application are handled through a *Handler* object that notifies the application classes whenever a change occurs to the device job list (i.e. completed/stolen/added), and the callback interface *ResultsRead*, which receives notification when all the results are collected. It is up to the application to provide the implementation of the processing of jobs and/or results. For example, in the Face detection app, Honeybee notifies the application activity whenever a new job is received, and this triggers the *doWork()* method containing the program specific logic.

Job Scheduling. Job scheduling is closely associated with the worker thread pool that was created in the resource discovery phase. Firstly, the job scheduler must start on executing own share of jobs, while assigning each connected worker their initial job list. As explained in Figure 1, stealing, or victim threads may also be created and run. It should be noted that all the aforementioned threads need to be carefully synchronized since (a)they all need access to the job pool, and (b)same bluetooth connection is used for all communications between a worker-delegator pair. An example of such a communication conflict is when a worker device starts transmitting results, and steal from the delegator simultaneously.

5   Experimental Evaluation

Our testbed contains a total of five Android devices of varying capabilities, including Nexus S[1], Ideos[2], and Galaxy SII[3]. We have implemented the following three applications using Honeybee framework to evaluate its performance and feasibility:(a)Distributed face detection, (b)Distributed mandelbrot set generation, and (c)Collaborative photography. We have selected these applications for their different job characteristics, that are listed in Table 1.

---

[1] http://www.google.com/nexus/#/galaxy/specs
[2] http://www.huaweidevice.com/worldwide/
    productFeatures.do?pinfoId=2831&directoryId=6001&treeId=3745&tab=0
[3] http://www.samsung.com/global/microsite/galaxys2/html/specification.html

Table 1. Job characteristics of applications used for evaluation

Application	Job type	Data size of I/O
Face detection	Machine centric: CPU and memory intensive	Big inputs/small outputs
Mandelbrot set generation	Machine centric: CPU intensive	Small inputs/big outputs
Collaborative photography	Human centric processing	Small inputs/big outputs

5.1   Distributed Face Detection

In this application, we run Android's native face detection on a collection of photographs. Face detection is heavy in terms of CPU cycles, and memory. The main objective of using Honeybee to distribute the face detection computations is to increase the performance in terms of speedup. Furthermore, because of its heavy memory allocation requirements, running face detection on a collection of images is difficult, and as we found, causes OutOfMemoryExceptions if we executed on low powered devices such as Ideos. But via Honeybee, such an Ideos device can achieve such resource intensive computations by offloading jobs to other more powerful devices.

Here, the job pool contains thirty images that are stored on the delegator. On a Nexus S, to run face detection takes around 74 seconds. We mainly focused on two sets of experiments; share with similarly capable devices, and share with more capable devices. In the first category, we used two other Nexus S devices and a Galaxy S, since they can be considered equals in terms of CPU and memory capabilities. In the second category, we used an Ideos as the delegating device, to offload work with the aforementioned more powerful devices.

Evaluation Objectives:

- Examine how the performance varies with job size.
- Examine the performance results for jobs with parameters that are large in terms of inputs. The outputs of this application is very small in terms of size. We have already discussed findings of an application (Mandelbrot) with opposite parameter characteristics (small inputs, large outputs) in our earlier work [9].Compared to Mandelbrot generation, Face detection's input parameters are of considerable size (at least $\geq$ 8MB).
- Implement an application with different job and steal parameters than for our previous work in [9]. We have extended Honeybee to implement applications with different types of jobs and job parameters.

Results and Discussion. The performance results are summarized in Figure 4 (a). In Figure 4 (a.1), where we show the 'time gain' versus the job size, using two devices, it is evident that the performance increases with job size. For example, for 30 images, the distributed implementation is only 4 seconds faster, but for 240 images, the shared version finished 63 seconds earlier. When comparing the

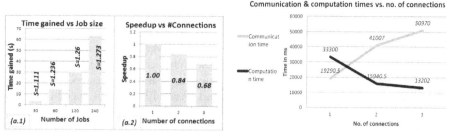

(a) Performance results for Face detection   (b) Time breakdown for Face detection

Fig. 4. Results of Face detection app

theoretical upper bound for this case (which is 2 as explained in Section 3.3), and the actual best result of 1.3 at 240 images, the effects of communication cost (of Bluetooth in particular) is evident. Figure (a.2) shows the variation of speedup results for a fixed job size (30 images) as number of connections are increased. In theory, more devices in the resource pool should have yielded better speedups. However the addition of devices seems to have degraded the performance.

Let us now examine the time breakdown that pertains to these results as shown in 4 (b). It is evident that the data rate drops considerably with the addition of new connections. The brunt of this communication time is spent on distributing the job parameters, i.e the data, to the worker devices. Although in all three cases, the amount of data transferred remains the same, managing additional connections has slowed down the delegator's throughput. Although the delegator's computation time does drop with each addition, this does not improve the overall performance. This is due to the fact that although the delegator steals jobs from workers, it still has to wait a long period of time until the jobs are distributed. This suggests using faster inter-device networking (e.g. WiFi-Direct which promises speeds up to 250 Mbps and longer range [2]) in our future work.

As another solution, dynamic initial job assigning can be explored. Instead of assigning equal jobs to all devices, the delegator is allowed to keep consuming jobs from the head of job queue. Meanwhile, jobs are transferred from the tail of the queue to workers, ensuring that the delegator's computation thread will not starve/wait till distribution is complete. In a sense, this is incorporating work stealing to the job consuming threads, since the delegator's worker thread and communication threads are consuming jobs from the same queue.

5.2 Distributed Mandelbrot Set Generation and Collaborative Photography

We have discussed the results of Mandelbrot set generation over a heterogeneous set of devices including Android and Nokia smartphones, and collaborative photography using crowd sourcing in our previous work [9]. The results of Mandelbrot experiments are summarized in Figure 5(a). By benchmarking each device in the Mandelbrot algorithm, we were able to determine that Nexus S and Nokia X6 performed the same, while both were around 6 times faster than Ideos. We have depicted this in the graph in the horizontal axis as resources in the distributed version relative to the monolith version. For example, when Nexus S shares work with an Ideos, new resources are $(1 + 0.2)x$ compared to initial $1x$ amount of resources (thus a negligible increase). We also experimented with adding a PC to the resource pool, and were able to gain speedups upto 23. These results show that even with communication overheads, Honeybee is always able to give a speedup.

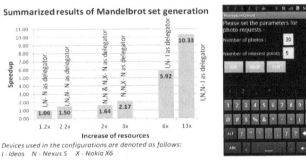

(a) Speedups for Mandelbrot set genera-   (b) Screenshots from Collaborative pho-
tion   tography

Fig. 5. Results of Mandelbrot set generation and Collaborative photography

Figure 5(b) illustrates main screens from the Collaborative photography app, which illustrates using work stealing concept in human centric computation. In this application, delegator specifies 'photo jobs' describing the requirements for photographs via 'interest points'. The faster photographers (talented/better cameras/good vantage points etc) will be able to steal additional jobs from slower workers, thus achieving load balancing.

6   Conclusions and Future Work

We present three main conclusions formed by our experiments: Firstly, results from initial prototype apps, implemented on Honeybee is evidence that a generalized framework for work/resource/expertise sharing on mobile crowd computing is viable. We have achieved this through abstracting jobs, and enabling parameterization for different types of jobs mentioned in Table 1. Secondly, for all three applications, load balancing has been achieved with work stealing, limiting device idle time. Thirdly, adding computational resources can prove to be ineffective in cases of large communication overheads. Therefore a small group of powerful devices achieves a better performance speedup than a large group of relatively weaker devices.

As future work incorporating stealing in initial job assignment should be explored to minimize the negative impacts of communication overheads. Handling incentives (social/monetary/reciprocal) and providing a secure platform is also essential for user participation. Although we have only used Bluetooth in this initial implementation, we hope to enable communications in WiFi direct as well. Furthermore, a degree of job redundancy needs to be supported to ensure robustness.

References

1. Amazon mechanical turk, https://www.mturk.com/
2. Wi-fi direct, http://www.wi-fi.org/discover-and-learn/wi-fi-direct
3. Afridi, A.H.: Mobile social computing: Swarm intelligence based collaboration. Lecture Notes in Engineering and Computer Science, vol. 2198 (2012)
4. Blumofe, R.D., Joerg, C.F., Kuszmaul, B.C., Leiserson, C.E., Randall, K.H., Zhou, Y.: Cilk: an efficient multithreaded runtime system. SIGPLAN Not. 30, 207–216 (1995)
5. Blumofe, R.D., Leiserson, C.E.: Scheduling multithreaded computations by work stealing. J. ACM 46(5), 720–748 (1999)
6. Chun, B.-G., Ihm, S., Maniatis, P., Naik, M., Patti, A.: Clonecloud: elastic execution between mobile device and cloud. In: Proceedings of the Sixth Conference on Computer Systems, EuroSys 2011, pp. 301–314. ACM, New York (2011)
7. Doolan, D.C., Tabirca, S., Yang, L.T.: Mmpi a message passing interface for the mobile environment. In: Proceedings of the 6th International Conference on Advances in Mobile Computing and Multimedia, MoMM 2008, pp. 317–321. ACM, New York (2008)
8. Fernando, N., Loke, S.W., Rahayu, W.: Dynamic mobile cloud computing: Ad hoc and opportunistic job sharing. In: 2011 Fourth IEEE International Conference on Utility and Cloud Computing (UCC), pp. 281–286 (December 2011)
9. Fernando, N., Loke, S.W., Rahayu, W.: Mobile crowd computing with work stealing. In: Proceedings of the 15th International Workshop on Mobile Cloud Computing Technologies and Applications (in NBiS) (September 2012)
10. Fernando, N., Loke, S.W., Rahayu, W.: Mobile cloud computing: A survey. Future Generation Computer Systems 29(1), 84–106 (2013)
11. Franklin, M.J., Kossmann, D., Kraska, T., Ramesh, S., Xin, R.: Crowddb: answering queries with crowdsourcing. In: Proceedings of the 2011 ACM SIGMOD International Conference on Management of data, SIGMOD 2011, pp. 61–72. ACM, New York (2011)
12. Howe, J.: The rise of crowdsourcing (2006), http://www.wired.com/wired/archive/14.06/crowds.html
13. Huerta-Canepa, G., Lee, D.: A virtual cloud computing provider for mobile devices. In: Proceedings of the 1st ACM Workshop on Mobile Cloud Computing & Services: Social Networks and Beyond, MCS 2010, pp. 6:1–6:5. ACM, New York (2010)
14. Jovanovic, N., Bender, M.A.: Task scheduling in distributed systems by work stealing and mugging - a simulation study. In: Proceedings of the 24th International Conference on Information Technology Interfaces, ITI 2002, vol. 1, pp. 259–264 (2002)
15. Lu, W., Gannon, D.: Parallel xml processing by work stealing. In: Proceedings of the 2007 Workshop on Service-Oriented Computing Performance: Aspects, Issues, and Approaches, SOCP 2007, pp. 31–38. ACM, New York (2007)

16. Marinelli, E.E.: Hyrax: Cloud Computing on Mobile Devices using MapReduce. Carnegie Mellon University, Masters thesis (2009)
17. Murray, D.G., Yoneki, E., Crowcroft, J., Hand, S.: The case for crowd computing. In: Proceedings of the Second ACM SIGCOMM Workshop on Networking, Systems, and Applications on Mobile Handhelds, MobiHeld 2010, pp. 39–44. ACM, New York (2010)
18. Ra, M.-R., Liu, B., Porta, T.F.L., Govindan, R.: Medusa: a programming framework for crowd-sensing applications. In: Proceedings of the 10th International Conference on Mobile Systems, Applications, and Services, MobiSys 2012, pp. 337–350. ACM, New York (2012)
19. Satyanarayanan, M.: Fundamental challenges in mobile computing. In: Proceedings of the Fifteenth Annual ACM Symposium on Principles of Distributed Computing PODC 1996, pp. 1–7. ACM, New York (1996)
20. Satyanarayanan, M., Bahl, P., Caceres, R., Davies, N.: The case for vm-based cloudlets in mobile computing. IEEE Pervasive Computing 8(4), 14–23 (2009)
21. Yan, T., Kumar, V., Ganesan, D.: CrowdSearch: exploiting crowds for accurate real-time image search on mobile phones. In: Proceedings of the 8th International Conference on Mobile Systems, Applications, and Services, MobiSys 2010, pp. 77–90. ACM, New York (2010)

A Trust Framework for Social Participatory Sensing Systems

Haleh Amintoosi and Salil S. Kanhere

The University of New South Wales, Sydney, Australia
{haleha,salilk}@cse.unsw.edu.au

Abstract. The integration of participatory sensing with online social networks affords an effective means to generate a critical mass of participants, which is essential for the success of this new and exciting paradigm. An equally important issue is ascertaining the quality of the contributions made by the participants. In this paper, we propose an application-agnostic trust framework for social participatory sensing. Our framework not only considers an objective estimate of the quality of the raw readings contributed but also incorporates a measure of trust of the user within the social network. We adopt a fuzzy logic based approach to combine the associated metrics to arrive at a final trust score. Extensive simulations demonstrate the efficacy of our framework.

Keywords: trust framework, participatory sensing, online social networks, data quality, urban sensing, fuzzy logic

1 Introduction

The rapid improvement in mobile phone technology, in terms of storage, processing and sensing, has resulted in the emergence of a novel paradigm called participatory sensing [1]. The core idea is to empower ordinary citizens to collect and contribute sensor data (e.g., images, sound, etc) from their surrounding environment. This new paradigm has been effectively used to crowdsource information about road conditions [2], noise pollution [3], diet [4] and price auditing [5].

For participatory sensing to be a success, a key challenge is the recruitment of sufficient volunteers. Typically there is no explicit incentive for participation and people contribute altruistically. In the absence of adequate contributors, the application will very likely fail to gather meaningful data. Another challenge, particularly for tasks which require domain-specific knowledge (e.g., takings photos of rare plant species), is the suitability of the participants for the task at hand [6].

One potential solution to address these challenges is to leverage online social networks as an underlying publish-subscribe infrastructure for distributing tasks and recruiting suitable volunteers [7,8]. This new paradigm, referred to as *social participatory sensing*, offers the following advantages. First, it makes it easier to identify and select well-suited participants based on the information available in their public profile (e.g., interests, educational background, profession, etc). Second, social ties can motivate participants to contribute to tasks initiated by

K. Zheng, M. Li, and H. Jiang (Eds.): MOBIQUITOUS 2012, LNICST 120, pp. 237–249, 2013.

friends. Third, incentives can be offered in the form of reputation points or e-coins [9] and published on the contributors' profile. A real-world instantiation of social participatory sensing was recently presented in [10], wherein, Twitter was used as the underlying social network substrate.

The inherent openness of participatory sensing, while valuable for encouraging participation, also makes it easy for propagation of erroneous and untrusted contributions. When combined with social networks, other trust issues arise. People normally have more trust on contributions provided by their close friends than casual acquaintances, since interactions with close friends provides more emotional and informational support [11]. In particular, when data of the same quality is available from two social network contacts, one a close friend and the other a casual acquaintance, it is natural human tendency to put more credence in the data from the close friend. Hence, in social participatory sensing, it is crucial to consider both, the participant's social trust and the data quality as influential aspects in evaluating the trustworthiness of contributions. While there exist works that address the issue of data trustworthiness in participatory sensing (see Section.2), they do not provide means to include social trust and as such cannot be readily adopted for social participatory sensing.

In this paper, we present an application agnostic framework to evaluate trust in social participatory sensing systems. Our system independently assesses the quality of the data and the trustworthiness of the participants and combines these metrics using fuzzy logic to arrive at a comprehensive trust rating for each contribution. By adopting a fuzzy approach, our proposed system is able to concretely quantify uncertain and imprecise information, such as trust, which is normally expressed by linguistic terms rather than numerical values. We undertake extensive simulations to demonstrate the effectiveness of our trust framework and benchmark against the state-of-the-art. The results demonstrate that considering social relations makes trust evaluation more realistic, as it resembles human behaviour in establishing trustful social communications. We also show that our framework is able to quickly adapt to rapid changes in the participant's behaviour (transitioning from high to low quality contributions) by fast and correct detection and revocation of unreliable contributions. Moreover, we find that leveraging fuzzy logic provides considerable flexibility in combining the underlying components which leads to a better assessment of the trustworthiness of contributions. Our framework results in a considerable increases in the overall trust over a method which solely associates trust based on the quality of contribution.

The rest of the paper is organised as follows. Related work is discussed in Section 2. We present the details of our fuzzy system in Section 3. Simulation results are discussed in Section 4. Finally, Section 5 concludes the paper.

2   Related Work

To the best of our knowledge, the issue of trust in social participatory sensing hasn't been addressed in prior work. As such, we discuss about related research focussing on trust issues in participatory sensing.

In a participatory sensing system, trustworthiness can be viewed as the quality of the sensed data. In order to ascertain the data trustworthiness, it is highly desirable to ascertain that the sensor data has been captured from the said location and at the said time. [12] has proposed a secure service which allows participants to tag their content with a spatial timestamp indicating its physical location, which is later used by a co-located infrastructure for verification. A similar approach has been proposed in [13], in the form of a small piece of metadata issued by a wireless infrastructure which offers a timestamped signed location proof. Since these works rely on external infrastructure, they have limited scalability. Moreover, neither approach will work in situations where the infrastructure is not installed. In our proposed framework, we assume that sensor data is tagged with GPS coordinates/system time before being stored in phone memory, which is then used by trust server for verification. Data trustworthiness has been investigated from another point of view which tries to confirm that uploaded data preserves the characteristics of the original sensed data and has not been changed unintentionally or maliciously. In particular, there are several works which make use of Trusted Platform Module (TPM)[14], which is a micro-controller embedded in the mobile device and provides it with hardware-based cryptography as well as secure storage for sensitive credentials. In [15], each device has a trusted hardware element that implements cryptographic algorithms for content protection. [16] presents two TPM-based design alternatives: the first architecture relies on a piece of trusted code and the second design incorporates trusted computing primitives into sensors to enable them sign their readings. However, TPM chips are yet to be widely adopted in mobile devices. There is also recent work that does not require TPM. [17] proposes a reputation-based framework which makes use of Beta reputation [18] to assign a reputation score to each sensor node in a wireless sensor network. Beta reputation has simple updating rules as well as facilitates easy integration of ageing. However, it is less aggressive in penalizing users with poor quality contributions. A reputation framework for participatory sensing was proposed in [19]. A watchdog module computes a cooperative rating for each device according to its short-term behaviour which acts as input to the reputation module which utilizes Gompertz function [20] to build a long-term reputation score. Their results show an improvement over the non-trust aggregation based approaches and Beta reputation system. However, the parameters related to the participants' social accountability have not been considered. As such, their system cannot be readily used in our context.

3   Fuzzy Trust Framework

In this section, we explain the proposed framework for evaluating trust in social participatory sensing system. An overview of the architecture is presented in Section 3.1 followed by a detailed discussion of each component in Section 3.2.

3.1   Framework Architecture

Since our framework attempts to mimic how human's perceive trust, we first present a simple illustrative example. Suppose John is a member of an online social network (e.g., Facebook). He has made a profile and has friended several people. John is a vegetarian. He is also on a budget and is keen to spend the least possible amount for his weekly groceries. He decides to leverage his social circle to find out the cheapest stores where he can buy vegetarian products. Specifically, he asks his friends to capture geotagged photos of price labels of vegetarian food items when they are out shopping and send these back to him. One of his friends, Alex decides to help out and provides him with several photos of price labels. In order to decide whether to rely on Alex's contributions, John would naturally take into account two aspects: (i) his personal trust perception of Alex, which would depend on various aspects such as the nature of friendship (close vs. distant), Alex's awareness of vegetarian foods, Alex's location, etc and (ii) the quality of Alex's data which would depend on the quality of the pictures, relevance of products, etc. In other words, John in his mind computes a trust rating for Alex's contribution based on these two aspects. Our proposed trust framework provides a means to obtain such trust ratings by mimicking an approach similar to John's perception of trustworthiness in a scalable and automated manner. This trust rating helps John to select trustable contributions and accordingly plan for his weekend shopping. Our framework also affords a list of trustable friends for the data consumer (e.g., John) for future recruitment.

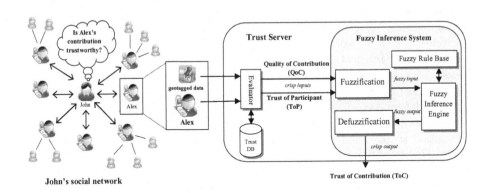

Fig. 1. Trust framework architecture

Fig. 1 illustrates the architecture of the proposed fuzzy framework. The social network serves as the underlying publish-subscribe substrate for recruiting friends as participants. In fact, the basic participatory sensing procedures (i.e., task distribution and uploading contributions) are performed by utilizing the social network communication primitives. A person wishing to start a participatory sensing campaign disseminates the tasks to his friends via email, message or by writing as a post on their profiles (e.g., Facebook wall). Friends upload their contributions via email or in the form of a message. We can also benefit from group construction facilities in Facebook or circles in Google Plus. The contributions received in response to a campaign are transferred (e.g., by using Facebook Graph API[1]) to a third party trust server, which incorporates the proposed fuzzy inference system and arrives at a trust rating for each contribution. This cumulative trust rating can be used as a criterion to accept/reject the contribution by comparing against a predefined threshold. Alternately, the ratings can be used as weights for computing summary statistics. Finally, ordered list of contributions according to their ToCs, or of participants according to their ToPs can be generated. ToP is also updated based on the quality of contributions. If below a specified threshold, participant's trust will be decremented by α; otherwise it will be incremented by β. Note that $\alpha > \beta$; since in typical social relations, trust in others is built up *gradually* after several trustworthy communications and torn down *rapidly* if dishonest behaviour is observed.

3.2   Framework Components

This section provides a detailed explanation of the framework components. In particular we focus on the trust sever and fuzzy inference system.

Trust Server. The trust server is responsible for maintaining and evaluating a comprehensive trust rating for each contribution. As discussed in Section 1, there are two aspects that need to be considered: (1) quality of contribution and (2) trust of participant. The server maintains a trust database, which contains the required information about participants and the history of their past contributions. When a contribution is received by the trust server, the effective parameters that contribute to the two aforementioned components are evaluated by the Evaluator and then combined to arrive at a single quantitative value for each. The two measures serve as inputs for the fuzzy inference system, which computes the final trust rating. In the following, we present a brief discussion about the underlying parameters and the evaluation methods.

Quality of Contribution (QoC)

In participatory sensing, contributions can be any form such as images or sounds. The quality of the data is affected not only but fidelity of the embedded sensor but also the sensing action initiated by the participant. The in-built sensors in mobile devices can vary significantly in precision. Moreover, they may not be correctly calibrated or even worse not functioning correctly, thus providing erroneous data. Participants may also use the sensors improperly while collecting data,(e.g., not focussing on the target when capturing images). Moreover, human-as-sensor applications such as weather radar in [10] are exposed to variability in the data quality due to subjectivity. For example, what is hot for one person may be comfortable for another. In order to quantify QoC, a group of parameters must be evaluated such as: relevance to the campaign (e.g., groceries in the above example), ability in determining a particular feature (e.g., price

---

[1] http://developers.facebook.com/docs/reference/api/

tag), fulfilment of task requirements (e.g., specified diet restrictions), etc. There already exists research that has proposed methods for evaluating the quality of data in participatory sensing. Examples include image processing algorithms proposed in [4] and outlier detection [23] for sound-based sensing tasks. Rather than reinventing the wheel, our system relies on the state-of-the-art methods for this evaluation. The result is a single value for QoC in the range of [0, 100].

Trust of Participant (ToP)

ToP is a combination of personal and social factors. Personal factors consist of the following parameters:

Expertise(E): It is defined as the measure of a participant's knowledge and is particularly important in tasks that require domain expertise. Greater credence is placed in contributions made by a participant who has expertise in the campaign. We employ expert finding systems for evaluating expertise. These systems employ social networks analysis and natural language processing (text mining, text classification, and semantic text similarity methods) to analyse explicit information such as public profile data and group memberships as well as implicit information such as textual posts to extract user interests and fields of expertise [21]. Dmoz[2] open directory project can be used for expertise classification. Expertise evaluation is done by incorporating text similarity analysis to find a match between the task keywords (e.g., vegetarian) and participant's expertise.

Timeliness(T): Timeliness measures how promptly a participant performs prescribed tasks. It depends on the time taken to perform the task (t) and the task deadline (d). To evaluate this parameter, inverse Gompertz function defined as $T(t) = 1 - e^{-be^{-ct}}$ can be used because of its compatible with timeliness evolution. In the original inverse Gompertz function, the lower asymptote is zero; it means that the curve approaches to zero in infinity. In our case, timeliness rate will only be zero if contribution is received after the deadline; otherwise, a value between x and 1 is assigned to it. It means that the lowest timeliness rating will be x if contribution is received before the deadline, and is zero if received after the deadline. So, we modify the function as Eq.1 to calculate the timeliness(T):

$$T(t) = \begin{cases} 1 - [(1 - x)e^{-be^{-ct}}] & \text{if } t < d \\ 0 & \text{otherwise} \end{cases} \tag{1}$$

Locality(L): Another significant parameter is locality, which is a measure of the participant's familiarity with the region where the task is to be performed. We argue that contributions received from people with high locality to the tasking region are more trustable than those received from participants who are not local, since the first group is more acquainted with and has better understanding of that region. According to the experimental results presented in [22], people tend to perform tasks that are near to their home or work place (places that they are considered 'local' to them). This implies that if we log the location of participants' contributions, we can estimate their locality. A participant's locality would be highest at locations from where they make maximum number

---

[2] http://www.dmoz.org

of contributions. In order to evaluate locality, we assume that the sensing area has been divided to n regions, and a vector V with the length equal to n is defined for each participant, where, $V(i)$ is number of samples collected in region i. In this case, locality of a participant to region i is calculated by Eq. 2:

$$L(i) = V(i)/\sum_{i=0}^{n-1} V(i) \qquad (2)$$

Next, we explain the social factors that affect ToP:

Friendship duration(F): In real as well as virtual communications, long lasting friendship relations normally translate to greater trust between two friends. So, friendship duration which is an estimation of friendship length is a prominent parameter in trust development. We use the Gompertz function to quantify friendship duration, since its shape is a perfect match for how friendships evolve. Slow growth at start resembles the friendship gestation stage. This is followed by a period of accumulation where the relationship strengthens culminating in a steady stage. As such, the friendship duration is evaluated according to Eq. 3, in which, b and c are system-defined constants and t is the time in months.

$$F(t) = e^{-be^{-ct}} \qquad (3)$$

Interaction time gap(I): In every friendship relation, interactions happen in form of sending requests and receiving responses. Interaction time gap, measures the time between the consequent interactions and is a good indicator of the strength of friendship ties. If two individuals interact frequently, then it implies that they share a strong relationship, which translates to greater trust. We propose to use the inverse Gompertz function shown in Eq. 4, to quantify the interaction time gap, where, b and c are system-defined constants and t is the time in months.

$$I(t) = 1 - e^{-be^{-ct}} \qquad (4)$$

The aforementioned parameters are combined by the Evaluator to arrive at a single value for ToP, as follows, $ToP = w_1 \times E + w_2 \times T + w_3 \times L + w_4 \times F + w_5 \times I$, where, w_i is the application specific weight of each parameter.

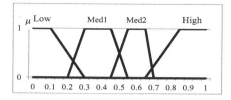
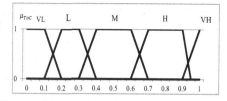

(a) Membership function for QoC and ToP   (b) Membership function for ToC

Fig. 2. Membership functions of input and output linguistic variables

Fuzzy Inference System. Our proposed framework employs fuzzy logic to calculate a comprehensive trust rating for each contribution, referred to as the Trust of Contribution (ToC). We cover all possible combinations of trust aspects and address them by leveraging fuzzy logic in mimicking the human decision-making process. The inputs to the fuzzy inference system are the crisp values of QoC and ToP. In the following, we describe the fuzzy inference system components.

Fuzzifier: The fuzzifier converts the crisp values of input parameters into a linguistic variable according to their membership functions. In other words, it determines the degree to which these inputs belong to each of the corresponding fuzzy sets. The fuzzy sets for QoC, ToP and ToC are defined as:

T(QoC)=T(ToP)={Low, Med1, Med2, High}, T(ToC)= { VL, L, M, H, VH}

Fig.2(a) represents the membership function of QoC and ToP and Fig.2(b) depicts the ToC membership function. We used trapezoidal shaped membership functions since they provide adequate representation of the expert knowledge, and at the same time, significantly simplify the process of computation.

Inference Engine: The role of inference engine is to convert fuzzy inputs (QoC and ToP) to the fuzzy output (ToC) by leveraging If-Then type fuzzy rules. The combination of the above mentioned fuzzy sets create 4*4=16 different states which have been addressed by 16 fuzzy rules as shown in Table.1. Fuzzy rules help in describing how we balance the various trust aspects. The rule base design is based on our experience and beliefs on how the system should work. To define the output zone, we used *max-min* composition method as:

$$\mu_{T(ToC)}(ToC) = max[\min_{\substack{X \in T(ToP), \\ Y \in T(QoC)}} (\mu_X(ToP), \mu_Y(QoC))], \text{ where } \mu_A(x) \text{ denotes}$$

the degree of x's membership to a fuzzy set A. The result of the inference engine is the ToC which is a linguistic fuzzy value.

Table 1. Fuzzy rule base for defining ToC according to QoC and ToP

Rule no.	if QoC	and ToP	Then ToC	Rule no.	if QoC	and ToP	Then ToC
1	Low	Low	VL	9	Med2	Low	M
2	Low	Med1	L	10	Med2	Med1	H
3	Low	Med2	L	11	Med2	Med2	H
4	Low	High	M	12	Med2	High	H
5	Med1	Low	L	14	High	Low	H
6	Med1	Med1	L	14	High	Med1	H
7	Med1	Med2	M	15	High	Med2	VH
8	Med1	High	M	16	High	High	VH

Defuzzifier: A defuzzifier converts the ToC fuzzy value to a crisp value in range of [0, 1] by employing the Centre of Gravity method (COG) [24], which computes the center of gravity of the area under ToC membership function.

To summarize, once a campaign is launched, participants begin to send a series of contributions. For each contribution, the Evaluator computes a value for QoC and ToP. These values are fed to fuzzy inference engine which calculates ToC for that contribution. The server utilizes the ToC to provide useful statistical results. For example, only contributions with a TOC greater than a certain threshold could be considered as trustable. Moreover, the ToP values could be used to select a list of trustable candidates for recruitment in future campaigns.

4 Experimental Evaluation

This section presents simulation-based evaluation of the proposed trust system. The simulation setup is outlined in Section 4.1 and the results are in Section 4.2.

4.1 Simulation Setup

To undertake the preliminary evaluations outlined herein, we chose to conduct simulations, since real experiments in social participatory sensing are difficult to organise. Simulations afford a controlled environment where we can carefully vary certain parameters and observe the impact on the system performance. We developed a custom Java simulator for this purpose. We simulate an online social network where 50 members participate in 200 campaigns, producing one contribution for each. In the ideal case, for each contribution, we would have computed the value of each of the underlying parameters discussed in Section 3.2 based on some typical probabilistic distributions. However, this would make the simulations quite complicated. Moreover, this exercise would digress from the primary objective of the evaluations: to evaluate if social trust is a useful contributor to the overall trust in social participatory sensing. For the sake of simplicity, we therefore, assign a random value of ToP to each participant and a random value of QoC for each contribution, both in the range of [0, 100], based on criteria specific to the scenarios and leave extra investigation for future work.

Recall that, the goal of the trust framework is to assign a trust rating to each contribution which is further used as a criterion to accept/reject the contribution. As such, in the evaluations, we artificially create circumstances in which, some participants contribute poor quality data for a certain number of campaigns. We want to investigate if our trust framework is able to identify this behaviour and revoke untrusted contributions in a robust manner. In order to create all possible combinations of QoC and ToP, we assume that participants belong to one of the following four categories, each of which resembles one type of friend in a typical social participatory sensing system:

Category 1: Participants with high ToP (ToP$\geq$50) and high QoC (QoC$\geq$50).
Category 2: Participants with low ToP (ToP<50) but high QoC (QoC$\geq$50).
Category 3: Participants with high ToP (ToP$\geq$50) but low QoC (QoC<50).
Category 4: Participants with low ToP (ToP<50) and low QoC (QoC<50).

The threshold 50 used above for a trustworthy participant/contribution has also been used previously in [19,25]. Friends that belong to Category 1 would generally be more willing to volunteer and contribute data. As such, we assume that Category 1 contains more participants (20), in comparison with the other 3 categories, which contain 10 participants each. In the first scenario, we assume that participants do not alter their behaviour and thus QoCs follow the category settings throughout the entire simulation. In the second scenario, we assume that participants can transition from one category to another (details in Section 4.2).

As mentioned in Section 3, a ToC rating is calculated for each contribution and those with ToC lower than a predefined threshold are revoked from further calculations. The ToCs for the non-revoked contributions are then combined to form an overall trust for that campaign. In other words, $OverallTrust = \frac{\sum_{i=1}^{n} ToC}{n}$ in which, n is the number of non-revoked contributions. ToPs are also updated based related QoCs. We consider the overall trust as the evaluation metric. The greater the overall trust the better the ability of the system to revoke untrusted contributions. Overall trust has a value in the range of $[0, 100]$.

We compare the performance of our framework against a baseline system, which only considers QoC for evaluating the trust of each contribution. In order to study the effect of other trust aspects, we incrementally add them to the baseline to see how considering each aspect influences trust. Specifically, we compare the following: (1) Baseline: where $ToC = QoC$ (2) Baseline-Rep: which follows the approach in [19] by calculating a reputation score for each participant according to the QoC of his successive contributions. This reputation score is used as a weight for QoC. In other words, $ToC = \sqrt{Rep * QoC}$ (3) Average: which includes ToP but computes the ToC simply as an average of ToP and QoC (4) Fuzzy: our proposed framework.

The revocation threshold is set to 50. Recall that, when ToP is updated, it is decremented by α if the QoC is below a threshold; otherwise it is incremented by β. We set the QoC threshold to 50 and α and β to 2 and 1, respectively.

4.2   Simulation Results

We first present the simulation results for the first scenario. Figure 3 depicts the evolution of the average overall trust as a function of the number of campaigns. As shown in the figure, our fuzzy trust method outperforms all the other methods. This confirms its success in mimicking the human trust establishing process by correct settings of fuzzy rules. In particular, we have set the rules in a way that results in early detection and severe punishment of untrusted contributions and also put greater emphasis on highly trusted contributions. The former has been done by assigning a very low(VL) value to ToC in case of low ToP and QoC (i.e., Rule no. 1 in Table. 1), whereas the latter has been obtained through assigning very high(VH) value to ToC in case of high QoC and above average ToP (i.e., Rule no. 15 and 16 in Table. 1).

Fig. 5 depicts two ordered lists provided by trust server. The first list sorts the participants in a descending order of their ToPs. This can be used as a suggestion list for data consumer for future recruitment of participants. The second list provides an ordered list of contributions according to the descending order of ToCs, which can help the data consumer to select the most trustable contributions based on a certain configurable threshold.

Next, we present results for the second scenario, wherein, the behaviour of the participants can change with time, which may result in a transition from one category to another. This scenario allows us to observe the performance of the schemes in the presence of noise. For example, consider a participant who is initially highly trusted and provides high quality data and thus belongs to

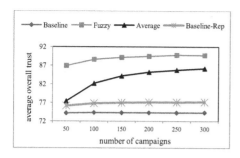

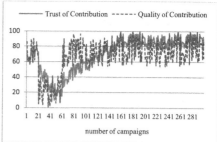

Fig. 3. Evolution of average overall trust for all methods, Scenario 1

Fig. 4. Evolution of QoC & ToC for one participant, Fuzzy method, Scenario 2

Participant ID	0	8	13	9	1	14	. . . .	41	28	43	44	45
ToP	100	100	100	98	95	93	. . . .	20	16	13	10	5
Contribution ID	450	451	458	457	466	470	. . . .	495	494	490	498	496
ToC	96.6	96.6	96.6	96.4	95.7	87.2	. . . .	25	23.8	23.2	8.6	7.7

Fig. 5. Ranked lists provided by trust server with Fuzzy method, Scenario 1

category 1. After some time, this participant contributes low quality data for some campaigns. This may be because of incorrect operation of mobile device for the purpose of the sensing task (e.g., capturing unfocussed pictures). In this scenario, we assume that 15 participants transition from category 1 to category 3. In other words, the total population of the 4 categories changes from (20, 10, 10, 10) to (5, 10, 25, 10). The transitionary period lasts from the 20th to 60th campaign. Following this, the 15 participants transition back to category 1 and we return to the initial population distribution.

Fig. 6 shows the evolution of overall trust as a function of the number of campaigns in the Average and Fuzzy methods (the two Baseline methods are excluded, since we want to compare ToP related methods). There is a decrease in overall trust for both methods in the transition period, due to an increase in the number of category 3 participants, who produce low quality contributions. However, the fuzzy method is more robust at limiting the effect of these bad contributions and still achieves an acceptable level of trust. This is due to the correct adjustment of fuzzy rules such as rule no. 6 in Table. 1 which assigns a low trust rating to low quality contributions, which leads to their revocation.

As can be seen in this figure, there is a small decrease in overall trust after the transitionary period. The reason is that when participants transition to category 3, they begin providing low quality contributions, which in turn, results in low ToP for them (Recall that ToP is updated according to QoC). By transitioning back to category 1, they resume providing high quality contributions. But since ToP is still low, the obtained ToC is a value that is lower than before, but greater than revocation threshold. So, these contributions are not revoked and considered in overall trust calculation, which makes the aforementioned decrease.

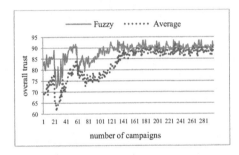 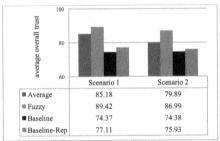

Fig. 6. Overall trust obtained in Fuzzy and Average methods in Scenario 2

Fig. 7. Comparison of average overall trust for all methods for both scenarios

Fig. 7 presents summary results for both scenarios, averaged over 300 campaigns. Observe that the proposed fuzzy framework outperforms all other schemes in both scenarios. In particular, our scheme demonstrates high robustness to noisy contributions (scenario 2), as compared to the other schemes under consideration.

5   Conclusion

In this paper, we proposed an application agnostic trust framework for social participatory sensing system. Our system independently assesses the quality of the data and the trustworthiness of the participants and combines them via fuzzy inference engine to arrive at a comprehensive trust rating for each contribution. Simulations demonstrated that our scheme increases the overall trust by over 15% as compared to the Baseline method. As future work, we plan to extend the simulation scenarios to demonstrate the robustness of proposed framework.

References

1. Burke, J., Estrin, D., Hansen, M., Parker, A., Ramanathan, N., Reddy, S., Srivastava, M.B.: Participatory sensing. In: WSW Workshop, ACM SenSys 2006 (2006)
2. Hull, B., Bychkovsky, V., Zhang, Y., et al.: Cartel: a distributed mobile sensor computing system. In: ACM SenSys 2006 (2006)
3. Rana, R.K., Chou, C.T., Kanhere, S.S., Bulusu, N., Hu, W.: Ear-phone: an end-to-end participatory urban noise mapping. In: ACM/IEEE IPSN 2010 (2010)
4. Reddy, S., Parker, A., et al.: Image browsing, processing, and clustering for participatory sensing: lessons from a dietsense prototype. In: ACM EmNets 2007 (2007)
5. Dong, Y., Kanhere, S.S., Chou, C.T., Liu, R.P.: Automatic image capturing and processing for petrolwatch. In: ICON 2011 (2011)
6. Reddy, S., Estrin, D., Srivastava, M.: Recruitment Framework for Participatory Sensing Data Collections. In: Floréen, P., Krüger, A., Spasojevic, M. (eds.) Pervasive 2010. LNCS, vol. 6030, pp. 138–155. Springer, Heidelberg (2010)
7. Krontiris, I., Freiling, F.: Integrating people-centric sensing with social networks: A privacy research agenda. In: IEEE PERCOM 2010 (2010)

8. Krontiris, I., Freiling, F.: Urban Sensing through Social Networks: The Tension between Participation and Privacy. In: ITWDC 2010 (2010)
9. Camenisch, J., Hohenberger, S., Lysyanskaya, A.: Balancing accountability and privacy using e-cash. In: De Prisco, R., Yung, M. (eds.) SCN 2006. LNCS, vol. 4116, pp. 141–155. Springer, Heidelberg (2006)
10. Demirbas, M., Bayir, M.A., Akcora, C.G., et al.: Crowd-sourced sensing and collaboration using twitter. In: IEEE WoWMoM 2010 (2010)
11. Hays, R.B.: The day-to-day functioning of close versus casual friendships. Journal of Social and Personal Relationships 6(1) (1989)
12. Lenders, V., et al.: Location-based trust for mobile user-generated content: applications, challenges and implementations. In: ACM HotMobile 2008 (2008)
13. Saroiu, S., Wolman, A.: Enabling new mobile applications with location proofs. In: ACM HotMobile 2009 (2009)
14. Trusted computing group, https://www.trustedcomputinggroup.org/home
15. Dua, A., Bulusu, N., Feng, W.C., Hu, W.: Towards trustworthy participatory sensing. In: HotSec 2009 (2009)
16. Saroiu, S., Wolman, A.: I am a sensor, and I approve this message. In: ACM HotMobile 2010 (2010)
17. Ganeriwal, S., Balzano, L.K., Srivastava, M.B.: Reputation-based framework for high integrity sensor networks. ACM TOSN 2008 4(3) (2008)
18. Commerce, B.E., Jøsang, A., Ismail, R.: The beta reputation system. In: Bled Electronic Commerce Conference (2002)
19. Huang, K.L., Kanhere, S.S., Hu, W.: On the need for a reputation system in mobile phone based sensing. In: Ad Hoc Networks (2011)
20. Kenney, J., Keeping, E.: Mathematics of statistics, part 1. Van Nostrand, Princeton (1962)
21. Alkouz, A., Luca, E.W.D., Albayrak, S.: Latent semantic social graph model for expert discovery in facebook. In: IICS 2011 (2011)
22. Alt, F., Shirazi, A.S., Schmidt, A., Kramer, U., Nawaz, Z.: Location-based crowdsourcing: extending crowdsourcing to the real world. In: ACM NordiCHI 2010 (2010)
23. Papadimitriou, S., Kitagawa, H., Gibbons, P., Faloutsos, C.: Loci: fast outlier detection using the local correlation integral. In: IEEE ICDE 2003 (2003)
24. Leekwijck, W., Kerre, E.E.: Defuzzification: criteria and classification. Fuzzy Sets and Systems 108(2), 159–178 (1999)
25. Shekarpour, S., Katebi, S.: Modeling and evaluation of trust with an extension in semantic web. Web Semantics: Science, Services and Agents on the World Wide Web 8(1) (2010)

Adapting the Obtrusiveness of Service Interactions in Dynamically Discovered Environments

William Van Woensel[1], Miriam Gil[2], Sven Casteleyn[1,2], Estefanía Serral[2], and Vicente Pelechano[2]

[1] Vrije Universiteit Brussel,
Pleinlaan 2, 1000 Brussels, Belgium
{william.van.woensel}@vub.ac.be
[2] Centro de Investigación en Métodos de Producción de Software,
Universitat Politècnica de València, Camino de Vera, 46022 Valencia, Spain
{sven.casteleyn}@upv.es, {mgil,eserral,pele}@pros.upv.es

Abstract. Due to the ubiquity of mobile devices, mobile service interactions (e.g., agenda notifications) may occur in any situation, leading to potential obtrusiveness (e.g., while in a meeting). In order to effectively adapt interaction obtrusiveness to suit the user's situation, the user's different situations should be defined in an unambiguous, generic and fine-grained way, while being valid across previously unknown, dynamically discovered environments. To realize this, we put the user in charge of defining his own situations, and exploit rich, descriptive environment information for defining and determining user situations. Our concrete approach aligns and extends two approaches, namely AdaptIO and SCOUT, to autonomously adapt mobile interactions in new, dynamically discovered environments. We supply a mobile user interface for defining situations, and validate it via an initial study with end-users.

Keywords: interaction adaptation, obtrusiveness adaptation, dynamic environment discovery.

1 Introduction

Mobile devices are an integral part of our lives. Improved battery life, screen resolution, input capabilities and computing power, as well as increased WiFi and 3G/4G coverage, have made them powerful and quasi-permanently connected computing devices. As a result, mobile devices are used at any time and everywhere, for instance to run general-purpose, resource-intensive applications (e.g., office applications, games) or to access online information and services.

Mobile service interactions comprise any interaction between mobile users and mobile services, where a service may proactively notify the user (e.g., agenda notification) or the user may directly contact the service (e.g., buying tickets from an e-ticket service). Because of their ubiquitous nature, mobile service interactions occur during a variety of situations, thus increasing their potential for obtrusiveness; for instance, loud notifications while the user is at a meeting or in a theatre. The necessity to reduce the obtrusiveness of mobile interactions is well recognized [1, 2]. In order to determine interaction obtrusiveness, most approaches currently either rely on

K. Zheng, M. Li, and H. Jiang (Eds.): MOBIQUITOUS 2012, LNICST 120, pp. 250–262, 2013.

(semi-)automatic learning techniques [3] or on designer knowledge [4]. Automatic learning techniques require training data and do not support cold-starts [5]; also, they require time to adjust to new user behavior. On the other hand, the designer cannot capture all situations that influence interaction obtrusiveness for all users, especially in a priori unknown environments without well-defined context or location models (e.g., at a theatre or at work). The only stakeholder with the required knowledge to define such situations accurately and unambiguously is the user himself. Furthermore, in order to effectively define situations across a priori unknown environments, we need to rely on rich environment data. In contrast, solely relying on local context, collected by sensors (e.g., microphones) or applications (e.g., agenda) [6], can lead to inaccuracy and ambiguity; e.g., simply turning up the ring volume in loud areas would not work while watching an action movie in a theatre. By relying on descriptive environment data, the user can specify he is in a "quiet-place" whenever he is inside a place of type "Theatre", thus defining situations in a more fine-grained and generic way.

Our goal is to adapt the obtrusiveness of mobile interactions in a priori unknown environments. To achieve this, the user is put in charge of defining his own situations, while rich environment context is exploited to define and determine user situations. Our approach aligns AdaptIO [7], a mobile obtrusiveness adaptation approach, with SCOUT [8], a mobile framework that dynamically discovers new (smart) environments, and autonomously collects context data. To ensure autonomy in any environment (potentially lacking middleware), all the components run on the mobile Android platform. Moreover, the AdaptIO approach has been extended in several ways. A user situation inferencing component has been added, which derives the user's current situation based on rich environment context. Furthermore, AdaptIO is extended with expressive user support for defining situations, via a user-friendly mobile interface. To validate the AdaptIO extension, where the user becomes a major stakeholder in mobile interactions adaptation, we evaluate the expressivity and usability of the interface by means of an initial study with real users. The developed software can be found at http://www.pros.upv.es/adaptio/dynamicenvironments.

2   Related Work

Some studies [3, 9] have been conducted on automatically adapting the modality configurations of mobile devices, based on user context. However, their focus is on context recognition, not on the modality configuration and how it influences obtrusiveness. Moreover, they rely on the designer to define the different user situations. In the same area of context-aware adaptation, [10] provides users with a UI to manually define new interactions in smart phones (e.g., gestures) and link them to device actions; however, interaction adaptation is not provided.

In the area of mobile interaction obtrusiveness, research focuses on minimizing unnecessary interruptions for the user [11]. This problem has been addressed directly by means of models of importance and willingness [4]. Also, [2] uses context-aware mobile devices to calculate the adequate timing for interruptions. Sensay [6] infers user's context from a variety of sensed data and determines whether or not the phone should interrupt the user while in regular communications. This research focuses primarily on determining *when* to interrupt for a particular application. In contrast, our approach dynamically adapts the obtrusiveness of interruptions to suit the user's current situation. Furthermore, as far as we know, no approach provides support for newly discovered services.

A number of approaches aim to facilitate mobile devices in interacting with newly discovered smart environments. For instance, the SOFIA project [12] interacts with new, heterogeneous smart environments (e.g., with legacy services, different data formats) by providing mobile applications with shared, interoperable information spaces. In [13], personalized service access is supported across different, heterogeneous environments. However, these approaches require environments to be outfitted with extra middleware, deploying their specific software. On the other hand, mobile ad-hoc networks (MANETS) allow mobile applications and services to directly discover and communicate with each other, without requiring an existing infrastructure (e.g., via event-based communication) [14, 15]. MANETS allow powerful ad-hoc and loosely coupled communication with newly discovered services; however, their approach-specific software needs to be deployed on each component.

In contrast, we rely on open, minimally outfitted and standards-based environments that do not require middleware; instead, services are semantically described, and any coordination work is delegated towards the client. In addition, by relying on well-known standards, any client can discover new services and interact with them, without requiring support for specific approaches.

3   Architecture Overview

Our approach adapts the obtrusiveness of mobile interactions in previously unknown environments. To determine and define fine-grained and generic situations in such environments, our approach relies on rich and descriptive environment context. Furthermore, the user is made responsible for specifying his own situations, allowing for accurate and unambiguous situation definitions.

Our integrated system (see Fig. 1) comprises three layers: the *environment discovery and management layer*, which utilizes SCOUT to discover and manage previously unknown environments; the *services layer,* comprising interactive mobile services; and the *obtrusiveness adaptation layer,* which employs AdaptIO to adapt mobile interaction obtrusiveness. The AdaptIO system has been extended to support our goals, and its components moved to the mobile platform to ensure autonomy. Below, we elaborate on each of the layers.

3.1   Environment Discovery and Management Layer

This layer discovers a priori unknown (smart) environments, interacts with them, and collects context data. To achieve this, it relies on SCOUT, a mobile, client-side framework for the development of context-aware applications. SCOUT runs autonomously on the mobile device and utilizes technologies such as Quick Response (QR) codes, RFID/NFC and GPS to dynamically discover new environments and collect information on the user's surroundings. Based on this detected information, SCOUT builds a client-side, integrated view on the user's environment called the Environment Model, which is expressed using Semantic Web technology.

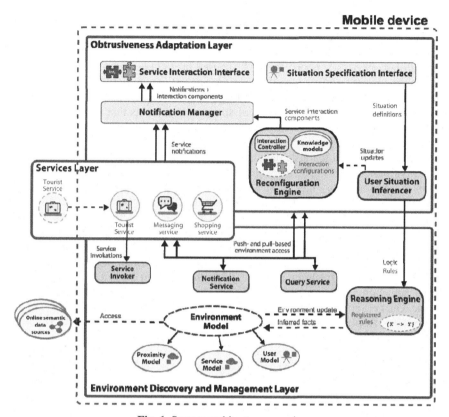

Fig. 1. System architecture overview

As shown in Fig. 1, four main information sources compose the Environment Model:

1/ *User Model:* This model contains the user's personal profile, including preferences, characteristics and device information (using ontologies such as FOAF).

2/ *Proximity Model:* This model encodes positional information about the user's environment, specifying which people, places, things and services are nearby.

3/ *Service Model:* This model keeps semantic descriptions of detected services in the user's environment (see below).

4/ *Online semantic data sources:* This includes RDF(S)/OWL data sources and semantically annotated websites, describing nearby people, places, things and services. SCOUT obtains references to these sources from the user's environment; for instance, by automatically reading URLs from QR codes or RFID tags, and by utilizing open online datasets such as LinkedGeoData[1], which link absolute coordinates (e.g., the user's GPS position) to online semantic information.

The SCOUT API provides mobile applications with access to the Environment Model in a push- and pull-based way, respectively via the **Notification Service** and **Query Service**. Data selection and caching techniques are in place to optimize data access

---

[1] http://linkedgeodata.org/

[16]. Finally, SCOUT provides applications with a general-purpose **Reasoning Engine**. Each time the user's environment changes, the engine (re-)evaluates the registered rules, potentially inferring new environment facts.

Regarding services support, SCOUT focuses on *lightweight* smart environments, i.e., environments outfitted with sensing, actuation and information services containing only the required service hardware and no external middleware. This way, SCOUT aims to support a wide range of smart environments that are cheap and easy to setup. SCOUT relies on environments that are fully standards-based and contain semantically described services; this way, any discovery, invocation and orchestration work can be delegated towards the client. In order to interact with newly discovered smart environments, SCOUT relies on the following semantic service stack. The W3C Semantic Annotations for WSDL and XML Schema[2] (SAWSDL) defines mechanisms to complement technical service descriptions (written using the W3C Web Service Description Language[3] or WSDL) with concrete semantics. WSMO-Lite[4] exploits the SAWSDL mechanisms, and utilizes a concrete ontology to semantically describe services. SCOUT converts and adds the online semantic service descriptions to the Service Model (see before) in RDF format, making it part of the Environment Model. In order to be alerted when certain services become nearby, mobile applications can register a discovery query with the Notification Service (or use the Query Service), to find services useful (nearby) services offering specific functionality. Applications interact with discovered services via the **Service Invoker**.

In order to convert WSDL descriptions (with SAWSDL annotations) to RDF, part of the SOA4ALL iServe[5] project code was extended and ported to Android. The Service Invoker uses the kSOAP2 library to interact with SOAP services, while the Reasoning Engine is based on the Androjena[6] general-purpose rule engine. We refer to [8] for more information on the SCOUT implementation.

3.2   Services Layer

This layer comprises local and remote services (see Fig. 1) that interact with the mobile user. Typically, plenty of local services or applications are running on a user's mobile device (e.g., agenda), which may for instance notify the user in case of important events (e.g., agenda deadline approaching). Remote services can also be plugged in, making their interaction capabilities available on the device. For instance, in Fig. 1, a local tourism application enables discovered remote tourist services to provide the user with information on good nearby hotel deals, and nearby points-of-interest. Such local applications register a discovery query with the Notification Service from the environment discovery and management layer (see Section 3.1). In case a relevant remote service is encountered, the application is notified, and utilizes the Service Invoker for remote communication. Based on the received data, the application provides notifications, for instance informing the user of good deals.

---

[2] http://www.w3.org/2002/ws/sawsdl/

[3] http://www.w3.org/TR/wsdl

[4] http://www.w3.org/Submission/WSMO-Lite/

[5] http://technologies.kmi.open.ac.uk/
soa4all-studio/provisioning-platform/iserve/

[6] http://code.google.com/p/androjena/

Local services can also utilize the environment discovery and management layer to enhance their own functionality. For instance, the shopping service (see Fig. 1) notifies the user in case a shop that sells products on his digital shopping list becomes nearby. To achieve this, the service registers a query with the Notification Service, to be alerted in case such shops become nearby. A number of service discovery scenarios and queries can be found on http://wise.vub.ac.be/Mobiquitous2012/.

3.3   Obtrusiveness Adaptation Layer

This layer adapts the obtrusiveness of mobile service interactions received from the *services layer*, depending on the user's current situation. This layer utilizes and extends the AdaptIO system, a mobile adaptation approach that adapts service interaction obtrusiveness at runtime. It is a model-based approach, where a service designer declaratively specifies the service's interaction adaptation behavior in knowledge models (see Section 4.1; for more information, we refer to [7]). In a nutshell, AdaptIO intercepts notifications from mobile services, chooses appropriate interaction resources (e.g., dialog, sound), and presents them to the user. Below, we elaborate on the main components (see Fig. 1).

Firstly, AdaptIO is extended with the **User Situation Inferencer**, which determines the user's current situation and notifies other components of changes. The user-supplied situation definitions (see Situation Specification Interface), expressed as logic rules, are passed to the environment discovery and management layer (Reasoning Engine), which uses them to accurately infer the user's situation. If a new situation is inferred, that layer's Notification Service notifies this component.

The **Reconfiguration Engine** determines which high-level interaction resources should be used for each service's interaction, based on the user's current situation. When alerted by the User Situation Inferencer of a new user situation, the engine consults the aforementioned *knowledge models* to retrieve the interaction resources that best suit the user's new situation. The **Interaction Controller** converts these abstract interaction resources (e.g., dialog) to concrete platform-specific (e.g., Android) interaction components, thus decoupling the models from the platform.

The **Notification Manager** receives notifications from mobile services and relays them, together with the service's latest interaction components (obtained from the Reconfiguration Engine), to the **Service Interaction Interface**. This interface displays the notifications to the user, employing suitable interaction components.

Finally, AdaptIO is extended with a **Situation Specification Interface**. This interface allows users to expressively define their situations, utilizing the environment context from the environment discovery and management layer. Situation definitions are passed to the User Situation Inferencer. In Section 4.2, we elaborate on the UI.

The Reconfiguration Engine is based on MoRE [12], which was ported to Android and is based on Autonomic Computing principles [17]. To query the knowledge models at runtime, we rely on a ported version of the Eclipse Modeling Framework Model Query[7] plugin. The model-handling operations are described in [18].

---

[7] http://www.eclipse.org/modeling/emf/

4   Methodology

In this section, we elaborate on the approach methodology and detail the tasks that need to be performed by the two stakeholders: the service designer and user. The designer is responsible for creating the knowledge models, which capture the service's desired behavior for adapting interaction obtrusiveness. On the other hand, the user is in charge of specifying his situations across which the obtrusiveness of interactions differ (e.g., in a meeting, in free-time). Service designers are not able to specify these situations for all users, especially in a priori unknown environments, without well-defined context or location models. To support this, our approach provides a mobile interface (called the Situation Specification Interface), which exploits environment context. Below, we elaborate on the designer's tasks. Section 4.2 discusses the Situation Specification Interface.

4.1   Service Designer: Adaptation Behavior Specification

In order to model the interaction obtrusiveness of services, we use the conceptual framework for implicit interactions presented in [19]. This framework defines two dimensions to characterize interactions: initiative and attention. Regarding the initiative factor, our approach focuses on proactive interactions (or notifications), where the system takes initiative and the user is potentially interrupted. The attention factor concerns an interaction's attentional demand, which can be represented on an axis. For the purpose of this paper, we divided the attention axis in three segments: *invisible* (user does not perceive the interaction), *slightly-appreciable* (user does not perceive the interaction, unless he makes an effort), and *user-awareness* (user is completely aware of the interaction, even while performing other tasks).

In our approach, the service's potential levels of interaction obtrusiveness correspond to the attention axis segments. Depending on the user's situation, the service's current (interaction) obtrusiveness level will vary. To capture this behavior, the designer creates the first knowledge model, namely an *obtrusiveness model*, which contains a state machine. Each state corresponds to an obtrusiveness level, and the guard conditions of the state transitions reference a user situation. The services' obtrusiveness models are checked by the Reconfiguration Engine (see Fig. 1) whenever it receives a new user situation (see Section 3.3); if any transition matches the new situation, it is fired, leading to a new obtrusiveness state for the service. In Fig. 2, we show the state diagram of a service that displays incoming messages.

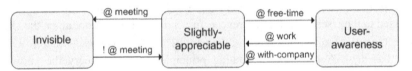

Fig. 2. Obtrusiveness state diagram for a messaging service

When the user arrives at work (*@work* situation), the messaging service passes to the *slightly-appreciable* state, thus reducing notification obtrusiveness when the user is working. When the system determines that the user is no longer working (*@free-time* situation), the service goes back to the *user-awareness* state, increasing notification obtrusiveness. In case the system determines the user is in a meeting (*@meeting*), the service passes to the *invisible* obtrusiveness state, making sure the user is not disturbed. In addition, if the user is in the company of others (*@with-company*) while the service is at maximum notification obtrusiveness (i.e., *user-awareness*), the messaging service transitions to the *slightly-appreciable* level, so the user is not overly disturbed while socializing.

Furthermore, each of the obtrusiveness states is supported by the appropriate interaction resources. In the second knowledge model, the *interaction model*, the designer associates interaction resources with one or more obtrusiveness levels (e.g., slightly appreciable: status bar icon, vibration). A service's interaction model is consulted by the Reconfiguration Engine (see Fig. 1) in case a transition fires and leads to a new state (see before); this way, the engine can retrieve interaction resources suiting the new obtrusiveness level.

The knowledge models are represented in XML Metadata Interchange standard (XMI)[8]. Examples of obtrusiveness and interaction models can be found on http://wise.vub.ac.be/Mobiquitous2012.

4.2   Service User: Situation Specification

In order to guarantee accurate and unambiguous situation definitions, the user is put in charge of defining his own situations. We developed a mobile interface that allows users to specify their situations in a generic and fine-grained way, based on environment context. To increase usability and support nomadic users in a wide range of environments, the interface also supports directly *capturing* user situations. Below, we first discuss how the user can manually specify situations, and then how he can use the "capture" functionality.

4.2.1   Manually Defining Situations

In the first screen (see Fig. 3), the user can choose to define a still undefined situation (referenced in a service obtrusiveness model), or edit an already defined one. In the second screen (see Fig. 4), he can define the chosen situation using two aspects: location and time. A third, more advanced "free-form" option allows the user to place arbitrary constraints on his environment (see below). Using the location option, the user describes the location(s) he is in while being in the chosen situation. For each location (see Fig. 5), the user specifies whether he is *inside* or *nearby* a certain place, person or thing (i.e. physical entity) in that situation, and provides a way to identify that physical entity via its type and/or unique identification (URI). The user is aided via auto-complete functions: the type field suggests terms from well-known ontologies, as well as synonyms of the ontology terms (provided by WordNet); while

---

[8] http://www.omg.org/spec/XMI

the URI field suggests URIs that identify physical entities the user has encountered (this information is obtained from the environment discovery and management layer; see Section 3.1). The user can also specify time intervals (i.e., days of the week and time span) during which he is in the situation (see Fig. 6).

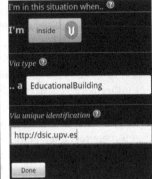

Fig. 3. Situation overview   **Fig. 4.** Specification options   **Fig. 5.** Define via location

The advanced, "free-form" option (see Fig. 7) allows defining situations in a more powerful and expressive way, by placing arbitrary constraints on the user's environment context. A constraint consists of a property and a value field. A user may arbitrarily constrain a property value, either by providing a concrete string or by linking its connector to other constraints. This free-form option, with connectable components, resembles the popular Yahoo! Pipes online mashup tool. In this example, the user is inside his office during the *@work* situation. To describe this in a generic way, the user specifies the *inside* property, and creates two constraints on the place he should be inside of. The first constraint states the *type* of the place should be "Office", while the second specifies the place is the user's office (via the *housesPerson* property). Using the constraint's connectors, the user connects the two new constraints to the first constraint's value field. The property and value fields are respectively backed by the same auto-complete functions mentioned above.

4.2.2 Capturing Situations

The "capture" option exploits the user's current environment to quickly and easily specify situations. In this option, the user takes a snapshot of his environment, fine-tunes it, and attaches it to a situation. For example, the user is sitting in a movie theatre, and one of the services produces a loud notification. The *obtrusiveness model*, defining the service's adaptation behavior (see Section 4.1), makes sure notifications are handled at the *invisible* obtrusiveness level in an *@quiet-place* situation (e.g., classroom). However, mobile users are typically nomadic and move in a wide range of (previously unknown) environments, making it difficult even for them to foresee every situation-relevant environment (e.g., movie theatre). After quickly (and manually) turning off the device's sound, the user selects the capture option. This option re-uses the screens from the previous "define" option (see previous section) and populates them, based on the user's current environment. The user selects the location aspect (see Fig. 8), and sees that the "inside MovieTheatre" location is present, as well as some other captured locations (e.g., "nearby Cafe"). He then removes the irrelevant locations, and also unchecks the time and free-form option, since they are not relevant in this case. In the final screen, the user attaches the fine-tuned context to the @*quiet-place* situation, thus making sure the *invisible* obtrusiveness level will be utilized in movie theatres as well.

Fig. 6. Define via time   **Fig. 7.** Free-form option   **Fig. 8.** Captured locations

5   Evaluation

We validated the usability and expressivity of the Situation Specification Interface by means of a user evaluation, where users had to specify six situations of varying complexity via the definition and capturing options (see Section 4.2). The final, most complex situation required using the more advanced free-form option. For detailed information on these situations, we refer to http://wise.vub.ac.be/Mobiquitous2012/.

In each user session, we took five minutes to shortly explain the interface, and then let the user specify the described situations. We noted the required time, as well as any encountered difficulties and errors during their task. After performing their task, the users filled out the Post-Study System Usability Questionnaire (PSSUQ) [20]. This questionnaire is a 19-item instrument for assessing user satisfaction with system usability. Specifically, it studies the following four dimensions: overall satisfaction with the system, its usefulness, information quality, and interface quality. A total of 8 subjects participated in the experiment (5 male and 3 female), between the ages of 25 to 35. All of them had a strong background in computer science, being students or researchers; they were also familiar with the use of a smartphone, and 4 out 8 owns an Android-based smartphone similar to the one used in the experiment.

5.1   Evaluation Results

Fig. 9 shows a summary of the PSSUQ questionnaire results; the complete dataset can be downloaded from http://wise.vub.ac.be/Mobiquitous2012/. Overall, users found the interface simple to use (questions 1, 2) and very easy to learn (7), while they also felt they could complete tasks effectively (3) and quickly become productive using the system (8). Users found the provided information more or less clear (11), easy to find (12) and understand (13), and clearly organized (15). Overall, around 80% of the users found the interface pleasant (16), and 75% liked using the interface (17). Averaging the questionnaire results, on a scale from 1 (strongly agree) to 7 (strongly disagree); overall satisfaction was 3.09, usefulness was 3.2, information quality was 3, and interface quality was 3.04.

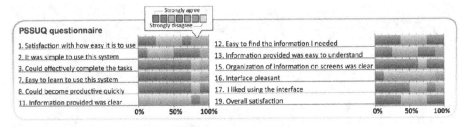

Fig. 9. Summarized questionnaire results

On average, users took about 13 minutes to specify all situations; since "capturing" the first five situations proved trivial, they were left out the remaining evaluations of the capture option. One user had initial difficulty with the location method (see Section 4.2.1); but the other users had no problems. Six out of seven users had difficulty using the free-form method while testing the define option; on the other hand, they found using this method easier when "capturing" situations.

In conclusion, the evaluations show the interface to be usable and expressive, allowing users to specify non-trivial situations within a short time span. Moreover, the capture option makes it very simple to specify most situations. The free-form method, which allows for more generic and complex situation definitions, proved to be more difficult to use and have a steep learning curve. However, using this option becomes much easier in the capture option, since users are able to fine-tune a given free-form specification instead of creating one from scratch.   We do note that this is a preliminary evaluation, and additional experiments, with a larger and more heterogeneous user group, are needed to confirm and generalize these results.

6   Conclusion and Future Work

In this paper, we presented an autonomous approach that adapts mobile interaction obtrusiveness across dynamically discovered, a priori unknown (smart) environments. The user represents a major stakeholder, being the only one with the required knowledge to accurately and unambiguously define his own situations. We provide the user with a mobile interface, where he can manually define or directly capture situations, based on expressive environment context. Our approach runs entirely on the mobile device, and does not require orchestrating or adaptation middleware.

Regarding future work, we are considering fine-tuning the mobile interface based on user feedback; more specifically, by improving the usability and learnability of the free-form option. Further user tests are still required to fully assess the usability of the interface, with a focus on users without computer science backgrounds. A major challenge is to allow users to specify interaction adaptation behavior as well, a task now exclusively reserved for the service designer. This way, the user could express custom adaptation behavior not initially foreseen by the designer.

Acknowledgments. This work has been developed with the support of MICINN under the project EVERYWARE TIN2010-18011 and co-financed with ERDF, in the grants program FPU. Sven Casteleyn is supported by an EC Marie Curie Intra-European Fellowship (IEF) for Career Development, FP7-PEOPLE-2009-IEF, N° 254383.

References

1. Chittaro, L.: Distinctive aspects of mobile interaction and their implications for the design of multimodal interfaces. Multimodal User Interfaces 3, 157–165 (2010)
2. Ho, J., Intille, S.S.: Using context-aware computing to reduce the perceived burden of interruptions from mobile devices. In: Proc. of CHI 2005, pp. 909–918. ACM (2005)
3. Valtonen, M., Vainio, A.-M., Vanhala, J.: Proactive and adaptive fuzzy profile control for mobile phones. In: Proc. of PERCOM 2009, pp. 1–3. IEEE Computer Society (2009)
4. Chen, H., Black, J.P.: A quantitative approach to non-intrusive computing. In: Proc. of Mobiquitous 2008, pp. 1–10 (2008)
5. Serral, E., Valderas, P., Pelechano, V.: Improving the cold-start problem in user task automation by using models at runtime. In: Proc. of ISD 2010, pp. 648–659. Springer (2010)
6. Siewiorek, D., Smailagic, A., Furukawa, J., Krause, A., Moraveji, N., Reiger, K., Shaffer, J., Wong, F.L.: Sensay: A context-aware mobile phone. In: Proc. of ISWC 2003, p. 248 (2003)
7. Gil, M., Giner, P., Pelechano, V.: Personalization for unobtrusive service interaction. Personal and Ubiquitous Computing 16(5), 543–561 (2012)
8. Van Woensel, W., Casteleyn, S., Paret, E., De Troyer, O.: Mobile Querying of Online Semantic Web Data for Context-Aware Applications. IEEE Internet Comp. 15(6), 32–39 (2011)
9. Assad, M., Carmichael, D.J., Kay, J., Kummerfeld, B.: Personisad: distributed, active, scrutable model framework for context-aware services. In: LaMarca, A., Langheinrich, M., Truong, K.N. (eds.) Pervasive 2007. LNCS, vol. 4480, pp. 55–72. Springer, Heidelberg (2007)
10. Korpipaa, P., Malm, E.-J., Rantakokko, T., Kyllonen, V., Kela, J., Mantyjarvi, J., Hakkila, J., Kansala, I.: Customizing user interaction in smart phones. IEEE Perv.Comp. 5, 82–90 (2006)
11. Ramchurn, S.D., Deitch, B., Thompson, M.K., Roure, D.C.D., Jennings, N.R., Luck, M.: Minimising intrusiveness in pervasive computing environments using multi-agent negotiation. In: Proc. of MobiQuitous 2004, Los Alamitos, CA, USA, pp. 364–372 (2004)
12. Toninelli, A., Pantsar-Syväniemi, S., Bellavista, P., Ovaska, E.: Supporting Context Awareness in Smart Environments: a Scalable Approach to Information Interoperability. In: International Workshop on Middleware for Pervasive Mobile and Embedded Computing, pp. 5:1–5:4. ACM, New York (2009)

13. Retkowitz, D., Armac, I., Nagl, M.: Towards Mobility Support in Smart Environments. In: 21st International Conference on Software & Knowledge Engineering, pp. 603–608 (2009)

14. Hadim, S., Al-Jaroodi, J., Mohamed, N.: Trends in Middleware for Mobile Ad Hoc Networks. Journal of Communications 1(4), 11–21 (2006)

15. Meier, R., Cahill, V.: STEAM: Event-Based Middleware for Wireless Ad Hoc Network. In: 22nd International Conference on Distributed Computing Systems, pp. 639–644 (2002)

16. Van Woensel, W., Casteleyn, S., Paret, E., De Troyer, O.: Transparent Mobile Querying of online RDF sources using Semantic Indexing and Caching. In: Bouguettaya, A., Hauswirth, M., Liu, L. (eds.) WISE 2011. LNCS, vol. 6997, pp. 185–198. Springer, Heidelberg (2011)

17. Kephart, J.O., Chess, D.M.: The Vision of Autonomic Computing. Computer 36, 41–50 (2003)

18. Cetina, C., Giner, P., Fons, J., Pelechano, V.: Autonomic computing through reuse of variability models at runtime: The case of smart homes. Computer 42(10), 37–43 (2009)

19. Ju, W., Leifer, L.: The design of implicit interactions: Making interactive systems less obnoxious. Design Issues 24(3), 7–84 (2008)

20. Lewis, J.R.: Ibm computer usability satisfaction questionnaires: psychometric evaluation and instructions for use. Int. J. Hum.-Comput. Interact. 7(1), 57–78 (1995)

Efficient Position Sharing for Location Privacy Using Binary Space Partitioning

Marius Wernke, Frank Dürr, and Kurt Rothermel

Institute of Parallel and Distributed Systems
Universitätsstraße 38, 70569 Stuttgart, Germany
{marius.wernke,frank.duerr,kurt.rothermel}@ipvs.uni-stuttgart.de

Abstract. Millions of users use location-based applications (LBAs) to share their positions with friends, request information from points of interest finders, or get notifications from event finders, etc. Such LBAs are typically based on location servers (LSs) managing mobile object positions in a scalable fashion. However, storing precise user positions on LSs raises privacy concerns, in particular, if LS providers are non-trusted. To solve this problem, we present *PShare-BSP*, a novel approach for the secure management of private user positions on non-trusted LSs. *PShare-BSP* splits up precise user positions into position shares and distributes them to *different* LSs of different providers. Thus, a compromised provider only reveals user positions with degraded precision. Nevertheless, LBAs can combine several shares from different LSs to increase their precision.

PShare-BSP improves on our previous position sharing approaches [4,15,17]: It uses a deterministic share generation approach based on binary space partitioning to avoid probabilistic attacks based, for instance, on Monte Carlo simulations. Moreover, it significantly decreases the computational complexity and increases the efficiency by reducing the update costs for succeeding position updates.

Keywords: Location based applications, position sharing, privacy.

1 Introduction

The widespread adoption of mobile devices with integrated positioning systems such as GPS has led to a drastic increase of the usage of location based applications (LBAs). For instance, points of interest finders such as Qype can be used to determine the next restaurant or gas station based on the current user position. Friend finder applications such as Loopt notify users when friends reach their vicinity. Moreover, geosocial networks such as Facebook Places, Foursquare, and Yelp let users "check-in" at locations to share their positions with friends.

LBAs typically make use of so-called location servers (LSs) to manage position information of mobile objects. Mobile objects send their position to the LS, and LBAs act as *clients* to query the LS for mobile object positions. LSs allow for the efficient and scalable management of mobile object positions, in particular, if position information is required by several clients since the LS relieves the mobile objects from sending positions to each client individually. A number of LSs are already provided on the Internet today, for instance, by Google (Latitude), Yahoo (Fire Eagle), and other service providers.

K. Zheng, M. Li, and H. Jiang (Eds.): MOBIQUITOUS 2012, LNICST 120, pp. 263–275, 2013.
© Institute for Computer Sciences, Social Informatics and Telecommunications Engineering 2013

However, providing precise user positions to LSs raises privacy concerns. These concerns are intensified by a number of incidents where private data was revealed [3] and where even providers that were deemed to be trustworthy did not succeed to protect private user data. Such incidents include attacks, leaking or losing personal information. As a consequence, we cannot trust any provider to protect our data. Thus, security mechanisms for the secure management of position information taking non-trusted providers into account are needed.

Spatial obfuscation [2,5] is a common principle to protect user location privacy in non-trusted systems. Instead of providing precise user positions to an LS, users degrade the precision of their positions and only provide this degraded information to the LS. However, such spatial obfuscation approaches limit the maximum allowed precision of a user position that can be provided to the clients of the LS by the trustworthiness of the LS. Consequently, we cannot provide a client with more precise positions than stored by the LS, no matter how much we trust the client. This might have severe impact on LBAs since usually the quality of applications might also degenerate with the quality of the provided position information. Furthermore, we cannot provide different precisions to different clients with different quality of service demands and trust levels.

Our position sharing approaches presented in [4,15,17] overcome this problem. Using position sharing, the mobile object splits up its precise position into a set of *position shares*, where each share represents an imprecise position, and distributes the generated shares to *different* LSs of different providers. Therefore, a compromised LS only reveals degraded position information, while clients can combine several shares to increase their precision. Thus, we can provide different precisions to different clients without storing precise positions at the LSs.

In this paper, we present *PShare-BSP*, a new position sharing approach based on binary space partitioning. We improve our previous position sharing approaches developed in our *PriLoc*-Project [11] as follows. In comparison to [4,15], *PShare-BSP* uses a deterministic instead of a probabilistic approach to increase robustness against attacks based on Monte Carlo simulations. Compared to [17], which is based on multi-secret sharing, *PShare-BSP* reduces the computational complexity by avoiding complex cryptographic operations. Moreover, we optimize the communication costs for position updates significantly by avoiding updating all LSs for each new position.

The rest of this paper is structured as follows: First, we present an overview of the related work in Sec. 2 and describe our system model in Sec. 3. Then, we introduce our new position sharing approach in Sec. 4 and analyze its security in Sec. 5. In Sec. 6, we present our evaluation results, before we summarize the paper in Sec. 7 together with an outlook onto future work.

2   Related Work

Approaches providing location privacy can be categorized whether they require a trusted third party or not.

Approaches with Trusted Third Party. The most prominent approach providing user privacy is *k-anonymity* [7] guaranteeing that a user is indistinguishable from $k - 1$

other users. However, *k*-anonymity and its extensions such as *l-diversity* [9] and *t-closeness* [8] usually require a trusted anonymizer, whereas we aim to provide user privacy without any trusted third party.

Approaches without Trusted Third Party. A simple approach to protect private positions is to store encrypted positions on LSs. This approach does not rely on any security mechanism of the LSs. However, the LSs cannot perform essential computations such as nearest neighbor or range queries on the server side.

Existing *dummy-approaches* such as [12] generate several false positions (dummies) and send them together with the true position of the user to an LS. However, the provided privacy of these approaches is reduced if dummies can be identified. As shown in [10], this is possible even if sophisticated algorithms are used for dummy generation.

Spatial obfuscation approaches such as [2,5] provide user privacy by sending positions of degraded precision to the LS. In general, obfuscation does not require a trusted third party. However, the maximum precision that can be provided to the clients is limited by the trustworthiness of the LS. Furthermore, an incremental precision increase for different clients as supported by our position sharing approach is not supported.

Our *position sharing* approach presented in [4] and its extension to maps [15] provide different precisions to clients by combining several position shares from different LSs based on random geometric transformations. Although these approaches provide sufficient privacy in many scenarios, an attacker can use a Monte Carlo simulation to derive positions of higher precision than intended with a certain probability. In contrast, we propose a deterministic approach in this paper that makes such attacks impossible.

In [17] we presented a position sharing approach using a multi-secret sharing scheme. In this paper, we present *PShare-BSP* that is based on binary space partitioning rather than cryptographic operations, which are less complex and thus increase computational efficiency. Finally, *PShare-BSP* also increases communication efficiency by implementing a protocol for optimized share updates.

3   System Model

The system model consists of three different components as depicted in Fig. 1.

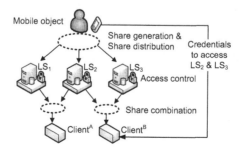

Fig. 1. System Components

The **mobile object** (MO) uses an integrated positioning system, such as GPS, to determine the current MO's position π. We assume that no malicious software component is running on the MO that can access π, e.g., using existing mobile trusted computing approaches such as [6]. We assume π to be a Cartesian point coordinate that is perfectly accurate and precise. To map ellipsoidal longitude and latitude coordinates to Cartesian coordinates, we can use a common map projection such as the Universal Transverse Mercator (UTM) projection, which divides the Earth into sixty zones, each representing a six degree band of longitude. In case the MO travels from one zone to another for a new check-in, the corresponding zone is changed as soon as the obfuscation area of the MO is completely covered by the new zone.

The MO executes a local software component for share generation splitting up π into a master share m_π, called m-share, and a set of refinement shares $S = \{r_{\pi,1}, \ldots, r_{\pi,l_{max}}\}$, called r-shares, by using the function

$$generate(\pi, l_{max}) = (m_\pi, \{r_{\pi,1}, \ldots, r_{\pi,l_{max}}\}).$$

Parameter l_{max} is defined by the MO and defines the number of $l_{max}+1$ different precision levels offered to clients. The MO's position of precision level l with $0 \leq l \leq l_{max}$ is denoted as $p(\pi, l)$. The m-share m_π defines position $p(\pi, 0)$ with a precision which is low enough to be published without raising privacy concerns. The r-shares can be used to increase the precision of the m-share ($p(\pi, 0)$) by providing refinement information stored in the r-shares. After shares are generated, they are distributed to different LSs of different providers. The communication between the MO and the LSs must take place over secure channels to avoid modification, sniffing, and message injection.

Location servers (LSs) store position shares and answer queries from different clients by returning the corresponding shares. Each LS implements an access control mechanism, as presented for example in [1], to manage the access of different clients to shares. The access rights are defined by the MO and provided to the clients as credentials to access a certain number of shares.

Clients query several shares from different LSs and use *share combination*

$$combine(m_\pi, \{r_{\pi,1}, \ldots, r_{\pi,l}\}) = p(\pi, l)$$

to increase the provided precision of $p(\pi, 0)$ to $p(\pi, l)$ with $0 < l \leq l_{max}$ by combining the m-share m_π and l r-shares from different LSs. The communication between clients and the LSs must also be protected by secure channels.

4   Position Sharing Approach

In this section, we present our position sharing approach *PShare-BSP* implementing the functions for share generation and combination introduced above. Then, we present an optimization reducing the number of required updates.

4.1   Basic Approach

Both share generation and combination depend on the concept of how to translate the exact MO's position π into an obfuscated position $p(\pi, l)$ of a certain precision level l.

Geometrically, an obfuscated position $p(\pi, l)$ of a given precision level l is defined as $p(\pi, l) = ((x_l, y_l), 2^{l_{max}-l})$ representing a square area that contains π (cf. Fig. 2). The tuple (x_l, y_l) denotes the coordinates of the lower left (south-west) corner of the square area, and $2^{l_{max}-l}$ denotes the side length measured in meters. The side length $2^{l_{max}-l}$ defines the precision of $p(\pi, l)$. We assume that a maximum precision of 1 meter, which is well below the precision of common positioning systems such as GPS, is sufficient for every practical application. Therefore, we set the precision of the position $p(\pi, l_{max})$ of the highest precision level l_{max} to 1 meter. What remains to be defined is how the coordinates (x_l, y_l) defining $p(\pi, l)$ are chosen based on the MO's precise position π with the coordinates $\pi.x$ and $\pi.y$. Numerically, $\pi.x$ and $\pi.y$ can be expressed in the binary numeral system with a system-defined bit length n as

$$\pi.x = \sum_{k=0}^{n-1} \alpha_k * 2^k = (\alpha_{n-1}\cdots\alpha_1\alpha_0)_2 \text{ and } \pi.y = \sum_{k=0}^{n-1} \beta_k * 2^k = (\beta_{n-1}\cdots\beta_1\beta_0)_2.$$

For $p(\pi, l)$ we define the coordinates (x_l, y_l) as the coordinates of $\pi.x$ and $\pi.y$ with the $l_{max} - l$ least significant bits set to zero. These bits are the undefined bits of $p(\pi, l)$. The position of the i-th undefined bit of a coordinate is equal to its $(l_{max} + 1) - i$ least significant bit. The precision value of $p(\pi, l)$ is set to $2^{l_{max}-l}$ defining the range of the $l_{max} - l$ undefined bits. The less undefined bits exist, the higher is the precision of a position. As an example consider Fig. 2 where the undefined bits of $p(\pi, l)$ that were set to zero are underlined for each level l and $l_{max} = 3$.

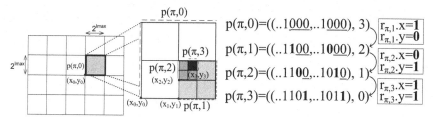

Fig. 2. Grid and refinement example for $p(\pi, 0)$ based on $l_{max} = 3$

The m-share m_π represents the coarsest obfuscation area $p(\pi, 0)$ with the coordinates (x_0, y_0) and the precision value l_{max}. By replacing the l_{max} least significant bits of $\pi.x$ and $\pi.y$ by zero when calculating $p(\pi, 0)$, l_{max} deterministically defines a partitioning of the movement area into a grid of cells with a side length of $2^{l_{max}}$ meter.

To increase the precision of the m-share m_π, the undefined bits of $p(\pi, 0)$ have to be defined. To this effect, we use a set $S = \{r_{\pi,1}, \ldots, r_{\pi,l}\}$ of $l \leq l_{max}$ r-shares, where each r-share $r_{\pi,i}$ defines the i-th undefined bit of the x and y value of $p(\pi, 0)$. At the same time the precision is improved by decreasing the side length value of $p(\pi, 0)$. Thus, position $p(\pi, 0)$ can be refined up to $p(\pi, l)$ by incrementally substituting the undefined bits of $p(\pi, 0)$ by the corresponding bits of the r-shares. The number of generated r-shares for each position update is defined by the value l_{max} such that the precision of $p(\pi, 0)$ can be increased up to l_{max} different precision levels from $p(\pi, 1)$ to $p(\pi, l_{max})$. An example is shown in Fig. 2 on the right.

Algorithm 1.	**Algorithm 2.**
PShare-BSP: Share generation	*PShare-BSP*: Share combination

Function: $generate(\pi, l_{max})$	**Function:** $combine(m_\pi, \{r_{\pi,1}, \ldots, r_{\pi,l}\})$
1: $m_\pi \leftarrow generateMShare(\pi, l_{max})$	1: $p(\pi, 0) \leftarrow m_\pi.p(\pi, 0)$
2: **for** $i = 1$ to l_{max} **do**	2: **for** $i = 1$ to l **do**
3: $r_{\pi,i} \leftarrow getBits(\pi, i)$	3: $p(\pi, i) \leftarrow setBits(p(\pi, i-1), r_{\pi,i})$
4: **end for**	4: **end for**
5: $S \leftarrow \{r_{\pi,1}, \ldots, r_{\pi,l_{max}}\}$	5: **return** $p(\pi, l)$
6: **return** m_π, S	

Next, we describe the share generation using function $generate(\pi, l_{max})$ (cf. Alg. 1). The m-share is calculated by function $generateMShare(\pi, l_{max})$ by setting the l_{max} least significant bits of $\pi.x$ and $\pi.y$ to zero. Each r-share $r_{\pi,i}$ with $1 \leq i \leq l_{max}$ defines the two bits of $\pi.x$ and $\pi.y$ corresponding to the bits at the position of the i-th undefined bit in $p(\pi, 0)$. These bits are returned by function $getBits(\pi, i)$.

The share combination function $combine(m_\pi, \{r_{\pi,1}, \ldots, r_{\pi,l}\})$ is implemented as shown in Alg. 2. It takes as input the m-share m_π representing the obfuscation area $p(\pi, 0)$ and a sequence of r-shares $r_{\pi,1}, \ldots, r_{\pi,l}$. In order to be able to refine the position up to a certain precision level l, the sequence of r-shares must contain all r-shares for the levels 1 to l. The refined position $p(\pi, l)$ is calculated by replacing stepwise the i-th undefined bit of the x and y values of $p(\pi, 0)$ by the bits of r-share $r_{\pi,i}.x$ and $r_{\pi,i}.y$ for $1 \leq i \leq l$. This step is implemented by function $setBits(p(\pi, i-1), r_{\pi,i})$.

To protect multiple position updates, we use the idea of delaying updates if they would reveal additional information to an attacker. For a detailed description of an attack on multiple position updates we refer to [5]. We analyzed the counter measure of delayed updates in our previous work [17] and use the same approach for *PShare-BSP* to resist attacks on multiple position updates.

4.2   Update Optimization

A drawback of position sharing is that multiple shares have to be updated per position fix instead of one. To alleviate this problem, we present an optimization called *PShare-BSP^{opt}* reducing the number of messages required for position updates significantly.

Existing position sharing approaches [4,15,17] and *PShare-BSP* presented in this paper need to update the m-share and all r-shares for each new position. The general idea of *PShare-BSP^{opt}* is that, initially, the m-share and all r-shares are updated once. For the following $k-1$ position updates, we re-use the r-shares to refine the positions of several m-shares and update only the m-share for every new position. To this end, an m-share contains a partially encrypted position that can be decrypted by the bits of the corresponding key that is split up and stored within different r-shares. Therefore, only one share has to be updated per new position rather than $1 + l_{max}$ (one m-share and l_{max} r-shares). In order to allow for the re-use of r-shares for the next $k-1$ updates, we have to include additional information for each r-share. The value of k can be defined by the MO and determines the number of times the r-shares can be re-used before they must be updated. For simplicity, we limit our explanations to the x coordinate. The y coordinate is handled identically.

For each position update we use a one-time pad encryption to protect the l_{max} least significant bits of $\pi.x$. Generally, a one-time pad encryption can be used to protect a secret by XORing it with a random set of bits defining the key of the encryption. The result of the encryption is a cipher that does not provide any information about the secret without the key. We define the secret s_x as the l_{max} least significant bits of $\pi.x$. The corresponding key is of length l_{max} and called *refinement-key* (r-key). The cipher c_x is calculated by bitwise XORing s_x with the corresponding r-key as $c_x = s_x$ XOR r-key$_x$. Cipher c_x is then stored within the m-share m_π in addition to $p(\pi, 0)$ as shown in Fig. 3. The idea is now to split up r-key$_x$ into its l_{max} bits and distribute them as part of the r-shares to different LSs. The refinement of $p(\pi, 0)$ to $p(\pi, l)$ for a certain precision level l requires the l most significant bits of the r-key$_x$, denoted as r-key$_x[l]$. The refinement is done by decrypting c_x with the combined r-key$_x[l]$ of the r-shares as shown in Fig. 4. The result of the decryption defines the l most significant bits of s_x, denoted as $s_x[l]$. Finally, $p(\pi, 0)$ is refined to $p(\pi, l)$ by substituting the l most significant undefined bits of $p(\pi, 0)$ by $s_x[l]$. The $l_{max} - l$ undefined bits remain zero.

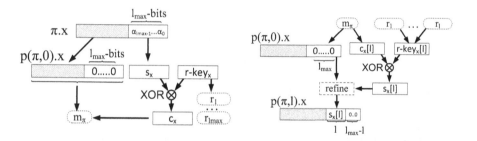

Fig. 3. Share generation overview   **Fig. 4.** Share combination overview

To fulfill the optimization goal, we provide within each r-share k bits that can be used to reconstruct the r-keys of k updates. Therefore, the r-share r_i stores the i-th bit of any of the k generated r-keys. The different r-keys are referenced by an id, denoted as r-key^{id}. The correlation of r-shares and r-keys is shown in Fig. 5, where LS_i stores the r-share r_i representing a secure random set of k bits.

Next, we describe the detailed algorithms for share generation and combination. The share generation presented in Alg. 3 checks whether a distributed r-key can be used for

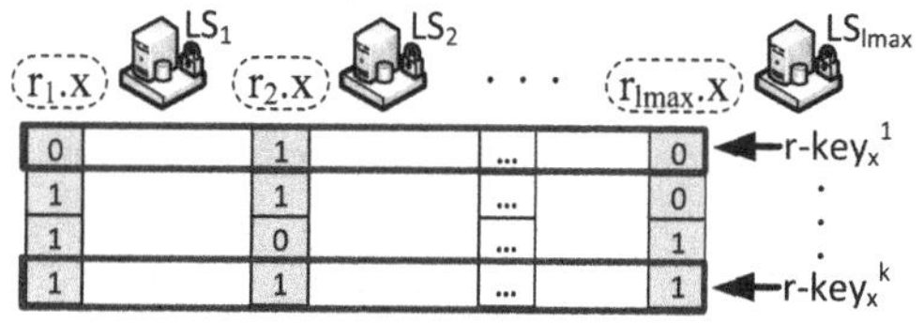

Fig. 5. Correlation of r-shares and r-keys

Algorithm 3.
PShare-BSP^{opt}: Share generation

Function: $generateSharesOPT(\pi, l_{max})$
1: **if** $noUnusedRKeyAvailable()$ **then**
2:     **for** $id = 1$ to k **do**
3:        $r\text{-}key_x^{id} \leftarrow getRandBits(l_{max})$
4:     **end for**
5:     **for** $i = 1$ to l_{max} **do**
6:        $r_i.x \leftarrow getBitsFromRKeys(i)$
7:     **end for**
8:     $S \leftarrow \{r_1, \ldots, r_{l_{max}}\}$
9: **end if**
10: $id \leftarrow getUnusedRKeyID()$
11: $m_\pi \leftarrow generateMShareOPT(\pi, l_{max}, r\text{-}key_x^{id}, id)$
12: **return** m_π, S

Algorithm 4.
PShare-BSP^{opt}: m-share generation

Function: $generateMShareOPT(\pi, l_{max}, r\text{-}key_x^{id}, id)$
1: $m_\pi \leftarrow generateMShare(\pi, l_{max})$
2: $s_x \leftarrow getXRefinement(\pi.x, l_{max})$
3: $m_\pi.c_x \leftarrow s_x$ XOR $r\text{-}key_x^{id}$
4: $m_\pi.rKeyID \leftarrow id$
5: **return** m_π

Algorithm 5. *PShare-BSP^{opt}*: Share combination

Function: $combineOPT(m_\pi, \{r_1, \ldots, r_l\})$
1: $r\text{-}key_x^{id}[l] \leftarrow getRKey(m_\pi.rKeyID, \{r_1.x, \ldots, r_l.x\})$
2: $p(\pi, l).x \leftarrow setXBits(m_\pi.p(\pi, 0).x, m_\pi.c_x[l]$ XOR $r\text{-}key_x^{id}[l])$
3: **return** $p(\pi, l)$

the next update. If no unused r-key is available, a set of k new r-keys and l_{max} new r-shares is generated. Then, the id of the r-key to use is set. Finally, Alg. 4 generates the m-share m_π including cipher c_x. After generation, the shares are distributed to the LSs.

Share combination presented in Alg. 5 reconstructs position $p(\pi, l)$ of precision level l by combining the m-share m_π with l r-shares $r_1, \ldots, r_l$. The l r-shares can be used to compose the corresponding $r\text{-}key_x^{id}[l]$ of length l. Then, cipher c_x of m_π is XORed with $r\text{-}key_x^{id}[l]$. The reconstructed refinement bits are then used as substitute of the corresponding undefined bits. The remaining $l_{max} - l$ bits are still undefined. Without knowing the missing $l_{max} - l$ r-shares and thus the corresponding parts of the *r-key*, it is not possible to further increase the precision of $p(\pi, l)$.

To guarantee the security of *PShare-BSP^{opt}*, it is essential that each r-key is only used once. Otherwise the encryption could possibly be broken. Therefore, we use each r-key only once and renew the r-shares after all k r-keys have been used.

5 Security Analysis

In this section, we present our attacker model and analyze various attacks.

5.1 Attacker Model

We assume malicious clients and malicious LSs that could be compromised as possible attackers. Malicious clients are a special sub-case of malicious LSs. We consider the case that the LSs storing the m-share and l r-shares are compromised and collude together such that the attacker knows an MO's position $p(\pi, l)$ of precision level l. An ideal position sharing approach will not allow an attacker knowing $p(\pi, l)$ to derive a position with a precision beyond the precision of $p(\pi, l)$.

We assume a free-space mobility model where each position π is equally likely. Different *probability distribution functions* (pdfs) of positions are part of our future work. For instance, an attacker could calculate a pdf for $p(\pi, l)$ using additional map knowledge and exclude non-reachable areas from $p(\pi, l)$.

5.2   Attacks on *PShare-BSP* and *PShare-BSP*^{opt}

PShare-BSP and *PShare-BSP*^{opt} both deterministically transform the MO's position π for a given value of l_{max} to position $p(\pi, 0)$. For each position $\pi' \in p(\pi, 0)$ it holds that the same position $p(\pi, 0)$ is calculated. This is guaranteed by mapping the l_{max} least significant bits of the x and y coordinate to zero, independent whether the bit was zero or one before. An attacker knowing $p(\pi, l)$ trying to increase his precision to level $l+1$ would have to determine the first unknown bit of the x and the y coordinate of $p(\pi, l)$. Thus, the attacker could try to analyze the undefined bits of $p(\pi, l)$ and try to calculate the inverse function of the mapping to zero values. However, as values of zero and one are both mapped to zero, no further information is revealed to the attacker without knowing the corresponding r-share r_{l+1}. The same holds for an attacker analyzing the four possible refinement areas of $p(\pi, l)$ on level $l+1$. All four areas are of the same size and share therefore the same probability to cover π. Thus, the probability of selecting the correct area on level $l+1$ is equal to randomly guessing a certain area on level $l+1$.

An attacker knowing m_π in *PShare-BSP*^{opt} also knows ciphers c_x and c_y. As proven in [13], the cipher of a one-time pad encryption provides no information about the protected secret, even if the attacker has infinite computational power. Thus, it is not possible for an attacker to increase precision from $p(\pi, l)$ to $p(\pi, l+1)$ without knowing r-share r_{l+1} defining the corresponding parts of the r-keys to decrypt c_x and c_y.

In addition to analyzing the undefined bits, an attacker could also try to analyze the generated positions. For instance, an attacker could try to use a *region intersection attack* [16] that can be successful on obfuscation-based approaches if different obfuscation areas are generated for the same position π. However, we deterministically generate for each position π and each level l always the same obfuscation area. For the MO's value of l_{max} and two different positions π' and π'' either the obfuscation areas of level l are equal, i.e., $p(\pi', l) = p(\pi'', l)$, or the areas do not intersect each other, i.e., $p(\pi', l) \cap p(\pi'', l) = \emptyset$. In both cases, an attacker cannot refine $p(\pi, l)$.

A *probability distribution attack* [14] calculates the probability that the MO is located in certain areas. It is most beneficial for probabilistic privacy algorithms that might lead to an uneven distribution of (possible) MO positions within the obfuscation area. For instance, the algorithm presented in [4] leads to a concentration in the center of the obfuscation area. We try to avoid such concentrations and strive for a uniform distribution within the obfuscation area. Our deterministic share generation algorithm guarantees that each position $\pi' \in p(\pi, l)$ would lead to the obfuscation area $p(\pi, l)$ with the same probability for a certain precision level l. Running a Monte Carlo simulation for the deterministic obfuscation and share generation algorithm over $\pi' \in p(\pi, l)$

leads to a uniform distribution over $p(\pi, l)$. Therefore, probability distribution attacks do not provide any additional information to the attacker.

By design, we only generate and update new position shares if they are not vulnerable to a *maximum velocity attack* [5] by using delayed updates as counter measure. Thus, an attacker cannot increase his precision by analyzing succeeding position updates using a maximum velocity attack.

6   Evaluation

Next, we analyze the computational efficiency of our approaches by measuring the performance of share generation and share combination using a prototype implementation of our system. Afterwards, we analyze the bandwidth efficiency of our approaches.

6.1   Performance Evaluation

Generally, the share generation is performed on a resource-constrained mobile device with limited CPU power and battery capacity. Even on such resource-poor devices, share generation must be possible in short time, which results in a small overhead in terms of energy. To show the performance of our approaches, we measured the overall time for share generation on a state of the art mobile device (HTC Desire HD). We measured the time to create one m-share and one to 15 r-shares and plotted the overall time over the number of r-shares in Fig. 6. As reference values we used the results presented in [4] for a random share generation algorithm (denoted as *RSG*) and [17] for *PShare-GLM* based on multi-secret sharing techniques. We limited the number of generated r-shares to 15, because a precision of 32768 m should be sufficiently coarse to provide user privacy. As we can see, the share generation of both approaches stays well below 1 milliseconds even when providing $k = 184$ different r-keys within the r-shares. Thus, we can state that the share generation is highly efficient and suitable even for resource-poor devices.

In contrast to share generation, the share combination is done by clients (location-based applications) that typically run in the infrastructure with no energy restriction and

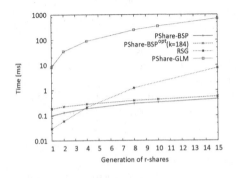
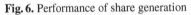

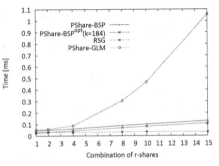

Fig. 6. Performance of share generation   **Fig. 7.** Performance of share combination

high computational power. We measured the time required to combine one m-share with up to 15 r-shares on a state of the art personal computer (Intel Core 2 Duo, 2.53 GHz, 3 GB RAM). As we can see in Fig. 7, share combination is calculated very efficiently in less than 150 microseconds even for a larger number of shares.

6.2 Bandwidth Efficiency

To analyze the efficiency of our approaches in terms of communication overhead, we compare the number of required update messages for both approaches. We assume that the MO performs a number of $k' \le k$ succeeding position updates using $l_{max} + 1$ LSs to store the generated m-share and the l_{max} r-shares. Then, for *PShare-BSP* the MO has to send in total $k' * (1 + l_{max})$ update messages, where each of the k' position updates triggers an update of the m-share and all l_{max} r-shares. For *PShare-BSP*^{opt} we update once the m-share and all l_{max} r-shares while for the next $k - 1$ updates only the m-share has to be updated. This results in a total number of $k' + l_{max}$ update messages. The r-shares are updated after $k' = k$ position updates were sent.

Next, we analyze the generated network load by analyzing the different share sizes and the overhead of lower level communication protocols. Each share has a share-ID (32 bits), a user-ID (32 bits), and a type definition (8 bits). In *PShare-BSP*, the m-share m_π adds position information (112 bits) and a list of ids defining the r-shares of m_π (l_{max} * 32 bits). An r-share r_π adds 2 bits for its refinement property. In *PShare-BSP*^{opt}, the m-share m_π^{opt} adds cipher c_x (l_{max} bits), cipher c_y (l_{max} bits), and the used r-key id (32 bits) to m_π. The additional payload of m_π^{opt} compared to m_π is denoted as Δm_π^{opt}. Each r-share r^{opt} consists of k (32 bits) and $2 * k$ bits to reconstruct r-key$_x$ and r-key$_y$.

The network load of *PShare-BSP* for k' position updates is $NL_{basic} = k' * ((size(m_\pi) + o) + l_{max} * (size(r_\pi) + o))$ bits, where o defines the protocol overhead introduced by lower level protocols for each message. The network load of *PShare-BSP*^{opt} is $NL_{opt} = k' * (size(m_\pi^{opt}) + o) + l_{max} * (size(r^{opt}) + o)$ bits. Comparing NL_{basic} and NL_{opt} leads to

$$k' \ge \frac{l_{max} * (size(r^{opt}) + o)}{l_{max} * (size(r_\pi) + o) - size(\Delta m_\pi^{opt})} \tag{1}$$

denoting the number of k' updates that have to be sent until *PShare-BSP*^{opt} outperforms *PShare-BSP* and $NL_{opt} \le NL_{basic}$ holds. The size of the message overhead measured for sending a share over TCP/IP is $o = 320\,bits$. For $l_{max} = 16$ generated r-shares and for example $k = 128$ this results in a value of $k' \ge 1.72$. This means that *PShare-BSP*^{opt} outperforms *PShare-BSP* as soon as the second MO's position is updated. By using Equation 1, we can calculate that *PShare-BSP*^{opt} outperforms *PShare-BSP* always with the second update as long as $k \le 184$. For sending $k' = k = 184$ position updates *PShare-BSP* generates a total network load of NL$_{basic}$= 172 040 bytes when also taking the TCP/IP overhead into account. *PShare-BSP*^{opt} at the same time only generates a load of NL$_{opt}$= 27 896 bytes. This results in a reduction of 83.8% of the generated network load. By considering the additional overhead required to provide secure channels by using TLS, the overhead of each message is further increased. Thus, reducing the number of messages by *PShare-BSP*^{opt} further increases its efficiency.

In addition to optimizing the updates of shares—i.e., the communication between MO and LSs—, PShare-BSP^{opt} also optimizes the communication between the LSs and the clients. A client has to query all of its accessible r-shares only once within k updates instead of querying the r-shares every time a new position of the MO is updated.

7   Summary and Future Work

In this paper, we presented a new position sharing approach protecting user privacy in non-trusted systems of third-party location servers (LSs) and clients. *PShare-BSP* splits up a precise user position into position shares of limited precision, which are distributed to different LSs of different providers. Different clients can then combine several shares and increase their provided precision. Our approach has the advantage that a compromised server only reveals positions of degraded precision instead of precise positions.

We improve existing position sharing approaches [4,15,17] by providing a deterministic approach using binary space partitioning to avoid probabilistic attacks and by decreasing the computational complexity significantly by one order of magnitude compared to [4] and by more than three orders of magnitude compared to [17]. Furthermore, we presented an extension for *PShare-BSP* reducing the number of required messages for multiple position updates significantly.

As future work we will consider map knowledge and semantic knowledge, for instance, periodic behavior of users, knowledge about points of interest, etc. that could be used by an attacker to increase precision. Furthermore, we will consider replication strategies to increase the availability of shares without decreasing privacy.

References

1. Bonatti, P.A., Samarati, P.: A uniform framework for regulating service access and information release on the web. Journal of Computer Security 10, 241–271 (2002)
2. Damiani, M., Silvestri, C., Bertino, E.: Fine-grained cloaking of sensitive positions in location-sharing applications. Pervasive Computing 10, 64–72 (2011)
3. DATALOSSDB (April 2012), http://www.datalossdb.org
4. Dürr, F., Skvortsov, P., Rothermel, K.: Position sharing for location privacy in non-trusted systems. In: Proceedings of the 9th IEEE International Conference on Pervasive Computing and Communications, PerCom 2011 (2011)
5. Ghinita, G., Damiani, M.L., Silvestri, C., Bertino, E.: Preventing velocity-based linkage attacks in location-aware applications. In: Proceedings of the 17th ACM SIGSPATIAL International Conference on Advances in Geographic Information Systems, GIS 2009 (2009)
6. Gilbert, P., Cox, L.P., Jung, J., Wetherall, D.: Toward trustworthy mobile sensing. In: Proc. of the 11th Workshop on Mobile Computing Systems & Applications, HotMobile 2010 (2010)
7. Kalnis, P., Ghinita, G., Mouratidis, K., Papadias, D.: Preventing location-based identity inference in anonymous spatial queries. IEEE Transactions on Knowledge and Data Engineering 19, 1719–1733 (2007)
8. Li, N., Li, T., Venkatasubramanian, S.: t-closeness: Privacy beyond k-anonymity and l-diversity. In: IEEE 23rd International Conference on Data Engineering, ICDE 2007 (2007)
9. Machanavajjhala, A., Kifer, D., Gehrke, J., Venkitasubramaniam, M.: L-diversity: Privacy beyond k-anonymity. ACM Transactions on Knowledge Discovery from Data 1, 3 (2007)

10. Peddinti, S.T., Saxena, N.: On the limitations of query obfuscation techniques for location privacy. In: Proc. of the 13th Int. Conference on Ubiquitous Computing, UbiComp 2011 (2011)
11. PriLoc-Project (November 2012), http://www.PriLoc.de
12. Shankar, P., Ganapathy, V., Iftode, L.: Privately querying location-based services with sybilquery. In: Proceedings of the 11th International Conference on Ubiquitous Computing, UbiComp 2009 (2009)
13. Shannon, C.: Communication theory of secrecy systems. Bell System Technical Journal 28, 656–715 (1949)
14. Shokri, R., Theodorakopoulos, G., Le Boudec, J.-Y., Hubaux, J.-P.: Quantifying location privacy. In: Proc. of the 2011 IEEE Symposium on Security and Privacy, SP 2011 (2011)
15. Skvortsov, P., Dürr, F., Rothermel, K.: Map-aware position sharing for location privacy in non-trusted systems. In: Kay, J., Lukowicz, P., Tokuda, H., Olivier, P., Krüger, A. (eds.) Pervasive 2012. LNCS, vol. 7319, pp. 388–405. Springer, Heidelberg (2012)
16. Talukder, N., Ahamed, S.I.: Preventing multi-query attack in location-based services. In: Proceedings of the 3rd ACM Conference on Wireless network security, WiSec 2010 (2010)
17. Wernke, M., Dürr, F., Rothermel, K.: PShare: position sharing for location privacy based on Multi-Secret sharing. In: Proceedings of the 10th IEEE International Conference on Pervasive Computing and Communications, PerCom 2012 (2012)

MES: A System for Location-Aware Smart Messaging in Emergency Situations

Alaa Almagrabi, Seng W. Loke, and Torab Torabi

Department of Computer Science and Computer Engineering
Latrobe University, Melbourne, Australia
aoalmagrabi@students.latrobe.edu.au,
{S.Loke,T.Torabi}@latrobe.edu.au

Abstract. Location is considered the most significant element of context in ubiquitous computing. Location information, besides system context information, can offer rich queries for handling information especially in emergency systems. This paper introduces the Mona Emergency System that uses context information in providing emergency services such as sending warning messages to an identified location. MES context information includes actor, danger and point of interest information. This paper describes the MES methodology to obtain and distribute warning messages during emergency situations. MES is a new approach that defines message targets and content using spatial relations.

Keywords: context-aware messaging and addressing, emergency systems, spatial information, ad-hoc communication, ontology.

1 Introduction

Emergency systems submit to the procedures that support effectively dealing with tragedy within society [1]. Recently, in communication, context information is utilized as substitute to previous addressing methods such as IP addresses [2]. Modern technology can assist in decision making and saving time in disaster management [3]. Government utilizes all the accessible resources to terminate hazards. For instance, in Australia 2009 [4], Victorian government employed all available resources to stop the bushfire. However, it reported at least 166 deaths. A lot of survivors stated that, they did not have enough information about where to go and the fire movements, which caused some panicking. In addition, rescuer teams did have enough knowledge about the survivors and the levels of threat encountered by these survivors. In addition, the rescuers do not have any clue about the survivor movements and personal information such as age and health conditions. This information can assist different rescue team that work together with information that can improve the rescue mission [5].

The contribution of this paper is to introduce an approach to highlight the significance and advantages of using context information for addressing and messaging purposes during hazard times. We designed the Mona Emergency System (or MES, for short) to improve the flow and the content of the messages during risky periods. MES proposes generating alert messages for actors within affected areas

K. Zheng, M. Li, and H. Jiang (Eds.): MOBIQUITOUS 2012, LNICST 120, pp. 276–288, 2013.
© Institute for Computer Sciences, Social Informatics and Telecommunications Engineering 2013

using context information. The MES compares and examines context information such as name, location, type and status to assist in the messaging process. It is assumed that the MES utilizes different sensors from mobiles to gain context information. We employ the use of spatial relations via the use of structured English expressions using words such as "close", "near", "far" and "away" to help describe the message receivers. MES provides a new approach to defining the message targets using spatial relations. We design the Mona-ont ontology to describe and organize knowledge about danger situations.

The paper is structured to present an extensive overview of the Mona Emergency system as follows: the MES concept and design, the MES architecture, the message exchange process for the context information and the Mona-ont ontology. In addition, the paper describes the MES message structures as well as services and techniques that assist in supplying the actors with the right alert messages at the right time with the right context information; we illustrate the concepts of the MES via screenshots.

2   The Mona Emergency System (MES)

2.1   Concept and Design

The Mona Emergency System is used to generate alert messages during danger situations. The MES designed to improve the flow of exchanged information between the actors within the system. The system uses real-time context information that are collected and stored in the MES database. The MES employs spatial relations, qualitative and quantitative, to determine the significance of message targets and content. In the MES, controlled English expressions identify destinations and content of messages using context. Mobile phones are used to report information about the actors within the system. Danger information is passed to the MES database via any institution. Furthermore, the POI information can be entered and modified manually in the MES database. The MES transfer RCC8 or Egenhofer relations[1] into understandable English expressions to describe emergency situations. We define MES spatial relations for the following reasons:

- assist in distributing the right message at the right time,
- define and address the message target during the hazard times using available context information,
- describe the alert message content using the spatial relations between the system entities such as survivor, rescuer, safe points and danger areas,
- present sufficient knowledge about certain events to the rescue team, and
- label some dynamic spatial relations in such a way as to describe an event.

MES spatial relations structure context to indicate the situation of actors in the rescue process. The context model can be modified according to the usage environment. MES utilizes various types of context related to entities within the system. Figure 1 demonstrates the entities expressed in the MES model, which includes actor devices, services, hazards information and points of interest.

---

[1] http://www.w3.org/2005/Incubator/geo/XGR-geo-ont-20071023/

Fig. 1. The MES spatial overall view over a fire at La Trobe University

Figure 1 presents the MES distributed entities and its spatial relation during fictional fire scenario. The MES messaging services structured depends on multi-context information gathered from MES entities included such as actor, dangers and points of interest information. This offers dynamically modified messaging services to the actors' mobile devices.

The MES uses the available context information that includes the actor, danger and POIs to compare and match the context knowledge. For example, the MES computes and contrasts the location coordinate information (latitude and longitude) of actors, POIs and the danger using the Haversine formula[2]. The context information relating to actors such as rescuer and survivor are actor ID, location, status as well as some personality information such as age and health condition.

Actor ID is used to recognize the actor and the location used to place the actor. In addition, status used to distinguish the actor's danger event such as "stuck" or "safe", and health condition illustrates the health situation about the actor such as "disabled" or "fit". During an emergency situation the MES categorize survivors into two types; general survivor, representing people within the region that may encounter a dangerous situation and flag-bearer, where in the case of launching new ad-hoc network connections, an actor (called the *flag-bearer*) can coordinate communication with other people who are unregistered with the MES on a peer-to-peer basis, in order to assist them with the right services, on behalf of MES (e.g., relaying messages, i.e., effectively, we see that messaging can be "crowd-sourced"). On the other hand, rescuer stands for organizations that are expected to help according to their specialty, such as evacuation support, policeman and fireman. In addition, the MES uses danger context information to classify the danger zones depending on the danger severity using the scale: Red, Yellow and Blue. Also, the status is employed to explain the danger situation such as "occurring", "starting", and "terminated". The type is used to show the danger type such as "bushfire" and "flood". Moreover, the MES uses context information to present the point of interest (POI) as a safe point in a rescue process such as name, location, current danger zone and status. The current danger zone in used to find the POI in the affected area, and the POI status used to label the "lost" or "destroyed" POIs in dangerous situations. The MES classifies POIs into positive and negative points of interest. For example, a lake can be allocated by the MES automatically as a positive POI, where the survivor can be directed to in a Bushfire scenario.

---

[2] http://www.movable-type.co.uk/scripts/latlong.html

2.2 MES Mona-ont Ontology

We develop the Mona-ont ontology [6] to capture, form and filter information about disaster conditions. The information is expressed by the use of context information in emergency situations such as about actors, dangers and safe points. Mona-ont ontology is utilized in emergency situations to:

- describe the targets/destinations/receivers for context-aware messaging,
- support explaining events in emergency situations,
- help defining the emergency situation concepts and its attributes,
- express and discover the spatial relations that link MES concepts,
- allow the spatial relations to be understandable by humans,
- assist in building and modelling the Mona Emergency System,
- defining appropriate message contents for actors (including directions for survivors),
- allow sharing information between concepts within MES, and
- assist simulating the scenarios.

We use the editing tool called Protege[3] to build the Mona-ont ontology. The Mona-ont ontology captures knowledge in disaster situations, to be used by possibly different organizations involve in a rescue operation. Figure 2 highlights Mona-ont relationships between MES concepts. The Mona-ont ontology contains concepts that may be involved in emergency situations. For example, region, disaster management, emergency situation, affected area, actors and points of interest. The region represents the area where danger is happening and a disaster management unit manages the region, aggregates the context information from actors and provides alert messages to the actors. Actors represent survivors and rescuers, and emergency situation represents context information about a danger (e.g., a bushfire, or a flood) such as type, range, direction and speed of the danger. Affected area refers to the hazard/danger zones. Finally, points of interest (POI) symbolize the geographical features (man-made or natural) that can assist in a rescue operation.

Figure 2 illustrates the Mona-ont ontology spatial relationships that link the system's concepts and express events at risky situations. The Mona-ont ontology represents knowledge that is shared between actors within ME system. The qualitative spatial relations are mapped to a variety of values that help the MES in performing practical messaging functionalities. For example, the relation "near" represents a scope of values between 100 meters and 250 meters (this mapping can be changed depending on the geographical scales intended for the messaging). This mapping assists in discovering and filtering target and content of the alert messages. The MES spatial relations described as follows:

- Danger_relation: describe emergency situation within region such as "in", "within" and "out of".
- Position_relation: define concepts positions within the Mona-ont ontology such as "near", "far", "next to", "close to" and 'away'. For example, it links an actor with POIs and affected areas within the region, and also to describe the relative positions between the actors themselves.

---

[3] http://protege.stanford.edu/

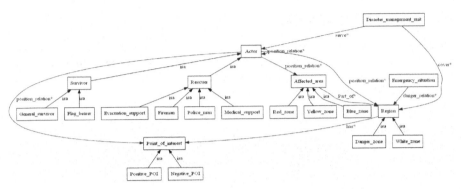

Fig. 2. Overview of the main concepts in the Mona-ont ontology

2.3   MES Architecture

Inspired by [7, 8], we employ numerous types of context-aware adjustment in the MES server side and the actor side. The MES employs a client-server architecture at the top level and multiple actors at the lower levels. The client-server architecture establishes the communication between the disaster management unit and the actor within the region while peer to peer communication occurs where the actors connect with each other via any type of ad-hoc communication. MES' overall architecture includes generally three main components, which are the actor; the disaster management unit and the database (see Figure 3).

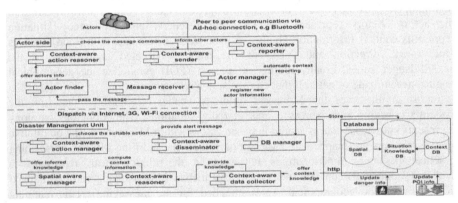

Fig. 3. MES architecture

The figure presents the MES architecture and the flow of information between the system entities and its component. The components are distributed into two levels. First, the actor side includes the survivor and the rescuer. Second, the server side includes the database and the disaster management unit. The database contains information about dangers area, actor and evacuation points. The evacuation points are particular points of interest (POI). The disaster management unit is responsible for the MES functionalities such as generating the automatic and the manual messages.

To start with, first, the database has the knowledge about the region including information about the emergency situation entities such as the danger information, actor and POI information. The database offer context knowledge to the disaster management unit via http. The data base consists of three parts:

- a spatial database includes the spatial relationships between emergency entities,
- a situation knowledge database with the spatial information and context information to be supplied to the disaster management unit, and
- a context database containing available context information about the system entities such as location, status and health condition, as noted earlier.

Second, the disaster management unit is responsible for the MES' main functionalities such defining the messages and the target of the messages. Also, capturing and filtering the context information about hazards situation. This information is used for the automatic and the manual messaging, presented on the relevant user interface forms. The disaster management unit components work as follows:

- *Database manager* (DB) responsible for registering the new actor information with the DB and keep updating the actor context automatically in a certain time,
- *Context-aware data collector* which collects the context information from the DB about the entities during danger time and passes the knowledge to the context-aware reasoner such as "there is survivor called Mr. Ahmed", and its current danger zone and POI information,
- *Context-aware reasoner* compares the collected context information that is ready for action such as computing that Mr. Ahmed's location falls within the red zone range,
- *Spatial aware manager* offers inferred knowledge and converts the quantitative information to qualitative aspects such as Mr. Ahmed is in the red zone "near" the hospital,
- *Context-aware action manager* constructs instructions or guidance information (in messages sent to actors) depending on context and decides the suitable action to be preformed such generating the automatic messaging to be sent to Mr. Ahmed in case of a lost POI, and
- *Context-aware disseminator* is responsible for sending the information to actors according to the context, providing the right alert to the actor at the right time using client server architecture via the obtainable connection method such as internet, 3G and Wi-Fi.

Finally, the actor side represents the survivor and the rescuer within the MES covered region. The actor side components are as follows:

- *Actor manager* is responsible for registering the new actor information and reporting the context information automatically,
- *Context-aware reporter* keeps reporting the actor context information to the disaster management unit automatically,
- *Message receiver* is in charge of the displaying the alert message,
- *Actor finder* searches for other actors within the available range using any communication tool such as Bluetooth in order to establish ad-hoc connection (peer to peer architecture),

- *Context-aware action reasoner* is responsible for choosing the message command by defining the right actor to forward the message to, and
- *Context-aware sender* is in charge of sending the message to the other actor within the available range.

This section describes the flow of information between the system's main components. Actors are required to register his/her information using an actor ID such as name, together with age and health conditions, with the disaster management unit which stores the information in its database. Once the danger occurs, the disaster management unit calls the information from the DB to be computed and processed. The MES disaster management unit identifies the danger zones, and the positive POI to assist in the rescue operation. The MES compares and matches location information and filters/selects the target actors depending on the available context in order to identify the message targets and contents. Once a message is received, the survivor can spread and share the message using peer to peer communication tools such as Bluetooth.

2.4   Message Exchange Process

This section gives an overview about the message content that been an exchange between the MES entities. The MES uses several type of contexts information in order to be widely aware of definite transformation in the region during the risk time (see Figure 4). Context information exchanged between the disaster management unit and the actor stored into the database. The context information depends on the actor category, the time and the event. For example, actors record location information more often according to their movement and the danger expanding, as oppose to when the actors are far from danger.

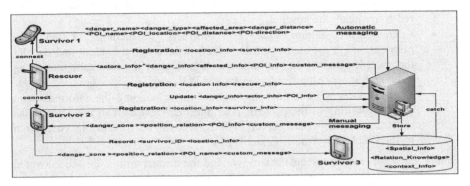

Fig. 4. Message exchange among the system's client-server components

Figure 4 describes the variety of context that has been exchanged between the MES disaster management unit and the MES actor. First, the context information at the registration level from the actor to the MES disaster management unit; the survivor registers using location information and survivor personal information such as ID, name, age and health condition. Furthermore, the rescuer registers using location information and personal information such as ID, name and institution. This context information is stored into the MES database via the MES disaster management unit. Second, relevant guidance context information is sent from the disaster management unit to the MES actor. There are two modes for messaging the survivors at this stage. In the automatic mode, the MES disaster management unit will send the danger information including danger name, danger type, affected area, danger distance and POI information such as POI name, location and distance. On the other hand, in the manual mode, the MES disaster management unit will send danger zone or the affected area, position relation, POI name and a custom message, such as "Mr. Alaa in a yellow zone near the lake please stay there". In addition, the rescuer will receive context information about the danger information and the survivors' information. Third, the guidance context information can be exchanged between survivors using peer to peer communication. A registered survivor is allowed to forward the alert message it received to other unregistered survivors, according to their context information. The unregistered survivors record their IDs and location information and that to the registered survivor in order to receive the alert messages (which include the automatically sent messages received from the MES in the automatic mode and custom messages sent manually). Finally, the disaster management unit updates the actor; danger and POI context information depending on the events during danger times.

3   MES Message Context Model Structure (EBNF), MES Services and Proof of Concept

3.1   Automatic Messaging

This mode provides an automatic alert messaging service to the survivors during hazardous situations, without involving human decisions. The MES automatic message content structure is designed as the following: first, the system decides on the survivor(s) that will take delivery of the message according to his/her (their) location(s). Then, the system informs the survivor about the existing danger type and zone, the distance from the danger (e.g., fire), the information about the related POIs that include the name of the POI and locations which clarify the areas (e.g., suburbs) that have the POI as well as the actual distance to the available safe POI and the direction. The structure of the automatically sent message is as follows (in EBNF):

<message>::=<actor1>+<danger_type><affected_area><danger_distance>
<POI_name><POI_location> <POI_distance>

    <actor1>::= <survivor_ID>.

    <danger_type>::= "fire" | "flood" | "earthquake" | "nuclear_danger".

    <affected_area>::= "red_zone" | "yellow_zone" | "blue_zone".

    <danger_distance> ::= REAL_NUMBER.

    <POI_name>::="lake"|"hospital"|"evacuation_center"|"school"|"playground".

    <POI_location>::= "Bundoora" | "Reservoir"| "Kingsbury".

    <POI_distance>::= REAL_NUMBER

The message target is defined according to several contexts during danger times. For instance, survivor 'aaa' is within a fire inside a red_zone, 945 meters from the centre of the fire as well as the name of the available safe POI name such as "Latrobe Hospital" and its location (which is in the suburb "Bundoora" and the actual distance to that POI which is 294 meters). Moreover, the MES messages survivor 'Alaa' about the danger type, current danger zone and the distance as well as the POI information. For example, 'Alaa' is in fire inside yellow_zone with 1050 meters from the danger centre next to CP3 building and its location (which is Bundoora and the actual distance to that POI which is 198 meters); see Figure 5.

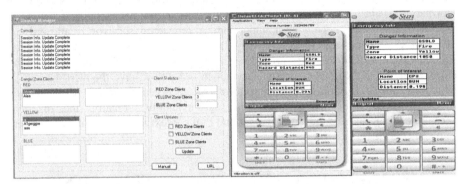

Fig. 5. Disaster manager for automatic messaging

Figure 5 shows the disaster management automatic messaging form which offers additional services such as providing a list containing the survivor IDs in the danger zone that they are located in. Additionally, it shows a summary of the number of the survivors positioned in the different zones. Moreover, the form updates the actor context information automatically according to the danger zone using the update options (e.g., messages containing location updates from actors, sent periodically). The automatic form offers visualization for the data via web services by the use of the URL command which will be activated in the future work to provide online services.

3.2   Manual Messaging

The manual message service offers custom message. The manual form requests the use of human interaction to define the message target and content via spatial relations. The spatial relation offer dynamic role to define messages for particular or group of survivor using structured English expressions. For example, the message target can be as the following; first, the system decides on the survivor(s) that going to receive the message according to his/her (their) location(s) and his spatial relation to danger zone. In addition, the target can be defined also using the survivor location and his POI spatial relation. The target of the manual message in EBNF is structure depend on the target as follows (in EBNF). For example, the administrator or the rescuer wants to send custom message the survivor according to the danger zone.

<message>:: = <Actor>⁺<Danger_relation> <Affected_area><custom_message>

<actor>:: = <survivor _ID >

<Danger_relation> :: = "inside" | "outside"

<affected_area> :: = "red_zone" | "yellow_zone" |"blue_zone".

Note: <survivor_ID> ∈ <survivor>.

Second example is the administrator wants to message the survivor according to the danger zone and the POI relation. For example,

<message>::=<actor>⁺[<Danger_relation><affected_area>]<POI_name><POI_position>
<custom_message>

<actor>:: = <survivor _ID >

<Danger_relation> :: = "inside" | "outside".

<affected_area>:: = "red_zone" | "yellow_zone" |"blue_zone".

<POI_name>::="lake"|"hospital"|"evacuation_center"|"school"|"playground".

<Position_relation>:: = "near" | " close to" | "far" | "away" | " next_to".

<custom_message>:: = STRING (e.g., "stay there").

The manual form helps filtering and capturing the information about the survivors depending on several contexts. For example, Alaa and Ahmed are survivors in the blue_zone, and we want to send a custom message containing the warning "fire coming". The manual form offers a choice to address a custom message to these survivors who are at same position relationships, such as "near the lake". The system then takes care of resolving the words "near" and the names "Alaa" and "Ahmed" to specific distance measures and specific mobile devices (see Figure 6).

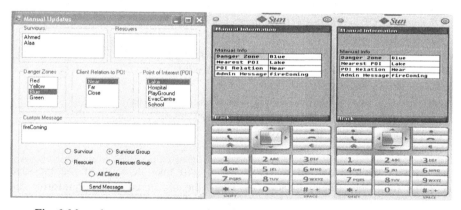

Fig. 6. Manual message to a group of survivors using particular spatial relationships

Figure 7 describes another service using the manual form such as sending a custom message only to one survivor such as Alaa who is located in yellow_zone at this stage and close to the lake, with message contents to say "stay there". The figure shows that only one survivor receives the custom message while the others keep receiving the automatically sent messages from the server.

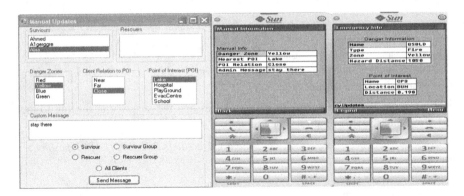

Fig. 7. Some survivors receive the automatied message

3.3   Peer to Peer Communication

The MES supports peer-to-peer emergency services by the use of ad-hoc communication. In the sense, an alert message can be forwarded from one actor to another depending on context using any peer-to-peer communication method such as Bluetooth. The message is forwarded from a registered survivor to unregistered survivor(s) according to location context information. The MES' peer-to-peer message content structure is designed the same as the automatic messaging mode plus a custom message as follows (in EBNF):

<message>::=<actor1>+<danger_type><affected_area><danger_distance>
<POI_name><POI_location> <POI_distance><custom_message>

  <actor1>::= <survivor_ID>.

  <danger_type>::= "fire" | "flood" | "earthquake" | "nuclear_danger".

  <affected_area>::= "red_zone" | "yellow_zone" | "blue_zone".

  <danger_distance> ::= "945" | "775" | "534".

  <POI_name>::="lake"|"hospital"|"evacuation_center"|"school"|"playground".

  <POI_location>::= "Bundoora" | "Reservoir"| "Kingsbury".

  <POI_distance>::= "0.25" | "0.775" | "0.999".

  <custom_message>:: = STRING (e.g., "stay there").

The survivor decides on the survivor(s) that will take delivery of the message according to his/her (their) location(s). Then, the registered survivor informs the unregistered survivor(s) about the existing danger information, including danger name, danger type, affected area, danger distance and POI information such as POI name, location, distance and a custom message.

Figure 8 shows the message flow starting from the disaster management unit and ending at unregistered survivor. For example, S represents the disaster management unit and C1 and C2 registered survivors, where C3 and C4 are unregistered survivors. S can send the alert message to C1 and C2 via SMS or Internet. In addition, C1 (as a

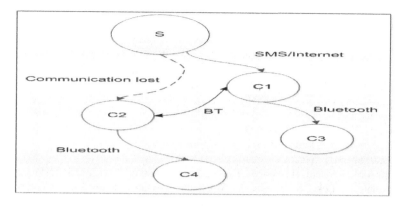

Fig. 8. Disaster automatic messaging via a peer-to-peer model

flag-bearer) can send the alert message to C3 via Bluetooth. Now, also, if C2 loses the communication with S, it will be able to receive the alert message from C1 via Bluetooth, and then C2 can send the alert message to the closest survivor C4. This service assists in spreading the alert messages around people in the danger area. It uses ad-hoc communication techniques in the case of unregistered survivors or lost communications with the disaster management unit (i.e., the main server).

4   Conclusion and Future Work

Context-awareness captures and represents the user's physical and social environments. In emergency situation there is an essential need to employ all obtainable information that may help in avoiding tragedy. The MES provides several techniques in order to send relevant emergency messages. First, the MES provides an automatic messaging service that will be generated depending on different contexts, from the disaster management unit to the actors. Second, manual messaging from the disaster management unit to the system actors can provide control and custom context-aware messaging for rescuers. Finally the system uses ad-hoc communication such as Bluetooth to send relevant messages to even those unknown to, or unregistered with the system, and so, creating greater robustness for messaging (even when some survivors are not directly reachable) – effectively crowdsourcing alert message delivery to actors (whom we call flag-bearers).

In the future, one of the main features that will be implemented within the system is sending geographical information using a map that will show the direction to the nearest safe POI as well as the danger locations, and this will be continually updated. Besides, we aim to provide online services to rescuers to access the MES via the mobile Internet, and to further evaluate the performance of our system.

References

1. Berry, J.: Spatial Reasoning for Effective GIS. John Wiley & Sons (1996)
2. Geiger, L., Durr, F., Rothermel, K.: On Context-aware Communication Mechanism, Communications. In: IEEE International ICC 2009 (2009)
3. Bonham-Carter, G.: Geographic information systems for geoscientists: modelling with GIS. Pergamon (1994)
4. Bushfire in Victoria Australia (2009),
   `http://www.boston.com/bigpicture/2009/02/`
   `bushfires_in_victoria_australi.html`
5. Howitt, A.M., Leonard, H.: Systems Failure. Crisis/Response 7(1), 22–25 (2011)
6. Almagrabi, A., Loke, S., Torabi, T.: Mona-ont: an Ontology for Smart Context-Aware Emergency Messaging (sent for publication at 23rd Australasian Conference on Information Systems)
7. Schilit, B., Adams, N., Want, R.: Context-aware Computing Applications. In: IEEE Workshop on Mobile Computing Systems and Applications, Santa Cruz, California, pp. 85–90 (1994)
8. Kortuem, G., Kray, C., Gellersen, H.: Sensing and visualizing spatial relations of mobile devices. In: Proceedings of the 18th Annual ACM Symposium on User Interface Software and Technology, UIST, pp. 93–102. ACM Press (2005)

Author Index